THE POLITICAL ECONOMY OF
WORLD ENERGY
An Introductory Textbook

World Scientific Series on Energy and Resource Economics
(ISSN: 1793-4184)

Published

Vol. 1   Quantitative and Empirical Analysis of Energy Markets
         by Apostolos Serletis

Vol. 2   The Political Economy of World Energy: An Introductory Textbook
         by Ferdinand E Banks

Vol. 3   Bridges Over Water: Understanding Transboundary Water Conflict,
         Negotiation and Cooperation
         by Ariel Dinar, Shlomi Dinar, Stephen McCaffrey & Daene McKinney

Vol. 4   Energy, Resources, and the Long-Term Future
         by John Scales Avery

Vol. 5   Natural Gas Networks Performance after Partial Deregulation:
         Five Quantitative Studies
         by Paul MacAvoy, Vadim Marmer, Nickolay Moshkin & Dmitry Shapiro

Vol. 6   Energy and International War: From Babylon to Baghdad and Beyond
         by Clifford E. Singer

World Scientific Series on
Energy and Resource Economics – Vol. 2

THE POLITICAL ECONOMY OF
WORLD ENERGY
An Introductory Textbook

Ferdinand E Banks

Uppsala University, Sweden

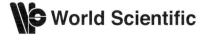

World Scientific

NEW JERSEY · LONDON · SINGAPORE · BEIJING · SHANGHAI · HONG KONG · TAIPEI · CHENNAI

Published by

World Scientific Publishing Co. Pte. Ltd.

5 Toh Tuck Link, Singapore 596224

USA office: 27 Warren Street, Suite 401-402, Hackensack, NJ 07601

UK office: 57 Shelton Street, Covent Garden, London WC2H 9HE

Library of Congress Cataloging-in-Publication Data
Banks, Ferdinand E.
    The political economy of world energy : an introductory textbook / by Ferdinand E. Banks.
        p. cm. -- (World Scientific series on energy and resource economics : 2)
    Includes bibliographical references and index.
    ISBN-13 978-981-270-036-0 -- ISBN-10 981-270-036-6
    ISBN-13 978-981-270-037-7 (pbk.) -- ISBN-10 981-270-037-4 (pbk.)
        1. Energy policy--Economic aspects. 2. Power resources--Economic aspects. I. Title.

HD9502.A2B3487 2007
333.79--dc22

2006048097

British Library Cataloguing-in-Publication Data
A catalogue record for this book is available from the British Library.

First published 2007
Reprinted 2008

Typeset by Stallion Press
Email: enquiries@stallionpress.com

Printed in Singapore by B & JO Enterprise

To Christian Otto, Claudia Soleil and Beatrice Gunilla

PREFACE

This is an elementary textbook on energy economics. Those who have completed a course in economics should have no problem reading all of it, and just as important, a large part of it can be easily understood by anyone with a serious interest in the subject, regardless of their academic background. The model for this volume is my textbook in international finance (2001), and Morton Davis' elementary presentation of game theory (1974).

Having taught long and intensive courses in elementary energy economics at the University of Stockholm and the University of Grenoble (France), I believe I can provide most of the readers of this book with the appropriate confidence and knowledge. I have also received important information about what readers with diverse qualifications can absorb from my lectures in Hong Kong and at the Royal Institute of Technology in Stockholm, and particularly at the ENI Corporate University in Milan, Italy.

As will be noticed, each chapter contains questions for discussion, with the exception of the chapters "Energy and Money" and "Economics and Electricity". These chapters contain exercises. As I mentioned in my previous textbooks, my presentation of these topics provides an indication of the lecturing style that I adopted early in my teaching career. To one extent or another, I have always favored a slight modification of the methods introduced at the Ecole Polytechnique (Paris) by Joseph Fournier, and similar arrangements that were employed at the United States Military Academy at West Point. Exercises are worked at the board by teams of two to four students, who then discuss their work, and answer both my questions and those of the remainder of the class. *Interactive teaching* is probably the best description of this approach.

In preparing this book, I received invaluable help from the comments on my articles and the articles of other contributors to *EnergyPulse* (www.energypulse.net), and the up-to-date articles on energy topics by Ken Silverstein in *EnergyBiz Insider*. I can also mention the informative letters by readers discussing those articles. Other important sources of energy information are the blog "Power Encounter" of Dr Jesus M. Martin-Giraldo, and the very important web publication *Energy Politics*, which features leading energy professionals.

An unidentified reviewer of my finance textbook accused me of making an easy subject difficult. This is an uncomfortable accusation, but fortunately it happens to be the opposite of the truth. As I tried to demonstrate when teaching mathematical economics in Australia and Portugal, nothing in that subject worth spending any time on is inherently difficult, and the same is true of energy economics, assuming that you keep an open mind, and you do not fall in love with some of the algebraic techniques used to discuss energy topics in other energy economics textbooks, many of which are completely irrelevant.

I also want to say something about studying economics, which is a very broad discipline. The best way to deal with this subject is to find out what you like, or perhaps need, and then devote your time to learning it perfectly — or at least nearly perfectly. Naturally, many students of economics do not appreciate this kind of advice, but if they are lucky they will eventually find out that it makes sense. I would like to remind readers of the remarkable power of "search engines" such as Google for obtaining information of all sorts, and also publications such as *The Geopolitics of Energy* and *PetrominAsia*. When in doubt, turn to Google!

Some question has come up as to the optimal length of a book of this nature. This is hardly a problem for me because of the comments that I have received about my previous book. What is required is a textbook that can be covered in a single term or semester, and which gives the persons reading it a distinct professional advantage over persons who are reading other textbooks. Someday, I hope, there will be a place in the undergraduate curriculum for energy economics textbooks of the length of the marvellous microeconomic volumes that we now have access to, but to my way of thinking, that time has not arrived. What I attempt here is to provide readers with a book that will give them the information they want and deserve, and in the shortest possible time. For example, oil is scarce, electric deregulation loony, and nuclear useful.

At this point I would like to thank the many persons who have engaged in lengthy dialogues with me, calmly or acrimoniously, in seminars, workshops and via e-mail — and often in comments on my articles that were published in *EnergyPulse*; and also comments on my comments in the same forum. At the present time, I find it difficult to understand how it is possible to be a serious teacher of energy economics without advising students to become involved with this platform. I am particularly grateful to those persons who detected mistakes and/or a lack of clarity in my work, and brought it to my attention.

Readers might also notice a certain amount of repetition in this book. This is intentional! One of the reasons for the gross lack of realism in matters such as oil and electric deregulation is the failure by the large number of persons who are greatly interested in these subjects, to become sufficiently acquainted with enough elementary economic concepts to be able to reject the many pseudo-scientific offerings that in some cases originate at the highest political and bureaucratic levels.

Let me put this another way — teaching energy economics is not as easy as it should be. As Professor Sean Flynn of Vassar put it: "too often students do not see the forest for the trees". This is a perfect description of the situation that we have had in energy and resource economics during the last 30 years, and is characterized by journals and textbooks being full of useless models dealing with exhaustible resources, and even worse, econometric and theoretical spin-offs of these constructions. "Old rubbish" was the way the late John Lennon (of Beatles fame) would have described some of this work, had he taken a deep interest in theoretical economics.

A few other acknowledgments are in order. First and foremost, students in my course in natural gas economics at ENI Corporate University in Milan (Italy), as well persons who attended my lectures in Hong Kong, where I was able to work out the shortcomings of electric deregulation while a visiting professor and university fellow at The Hong Kong Energy Studies Centre (of Hong Kong's Baptist University). Here I would like to thank Professors Sandro Furlan in Milan and Larry Chow in Hong Kong. I would also like to express my gratitude to Professor Tony Owen in Sydney, whose book on nuclear energy is still the best economics book on that subject. I can also mention Åke Qvarfort of Uppsala University, and my daughters Amelie and Madeleine for their help with my computer difficulties. Unfortunately I was, and remain, a very poor student of that subject — hopeless actually. And of course, Gunilla and Thomas Banks, of whom the latter still functions as my personal trainer.

Finally, I want to call attention to the editor of this book, Yvonne Tan, and World Scientific Publishing, without whom this book would not have come into existence. As James Clerk Maxwell pointed out, "Energy is the go of things": for me, Yvonne Tan and World Scientific provided that "go". And although I paid my dues to *EnergyPulse* earlier, this book would not be complete without naming some of the brilliant commentators/authors who discuss — sometimes at great length — the many energy topics that are published on that site: Alan Caruba, Arvid Hallén, Dennis Moran, Don Giegler, Edward A. Reid, Graham Cowan, James Hopf, Jeff Presley, Jim Beyer, John Sutherland, Jose Antonio Vanderhorst-Silverio, Joseph Somsel, Len Gould, Malcolm Rawlingson, Ronald R. Cooke, Tam Hunt, Todd McKissick, Tom Tanton, Warren Reynolds, and many more.

Dr Ferdinand E. Banks
ferdinand.banks@telia.com

CONTENTS

Preface   vii

**Chapter 1.   A Long Introductory Survey of Some
                Aspects of World Energy**   **1**

  1. An Introduction   2
  2. Victory Begins Here (Sign over the Gate at Fort Jackson,
      South Carolina)   4
  3. A Preliminary Look at Oil and Gas, and Also Wind   14
  4. California's "Deregulation Plan" and "Tough Love"   26
  5. Oil and Economic Logic   34
  6. Great Expectations: A Brief Perspective on Natural Gas . .   47
  7. A Nuclear Energy Tale   59
  8. Kyoto and Its Discontents   65
  9. "The Financialization of Energy"   70
 10. More Deregulation Blues   76
 11. Final Remarks and Conclusions   79
 Appendix: Observations on the Main Text — Units and
    Equivalencies   84

Chapter 2.   Economic Theory and World Oil: A Survey   **93**

  1. Some Absolutely Essential Background   97
  2. More of the Same   103
  3. Some Further Aspects of Oil Production   108
  4. Some Algebraic Aspects of Production and Pricing   110
  5. A Few Comments on OPEC   113
  6. The Refining Gap   119

7. Ancillary Issues 123
8. Comments on Oil Derivatives and the War Against Risk . . 125
9. Final Remarks and Conclusions 129
Appendix: Some Quantitative Matters 132

Chapter 3.   Oil and Saudi Arabia, Russia and Africa   141

1. Introduction 142
2. A Few General Observations 144
3. The Annoying Truth about Saudi Arabia and Oil 148
4. Some Aspects of Russian Oil 152
5. A Beautiful Myth 154
6. Near and Far 158
7. African Skies 162
8. Some Conclusions 166

Chapter 4.   An Introduction to Natural Gas Economics   171

1. Introduction 172
2. Simple Geology and Economics 180
3. Supply and Demand 184
4. Gas and Microeconomics 187
5. Storage, Hubs and Market Centers 193
6. Some Economic Aspects of the Russian Gas Puzzle 200
7. Liquefied Natural Gas (LNG) 204
8. Some Unpleasant Gas Market Vibrations in the United States 208
9. Some Aspects of Risk Management 211
10. Final Observations and Concluding Statement 218
Appendix: The Deregulation of Natural Gas 221

Chapter 5.   Coal and Its Discontents   229

1. Some Background 230
2. The World Coal Scene 238
3. Coal Prices and Price Theory 243
4. From Coal to Liquids 249
5. Environmental Issues 251
6. Concluding Remarks 256

Chapter 6.   An Introductory Survey of Economics and Nuclear Energy   261

   1. Some Basic Physics and Economics of Nuclear Energy . . . 266
   2. The Uranium Price, the Fast Breeder and MOX 272
   3. Nuclear in the Light of "Kyoto" 275
   4. A Conclusion 283
   Appendix: Swedish Nuclear Energy 285

Chapter 7.   Economics and Electricity   303

   1. A Preliminary Discussion 303
   2. Basic Investment Theory 306
   3. The Cost of Fuel 312
   4. Investment and Capital Cost 316
   5. Capacity Factor, Efficiency and Some Thermodynamics . . 319
   6. The Economics of Load Division (1) 323
   7. The Economics of Load Division (2) 327
   8. Final Remarks and Conclusions 330
   Appendix: Deriving an Important Equation, and Some Aspects of
   the Discount Rate 333

Chapter 8.   Energy and Money   339

   1. A Futures Market Fable 340
   2. The Basic Mechanics of Futures Markets 346
   3. Simple Options Theory 353
   4. Another Look at Futures 359
   5. Basis Risk 367
   6. Some Further Aspects of Options 372
   7. Three More Topics: Exchange of Futures for Physicals,
   Options on Futures and Swaps 376
   8. A Final Comment 381
   Appendix: Some Further Aspects of Hedging and Options, and
   the Optimal Hedge Ratio 381

Chapter 9.   A Faith-Based Approach to Global Warming   389

   1. Introduction 389
   2. Climate Change and Politics 394

3. Emissions Trading 397
4. Kyoto and Nuclear 401
5. Final Comments and Conclusions 405

Chapter 10.   An Energy Message for the 21st Century   409

1. More Aspects of World Energy and the 21st Century 413
2. A Loose End: Option Value 427
3. Final Statement: Sweden's Electric Deregulation Failure . . 431

Index   441

CHAPTER 1

A LONG INTRODUCTORY SURVEY OF SOME ASPECTS OF WORLD ENERGY

Perhaps the three most important topics in energy economics at the beginning of the new millenium were the availability of oil in the near future, the deregulation of electric (and perhaps also natural gas) markets, and last but very definitely not least, global (or climate) warming. The supply of natural gas in the long run also deserves some attention. As a result, this long introductory chapter will concentrate on a non-technical presentation of these items, although my aim in this book is to give readers enough insight into the logic and rhythm of energy economics, so that they can fully comprehend the most important aspects of a topic that has started to receive the attention that it deserves. I would like to do the same for environmental economics, but this book is too short for me to provide serious readers with more than a few comments.

Where the debates concerning oil and global warming are concerned, the most important thing just now is the utilization of an informal Neumann–Morgenstern (1944) approach which emphasizes the significance of avoiding unfavorable (and irreversible) outcomes. To me, this means that the value of nuclear energy should not be underestimated, the Kyoto Protocol — and particularly the trading of emissions permits — should be regarded with considerably less enthusiasm than at present, and the growing "scarcity" of conventional oil should be recognized and carefully studied. Furthermore, I would like to see global warming dealt with at the highest governmental levels, on a continuous basis, instead of in mammoth conferences attended by persons who often lack a suitable background in science or the kind of economics presented in this book.

1

1. An Introduction

Things move fast in the great worlds of energy and finance. In fact, there are many observers who believe that they often move *too* fast, and in the wrong direction. One of the reasons for this is the surprising increase in the price of oil that began in 2003–2004, as well as an alarming increase in the price of natural gas.

After the good news of the 1990s for financial markets, there is a palpable risk that at any time the global macroeconomy may take on a different complexion. Although recoveries sporadically appear to be underway, unemployment in Europe remains comparatively high, and in their attempt to restore the situation, governments in many countries are systematically reducing welfare. (For example, pension "reform" has become a favorite mantra of the political movers and shakers.) It also needs to be emphasized that in terms of price-earnings ratios and interest rates (considered on the basis of average values over the last 30 years), share and bond markets could still be out of equilibrium. On this point I can refer readers to my elementary international finance textbook (2001).

Although the energy picture is, to a considerable extent, dominated by unexpected increases in the price of oil and natural gas, and to a lesser degree coal, from the point of view of mainstream economics these price rises were inevitable: the effective supply of comparatively inexpensive *petroleum* (i.e., oil + gas) reserves is probably well under the level predicted by many optimists a few years ago. This is due to both inadequate investment in exploration and production, as well as an actual shortage of oil and gas in the crust of the earth relative to the amount that will be required in the distant *or* near future. Observe that when I say *reserves*, I am talking about known and *exploitable* oil and gas, and not hypothetical resources!

There have also been electricity deregulation miscarriages in many parts of the world (e.g., California, Ontario, Brazil, South Australia, Sweden, etc.), and of course the bankruptcy of the giant energy trading firm Enron. As I have pointed out at many conferences and seminars, it is nothing less than amazing how voters and their representatives allowed themselves to be beguiled for so long by deregulation enthusiasts and their paid and unpaid propagandists. The so-called "opening up" of the electric and gas markets to "liberalization" is in many respects a gigantic blunder, because it is very possible that *smart* regulation of these two quite special industries is the best friend of a free-market system. For one of the best pedagogical treatments of this topic I can recommend a working paper by Coppens and Vivet of the National Bank of Belgium, titled "Liberalization of network industries: Is electricity an exception to the rule?" (2004). As stressed in this textbook, and more extensively by these two authors, electricity is definitely an exception, and the same may be true for natural gas.

At the present time, with newspapers and television constantly assuring us that we live in a new world as a result of the 9–11 attacks on the World Trade Center and the Pentagon (2001), some of us hope that this new world will include a less nonchalant approach to certain crucial economic phenomena, to include those having to do with energy. The latter may now be possible, since President Bush wisely designated energy a "national security concern". It could be argued that until recently, there were excellent reasons (of a "game-theoretical" nature) for several directors of the leading oil companies to pretend that there is still a large amount of inexpensive oil that can eventually be located and brought to the surface, but some question has to be asked as to why so many academics elected to join in the elaboration and spreading of this dangerous myth. In the present context, the expression "game-theoretical" means large firms trying to convince smaller firms (as well as other large firms) that there will be a big supply (and concomitant low price) of oil in the near future, and as a result they should consider selling various production assets to these large firms.

Many of the same academics are also deregulation enthusiasts, but the unmistakeable succession of deregulation miscarriages might eventually cause them to reconsider their loyalties. Lamentably though, it is still too early to conclude that the illogical attachment to electricity and gas deregulation has run its course. At the Barcelona "summit" of the European Union (EU), a former president of France emphasized that Sweden was a good example of a country where, contrary to expectations, (consumer) electricity prices have greatly increased since deregulation, but as it turned out, he was wasting his breath. The shocking visibility of the California meltdown and its aftermath resulted in the EU's energy overseers becoming almost frantic in their efforts to deregulate their unperceptive subjects into the emergency room. What we have here is a simple refusal to acknowledge the many deregulation failures that have taken place around the globe, despite an overwhelming accumulation of both anecdotal and scientific evidence. On a somewhat higher plane, we are encountering a disturbing absence of the requisite microeconomic knowledge.

There are many energy topics in this book. Among other things I have attempted to eliminate a few of the gaps in my (intermediate level) energy economics textbook (2000), as well as to refine or simplify some of the arguments in that book. A small amount of elementary mathematics could not be avoided, but I have attempted to place at least some of this algebra where it can be ignored by readers who find this departure annoying. A minor exception is made in the chapter dealing with electricity, and also in the chapter titled "Energy and Money". However, even here most readers should experience no difficulty in following the discussion.

2. Victory Begins Here (Sign over the Gate at Fort Jackson, South Carolina)

The following quotation introduces an energy survey in *The Economist* by Vijay Vaiteeswaran (10 February 2001): "The world of energy is being turned upside down. The best thing governments can do is to get out of the way". Unfortunately, however, an authentic picture of world energy and environmental problems would reveal the necessity of government involvement. For instance, in the United States, the absence, until recently, of a governmental energy policy was strongly deplored by many executives in the industrial sector, to include the major oil companies, while the executive director of the International Energy Agency (IEA), Claude Mandil, has argued that governments should not leave the development of, e.g., renewables to the market. As he pointed out, "There is too much at stake".

The most commendable aspect of Mr Vaiteeswaran's survey is that he has approached several "hot" topics in energy economics — such as oil, electricity and nuclear energy — that are important for this book. As far as I am concerned, his conclusions about oil are not always correct, just as I certainly cannot agree with most of what he writes about the electricity market; but even so, an hour or two spent reviewing his work will provide a partial introduction to these and other issues. In addition, his comments about nuclear energy were fairly valuable, although it would have been a good idea if a modicum of attention had been paid to a former Secretary General of the OECD.

According to Donald Johnson, greenhouse gas emissions, together with the predicted growth in global population, are "putting the world on a fast track to (unhealthy) global consequences for future generations". As a result, he concludes that "if we are to hand on to future generations a planet that will meet their needs, as we have met ours, it can only be done by incorporating the nuclear option". A similar opinion has also been put forward by a number of eminent international civil servants, as well as many conscientious politicians and journalists who have made a thorough as opposed to a superficial study of energy markets, which means that expressing these sentiments has become a great deal more respectable than was the case just a few years ago.

They might have added that global power capacity is expected to increase by about 45% in the next 14 years, and it will have to grow by a larger amount if the hundreds of millions of households that have *no* reliable access to electricity today (plus those that will be added by population growth) are to be able to obtain a minimal amount of that indispensable "good". (At the present time, about two billion persons in developing countries rely on traditional biomass — such as wood and agricultural residues — for their basic energy needs, and two billion is also Lester Brown's estimate of the number of the world's poor.) Global demand for electricity grew by 2.2%/year between 1990 and 1997, and future demand growth is expected to reach an average rate of 2.5%/year by 2020 (as compared to an expected global population growth of about 1.6%/year). Dealing with this problem without placing an undue burden on the environment will almost certainly call for more nuclear capacity and renewables, with the emphasis on more environmentally friendly motor fuels.

Despite the constant reminders in this book of the importance of nuclear power, I in no way want to downgrade the significance of renewables. Renewables have a crucial role to play in the immediate energy future, but, e.g., the great mistake by many environmentalists is the belief that they are ready to do everything (or almost everything) by themselves, which to me means that economics (i.e., cost) is not being given its proper consideration. As Claude Mandil noted, "Renewables can make major contributions to the diversity and security of energy supply, and to economic development". In particular, his organization emphasizes wind turbines, whose production costs at the beginning of this century were reputedly somewhat less than a quarter of what they were in 1981. According to the American Wind Energy Association, in the US, in 2005, a new wind-generating equipment of worth more than three billion dollars ($= \$3\,bn$) was installed, and the IEA apparently believes that by 2030, the global share of renewables in electricity generation should be almost 20% of a very large output of electric power.

Where other renewables are concerned, I do not consider myself qualified to venture an inclusive judgment. The IEA seems to have great faith in solar energy, and it seems likely that in 15 years, the first large US solar plant may soon be constructed in Nevada (and will be called "Nevada Solar One"). Its capacity is 64 megawatts ($= 64\,MW$), and the project is estimated to cost \$106 million. The installation uses mirrors to concentrate heat from the sun, and to raise to a very high level the temperature of a special fluid. This fluid then transfers the heat to a steam generator that will produce electricity. It is predicted that the plant will generate electricity for about 12 cents per kilowatt hour ($= 12$ cents/kWh), which can be compared to 5–8 cents/kWh for coal-fired plants in the region.

All these sound promising, but I heard the same sort of thing about 20 years ago when I gave a short course at the Australian School of the Environment (in Brisbane). As it happens, the Nevada solar facility is not particularly large, and that state has certain advantages with regard to weather that are not enjoyed by many other regions in the US. It might then be suggested that this facility should be considered a pilot installation for similar projects close to Las Vegas, which is one of the most rapidly growing communities in the US. If Nevada Solar One performs according to expectations, then ideally the system will soon be scaled up for use both in Nevada and in other suitable localities.

Something worth mentioning here is that the noble goals of the United Nations and others as to poverty elimination do not make any sense at all without an adequate supply of electricity being available for households, small and large businesses, and industries. A similar observation applies to the availability of oil: oil is used everywhere, and without a large supply many fundamental activities (e.g., transportation, and the production of chemicals) would have to be operated at less than a desirable level. To paraphrase Georges Monbiot, for the foreseeable future, oil is the commodity on which our lives are built.

Unless I am mistaken, the basic *contretemps* will turn out to be when and how governments go into reverse where their present attitude toward nuclear energy is concerned, because for various reasons that will be spelled out in this and future chapters, the irrational ostracizing of nuclear energy cannot be continued indefinitely in a world where voters want less carbon dioxide (CO_2), but where — according to a UN forecast — there will be at least a doubling of the demand for energy over the next 25–30 years. Eventually, this might become apparent to even the Swedish government, and it will be admitted publicly that initiating their nuclear retreat was ill-timed. Moreover, when a new generation of safe nuclear equipment is ready to be put into operation (which may be soon), their present position should be reassessed — and this is especially true if vehicles exploiting a more environment-friendly technology are not available on a *very large* scale.

This latter situation may be a long time coming, given the present age structure of the global vehicle inventory. Similarly, as yet, sales figures for new trucks, automobiles and motorcycles show no signs of attenuating, despite the increase in the price of vehicle fuel. Notice the emphasis above on "very large". For example, a number of major automobile companies have unveiled impressive "hybrid" electric vehicles and as a result of expectations about the oil price, doubts about their commercial prospects are gradually being dispelled. (Hybrids are vehicles where a conventional gasoline-driven motor is placed alongside an electric one powered by batteries that are recharged whenever the vehicle coasts or brakes. One of the best known examples is Toyota's "Prius" hybrid. Considerable emphasis is now being placed on plug-in hybrid vehicles, whose batteries can be recharged overnight via the electric grid, and thus take advantage of low off-peak power prices.)

Hopefully, the hybrid market will soon be expanding rapidly enough so that producers will be able to fully exploit increasing returns to scale in the manufacture of these vehicles, which in turn will permit them to offer lower prices. At the same time, there have been claims that hybrid vehicles should be regarded as an intermediate technology, and in the long run hydrogen fuel-cell vehicles may be preferable because fuel cells are twice as efficient as combustion engines. Another factor working to make hydrogen the fuel of choice is its availability: some observers insist that it takes just one-and-a-half gallons of water — one toilet flush — to create enough hydrogen for a day's driving of 30 miles (= 48 km). Let us put it this way: hydrogen is very definitely going to be an important energy resource, but where vehicles are concerned, the long run could be longer than we anticipated a few years ago as a result of hybrid technology becoming more impressive.

In July 2001, Mr Brian Wilson — the newly appointed UK energy minister — visited the US in order to discuss energy security with the US vice president and the US energy secretary. These gentlemen wanted to see more nuclear facilities in the energy portfolios of their countries; however, environmentalists in both the United States and United Kingdom, their sympathizers, and most importantly their political "support", indicated that they will do everything possible to block any and all actions having to do with nuclear energy. As Marcel Boiteux (the eminent French economist who at one time was president of Electricité de France) once remarked: "In the United States and elsewhere, they have succumbed to the dictatorship of the anti-nuclear minority". In almost every country in the world, this minority is busily claiming that it is possible to achieve energy and environmental goals without initiating a renewal of nuclear power station construction. Instead, they insist, attention should now focus on an accelerated provision of renewable energy.

But they began saying this at least two decades ago, and in my opinion they are still too impetuous. At the same time though, it needs to be made clear that at some point in the future — and perhaps the not-too-distant future — they will see the light: *renewables are indispensable, but so is nuclear energy.* Moreover, the science academy of the UK Royal Society has warned the UK government of the inadequacy of proposals to put the main weight of reducing global warming on strategies like the soaking up of carbon dioxide (CO_2) in forests and farmlands (i.e., "carbon sinks"), and to this should probably be added funneling CO_2 into the depths of the ocean. These are not entirely futile initiatives however, and are probably justified to a limited extent. Similarly, the suggestion of President Bush, Sr, that efforts should be made to plant a billion trees undoubtedly deserves consideration, but as far as the academy is concerned, none of these are long-term substitutes for unequivocal reductions in CO_2 emissions — although at the Bonn Meeting on climate control, in order to obtain some sort of compromise that would be acceptable to several important industrial countries, a number of misleading assumptions had to be treated as indisputable scientific reality. According to the academy, achieving a meaningful decrease in carbon emissions can only come about if, among other things, there is more emphasis on the construction of carbon-neutral energy sources such as nuclear power and wind turbines.

My thoughts on these matters move in several directions. I find it hard to believe that we will *not* have to experience what Professor Ken-Ichi Matsui calls the Seventh Energy Revolution, which he pictures as being based on nuclear energy; but it could happen that it will become possible in the not-too-distant future to efficiently "store" large amounts of electricity (in one form or another), and in these circumstances, options like wind turbines could become much more important in the world energy picture than they are at present. Someday, readers of this book might be in a position to help decide exactly how important.

The chapter on natural gas is the longest in my previous energy economics textbook (2000), but it needs to be emphasized here that some people are likely to be disappointed about the long-run availability of "the fuel of the future", to include observers who believe that large, centralized power plants are passé, and small-scale distributed-power-generation plants burning natural gas are the wave of the future. At the turn of the century, global electric power generation was about 40% coal-based, hydro and other renewables were 20% of the total, nuclear 15%, natural gas 15%, and oil 10%. By 2020, the share of gas in global power generation could be well over 20% of a much larger total. *Ceteris paribus*, this could have a dramatic impact on gas prices everywhere.

Present predictions are still that the growth rate for oil consumption should be on the order of 1.5%–1.75%/year, although it could move above that level, largely due to the exceptionally high macroeconomic growth in China, as well as the striking economic progress that seems to be taking place in India and which could easily take place in Russia. I can, however, accept the argument that in many isolated regions it may be economical to rely on small-scale power sources, since it might be too expensive to expand or extend the main power grid. Something that deserves to be carefully observed is that while at the present time coal accounts for slightly more than 50% of the fuel input for power generation in the US, some estimates have this eventually reaching 60%. We can only hope that higher authority has studied in detail the environmental consequences of a coal intensity of that degree.

Now let us complicate the discussion slightly by noting that 1000 cubic feet ($= 1000\,\text{ft}^3$ or 28.3 cubic meters) of gas has an average heating value of approximately 1,000,000 ($= 1$ m) British Thermal Units (Btu). (The exact figure is 1,035,000 Btu.) One barrel (b) of oil has an average heating value of 5,800,000 Btu. Several years ago, OPEC expressed the intention to keep the world oil price between $22/b and $28/b, and so we can immediately calculate that this corresponds to an energy-equivalent gas price of $3.8 dollars per million Btu ($= $3.8/mBtu) to $4.8/mBtu, considering only heating values. (As pointed out in the appendix to this chapter, which some readers should consider looking at now, heating values are often measured in "joules" rather than Btu.)

When oil prices began what appeared to be a definitive escalation several years ago, OPEC "unofficially" raised its price target to more than $50/b, citing among other things a lack of economic damage (to oil importing countries) from high oil prices. Using the figures given above, $50 a barrel for oil corresponds to a natural gas price of almost $9/mBtu. When I began writing this chapter, the gas price was hovering around $14/mBtu; but while the price later "collapsed" to $5.5–6/mBtu, nobody really expects it to stay there. Readers should immediately calculate an energy-equivalent oil price for gas at $14/mBtu, whereupon they may draw the conclusion that a sustained gas price at this level is not a very appetizing prospect. It is interesting to note that only a few years ago, a sustained price of $6/mBtu for gas was considered by some observers to be high enough to endanger the global macroeconomic stability.

At one spot sale in California at the beginning of this century, the price of gas spiked to $60/mBtu (according to the *International Herald Tribune*, 10–11 February 2001). Using the information above or the table of equivalents in the appendix to this chapter, the reader can easily calculate that in terms of energy content, this is the equivalent of oil selling for $335/b, which is indisputably destructive. In fact, it has been correctly pointed out that the increased price of electricity in California (and elsewhere) reflects to some extent the large and unexpected rise in the price of gas. As to be expected, these prices influenced the price of coal (since coal can substitute for gas in, e.g., heating applications), which in turn led to certain industries in the United States and Europe beginning to make plans to move all or a part of their operations to places in the world where they believed (or hoped) that gas prices were (and could remain) on the order of $4/mBtu or lower.

This may well be one of the main reasons why President Bush decided that the US should not support the Kyoto Protocol. Although a major part of new US generating capacity was supposed to be fueled by gas, increasingly expensive gas could eventually lead to an increase in the reliance on coal, which the US still possesses in abundance within its borders. As compared to oil and gas, coal is a comparatively low-priced resource; but *clean* coal might turn out to be fairly expensive, and this is something that cannot be ignored since a great deal of it might have to be consumed. To avoid having to confront choices that might be distasteful from a political point of view, the chief executive apparently decided that while global warming is a fact, the extent of the dangers posed by this phenomenon need to be confirmed by further research before his government can accept comprehensive emission controls of the kind presumably stipulated in the Kyoto proposals.

This is an extremely important subject, and it deserves the attention of everyone concerned with the future of themselves and future generations. Science is ultimately a matter of *bona-fide* scientists, and a huge major-ity of the world's scientific elite say that global warming is a potentially dangerous phenomenon, and that a large part of it has an *anthropogenic* (i.e., man-made) background. Many of them also say that drastic measures should be taken to address this threat as soon as possible — where by "drastic measures" they are alluding to a more straightforward approach than procedures written into or derived from the Kyoto Protocol.

By way of contrast, a scientist who caught President Bush's ear for a while, Professor Richard Lindzen, not only rejects the dangers that are implicit in the present rate of global warming, but he has also made some strange pronouncements about an important medical problem (involving smoking), which under normal circumstances might have made that gen-tleman and his judgments *persona non grata* at the White House. What we have here is a situation of the type that appeared following Albert Einstein's presentation of the theory of relativity, when a handful of scientists, sev-eral of whom had done outstanding work, decided that an overwhelming majority of the world's top physicists had taken leave of their senses in accepting Einstein's triumph.

A few topics referred to in this section require some elaboration before we move on. In 2006 there were more than 200 million vehicles in the US, and although there was nothing to match this in China, automobile ownership in the latter country may grow five times by 2025, which means 200 million cars in Chinese ownership at that time. The private automobile has also become a fixture in the dreams of many Russian and Indian households, and if these dreams are realized it should easily move the number of vehicles globally from the 800 million estimate by Lester Brown (of the Earth Policy Institute) to well over a billion.

China and India provide a significant insight into the future. Their present and expected demand for conventional motor fuel is so strong that it could virtually overwhelm any conservation efforts that are being made in the totality of smaller countries. As is increasingly pointed out, if the per-capita consumption of oil in China and India reached that of comparatively indigent Mexico, they would require more than 40 million barrels of oil a day. The oil price would then move off the Richter scale.

I have already mentioned hybrids and hydrogen, but despite the relatively low operating costs, hybrids are still not especially a price-competitive buy: after five years in the market they still only amounted to 1.2% of the US vehicle sales. Even the Toyota hybrid mentioned earlier requires that the average buyer in the US might have to wait about five years before recovering the additional cost (or *premium*) over a "standard" model, but this figure will almost certainly decline. The point is, however, that more and more effort is being directed toward improving the technology of these vehicles, and it may be true that OPEC and the large oil companies will realize it could pay off in the not-too-distant future. This might be the reason why they have become prone to claim that there will not be a serious shortage of oil in the future, and so automobile buyers can stick with the orthodox technology.

In the short run, a greater consumption of *conventional* diesel fuel may be the most cost-effective option for reducing what has come to be called "the dependence on oil". The problem here is that environmentally this fuel is not considered ideal, and is unacceptable in a large part of the US. The cleaner-emission diesel that is becoming available may be acceptable to both buyers and authorities, but it is not clear at the present time whether the increased cost of a diesel (car) will be substantially outweighed by fuel savings. Note the term "conventional" above: there is also biodiesel, which is a diesel equivalent fuel derived from biological sources.

In the important debates taking place on *EnergyPulse*, it has been stressed that producing hydrogen is an extremely energy-intensive activity, but it is possible that, e.g., wind and solar technologies may be capable of alleviating the dilemma caused by a negative or near-negative output–input energy relationship in the production process. Another annoyance is the difficulty (i.e., expense) of safely storing and transporting hydrogen in vehicles. As a result, it appears that the hydrogen optimism of a few years ago has to a certain extent been replaced by pessimism. The feeling here though is that hydrogen's availability, along with the relative ease with which it can be directly converted into electricity and water via fuel cells, will eventually allow it to prevail.

In his long awaited energy policy speech in 2006, President George Bush decried the "addiction" to oil and emphasized an increased resort to ethanol, which at the time supplied about 2% of US fuel requirements. Ethanol is probably the best known "biofuel", where the two relevant "brands" of this commodity are ethanol from grains (mostly corn), and cellulosic ethanol made from high yield crops or plant waste. *Switch grass* and *forest thinning* are often mentioned here, as is sugar cane, sugar beets, etc. In the last few years this fuel has had an impressive history in Brazil; but in, e.g., the US, corn-based ethanol gives the appearance of being fairly expensive, and while it is believed that cellulosic ethanol will be cost-effective, it may require as long as a decade of research and development before it can be introduced on a mass basis. In addition, research at the University of Minnesota shows that biodiesel has less impact on the environment, and a much higher net energy benefit than corn-based ethanol.

Peter Huber, writing in *Forbes* (10 April 2006), is of the opinion that cellulosic ethanol — when it becomes economical — will be an environmental catastrophe. To his way of thinking, once science and technology have made its production economical on a large scale, forests and grasslands will be savaged in order to obtain raw materials. Whether this will happen to Washington Park in Chicago or the Bois de Boulogne in Paris is dubious, but in the Third World there could be some very undesirable outcomes.

Some questions as to the ultimate utility of corn-based ethanol also need to be asked. The US is the largest exporter of corn in the world, and expectations are that beginning in 2007 they will convert at least as much corn into ethanol as they sell abroad. Moreover, US energy legislation requires ethanol production to reach 7.5 billion gallons by 2012, which will require a huge amount of raw materials that in turn will drive up the *global* price of corn that normally would be consumed as food. What is happening now is that with higher than expected price of oil, farmers will be converting wheat, soya beans, sugar cane and corn into vehicle fuel. This is not what advocates of ethanol as an environmentally friendly fuel had in mind, nor will it ease their minds to know that according to David O'Reilly — CEO of Chevron — 15% of the US corn crop goes into producing fuel, but it produces only 2% of the fuel. Brown (2006) provides another approach. He sees an "epic competition" between motorists who want to protect their mobility, and "the two billion poorest people in the world who simply want to survive".

I see no reason to claim an expertise that in reality I lack in the matter just above, but on the basis of the information at hand, nuclear and hybrids appear to be the way to go. Biofuels (e.g., ethanol and butanol) must also progressively be given an opportunity to show what they can do. Hydrogen's turn has not arrived yet, but it will come.

3.   A Preliminary Look at Oil and Gas, and Also Wind

Contrary to general belief, oil is found in open spaces (pore spaces) in permeable reservoir rock, and not in large open caverns. An oil field consists of one or more distinct accumulations of this nature which, inappropriately, are called pools. If sufficient gas is dissolved in the oil, and the confining pressure is high enough, a well (i.e., pipe) driven into this oil will drive the substance to the surface, sometimes in the form of a gusher. (James Dean was the lucky if unpleasant owner of one of these bonanzas in the film "Giant".) In this situation the oil does not have to be pumped, at least during the early life of the field; however, the rate of production that can be sustained from any particular reservoir tends to decline as the oil in it is depleted, and the underlying pressure decreases.

This arrangement is normally called "free flow". In an extremely valuable paper, Cairns and Davis (2001) stated that between 5% and 10% of the wells in the US fit this description, and a much larger percentage in the Middle East. Unfortunately, the mathematical content of their paper will probably limit its popularity.

If the natural pressure of the field becomes insufficient, the oil is pumped out. The two arrangements mentioned here (natural release and simple pumping) are called primary production. In fields where primary production results in an inadequate yield, secondary methods are also employed. These could involve pumping water into the stratum below the pool, or pumping gas into the layer above, with the intention of flushing out the crude oil clinging to the reservoir rock, or a combination of the two, or even something more exotic. What needs to be appreciated at this point is the crucial difference between reserves and oil-in-place. At the present time, with the available technology, the global average for the oil that is actually available (i.e., reserves) from oil-in-place is about 35%, and this varies from country to country. It also happens that some economists prefer to talk in terms of resources, which includes oil that is likely to be discovered, or even oil which has been discovered but is too costly to exploit at the present level of technology. The so-called "heavy oil" of Venezuela and the so-called "shale oil" in the western US might fit this description. As David Korn pointed out in a letter to *The Atlantic* (October 2006), "The cheap and easy oil — the light, sweet crude that gushes from wells under its own pressure — is a thing of the past. What's left is ever harder and more costly to extract, and ever lower in quality".

When I published my oil book (1980), a great deal was expected from the exploitation of tertiary methods, which involved such things as injecting gases like carbon dioxide or nitrogen into deposits, or using chemicals called surfactants to wash the droplets of oil from rock pores. In the US, these methods have been used more liberally than elsewhere, but even so the results are not particularly impressive. Hope is something that remains eternal, however, and some observers still believe that improvements in technology will make it possible to raise the recovery ratio to about 40%. This is something that I do not expect to take place in the near or medium future, but even if it came to pass it would not change a great deal, given the high rate of growth of oil consumption. It certainly would not mean as much as some people believe that it would mean where such things as production and price are concerned.

Although crude oil is a clearly defined commodity, it is often useful to distinguish a number of varieties. The most widely used criterion for classifying petroleum products and crude oils is the American Petroleum Institute (API) grading scale, which essentially describes the specific gravity of a liquid in terms of an API number that decreases as the specific gravity increases. Thus, Venezuelan *conventional* crude has an API of about 26, which means that it is very heavy, while Algerian crude has an API of about 41, which means that it is very light. By way of contrast, the plentiful Venezuelan resource known as heavy oil — which belongs to the unconventional category — has an API number that is extremely small, whereas gasoline — whose specific gravity is 0.74 — has an API of 60. The principal fuels derived from crude oil are gasoline (i.e., motor fuel) and fuel oil, and these are referred to as oil products. Obtaining them involves refining crude, where the fundamental activity in the refining process is the distillation that separates the various ingredients. Oil and oil products can be moved to markets in a number of ways, of which the two most prominent are large tankers (for transportation between seaports), and pipelines, but trucks and trains are also used for smaller amounts.

It has become clear that even greatly increased drilling may not appreciably increase the present or the near-future supply of gas (or oil) in many large producing areas. A majority of geologists now openly say that the geological prospects for (conventional) petroleum (= oil + gas) in *all* of North America — and perhaps even Mexico — are discouraging when anticipated demand is given adequate consideration. We still occasionally hear claims that Mexico is gas-rich; however, the *imports* of gas into that country could double in the near future, and "listed" Mexican oil reserves have not grown appreciably in nearly two decades. On the contrary, the huge Canterell field (in medium deep water), which may still be the second largest oil producer in the world, has definitely peaked. (The largest field in terms of production and reserves is the Ghawar in Saudi Arabia.) In the US a few years ago, a cycle of frenzied drilling enabled small but important increases in reserve levels to be registered, but while it was expected that the recent near record "nominal" (i.e., money) prices would lead to every available drilling rig being immediately pressed into service, this did *not* turn out to be the case. The main reason was that the major oil companies are not really interested in spending billions of dollars in regions where their geologists have told them that there are no extremely large deposits of crude waiting to be harvested.

Just as interesting, however, when it appeared that the oil price could escalate to almost any level, capital expenditures on energy exploration and more intricate production methods increased throughout the world, and every available rig was pressed into service, sometimes at a very great cost. But even so, only a very modest amount of new oil was discovered. The simple tale here is that the reservoir base is no longer as abundant as it was two decades ago when another exploration boom took place.

The largest oil strike of 2004 involved an estimated one billion barrels of oil in India. *A priori*, a student of oil economics might have thought that a discovery of this magnitude would have taken place somewhere around the Caspian, or off the west coast of Africa; but considering that its location is in oil-poor India, which is now achieving a high rate of economic growth, this leads some of us to conclude that the situation regarding oil reserves is even more abysmal than many geologists believe, because India — like China — will be an increasingly significant oil importer. Interestingly enough, one of the most important international business publications has become very pessimistic about oil and went so far as to claim that *oil discovery* could peak around 2010. In point of truth, however, global (conventional) oil discovery peaked in the mid-1960s. Some students of the oil scene have chosen 2010 as the year when *output* peaks, which is a far more disquieting event. In my opinion a peak this early is unlikely, but far from impossible. This might be the reason that the mayor of Ottawa (Canada), Bob Chiarelli, said: "Finding solutions (to the peaking problem) is a race against the clock". Unlike many politicians, the mayor understands that even in rich Canada, a global oil peak could bring severe social and economic discomfort in its wake.

Until recently, certain observers were constantly talking about the miracles that new technology will achieve in the UK North Sea, but in 2004 the UK imported more gas than it exported for the first time in 11 years, and oil production in the UK definitely peaked around the turn of the century. In a few years that country will be a major importer of both oil and gas, which was inconceivable in the popular imagination just a decade ago. Many corporate insiders and a few other observers knew that this was going to happen, even if they preferred not to discuss it, since they were not enthusiastic about seeing the estimated market values of any North Sea assets they owned decrease. (For what it is worth, I knew that it was going to happen when the trading in North Sea properties suddenly and drastically declined.) One of the most interesting characteristics of the oil business in the recent past was the selling of oil properties by large companies to small companies: the large companies obtain cash that can be used to exploit expensive but in their opinion high-value schemes in one part of the world or the other, while the small companies obtain properties that have seen their best days, but still can yield attractive profits if they are managed by highly competent executives who have access to skilled technical help.

Most of North America is, geologically speaking, a mature production area. This becomes obvious upon viewing the large *natural decline* (or natural depletion) rate for oil and gas in that region, and just as important, though often overlooked, the increase in this rate from its already high level for natural gas in the Gulf of Mexico, which accounted for about 20% of US gas supplies, and 26% of US oil. The last time I inquired, there were 4000 oil platforms and 33,000 miles of underwater pipelines in the Gulf of Mexico, but some influential observers claim that deepwater fields in this region *average* only about a fifth of the reserves in similar deposits off the West Coast of Africa. This is one of the reasons why billions are being spent on the right to look for oil in many parts of Africa, and prospects considered not worth being bothered with a few decades ago are now the object of intense scrutiny.

The "decline rate" can also be touched upon here. The subject categorization is the *natural decline rate* or *natural depletion rate*, and here it might be useful to speak of a "recovery factor", which can be defined as the ratio of the amount of oil expected to be recovered to the amount of *oil-in-place* in a deposit. Normally, this ratio decreases with production, but as far as can be determined, the magnitude of the decrease exceeds that which can be directly attributed to production, which immediately suggests that there is another "force" at work: this is natural decline (which in economic theory is akin to "depreciation by evaporation"). Occasionally we hear of something called the "compounding effect", which includes both the decline rate and the rate of demand growth. This has outwardly become so large that Mr Lee Raymond — the former CEO of ExxonMobil — stated that enough reserves must be located during the first decade of the 21st century to replace about half of the decade's oil and gas production, assuming that it is desirable to satisfy the expected oil demand in the second decade of this century without very large price rises. Another expert, Mr Robert Odd — Vice-President of the oil and gas department of the Bank of Montreal, and a petroleum engineer — informed me that for the world oil economy to remain healthy, an absolute minimum of 4 mb/d might have to be located annually to compensate for the compounding effect.

It would be interesting to obtain a candid outline of Mr Raymond's views on US gas, because some observers feel that US energy professionals and gas consumers are badly in need of a wake-up call on this subject. (Russia, Iran and Qatar have 58% of the world's gas reserves, while the US has only 3%.) Admittedly, Canadian gas sales to the United States may show a palpable increase during the present decade, especially since the US Congress has approved credits to the enterprises that will become engaged in constructing a new pipeline. There is also increased talk of a multibillion-dollar pipeline from Alaska's North Slope down to Chicago, carrying 4.5 billion ft^3/day of gas, but this project was being discussed when I began writing my gas book more than two decades ago. Assuming that these conduits come into existence and are filled, they will still be unable to overcome the North American gas deficiency, and in addition, the gas being transported will be much more expensive than originally conceived. Moreover, if approved, an Alaska–Chicago pipeline might take 10 years to construct.

The same applies even more rigorously to liquefied natural gas (LNG). The LNG that will be transported in very expensive ships from the "new" Norwegian field "*Snow-white*" to buyers in Europe and the US will not be bargain-basement gas. In fact, in the above-mentioned talks between the US and UK energy ministers, it was clearly noted that both countries could be facing a very large continued fall in their domestic natural gas production, which means that in the next few years there may be a much larger reliance on natural gas imports than was anticipated just a few years ago. With this in mind, the government of Qatar just announced that they intend to become the most important supplier of LNG in the world. As is clear from many of the important comments offered by the forum *EnergyPulse*, there are a large number of persons in the US who are less than pleased about their country increasing its imports of gas from the Middle East, and in some cases do not want LNG imported from any source.

As many readers of this chapter know, increased pressure is being put on the US government to open more land to drilling. (Altogether, the federal government owns about one-third of US land.) After Mr Bush won a second term, this alternative was clearly available. However, the theory here is that if there were adequate seismological evidence that this federally-owned land really contained a huge amount of oil and gas, drilling would have commenced a long time ago. Just as important, the exploitation of the extremely rich oil deposits of Alaska did not enable the 1970 production peak in the US peak to be reattained. The estimates of "oil experts" given in *Business Week* (29 October 2001) are not particularly dramatic where future supplies are concerned: 6–16 billion barrels (= 6–16 Gb) of "untapped" oil in the Arctic, 4 Gb in the "lower 48", and with "advanced technology" perhaps 59 Gb somewhere offshore. Some of the oil mentioned here is in areas that are highly sensitive from an environmental point of view, and the "advanced technology" would have to be extremely advanced if environmental sustainability were respected. (As is noted in the Appendix, the "G" above signifies "Giga", or billions.)

According to a declaration of the executive vice-president of Alstom Power, "Nuclear is dead in the water. The capital costs of building a nuclear station are three times those of a gas-fired equivalent, which is why the market is dominated by gas in the developed countries" (*Financial Times*, Tuesday, 20 June 2000).

The present-day (2006) market is *not* dominated by gas in the manner implied by Mr Vice-president, even though just about everywhere in the world there are plans to use as much gas as possible. This kind of decision, however, is as much influenced by political considerations as those having to do with economics. It reflects the political strength of the environmental movements, to include the vocal support and encouragement that they receive from persons who do not vote for the "Greens" — "fellow travellers" they would have been called at the beginning of the Cold War. However, if there should be a shortage of gas in the next 10–20 years, then the sponsors and advocates of gas-based installations may have a great deal of explaining to do, because it is highly unlikely that there will be any shortage of nuclear fuel during this century. And there *could* be a shortage of gas, because according to both the IEA and the work of Al-Fattah and Startzman (2000), the global output of natural gas could peak before 2020 if demand continued to expand at the present rate.

The IEA has also collected some useful cost figures. They say that operating (i.e., variable) costs in the US are 1.8 cents/kWh for nuclear, 2.1 cents/kWh for coal, and 3.5 cents/kWh for gas. On the other hand, what they call capital costs are \$2000/kW for nuclear, \$1200/kW for coal, and \$500/kW for combined cycle gas equipment. In my previous energy textbook, and in this book in Chapter 7 on electricity economics, I call these *investment costs*, and show how capital costs (in \$/year) are calculated from them. Calculations have been made by the World Nuclear Association suggesting that in the US, construction costs, *before interest charges*, need to fall to \$1000 a kilowatt in order for atomic reactors to be economic. However, a rising price of gas (and coal), a "life" for new nuclear installations exceeding 60 years, shorter licensing and construction times and more emphasis on CO_2 suppression would allow that figure to be increased: if fossil fuels were taxed in such a way as to obtain compensation for their external costs (e.g., pollution), the attraction of both nuclear energy and wind would be greatly increased.

I also want to emphasize that many of the figures given above and elsewhere in this book may only be approximations: diligent readers encounter all sorts of figures where things like energy costs are concerned. But even so, just about everything available is presented here in order to introduce readers to the terminology and the general thinking about energy issues. I therefore suggest that persons who require up-to-date information about the cost of nuclear power relative to, e.g., gas, should examine the cost of producing power at the new Finnish atomic installation, whose capacity (of 1600 MW) is the largest in the world. Given Finland's proximity to very large reserves of gas in Norway and Russia, I suspect they would learn that nuclear power is the most economical.

They might also learn something about renewables. Admittedly, wind may ultimately become one of the "flavors of the month" in that country, as in the rest of Northern Europe, but it is well-known by unbiased observers in Scandinavia that the early adoption of wind in Denmark was due to its competing against high-cost, high-polluting coal, while at the same time receiving a favorable tax treatment. Favorable tax treatments and subsidies explain a great deal where the adoption of wind-based electric generation is concerned in a number of countries, but although we have every right to expect a great deal from this energy source, I suggest that it is best for all concerned if we do not overestimate its capabilities.

In the Northwest United States, hydroelectric-installations (which can be quickly turned on and off) do not have enough remaining capacity to supplement and smoothen the up-and-down generation patterns of new wind farms, and the same may be true of gas-based facilities. As a result, the cost of wind power — including the costs of using other power sources to ensure a stable power flow even when the wind is not blowing — could be much higher than commonly realized. Here it can be pointed out that the maximum rating of a wind turbine is not very useful in considering whether that turbine should be installed, since its "capacity factor" might be as low as 25%. Wind power is probably optimal when used as a power source for non-time-dependent applications such as irrigation, and perhaps as an input for producing hydrogen. (The capacity factor is discussed in Chapter 7.)

At the present time (2006), the Horse Hollow wind farm in Texas (662 MW when functioning at rated capacity) is the largest wind farm in the world. Another large wind facility is located at Storm Lake, Iowa (US), where 257 turbines are deployed across more than 100 farms. Many knowledgeable observers believe that with present technology, this is the optimal arrangement. However, some years ago the UK energy economist Michael Grubb published a paper in which he said that wind installations were ideally suited for supplying the electric *base load* — i.e., the load that is on the line every hour of the day. (He concluded, and correctly, that relying on wind power for peak loads of only a few hours per day was questionable, given the lack of reliability of wind, but like many other economists he overlooked what could be a very sizable "intermediate load" — which might be on the line many hours, and together with the base load could mean a very large total load. It might be worth mentioning here that one of the reasons why gas-based equipment has always played such an important role for the peak load is the rapidity with which it can be brought into effective use.)

Exactly how Professor Grubb came to his conclusion about the relation of wind to the base load is a mystery. The base load is on the line 24 h/day, while the wind blows when it feels like it. That makes wind a comparatively unreliable source of power because for base load use, a "backup" would be mandatory that (in theory at least) might have to be large enough to carry the entire base load if the wind stopped blowing. What he should have said was that wind should be able to *contribute* to supplying the base load: in a sophisticated system it could possibly be "switched in" to replace some fraction of the output of conventional base load equipment, perhaps on a continuous basis, and thus reduce the variable cost of running this equipment. This assumes, of course, that when wind-based power is injected into an electric network, it does not upset what power engineers call "the stability of the system".

Apparently, the initial satisfaction accorded wind power in Germany has encountered some "snags". With 18,428 MW of capacity, Germany was the largest user of wind power in the world in 2005. (Spain was next with 10,027 MW and the US had about 9350 MW. Total global capacity was about 60,000 MW.) Unexpectedly though, the *Deutsche Energie-Agentur* (Dena), a government agency, recently concluded that wind power is in certain respects uneconomical and technically unsatisfactory, and intimidated that its technical deficiencies were played down by the media, and German taxpayers were largely unaware of the large subsidies that it has obtained. This was a very unwelcome surprise for the "Greens" in the UK, who have made a point of praising German wind power efforts to the high heavens. Texas has the most wind power in the US, or about 2400 MW (which they claim can supply electricity for 600,000 homes), and California has slightly less. Wind, though, only supplies about 1% of the power in the US, and it will not supply much more if tax credits for wind power entrepreneurs are not renewed. It has also been calculated that about 20,000 large turbines could supply the demand for power in Paris (France). Exactly what that would mean in terms of "backup", however, remains to be seen, and it is best not to discuss how Parisians would feel about their marvellous city being surrounded by 20,000 large wind installations.

An interesting discussion of wind power was initiated in an article by David Dixon in a recent edition of *EnergyPulse* (September 2006) with the title "Wind generation's performance during the July 2006 California heat storm". The comments on this article suggested, however, that wind has been greatly overrated. According to Rod Adams (2006), it often happens that the capacity factor of wind is only 4–10% at the time when it is most needed, and in addition, "Taxpayers have provided huge quantities of cash to wind turbine operators, constructors and salesmen" that, presumably, could have been better deployed. Len Gould (2006) added to this criticism the uncomfortable fact that "the capital cost of every wind unit must have added to it the cost of its required backup unit". (As noted, the capacity factor is discussed in Chapter 7 of this book.)

At the same time, the goal for wind power in the UK is fairly modest — i.e., about 10% of total energy use — and given the supply of wind in the vicinity of Britain, this should turn out to be manageable. Note the expression "supply of wind", because this is seldom used; but it appears that in Germany there is a "repowering" of some wind installations, with larger units replacing smaller and older turbines at sites with strong wind conditions. In other words, even in the windy north of Germany, wind conditions are not uniform, and there is not a large supply of sites where wind turbines are appropriate.

The first offshore wind farm in the US was planned for the Northeast Coast (south of Cape Cod), with construction scheduled to be completed sometime in 2006. Capacity would be 420 MW, and the expected cost is $600 million. (The largest proposed installation is in Ireland, with a capacity of 620 MW.) The expected per-kilowatt (capital) cost at present rates of interest comes to about $1400, and with hardly any variable cost, this is quite attractive. Little has been said, however, about capacity factors, backup costs, etc., and some observers think that a smaller project makes more sense at the present time. Of course, on the positive side, if this wind farm is economical, it can perhaps be expanded. It should also be noted that wind might turn out to be ideal for supplying the energy input needed to obtain hydrogen, assuming that storing the hydrogen is, or will eventually become, a cost-efficient proposition.

I can say here that my way of viewing energy and environmental economics turns on the work of Neumann and Morgenstern (1944). Conjecture about, e.g., oil should focus on the possibility (or probability if it can be determined) of something going wrong, and the kind of shortage suddenly materializing that weakens the macroeconomy, perhaps causes a traumatic adjustment of financial markets, and could lead to dangerous political tensions between oil exporting and importing countries, as well as within importing countries. For more on these matters, see Beyer (2007), Giegler (2007), Gould (2006), Hopf (2007), Hunt (2007) and Kok (2007).

The same type of (cautionary) observation, multiplied by a very large number, applies to global warming where, if some really bad news were to appear, it could be too late to do anything about it. In his review of climate policy (1995), Professor Richard Cooper of Harvard University spoke warmly of the ability of humans to make optimal adjustments in the face of approaching disaster. However, history has provided sufficient counter-examples to show the almost total incorrectness of this belief. Had Professor Cooper been given the opportunity that some of us enjoyed to view various post-war vistas in Europe and Asia via the sponsorship of the US Army, he might have come to a very different opinion.

In these circumstances, it may be appropriate to suggest that, ideally, thoughtful voters should do as much as they can to encourage the election of political leaders who have a predilection for making the right decisions in the face of excruciating uncertainty. The kind of uncertainty that cannot be completely eliminated, but which — even so — must be intelligently *managed*. Managed how? By deciding under what circumstances considerable amounts of resources should be taken from other uses, and deployed to reduce uncertainty. In other words, in order to reduce (the output of) pollution, relatively less efficient (or more costly) production processes might have to be accepted. This may sound abstract, but actually it amounts to no more than being aware that if data indicating that human activities are responsible for the major part of global warming turns out to be accurate, emissions curbs are inevitable, and the longer they are put off, the more draconian (i.e., costly) they will probably be.

Utilities often tend to be against regulation, but faced with the prospects being alluded to here, even important firms like the American Electric Power Company (AEP) have concluded that "establishing reasonable regulations is better than continuing in the present state of uncertainty" (*Business Week*, 9 April 2001). Needless to say, the insurance industry has become the most outspoken component of the business community where this issue is concerned, and its executives make no secret of the fact that they are in favor of a drastic change in energy use if this is what it takes to bring carbon emissions under control.

Arriving at an optimal set of answers to the *economic* dilemmas that are discussed in this book requires considerable imagination and a reasonable amount of creative intelligence. It will also require a great deal of work, because not only do certain influential energy and environmental economists know so little, but because they also know so much that is irrelevant, and they continue to get such lovely opportunities to publicize their bizarre opinions and promote their equally bizarre policies.

When using the expression "bizarre opinions", very little in modern times can match those associated with the deregulation of electricity. The initiation of this experiment suggests to me that large portions of the human race no longer take seriously the adage "self preservation should be the first law of nature". On this point, see David Walters (2007).

4. California's "Deregulation Plan" and "Tough Love"

California is a key state in the United States. In 2006 it may have produced approximately 14% of that nation's output, or more than the smallest 22 US states combined. In addition, with a Gross Domestic Product (GDP) of $1.5 trillion (in 2006), it ranked eighth in GDP — just behind China (and with the US on top). As a result, it is important for the entire world economy as well as the economy of the US. Assuming that decision makers on the US energy scene have partially come to their senses as a result of scrutinizing the deregulation failures in California and elsewhere, it might eventually become possible to take the steps that will facilitate an optimal energy policy for the entire United States. This, in turn, could benefit in a number of ways the citizens of many other countries.

Perhaps the best way to commence an examination of this topic is to look at the deregulation experiment in California, which along with Sweden and the UK was supposed to provide a model for the rest of the world. California started out with an electric industry which was typical in that *utilities* (i.e., electricity suppliers) were regarded as natural monopolies consisting of three major integrated components: electricity generation in very large power plants, transmission in high-voltage and very expensive power lines, and distribution to final consumers via low voltage lines. (Generators are sometimes called wholesalers, and distributors are called retailers.) Utilities were almost always described as *natural monopolies* because not only did they display increasing returns to scale, but potential rivals would have to make huge investments in order to become serious players. Regulation came about in order to keep natural monopolies from abusing the market power they attain as a result of their being in position to function as "price makers" as compared to "price takers".

(Increasing returns to scale means that *average costs* fall with increasing size, and thus a very large electricity supplier could outcompete several smaller firms supplying the same load because the large firm would have a lower unit cost than the smaller firms. Furthermore, if the smaller firms could not accept this reality and tried to compete, they would be risking a great deal of money due to the large expense associated with entering a very capital-intensive industry.)

The California deregulation show hit the road when it was decided that the retail market could and should be opened to competition. The strategy here was that geographical limits on power supply would be removed, and so independent retailers (or for that matter a new form of utility in the form of transmission firms with some retail outlets) could buy power from both local and out-of-state generators (who were later called out-of-state criminals by California Governor Gray Davis, when they began to "game" the market by withholding power, which naturally caused its price to increase). Ideally, the comparatively few retailers would become very many, and at the same time be able to buy electricity from many generating firms. The market would also be altered so that everyone had the legal right to transmit power through any "wires" that had available capacity, as long as they paid the market price.

Why would there be many generators? The reason offered by the deregulation booster club was that technological development reduced and in some cases eliminated economies of scale in electric generation. If so, there was now scope for the mass introduction of relatively small combined-cycle gas turbines, which also meant that wholesalers (i.e., generators) could become smaller. (Brazil was a country in which there were great expectations along this line.) In addition, it was postulated that in the best of all possible worlds, large industrial firms could generate their own power and even sell some of it to external buyers.

Now we can examine some price theory. Competition among retailers was supposed to lower prices to households and small businesses, while competition among generators — of which there would now be many both locally and in the surrounding states — would lower prices to retailers. The key element that was supposed to make everything work smoothly was the increase in efficiency that deregulators claimed was inevitable when competition worked its wonders. This arrangement has overtones that are similar to what a California journalist described as throwing a letter intended for foreign shores into the ocean, and hoping that friendly tides will take it to the intended destination.

Since the Enron bosses had promised the governor and people of California that retail prices would fall by 40%, the retail price was "regulated" down by 10% in order to convince doubters among voters and legislators that everything would go as promised. This annoyed retailers, but they maintained their composure because they expected that competition among a fairly large number of generators would reduce the cost of the electricity they purchased.

The actual outcome was that generators got rich, while retailers suffered losses amounting to billions of dollars. In San Diego, competition was allowed to determine the retail price, and that price increased by so much that it led to demonstrations and consumers refusing to pay their electric bills. Eventually the price in that city had to be capped, and the legislator who had led the fight to introduce deregulation deserted the deregulation booster club and signed on with the opposing side (led by Governor Davis). Similarly, on the East Coast of the United States, Senator Ernest Hollings brusquely abandoned the deregulation sinners who had seduced him into the ways of competition and began to call himself a "born-again regulator". Quite possibly, the senator noticed that as the smoke was clearing from the California meltdown, one of the old sayings introduced aboard some unlucky US Navy ships in World War II began to apply: "When in danger, when in doubt, run in circles, scream and shout".

It has been suggested that factors other than deregulation were at work in the California meltdown, such as rising fuel costs and drought (in the Pacific Northwest). There was no drought in New York (State), where a California-like deregulation scheme boosted retail prices, nor were there fuel shortages in Sweden and South Australia where deregulation fiascos took place. What there was in these and all other deregulation showplaces was the gaming of the system (i.e., price manipulation) by generators who — to use the words of the Irving Berlin song — were only doing what comes naturally. The *market power* of generators is not a fiction but a reality, because the returns to scale that deregulators said did not exist actually do exist, and they became relatively more important when natural gas prices increased by a very large amount. Something else that was real were the rolling blackouts that were experienced as capacity fell or stagnated or was "gamed down" while at the same time demand increased, as tends to happen in regions that become larger and/or richer.

The reaction of the deregulation booster club to these events was not unexpected. Consider, for example, Ms Laura Cohn of *Business Week* (19 February 2001), and Mr Spencer Abraham, the former US Energy Secretary. They immediately concluded that what they called the Bush Administration's "tough love" gambit was capable of resolving California's electric deregulation fiasco. By that they meant that the government would show its love for the citizens of California by not interfering with their problems. In other words, they rejected the opinion of the governor of Washington (State), Gary Locke, who said that "Energy deregulation began with the federal government, and that is where the problems created by failed deregulation efforts must be addressed".

Secretary Abraham could be expected to reject it, because when he was a US Senator he sponsored legislation to abolish the Department of Energy. He was also sympathetic to persons in the US automobile industry who, according to Bill Ford, chairman of Ford Motors, ". . . did the minimum to comply with the (fuel economy) law and fought virtually every (congressional) initiative".

Neither Ms Cohn or Mr Abraham seemed even faintly aware that the analysis of a typical electric grid should begin with physics as well as economics, because electricity is different: it cannot be readily confined to a *linear* path, which greatly complicates the *access* issue — i.e., the ability of consumers in a given district to obtain the amount desired at the lowest quoted price by simply stringing a wire between their location and the "point" featuring the most attractive price. Put another way, it might not always be possible to economically integrate markets in *different* locations into one large "competitive" market, with "the law of one price" being valid (or almost valid) within the limits of transportation and various transaction costs, and as a result the theoretical benefits associated with this scheme becoming available for everyone.

(In its least sophisticated form, the law of one price states that in a "perfectly informed" or price-wise transparent competitive market, if there were two or more prices for the same good, then it would make sense for some market actor to buy at or slightly above the lower price, and sell at or just under the highest. This *arbitrage* should tend to eliminate price differences. In addition, there would be a positive welfare effect due to goods being transferred into the possession of buyers who valued them the most, in return for a sum of money equal to or greater than that reflecting the value placed on these goods by the seller. As already noted, the ostensible fall in electricity prices would not dishearten generators and distributors, because the increase in efficiency that supposedly would accompany deregulation would result in lower production costs. Needless to say, most of this is an elaborate falsehood.)

Unfortunately, even if the physics could be played down and if supply were boosted, there is still the matter of the extreme volatility of electric prices. Why should households and small businesses acquiesce in the establishing of a system in which price spikes were automatically passed along, when it would probably mean that they might occasionally find themselves being requested to pay enormous amounts of money for their electricity? If we take this as a question, then the answer is that they would almost certainly not do so if they bothered to become aware of the personal misfortunes that this choice could bring about. *This is the undesired lesson that households in both Sweden and Norway have received the past few years.* However, experience seems to show that the experts who could assist them in avoiding this kind of mistake are often less than helpful. For instance, one of the most conspicuous finance icons of the 20th century is the former governor of the US central bank (i.e., the Federal Reserve System), Alan Greenspan. During his period as an aggressive libertarian, Mr Greenspan wrote that "The basis of regulation is armed force" (*The Economist*, 27 November 1999). Once it becomes profitable for academics and the business press to spread this particular variety of wisdom, then anything can happen.

The persons mentioned above, and others, cannot envisage how a restructured electric sector would function in the *real* as opposed to the *textbook* world. Under the new system, long-term arrangements (where electricity was contracted for over a long period) between utilities (i.e., distributors) and generators were supposed to be played down, and spot contracts (involving spot prices) promoted. (A spot price is the price for the immediate or near-immediate delivery of a commodity.) Unfortunately, this means that given the invariably faulty *derivatives market* in which futures and options contracts for electricity are traded, participants will find it difficult or even impossible to optimally *hedge* against price uncertainties. According to Professor Laura D'Andrea Tyson of the University of California and London Business School, the California deregulation plan included abolishing long-term arrangements (*Business Week*, June 2001). However, this ivory-tower agenda could not be sustained. The same is true in Brazil, where price volatility and inadequate investment soon caused the government to change its mind about the desirability of spot arrangements.

To make matters worse, the deregulation theorists were, and are, completely unable to grasp that the so-called "waste" that deregulation was supposed to eliminate could be magnified by the kind of investment program that would be necessary to compensate for and/or correct the badly conceived and orchestrated departures from vertical integration that were initiated in California and elsewhere.

It might be educational here to observe what happened in Australia when the government decided to sell some electric assets: the market immediately established the value of these assets at only a fraction of that which was expected. The underlying economics is simple, although it seems to be missing in most of the learned expositions on deregulation. The initial value of these assets was based on their integration into an existing, *comprehensive* electric supply network. When fragmented, their technical viability was reduced, and so (*ceteris paribus*) their economic values had to decline.

Before continuing, let me offer a comment on what happened in places like California, Brazil and energy-rich Alberta (Canada) where, with the help of a barrage of clumsy falsifications, a few influential economists and commentators succeeded in convincing both decision makers and voters that there would be a sizable fall in electric prices once networks were exposed to what they call "competition". Brazil, for example, soon found itself facing an energy crisis of the California variety because the Brazilian energy bureaucracy foolishly came to believe that "liberalization" would provide a miracle cure for potential energy supply deficiencies (via increased investment). Instead, a worsening energy crisis and chronic underinvestment threatened to cut economic growth by half, which brought Brazilian politicians at least partially to their senses. (An important element in this crisis was the belief that gas-based power could be less expensive than nuclear or hydro-based electricity, and given the opportunity via deregulation, private firms would detect this and invest accordingly.)

But as a minister (Pedro Parente) said, "The market is not enough to ensure an increase in the power supply. You need a bigger state role in regulation and supervision". Someone who agreed, to the surprise of everyone, was Lutz David Travesso, the president of AES, which is an American-owned power company operating in Brazil. He said that: "The market has not been working. Postponing liberalization is not bad but prudent, and for us even positive" (*Financial Times*, 17 January 2002).

At one time it appeared that the winners in the Swedish exercise would be large industrial and commercial firms (which is good for the economy as a whole), but as things turned out when electricity prices began to escalate, there was talk of energy-intensive firms forming a syndicate to buy power from coal-based installations in East Europe and Russia. Households now fully comprehend that they are losers and furthermore, Haas and Auer (2001) argue that almost all price decreases scheduled for Western Europe would, if realized, be temporary, since mergers, uncertainty, unbundling, etc., could lead to a (relative) fall in generating capacity as firms become more intent on acquiring the assets of other companies instead of expanding (through physical investment) their productive facilities.

This kind of spectacle is also visible in the international petroleum industries. Newly merged entities have often lowered exploration and drilling budgets below those existing in pre-merger conditions: in other words, the exploration and drilling whole became less than the sum of the parts. As pointed out in *Business Week* (10 March 2003), large producers found it more expedient to "merge and cut costs than to invest the time and money to bring new fields on line". What that discussion did not say was that the reason for this approach was they had become convinced there were no large new fields to be found.

Some state governors in the US asked Mr Abraham to impose a temporary ceiling — or "price caps" — on *wholesale* (i.e., generator) electric prices. The former Secretary — who preferred a large *retail* (final user) price rise — rejected these requests, maintaining that price controls would only aggravate the supply crisis. By way of supporting him, Ms Cohn turned to no less an authority than Paul W. MacAvoy, a Yale School of Management professor. MacAvoy called the price caps that Senators Dianne Feinstein (a Democrat) and Gordon Smith (a Republican) requested a "bad, bad disease".

I remember MacAvoy's previous intrusion into energy economics. Several decades earlier, he (and Professor Robert Pindyck of MIT) did some econometric work which led them to believe that taking away price regulations would lead to a sizable increase in the reserves of natural gas in North America. What they unfortunately failed to consider is that in the last analysis, the amount of reserves available from wasting assets like gas or oil are determined by geology, and not econometrics. In these circumstances, I sincerely doubt whether Professor MacAvoy's qualifications improved to an extent that they matched the identikit profile of a world-class expert on the very important topic of deregulation.

But even the most conscientious "servant of the people" — to use an expression mouthed by John Wayne in the film "McQ" — is susceptible to error when in the grip of the deregulation mania. "The best energy policy in the entire world", is how Ms Hazel O'Leary, a former US Secretary of Energy, described the newly deregulated Pakistan electric industry. According to the anti-corruption authorities in that country, it was better than the best if the financial benefits were flowing in your direction. Otherwise it was an abomination in practice and misleading in theory, although it was not until various market actors began to shoot at each other with real guns and bullets that Madame Secretary realized that her judgment had been a trifle premature.

In the old days, most love stories had a happy ending — even those involving tough love. The same is true here. With bad news expected everywhere on the energy front, President Bush imposed what was termed a "market-based mitigation plan" (for prices) that was extended to 11 Western states. The hated price caps thus made their appearance, though under a new name. "A rose is a rose no matter what it is called", Senator Dianne Feinstein remarked, and so another electric market that had gone wild was tamed by the toughest regulator of all: political expediency.

5. Oil and Economic Logic

"To look is to think"
— *Salvador Dali*

I picture this chapter as a long and important review of topics that many readers will someday extend and present to students, colleagues, friends and even enemies. For instance, imagine my surprise (and near panic) when I was severely chastised (at the 22nd international meeting in Rome (Italy) of the International Association for Energy Economics) for daring to express my belief in an interpretation of the Reserve-Production (R/q) ratio for petroleum similar to that which will be presented in some detail in this book.

I also became the object of some "attitude" on the part of other delegates when I made a friendly remark about the work of Dr M. King Hubbert that dealt with the ultimate availability of petroleum. Among other things, I was sanctimoniously informed that oil reserves are "dynamic", and basically are dependent on human ingenuity (i.e., technology) — which as all thoughtful persons are supposedly aware, would ultimately come scampering to the rescue in case the energy wolf appears at the door. Finally, I was assured that economics and technology were always the correct aperture through which oil reserves should be scrutinized. Geology was taken to be of minor importance. ·

A passing comment in the survey of environmental economics by Professor Richard Cooper indicated that he was prepared to take a similar position — at least when that survey was produced (1995). To his way of thinking, oil was certain to be cheaper in the future because technology would reduce costs. The matter of oil exhaustibility apparently did not occur to him, although even at that time oil production in the US was on a downward trend from which there was no recovery. Of course, the events of the past few years have probably changed his mind about a lot of things having to do with that commodity. At the present time there is a hectic scramble for oil, with China, India, South Korea and Japan together importing more than the US (or about 12 mb/d). Their import dependence is rising faster than that of the US, even though China and India — the two most populous countries in the world — are far behind the US in per-capita income and per-capita consumption of oil.

As a comment on this situation, the *Financial Times* (10 January 2005) said that western oil consumers will be able to deal with the competition for Middle East oil by countries like the above foursome by turning to non-OPEC sources such as the North Sea, Gulf of Mexico, West Africa, the Caspian and Russia. One certainly hopes that the governments of the "western" countries do not take this kind of advice too seriously because in about a decade, by my calculations, all of these will be of greatly reduced significance where the ability to export oil is concerned. In fact the UK North Sea is already in irreversible decline.

One of the reasons why we have to suffer so many errors of judgment on the part of various observers of the oil scene is that their fundamental mode of thought is still many years in the past, when the global consumption of oil was, e.g., 50 million barrels per day (= 50 mb/d), and could fairly easily be raised an extra million barrels or so (per day) by increased exploration and drilling, and/or a wider and more intensive application of various scientific or technological improvements to existing deposits. During the year in which this is being written, however, with consumption approaching 86 mb/d and a predicted need to add well over a million barrels per day to output every year over the foreseeable future, it could be a momentous indiscretion to accept or to even contemplate theories claiming that new projects in exotic locales can compensate for the near stagnation in production that could take place in certain oil-rich countries if these states decided to exhibit the same interest in their own long-range economic development as they have graciously shown in ensuring that adequate quantities of this vital commodity reach their clients.

For example, both the IEA and the US Department of Energy once suggested that one of the reasons why there will not be a peaking of global oil production in the next two or three decades is because Saudi Arabia has the capacity and willingness to produce 20 mb/d of oil in the not-too-distant future. However, as I point out in Chapter 3 of this book, it is unlikely that the Saudis would sign up for a *sustained* output of more 12 mb/d. As for their capacity to go much higher, even if they were willing, this is also dubious according to influential observers of the oil markets like Matthew Simmons, a Houston (Texas) investment banker and former advisor to President Bush, and one of the leading oil consultants, Herman Franssen (2005).

Furthermore, although one well-known oil optimist is correct when he repeatedly points out that "we keep looking for more oil, and finding more oil", he invariably forgets to note that, in terms of quantity, the aggregate amount of oil discovered is on a falling trend. Nearly 365 billion barrels were discovered in the 1960s, about 275 billion barrels in the 1970s, 150 billion in the 1980s, and the figures that I have seen for the 1990s suggest that less than 40 billion barrels were put on the books. My lectures on oil always begin with this unpleasant piece of information. At the present time, only one barrel of oil is being discovered for about every three being consumed, which I choose to interpret as the worst possible news for anyone on the buying side of the oil market, regardless of the relationship they may have to goods and services using oil.

It should also be noted that even if it were true that technology is "overwhelming natural depletion" — as some oil optimists still claim — and reducing costs all along the line, without an increase in the amount of oil discovered, preferably in the form of larger deposits, production cannot continue to rise. This is one of the major results derived from the work of M. King Hubbert, and clearly explained in this book as an *economic* as compared to a geological phenomenon. It is probably worth mentioning that few, if any, executives of the major oil companies in any part of the world expect a major alteration in the existing supply–demand picture, regardless of what they may say when the TV cameras are turned in their direction.

Let me emphasize for those persons who are uninterested in geological or economic arguments, and have no desire to read the next few chapters in this book, that a close look at the figures does not substantiate the exasperated point of view put forward by the oil optimists when they encounter opposition to their pet "theories". Since 1981, US oil output has fallen from 8.6 mb/d to less than 6 mb/d, although firms now drill deeper (to an average of 6105 ft, as compared to 4512 ft 20 years ago). Moreover, the cost of the average production well declined to about $769,000 as compared to $855,000 (in real terms) in 1981, and the success ratio has reached 80% as compared to the earlier 70%. (These figures apply to the beginning of 2002.)

The profitability of some international operations is also impressive. BP's return (i.e., yield) on investment and exploration seems to have reached a new record in 2005. The story behind its ability to do so well turns on the relatively inexpensive reserves that this firm succeeded in obtaining, as well as its ability to keep production costs lower than for major competitors ExxonMobil and Shell. [As in game theory, I often explain the cause of this situation as a combination of strategy, skill, and luck — and particularly the latter. In a world in which oil in the ground is becoming scarcer, BP's *bets* (on, e.g., the West Coast of Africa) paid off, although a key factor in explaining the value of West African oil to large foreign companies is corruption in the countries possessing this oil.]

At the same time though, BP's earnings (i.e., profits) in 2005 were only $22 billion as compared to $23 billion for Shell and $36 billion for Exxon-Mobil. (Here it can be mentioned that in 2005 all the major automobile makers together earned about $21 billion.) Despite all this money, Shell and Exxon have experienced some disappointments. Shell replaced only 60–70% of its production in 2005, while ExxonMobil managed only 19% in 2004. One conclusion that can be drawn here is that despite enormous capital resources, the failure by these firms to replace production is a sign that even worse tidings might eventually appear, although since BP's Lord (John) Browne (of Madingly) would not deny the possibility of oil costing $100/b at some point in the future, I doubt whether, e.g., ExxonMobil will be deprived of its position at the top of the corporate income league. Moreover, 2006 was an even better year for Big Oil, although voices were heard suggesting that Lord Browne should begin shopping around for another line of work due to some problems with BP's Alaskan assets.

One of the points being made in the above discussion is that since it is not unreasonably expensive to look for, find and produce conventional oil, the root of the oil problem in, e.g., the United States, is an incurable shortage of *large quantities* of conventional domestic reserves, and the same thing now also applies to, e.g., the North Sea (where just a few years ago journalists still talked about "exciting" prospects). At that time, certain oil companies heavily endorsed the idea of plentiful future oil (which implies low oil prices in the future) because they understood that merger-related cost reductions were more sensible than looking for "cheap" oil that is not there. In addition, if expectations are that oil prices will more likely fall than rise, then (*ceteris paribus*) the objects of their affection might find proposed mergers a great deal more attractive. The shares of the "target" firm might also be cheaper.

Put as simply as possible, some firms are to all intents and purposes looking harder than ever for oil, and it is not unthinkable that they will succeed in finding more; but collectively they are moving farther away than ever from finding enough. Take as an example the Russian Federation. It was recently announced that the largest discovery in 10 years has been made in the Caspian Sea. What this "find" comes to in production terms might eventually be 100,000 b/d, which is paltry: it amounts to only slightly more than 1% of present production. (I can add that with economic growth picking up in Russia, and additional energy required for electric power and vehicle fuel, the position of that country as an oil exporter is destined to weaken.)

The fallacy of composition comes to mind here — the simple fact that if something can be done on a small scale, it causes inattentive observers to jump to the conclusion that it can be done on any scale; however, you can be confident that the persons in the executive suites of the large firms that are active in places like North America, the Caspian region, the Gulf of Mexico — or any other region or gulf — are not confused by incidental statistics, nor the fallacies to which they may give rise. With a huge number of wells drilled, every large firm in the US, as well as the government of that country, now realizes that even a much higher success ratio cannot keep the (domestic) production/import ratio of the US from descending. During the periods reviewed above, US imports of crude and refined products moved from being important to being crucial.

A concept that most executives are familiar with — and which will be treated later in this section — is a "rule" associated with M. King Hubbert, which might be called the "mid-point depletion rule": in a given oil-producing region, *when half the oil discovered and likely to be discovered has been produced, production will level off and begin to decline.* A short discussion in the next chapter argues that this is as much an economic as a geological phenomenon; however, I want to state now that while Hubbert's geometry appears to work well for a majority of large deposits, this is because it is not the mid-point of reserves (50%) that is relevant, but a band around the mid-point from about 40% to about 60% of ultimate reserves.

An item that should never be overlooked is the location of oil. Global proved reserves in the low-cost, easily accessible class are overwhelmingly located in the Middle East, and according to Teitelbaum (1995), some very rich investors in the United States staked a great deal of money that a large fraction of those reserves will stay in the ground unless buyers in the oil-importing countries were willing to pay realistic prices for their extraction. As the Texas billionaire Richard Rainwater stated when he began purchasing oil assets five or six years ago, the rising global demand "paints a picture for me that doesn't have any other outcome. The price of oil is going to have to come up". His optimism definitely seems to have paid off, since beginning in the last quarter of 1999 the long-shunned gas and oil sectors generated profits at a lovely pace. Besides, as another billionaire — the late Marvin Davis — generously informed the inquisitive, "you don't have to be a cockeyed genius to see this coming".

Some attention can now be paid to the R/q ratio (which actually ties in with the work of M. King Hubbert). The concepts that are presented below are gradually being understood to the extent that they deserve, although not fast enough as far as I am concerned, which is one of the reasons that I make it my business to repeat them as often as I can. An irritating problem here is that even the many outstanding microeconomic textbooks to which our students have access insist upon treating the production of depletable resources in terms of an almost completely inappropriate model developed by a brilliant economist, Hotelling (1931). This exaggerated and scientifically meaningless respect for elegant irrelevance is one of the major reasons why academic economics is increasingly subjected to ridicule. "Narrow rationality" is what the superstar physicist Murray Gell-Mann has termed this kind of behavior, which features (easily) quantifiable nonsense being rated far above non-quantifiable plausibility.

The story of the R/q ratio is simple. When it falls below a "critical value" — 10 was the number assumed in the seminal article of Flower (1978) — this ratio will determine production in the sense that production should adjust in such a way as to hold the R/q ratio constant (or more realistically, nearly constant). If this were not done, then it would be tantamount to "overworking" the deposit, and as a result of accelerated (physical) depreciation, reducing the amount of oil that can ultimately be obtained. Let us put this in a slightly different way: if the R/q ratio falls below a certain level — probably somewhere between 10 and 15 — then the deposit is being "damaged" in the same manner that sucking too hard on a straw will damage an ice-cream soda (or — to take a more unpopular metaphor — firing a rifle on automatic will, *ceteris paribus*, reduce its length of its useful life relative to firing single shots). This particular R/q ratio can be designated the *critical R/q ratio*, or θ^*, and for simplicity I always take it as 10 — although Flower (1978) prefers the higher figure. This topic receives a short comment in this chapter's appendix, and will be treated with some simple algebra in the next chapter.

What happened in the US was that the reserve–production ratio fell below 10, and surprisingly continued downward until it was approaching 9. At that point the inevitable happened in the form of one of the largest declines in US oil output in modern times. Of course, oil production in the US had begun falling many years earlier. In 1962, Hubbert published an updated version of a highly controversial report in which he had claimed that oil production in the "lower 48" of the United States would peak between 1966 and 1970, at a point where approximately half of the *total* amount of US reserves had been produced. (Total here means the sum of the amount of oil already extracted *plus* proved existing reserves.) The peak came about the end of 1970, and in the "lower 48" has been trending down ever since.

Hubbert's warning of potential oil shortages was in general ignored because of an ingrained — and to a considerable extent understandable — belief by his potential readers in the efficacy of the price system: higher oil prices should supposedly speed up the introduction of a superior oil recovery technology, and at the same time increase exploration as well as the amount and intensity of drilling. The main difficulty here is that technological progress cannot find (conventional) oil that does not exist. (It can, admittedly, locate and produce "heavy" oil, oil from tar sands and unconventional oils from, e.g., shale; however, these resources are in a higher cost class.) It also needs to be carefully noted that the formation of the "efficiency" prices that are explained in advanced undergraduate or graduate courses in economics — and which convey the kind of information that will induce a logically meaningful reaction from producers and consumers — does not always take place in the presence of uncertainty, and this definitely applies to geological uncertainty. Before oil supply curves move to the right — i.e., before production will actually increase following a rise in prices — some of this uncertainty might have to be dispelled by increased seismological and/or drilling activities. (Supply curve movements to the left often seem less complicated. For example, when the oil price declined in 1998–1999, 136,000 of the 574,000 oil wells in the US were shut down temporarily or "permanently". High oil prices, though, may have cancelled this permanence.)

A few observations were offered earlier about the comparatively low recovery factor of oil reserves from oil-in-place. This is not a satisfactory state of affairs, but there is not much that can be done about it in the short run. The production of conventional oil involves reservoir fluids flowing under pressure out of the reservoir rock into a production well (or borehole). Initial production tends to be constant for a period ranging from several days to several years. Then, as the pressure drops and the oil has to move a longer distance through the reservoir rocks in order to reach a given borehole, the output will tend to decline — *ceteris paribus*. One of the things that will reduce the pressure is a too rapid depletion. This can result in the deposit being damaged, which in turn makes the oil more difficult to extract (for the same cost), as well as decreasing the ultimate recovery factor. Now we see why the R/q ratio is so important: when operating below the *crucial R/q* ratio (= 10 in the previous discussion), we are overworking the deposit. Something else that should be recognized is that petroleum engineering is a serious profession, and few economists have the background to understand the more abstruse facets of oil production. Thus, for economists, levels and changes in the R/q ratio can, if properly interpreted, sum up considerable important geological information.

This discussion can be slightly extended. As shown in my previous energy economics textbook, the production profile for a typical oil field — where a field is a group of reservoirs in the same general area — usually exhibits rising production, a plateau, and then falling production. Obtaining this profile calls for drilling a number of production wells. Initially, the flow from successive wells exceeds the depletion (i.e., production decline) of those already drilled, and so we start out with a rising production pattern. Then, new drilling takes place at a pace that is designed to keep output more or less constant; and finally drilling slows because as the amount of oil remaining in the field declines, the cost of extra wells is high compared to the additional amount of oil obtained. The downturn in drilling accounts for the declining portion of the profile. Naturally, this exposition also applies to gas.

A few statistics might be useful. The conventional oil already produced is close to 1000 billion barrels (=1000 Gb). The consensus figure for *proved reserves* available now is somewhat over 1000 Gb. The (estimated) amount that will still be found is 300–500 Gb, and thus *ultimate* reserves — the total amount available past and future — can be put at about 2400 Gb. Optimists, however, say that ultimate reserves are closer to 3000 Gb, and pessimists say 1900 Gb is a better estimate. If we look at the forecasts of the IEA for world demand, we see crude oil demand in 2010 at 95 mb/d, and in 2020 it reaches 115 mb/d. Taking ultimate reserves as 2400, and applying a variation of Hubbert's rule, the peak production year turns out to be somewhere around 2010, with the production of conventional oil at 95 mb/d (as compared to about 85+ mb/d just now). Thus, using the assumptions of this forecast, enough additional reserves would have to be found to enable an extra 15 mb/d of conventional or unconventional oil to eventually be produced in order to push the peak out to 2020. (2010 for peak production is too early to suit my taste. 2015 strikes me as more reasonable.)

Like most forecasts of future oil production and/or consumption, the above estimates may turn out to be quite far from the *ex-post* values, but even so this kind of approach has led some very serious people to believe that the age of (conventional) oil — in the most comprehensive sense — is slowly drawing to an end. Let me suggest, however, that it is highly unlikely it will draw to an end before 2010, and the same applies to 2020, or for that matter 2030, since plenty of oil will be produced and used after that time. Furthermore, some "back of the envelope" calculations that I once made assure me that we will not see a global production peak before 2015, although in case you are exceptionally impatient, I consider it unlikely that you will have to wait until 2020 to experience this traumatic event.

Now for one of the most important concepts in the widespread debate on the future availability of oil, which deals with the global oil supply. In the American Army, the United States at one time was frequently referred to as "The World". (In fact a former heavyweight boxing champion, Mohammad Ali, actually used that expression in public on one occasion.) Let us begin the analysis by pretending that the United States is actually the entire world, and take a brief look at what happened to its production of oil. If we examine the "lower 48" to begin with, we know that the modern oil age began in Pennsylvania (and perhaps also on the shores of the Caspian Sea). Output peaked in that region in a short time, and eventually also in California and

Oklahoma, and perhaps elsewhere in the US. But in the huge oil province of East Texas, output continued to rise, and as a result, if we examined the production curve for the entire lower 48, we would see the output of oil continuing to rise.

Though generally unexpected, output also peaked in East Texas, and in these circumstances it became impossible to maintain a rising production in the lower 48. Once the production of Alaska (where reserves were twice as large as East Texas) began to accelerate though, and this output was added to that of the lower 48, then the aggregate production curve for the *entire* US began moving up again, but even so it never attained the 1970–1971 maximum. Thus eventually, and even before output peaked in Alaska, the output curve for the US (i.e., the entire 50 states) peaked again (though not as high as the previous maximum). Equally as significant, although the huge Prudhoe field in Alaska was discovered as late as 1968 (with reserves estimated at 25 Gb), it peaked only 20 years later.

What happened in the US will happen in the entire world sooner or later. It will almost certainly happen when or even before output in the Middle East begins to slide. (Saudi Arabia is roughly operating on an undulating plateau at the present time, and while perhaps — *perhaps* — that plateau will move up by another million barrels a day or thereabouts, it might be possible to argue, as Matthew Simmons argues, that the bad news has already arrived.) Of course, what we would like to know is when (*ceteris paribus*) the output of the Middle East more or less duplicates the pattern exhibited as in the US.

There is some talk of a composite peak happening around 2030, but I would be very surprised if anybody in the executive suites of the major oil companies believes that it will take so long, and the same is true of many top politicians in North America and Europe, and perhaps elsewhere. Once again we can turn to Neumann–Morgenstern reasoning: regardless of when it actually happens, in the light of information shortages and the inexactness of calculation techniques, it is asking for trouble to count on it happening later rather than sooner. There is also some opinion coming from the IEA that Chinese imports will be as large as those of the US in 2030. Maybe so, but regardless of the actual quantity, these imports will not be rising because globally, there is not likely to be sufficient oil to support an increase in imports of the extent implied in that estimate.

A superficial examination of many oil production curves gives the impression that the decline from the peak tends to be more rapid than the approach to the peak. An interesting suggestion as to why this is so follows from an observation by Ali Samsam Bakhtiari of the National Iranian Oil Company: "it's not that you've eaten half of the pie, you've eaten the good half".

Until recently, energy economics featured an acid-like debate on the subject of oil depletion. This continues to a certain extent, and in citing my many contributions to this dispute I always enjoy pointing to the situation in neighboring Norway, where fewer exploratory wells were drilled in 2003 than in any year since 1977 — despite high and rising oil prices. Only a third of these ventures were judged successful, as compared to a half the previous year, and gas rather than oil was the principal discovery: in fact, it has been at least 11 years since a significant amount of oil has been discovered in the vicinity of Norway. That rich oil province has seen its best days, and from here on in the accent is going to be on gas.

I occasionally hear from people who have a different opinion from mine about the future of oil in the Norwegian North Sea. I have even heard it claimed that the unexploited field "Goliath" may contain five times as much oil as previously calculated. The probability of that being true is certainly greater than zero, although I intend to continue to believe that this estimate is unsubstantiated balderdash of the kind that is often circulated in order to increase share prices and/or obtain more investment dollars.

Similarly, there is a new twist (or spin) that deserves our consideration. Many of the optimists have become vaguely aware that technology and investment cannot overwhelm the laws of physics, and thus locate resources where in reality none exist. As a result, considerable attention is now focused on oil from Canadian tar sands. In stock form, these unconventional resources contain an amount of oil/energy that matches — and perhaps exceeds — the proved resources of Saudi Arabia and Iraq. I have nothing at all against believing that someday a technology will appear that will permit these unconventional assets to be economically exploited on a much larger scale, but thus far there is a shortage of proof. As far as I can tell, the production of oil from tar sands is increasing at a rate that is only slightly larger than the rate at which the output of conventional oil is declining.

The key word above is "someday", which in this context does not mean tomorrow: it means — in the best of cases — a long time in the future. Even in the most auspicious situation, the Canadian output will likely be well under 3 mb/d in 2010, and under 4.5 mb/d in 2020. Furthermore, regardless of when this oil becomes available, there is still this matter of the *energy return on energy invested* (EROEI), which involves calculating the "yield" from both the direct and indirect energy inputs employed in the production process. Professor Ugo Bardi of Florence University (Italy) has emphasized this approach in his recent work, and suggests among other things that it casts doubt on the viability of the "hydrogen economy". [You can refer to his on-line paper (in Italian), "A critical approach to the concept of a hydrogen based economy", at www.aspoitalia.net.]

According to some observers, the EROEI — which might be thought of as a kind of energy profit — tends to decline over time for all energy resources examined. They cite an EROEI for oil and gas in the United States of 17 today, as compared with 100 for the 1930s. More relevant for the present exposition, they say that the energy input required to produce conventional oil from the heavy oil in Venezuela and tar sands in Alberta is almost equal to the energy content of the final product. (To be specific, the long-chain hydrocarbons of the oil obtained from tar sands must be split into lighter, more usable molecules. This not only decreases the net energy yield, but greatly increases the amount of carbon dioxide released into the atmosphere.) I have also heard it said that an EROEI that is "much greater than one-to-one (1 to 1) is needed to run a society".

The expression "run a society" does not sound particularly elegant to my ears, even if it turns out to be important for the sequel. What we want to consider at first-hand is the flow of energy through a system in such a way as to locate all of the energy inputs relevant to the output of a well-defined good or service. In the case of conventional or unconventional oil, there is a direct energy cost of obtaining the item, to which are added the various energy costs associated with processing, transportation, etc. Slesser (1978) provides a useful introduction to these matters, and among other things notes the utility of input–output (I/O) analysis. Once this expression (I/O) enters the discussion, it becomes possible to think of a modified version of the Hawkins–Simon (H–S) condition (1949), which — though generally ignored — can provide a partial theoretical basis for EROEI.

We can look closer at this phenomenon with an observation from one of the most important economics books of the 20th century, *Linear Programming and Economic Analysis* (1958). The H–S condition turns on the theme that it should not "take more than a ton of coal to make one ton of coal". (You can use barrels of oil here instead of tons of coal.) Thus, "if we add up the direct and indirect inputs of coal that go into a ton of output (the coal to make coal, the coal to make coal to make coal, the coal to make the steel used to make coal . . . etc., *ad infinitum*), this should be less than one ton". Essentially, this is equivalent to the (less than of equal) one-to-one EROEI specification alluded to above, and intuitively it makes considerable sense on the "social" level — i.e., the level dealing with social rather than private profit.

However, if we leave coal (or oil) and think in terms of energy, then even if a barrel of produced energy contains, directly and indirectly, more than a barrel of energy inputs — with outputs and inputs measured in an energy unit such as Btu or joules — we might still find it attractive to do business, at least in the short run. This is because the barrel of energy at the output point might be different in composition from that used as an input. For instance, the output might be a barrel of oil from tar sands, and the input two barrels of coal containing more Btu than the oil obtained. If the price of oil were high, while coal was cheap, then it might be good economics to pump billions of dollars into the production of this liquid, even if in the fairly long run a negative energy yield could not be avoided — or, to use the terminology above, we are embarking on a bad way to run a "society". In the very long run, however, we are riding for fall with this particular arrangement.

(Of course, in the great world of neo-classical economics, it is unnecessary to worry about this kind of dilemma, because a comprehensive set of perfectly competitive spot and futures markets are theoretically capable of providing rational producers and consumers with the *scarcity prices* needed to make perfect decisions. As noted in a later chapter, in the real world we do not have — nor will we expect to have — anything approaching this ideal.)

It so happens, though, that despite their public affirmations, in private many geologists, petroleum engineers and executives of the large oil companies are sufficiently acquainted with technological realities to still believe that it makes more sense to search for large quantities of oil on the floor of the oceans than to invest as much as $30,000 per barrel per day for oil originating in the sensual north of Alberta (Canada). They may also be aware that, according to the opinion of Professor Bardi (and probably other physicists), the EROEI is based on thermodynamic factors, and thus in some sense may turn out to be largely (or nearly) impervious to the upgrading of technology. (See also the editorial in *Petromin*, October 2004).

One well-known executive, Mr T. Boone Pickens, recently informed a "60 minutes" interviewer that if we cannot get the oil that we need from the Alberta tar sands, then we are going to have to do without. I suspect that not a great deal of attention was paid to this remark, which conceivably was passed off as "infotainment", however the record shows that Mr Pickens is the kind of man who goes to a great deal of trouble to avoid making mistakes where items like oil or money are concerned.

What it comes down to then is whether the reader believes these oil industry decision-makers or, by way of contrast, assorted pundits (i.e., people whose opinions are relentlessly solicited by others), who refuse to accept that in reality the crust of the earth is not overflowing with inexpensive oil. According to their cheerful way of looking at these proceedings, if by some odd twist of fate a supply predicament should emerge, all you will need is enough dollars to finance the digging of an additional hole, following which you stand there with a bucket and your oil dreams will come true.

Given the social and political consequences of a sudden peaking of global oil, in addition to my almost complete inability at the present time to envisage even the tinge of a solution for this potentially explosive situation, I am afraid that it is completely impossible for me to side with my fellow academics.

6. Great Expectations: A Brief Perspective on Natural Gas

Since the publication of my book on natural gas (1987), dramatic changes have taken place in this market. The growth rate of the demand for gas exceeds that of all energy media except renewables, and unlike the situation 15 years ago, gas is highly recommended as an input for power generation. The reason is the advent of *combined cycle* gas-burning equipment with a very high efficiency. What happens here is that in addition to the gas turbine, there is a secondary turbine producing steam from the waste gases/heat of the gas turbine, and this enables the generator to produce additional electricity. At the same time, it should be recognized that if recent price tendencies continue, they could drastically alter the favorable economics of gas-based power generation that resulted from advances in combined-cycle technology, and in many cases made gas a competitor to coal and nuclear in generating the base load.

As bad luck would have it, there are very many misconceptions in circulation about natural gas, to include those having to do with its deregulation. Some question needs to be asked as to why and how these misconceptions came into existence, and it appears that the answer has to do with the very short time horizons of producers, as well as the short time horizons and carelessness of consumers. In some parts of the world, producers have expressed and conducted themselves in such a way as to suggest that there is a near infinite amount of natural gas reserves available for exploitation, when in truth, in many regions, demand could outrun local supply in a comparatively short time. For instance, in much of the US, exploration and production have started to yield disappointing results; and expectations about, e.g., the Gulf of Mexico, often have an air of unreality about them. With certain exceptions, many gas buyers are almost totally unaware of how supply and demand could develop in even the present decade, and instead continue to make plans for a future which they envisage as featuring all the moderately priced energy they believe they will need.

This might be a good place to repeat that in Brazil, deregulators counted on gas-based power being cheaper than hydroelectricity. As they now admit, this supposition was completely wrong. The problem in Brazil, as in many places, is that huge investments are required to move gas from seller to buyer. "Shortages amid plenty are the underlying irony of it all", was how Jed Baily of the Cambridge Energy Research Associates (CERA) of Boston described the situation (*The Economist*, 11 February 2006). There is plenty of gas in Venezuela and Bolivia, and perhaps also in Peru, where the largest gas field in South America (the Camisea Field) is located, but the question is whether it is more economical to transport a large part of this gas by pipeline or in the form of LNG. *The Economist* concluded that once distances exceed 3000 Km, LNG makes more sense than pipelines. However, on the basis of today's technology, the figure is probably greater than 4000 Km. Given the location of gas in South America though, the most economical transport pattern might involve both fairly long pipelines *and* sea transportation. Exactly how dramas of this nature will play out remains to be seen, because although 20 years of discussions and studies seem to have finally resulted in agreements to construct some very large pipelines from Canada and Alaska to the US mid-west, it may still take a decade before this gas starts flowing.

According to the IEA of the OECD, fossil fuels will account for 90% of the world primary energy mix by 2020, which is a big increase over 1997. Gas demand could rise by 2.7%/year, and its share in world energy demand move from 22% to at least 26%. (Oil's *share* should fall, but this might be more than compensated for by the increase in world oil demand.) Gas is expected to surpass coal after 2010, with its total demand rising by 80% between 1997 and 2020, but clearly in the long run the large availability of coal should assure its primacy. (The IEA base year is 1997.) Pipelines are expected to continue to handle the greater part of international trade, and gas-fired power generation could greatly increase, although the recent gas price increases may change this picture in that they change expectations, regardless of occasional price declines. In the OECD, imports of gas are expected to continue to expand, and OECD Europe alone could account for about 19% of the increase in world demand in the period 1997–2020. There is also an assumption by the IEA that higher natural gas use will reduce carbon dioxide emissions by 10% in 2020. The population basis for these estimates turns on an expected global figure of 7.4 billion persons in 2020.

Russia, which provides more than one-third of global gas exports, will continue to be Europe's main gas supplier, but will also probably contribute to the increased imports that will be required by — among others — China and Korea, especially if it becomes possible to construct large pipelines through North Korea to South Korea. In examining expected growth rates of gas demand, China, East Asia and South Asia stand out from the rest of the world. In the long run, their high rates of growth could have an important effect on the supply of gas to OECD Europe and North America, and if the gas deregulation plans of the EU energy directorate are carried out, there could be some ugly surprises where gas prices are concerned.

The IEA also deserves to be mentioned here. That organization has mostly got it wrong where oil and the liberalization of the electric sector are concerned, and as a result it is difficult to respect their ability to analyze the structure and mechanics of world gas. However, since even the experts of the IEA are capable of comprehending that major uncertainties exist about the ability to develop and transport the more distant gas reserves, then it might be appropriate to suggest that no capricious ideas about restructuring should be allowed to get in the way of sound engineering practices. After pointing out that the question of electric industry reform has several dimensions, to include technical, environmental, economic, social and political, Deepak Sharma (2001) goes on to note that "The ongoing debate ... is being conducted exclusively in the economic realm, which for practical reasons has been further relegated to the economic indicator of price. The underlying assumption is that economics encapsulates all relevant dimensions of reform. This is shortsighted and likely to be potentially damaging to the overall health of the economy".

To this it can be added that where natural gas reform is concerned, the economic debate is not particularly impressive, and in some cases is conducted by persons without the slightest feel for either the economics or the engineering aspects of natural gas industries, and this includes economists with a modicum of engineering training in their background. They have not bothered to find out, for example, that an important component of the financial sector — in the form of several leading investment banks that are heavily involved with commodities — are scaling down their risk management commitments in some commodity markets. Warburg Dillon Read — the investment banking arm of of the large Swiss bank UBS — closed down its electricity derivatives business as early as 1999, and in the same year Merrill Lynch announced its withdrawal from over-the-counter derivatives in natural gas. (Once again, *derivatives* are paper assets such as futures and options contracts associated with physical items such as electricity and gas, which are called the *underlying*.) The decision about electricity may have been reversed later, but if so, this is a comment on the gullibility of their clients rather than a boost in the efficiency of this market.

While this was going on, a consensus of commodity traders and analysts were still willing to wager that derivatives activity in gas and electricity would take off once market liberalization achieved a *critical mass*, and as it turned out, in electricity that condition was not too long in coming, although it did not turn out to be durable: it barely lasted long enough for the most important commodities exchange in the world (NYMEX in New York City) to declare its electricity futures contract hopeless, and also to dump one of its natural gas contracts. Some of this language may sound excessively informal, however later in this book readers will find a fairly long but elementary chapter in which I attempt to examine futures and options with the help of some simple algebra.

Like oil, natural gas is a high-quality energy resource and is probably much more valuable to society than was indicated by its (exceptionally low) price at the beginning of this century. The argument here turns on its superior environmental qualities as well as the comparatively large amount that is available in Russia and the Middle East, although occasionally there is some confusion on this point. The Chairman of the Ford Motor Company, Bill Ford, is concerned about the possible shortage of conventional energy sources in the not-too-distant future, and wants his corporation to lead the way into a hydrogen economy rather than to fuel Ford vehicles with, for example, compressed gas. However, it should not be forgotten that hydrogen is a derived energy source: it is extracted from, e.g., gas, coal or water, and the energy cost of this transformation is as yet considerable. On the other hand, in the long run, given the rate of population growth, it seems almost certain that hydrogen will have to play a major role in the world energy economy. Readers desiring interesting discussions of this topic are referred to *EnergyPulse* (www.energypulse.net).

At the Third Ministerial Meeting of the Gas Exporting Countries' Forum in the Qatari capital Doha in 2003, the Emir of Qatar, Sheikh Hamad Bin Khalifa Al Thani, noted that world gas consumption was growing at rates higher than oil and coal, and the share of gas consumption in total world energy use would continue to rise. He also mentioned that the Middle East possessed about 40% of the world's gas reserves, and since the consumption of the region is low, its potential export capacity is immense. The same observation — though on a lower quantitative level — applies to Bolivia, Peru and Venezuela in South America. These are countries where domestic consumption is far under production possibilities, though the opposite disposition prevails for Argentina, and perhaps Brazil.

Among the countries identified as a very large market for gas from the Middle East was the United States. At the time that I was writing my gas book, it was almost unthinkable that the US would import large amounts of that commodity from countries on the other side of the globe; but unthinkable or not, it is in situations of this type where we see that economics is different from other academic disciplines: the quandaries imposed by uncertainty and information shortages — and in particular those due to the special nature of geology and the irrationality of some market actors — are enormous, and despite what your favorite teachers of mathematical economics may tell you, we are no closer to dealing with them today than we were a quarter of a century ago. This is one of the reasons why it is so difficult to judge the quantity and quality of the energy assets that we will have at our disposal at any given time in the future.

As an example, we can cite the reputedly huge unconventional resources of natural gas languishing in or beneath such things as coal, shale and sandstone deposits, or mixed with salt water and buried under tremendous pressure beneath the Gulf of Mexico and perhaps other bodies of water. Despite the optimism of many important economic researchers, they continue to elude energy companies that are desperate to renew their reserves. This desperation has to some extent turned to resignation, since many of these organizations are now concentrating on maintaining profit *rates* rather than expanding reserves or production. It has also become clear that the new resources that were supposed to come into existence because of gas market deregulation are as non-existent as ever. Fortunately, the failure of electric deregulation is so shocking and extensive that gas market deregulation has been held in check to some extent.

Among the observers of the gas scene who have chosen to go public with their apprehensions is the former Chairman of the US Federal Reserve, Alan Greenspan. On several occasions he has warned of possible traumatic spikes in the price of gas that could have disagreeable macroeconomic consequences. He has also said that North America will forever be condemned to a volatile and inefficient gas market unless it enjoys a guaranteed access to the vast reserves of gas located far from its borders. The same kind of opinion is undoubtedly circulating in some upscale localities about oil.

Many persons still have some difficulty in accepting that the rapid increase in the price of oil might be sustainable. However, countless managers of gas-based electricity generating installations are thinking seriously about restoring gas to its traditional place in the electricity-generating merit order.

To understand what this is all about, it is useful to recall that until the availability of very inexpensive gas and very efficient combined-cycle gas-based generating equipment, natural gas was customarily used to generate the peak load, while the base load — the load that is on the line 24 hours a day — was customarily serviced by coal, nuclear or hydro. As explained in my earlier textbook, and will be repeated in Chapter 7 of this book, the logic here turned on gas-based equipment displaying low capital costs and high variable (i.e., fuel) costs, and in addition this equipment was easy to turn on and off. What happened with the appearance of combined-cycle technology and cheap gas was the promotion of gas to generating the base load (which, among other things, meant a much larger daily input of gas). For instance, in California, a very large fraction of all new power investment in the 1990s involved fairly large gas-based installations. Somewhat earlier in the UK, the "dash for gas" was a similar spectacle.

Once again we get a glimpse into the force of uncertainty in economic theory. When gas prices suddenly increased, these gas-based facilities were often judged to be sub-optimally deployed: the base load was perceived as being generated with the wrong equipment, particularly in situations where the price of the gas being used had not been locked in by long-term contracts. As bad luck would have it, these are the kind of contracts that deregulation/liberalization was dedicated to eliminating, because according to the offbeat gospel of deregulation, they were at least partially responsible for the inefficiencies that supposedly plague the electricity and gas markets.

The electric deregulation circus got under way in Europe — in Scandinavia and the UK — while natural gas deregulation began in the US about 20 years ago, but comparatively slowly. I make no secret of the fact that I am an opponent of almost all electric and natural gas deregulation, but at the same time I am sympathetic to the natural gas buyers and others in the US who felt that the regulatory climate at the time of the "gas bubble" in that country did not correctly address either efficiency or equity concerns. What eventually happened though was that a claque of economists, consultants and various "researchers" were provided with a forum in which they could unleash a barrage of pretentious ideas for correcting what they construed as intrinsic shortcomings, while at the same time promoting a radical transformation of the entire natural-gas sector — from "wellhead" to "burner tip".

How does one treat a collection of misunderstandings and blunders of the magnitude and extent involved here? In the courses on energy economics that I taught in Sweden and France, and in my previous textbook, I did not treat them at all, because unlike the deceptive electric deregulation circus, gas deregulation has not been able to get up full steam. Hopefully this will continue to be the case.

One of the reasons for this was that in the US, and perhaps elsewhere, some important politicians and industry people and genuine experts from the academic world took issue with gas deregulation proposals. For instance, when Professors Arthur DeVany and W. David Walls claimed that the natural gas market in the US was informationally efficient — in the sense that spot gas prices at widely separate points follow each other so closely that it is possible to conclude that these points are in *one* market — their conclusion was disputed by John Herbert and Erik Krell of no less than the US Energy Information Administration, which is an establishment that would like nothing better than to turn the assertions by DeVany and Walls into a holy writ. Instead, Herbert and Krell (1996) found it necessary to state that "it is not clear why they make the claim that the price paid by gas customers is the same, adjusted for a constant basis differential, for all gas markets. Moreover, they do not address some key issues and problems in the operation of gas markets".

It may not be clear to those two researchers, but it is clear to me. DeVany and Walls had an agenda to sell, although to my way of thinking, instead of writing a book, they should have settled for a video clip. How, for example, should we interpret the following statement? "The good news is that the futures market is alive and well, and its price discovery mechanism is reliable and unbiased". If that were true it would indeed be something to shout about; however, in reality, the gas futures market in the US is desperately unwell. Moreover, if a former CEO of British Gas was correct in his contention that the "half-baked fracturing" of the gas markets in order to bring about competition is essentially counter-productive, then a gas futures market is greatly diminished in status, and should expect to eventually be reduced to considerably less than its originally conceived magnitude.

As interesting as various misunderstandings about derivatives markets are for me as a teacher of finance, they are paltry in comparison to uncertainties created by the transition from what DeVany and Walls call "planning" to what they interpret as the "freedom" of spot markets. As far as I am concerned, large and complex gas systems operating in a climate of uncertainty are most efficiently run on an integrated basis that emphasizes long-term contracting. This kind of arrangement promotes optimally dimensioned installations, although this may not have received enough emphasis in your economics textbook.

If pipeline-compressor processing systems which fully exploit increasing returns to scale in order to obtain minimum costs are to be financed and constructed, then — as I interpret the evidence — the kind of uncertainties associated with short- to medium-term sales arrangements should be kept to a minimum as much as possible. Failing to do so could cause a reduction in physical investment, and in the long run higher rather than lower prices. It was the proposed shift from bilateral transactions to spot markets that contributed to what I call *deregulatory uncertainty*, and a possible shortage in local (generator) capacity in California and Alberta (Canada).

In Europe, the EU Commission first mandated the completion of gas market restructuring by 2005. While I can imagine that they were serious when they concocted this pipedream, I would be very surprised if they believe any longer that restructuring can be taken any farther than liberalization, by which they mean that anyone, anywhere, should be able to buy anything that they can afford; and if this "anything" is not for sale, then the rules should be changed so that it could be put on the block if the price is "right". The rest of the restructuring package — bringing into existence what they originally announced would be the kind of "gas-to-gas" competition that is supposed to provide consumers with huge savings — will have to wait, and probably indefinitely. One of the reasons for this is almost certainly a morale problem in the deregulation booster club due to the widespread failure of electric deregulation, but another is the negative attitudes displayed by high-profile industrialists and their experts, and lately some influential politicians.

An example of the experts is Mr Ron Hopper, who was with the US government's Federal Energy Regulatory Commission (FERC) for 11 years, and as a private consultant was an advisor to the EU Energy Commissioner, and also OFGAS (in the UK). Hopper calls himself a strong believer in deregulation, but even so he said that "It is difficult for me to see the potential for pipeline-to-pipeline competition".

I am sure that it is difficult, because he knows as well as I do — and most likely much better — that "looping" and/or increasing compression is often a viable alternative to constructing the new pipelines that deregulation might entail, unless large increases in demand are anticipated. Hopper has also pointed out on several occasions that there can be considerable difficulty in obtaining rights-of-way.

I would be very surprised if Mr Hopper failed to share some of his knowledge of the trials and tribulations of FERC with his EU employers. If so, I hope that he remembered to tell them about a very odd claim by FERC that it had prepared an extensive economic analysis detailing the benefits that would accrue to the national economy in general and gas consumers in particular, if the natural gas sector was restructured. That "claim" led to FERC being sued by Citizen Action — a US consumer organization — and eventually "deciding" to assert that no comprehensive analysis had taken place. This raises an important question: why had there *not* been an in-depth study by FERC's economists or outside consultants? The answer to that must be that there almost certainly had been — it could not have been avoided; and perhaps it was carried out by someone as competent as Ron Hopper.

Assuming that such was the case, then what that unacknowledged study had to reveal was that local distribution companies and consumers would be forced to pay the billions of dollars in transition costs that would be involved in going from regulation to re-regulation. Note: *not* in going from regulation to deregulation, but in going to a different brand of regulation. Incidentally, this is exactly what happened. Consumers and distribution companies (i.e., utilities) *were* burdened with higher costs, *and* found themselves assuming more of the price risk that accompanied the various changes that were made. One of the reasons why things turned out this way is because, according to the deregulators, consumers and distributors were going to be big winners due to the changes being made — though perhaps later rather than sooner. Incidentally, the matter of reliability was simply overlooked, although as *Forbes* (22 January 2001) intimated, deregulation has "whittled away" at the guarantee that many gas users had of a secure gas supply, since, e.g., pipeline companies no longer had the incentive to resort to as much expensive underground gas storage as before, nor to use long-term contracts (with producers) to the same extent.

Edward Feigenbaum, the "inventor" of artificial intelligence, based his work on the belief that human intelligence does not spring from rules of logic, but from knowledge about specific problems, and about the world in general. This may well be so; however, the high-spirited promotion of twisted logic is far from irrelevant for anyone having to deal with the supply side of a market like the gas market. If a conclusion needs to be offered about the deregulation of gas (and electricity), I can only say that what it reduces to is an irrational novelty.

A few years ago, the price of natural gas in the United States averaged $2.2/mBtu, and there were some rumours that it might eventually climb to $4/mBtu. Since almost half of all US homes are heated by gas, this information was looked upon with some apprehension. What happened in early 2003, however, changed apprehension to alarm, because prices suddenly leaped to $6/mBtu, and that was only the beginning — although later they "descended" to about $6/mBtu.

By the end of 2005, gas prices had more than doubled, and the CEO of Dow Chemical told a Senate committee on 6 October that the United States was in a "natural gas crisis". He and his executives gave some indication of what they thought about all this by closing what they called 26 "inefficient" plants in North America and moving them to places where they considered gas to be plentiful (and cheap), which included Kuwait and Argentina. According to *Forbes* (21 October 2005), CEO Andrew Liveris asked the Senate, "How can I recommend investing here?" in the course of attempting to explain why, on that occasion, the global chemical industry had 120 projects under way, with only one in the United States. Among the places where Dow launched joint ventures were Oman and Qatar, where gas was selling for less than a dollar per million Btu.

As implied earlier, the economics taught in Econ 101 will not help serious readers to fully understand the short-run pricing of crude oil, and the same is true where the pricing of natural gas is concerned in, e.g., North America. Once again the availability of gas inventories (stocks) is crucial, and the logic here is about the same as that for oil, which will be taken up at some length in Chapter 2.

In the autumn of 2005 it was estimated that an exceptionally cold winter could reduce stocks of gas in the United States to 500 billion ft^3, which was not a great deal in excess of the amount of gas a pipeline system must have to maintain pressure. Had this happened, a sharp price escalation might have resulted, but fortunately the following winter turned out to be comparatively mild, which also helps to explain the slight decreases in oil and gas prices. The upshot of this is that weather is important for understanding oil and gas prices.

Liquefied natural gas (LNG) from every part of the world is looking increasingly attractive to the United States at the present time, although like the young person across the dance floor, it is impossible to be completely sure of its charms. Price is just one part of the puzzle here, because things like explosions and fireballs are often referred to when discussing the location of LNG terminals. This is perhaps the best place to refer you to an article recently published in *EnergyPulse* by Tam Hunt (2006), and particularly the brilliant comments/discussions on that article published immediately below it. Hunt discusses a few of the arguments against introducing more LNG into California, but it so happens that in this matter the energy consumers of California will have the last say, and they will almost certainly conclude that they cannot do without more gas.

Some statistics might be in order. IEA estimates are that in 2010, (conventional) gas consumption will be 3.2 trillion cubic meters per year ($= 3.2\,\text{Tm}^3/\text{y}$), as compared with the present $2.5\,\text{Tm}^3/\text{y}$; and in 2020 forecast demand will be $4.4\,\text{Tm}^3/\text{y}$. As for reserves, the amount already produced is $60\,\text{Tm}^3$, while *proved* (i.e., remaining) reserves are about $140\,\text{Tm}^3$. The estimated amount that is still to be found is $60\text{–}120\,\text{Tm}^3$. *Ultimate* reserves are thus $260\text{–}320\,\text{Tm}^3$. This may or may not be the actual situation, but readers should get used to seeing and working with this kind of terminology.

Coal will not be taken up in this introductory survey, but this might be the place to mention integrated coal gasification combined cycle (IGCC) technology. What we have here is the gasification of coal which, after processing, is transmitted to a combined cycle power plant. One of the things making this special is that the intention is to remove CO_2 from the coal during the syngas conversion process and store (i.e., sequester) it in underground geologic formations. Some of this is probably being done now, and more will be done later, but in terms of solving the excessive CO_2 problem, it is strictly provisional.

7. A Nuclear Energy Tale

I think it safe to say that while every researcher has his or her private idea of what constitutes success, an intense desire to avoid falling out of favor with the decision makers is something that most of them have in common. This is why in Sweden where, although almost half of the domestic supply of electricity originates in the nuclear sector, there are few economists who take an active part in the nuclear debate. It has been made clear to these ladies and gentlemen that the exposure they prize above all other things in their professional lives will be in the danger zone if they become too friendly toward the "friendly atom".

To get some idea of how this matter is viewed in the "land of the midnight sun", it is useful to know that every year, in conjunction with the awarding of the Nobel prizes, the new laureates participate in a TV program called *Snillen Speculerar* (Genius Speculates), where they discuss various scientific topics that supposedly are of interest to a broad audience. In reality, a large part of this "broad audience" that the program hopes to reach would rather have these matters discussed by Sir Elton or Madonna, which is one reason why only a relatively few of them — including academic economists — are sitting in front of their TVs when this distinctive intellectual event takes place.

A few years ago the dominant voice among the laureates was that of the physicist Robert Laughlin, who at one stage of the discussion expressed outrage that in Sweden, scientists who receive their salaries from the government are discouraged from discussing nuclear matters in a serious (i.e., technical) fashion, just as they are prevented by law from participating in organized nuclear research. Of course, if they had conclusive proof in one form or another of the economic and/or technical shortcomings of nuclear energy, then it is likely that they would be warmly welcomed to the corridors and restaurants of government power. However, as many of us are aware, such proof is difficult to acquire.

Social Democratic governments in both Sweden and Germany have now announced that they intend to dismantle their nuclear sectors, although they were deliberately vague about the time frame. As noted earlier, behind this flagrant irrationality are the small but vocally active and politically important environmentalist parties: in Sweden, acceptance of an eventual nuclear retreat is still part of the price that must be paid by the Social Democrats for the political cooperation of the Green party, although in Germany — now that the Social Democrats have entered into a coalition with the Christian Democrats — they may be in a position to alter their anti-nuclear stance. Another part of the price is having to keep a straight face while entertaining the absurd theories that are often launched about things like the economic feasibility of "green electricity", which is an idea whose realization beyond a minor extent is highly unlikely in either Sweden or Germany in the near future.

As already noted, wind power plays an important part in the Danish energy mix because of subsidies, guaranteed access to the wholesale energy market and, especially, the high cost of energy in Denmark — which to a certain extent results from nuclear abstention and a reliance on coal. Similarly, across the Baltic in Germany, it appears that a large part of the present wind power capacity can be attributed to large subsidies. In fact, many of the production costs associated with the so-called *economical* large-scale wind installations in the world are subsidized in one way or another. The claim that we hear quite often these days is that new technologies will soon enable substantial *amounts* of "competitive" power to be produced from wind installations, and therefore subsidies will be unnecessary; however, even if this turns out to be true — which is definitely possible — it will only change the power supply picture marginally, because the "large amounts" that are mooted are not really large at all, given total power demand.

It appears that approximately 70% of the global output of wind power can be attributed to Europe, almost 20% to North America, and about 10% to the Asia-Pacific region. Wind-generating capacity is still growing at a higher rate than any other energy source, but it is not certain that this can continue. The total power generated by one of these installations is a function of wind speed cubed, and as a brief calculation will show, there is a world of difference between Patagonia with its near-steady 40 km/h airstream, and the supposedly wind-favored North Europe with its 27 km/h gusts. There is also the matter of the low *capacity factor* of wind turbines: as any wind surfer will tell you, there are days when there is practically no wind. The operative word is *intermitancy*!

Sweden and Norway are generally credited with having the most inexpensive electricity in the world in terms of cost, but there is an important difference. Norway's electricity is about 95% hydro-based, while Sweden's is approximately 43% nuclear-based, with most of the remainder being hydro, which is generally considered the most inexpensive power. The closeness of the cost of electricity in these two countries should make it clear that electricity produced in *best practice* nuclear facilities is more economical than that produced in fossil fuel installations, regardless of what you may have heard or read about the inexpensiveness of electricity generated from coal or natural gas; and this is even more true at the present time than it was in the past because the nominal "life" of high-quality nuclear plants have been extended to more than 60 years, as compared to the estimated 40 years that was common in the not-too-distant past, and I see no reason why the "life" of new plants cannot be longer. The reason for the lower cost is discussed in Chapter 7 of this book using the annuity formula.

Of course, there is no getting away from the fact that when I say that best practice nuclear power is less costly than fossil fuels and renewables, I am assuming that the scientific establishment is correct when they claim that nuclear "waste" can be safely warehoused over the indefinite future, and more importantly, new reactors are on the drawing board that produce much less waste. What I would like to hear though is that this "waste" will someday be taken out of storage, and the energy in it exploited. In other words, that the nuclear cycle will be "closed" in that waste will be continuously reprocessed until there is almost no extractable energy left in it. In these circumstances, its radioactivity might be reduced to a near trivial amount.

Clearly, a large part of the TV audience seems to exhibit a curious nonchalance about this issue, even though it happens to be extremely importantly for their daily lives. There is also an unrealistic approach to global warming, even though several of the largest reinsurers in the world (e.g., Munich Re and Swiss Re) appear convinced that climate change could bring about a substantial escalation in the number of natural catastrophes in the *present* decade, as well as continuing to pose over the indefinite future a mounting threat to the most populated regions of the globe. [According to McKibben (2001), the insurance industry has seen its payouts increase from about two billion dollars annually in the 1980s, to an average of 30 billion dollars annually between 1990 and 1995.] Much less attention seems to be paid to this nearby menace than the possibility that something could go wrong a thousand years from now in some remote underground storage site for nuclear waste — by which time it is very likely that science and competent governments will be well prepared to do what has to be done to eliminate threats by this waste to life and property.

Although there is no genuine evidence that science and technology is capable of greatly changing the demand or supply for world oil except in the fairly long run, it seems almost certain that safe reactors of virtually any size can eventually be built (employing, e.g., the "pebble-bed" technology). In fact, they could be built in Sweden in the not-too-distant future if many persons in this country adopted a less resentful attitude toward the scientists and technologists who have been instrumental in providing them with one of the highest standards of living in the world, and an even higher quality of life. As for nuclear waste, it may someday be possible to construct reactors (based perhaps on some variant of the Accelerator-Driven Transmutations-Technique technology) that consume so much of their uranium input that there is little or no residue; but even if there were no such things as absolutely safe reactors and it was extremely expensive to safely store "spent" uranium, there is still the matter of global warming.

Consider the situation in France, which around the turn of the century generated between 70% and 80% of its electricity in nuclear installations. According to Dr Hans Blix, the former director general of the International Atomic Energy Agency (and once a Swedish foreign minister), the emissions of CO_2/kWh (of electricity generated in that country) are about 64 g, while in the UK, which employs an energy mix of coal, gas and a small amount of nuclear energy, the CO_2 emissions are 10 times as large. It deserves to be noted that in Sweden the emission of CO_2/kWh of electricity generated is 59 g, while in Denmark the figure is about 920 g. The reader should take this into account when he or she hears about the resounding success of wind-generated electricity in that country. Dr Blix also noted that on a global basis, nuclear power helped to avoid the emission of some 700 million tonnes of CO_2 per year.

At the present time, there are 441 reactors in operation globally. There are, however, a number under construction, and most of these are in Asia. World energy demand is expected to rise by about 2%/year (net), and according to the IEA, developing countries are expected to account for two-thirds of this, with carbon emissions rising even faster than overall energy demand. If this is true, then instead of opposing nuclear energy, environmental movements should commence working immediately to convince all governments and international organizations that they should be preparing a crash-program to construct a great deal more as soon as large-scale versions of "safe" equipment (such as "pebble bed" or the Swedish PIUS and SECURE designs) have been perfected. Surely it must have occurred to them that if the water should ever start rising on Canal Street in Amsterdam or the Reeperbahn in Hamburg, then the good residents of those cities would have about the same chance of reversing the situation as King Canute had when he ordered the tide out.

Given my expectations for natural gas prices, I consider best practice nuclear plants indisputably more economical as combined cycle gas plants (which many observers think the most competitive on a unit cost basis). But even so, at least some of the new facilities that will be making an appearance soon will be even more cost-effective. As for nuclear waste disposal and/or reuse, the open or once-through nuclear fuel cycle employed in most countries can possibly be improved without introducing radical new arrangements. In one proposed scheme, used fuel is recycled to recover uranium and plutonium, after which it is transformed into new fuel using a process called PUREX (i.e., plutonium uranium extraction). This activity is capable of doubling the amount of energy recovered from the fuel, in addition to removing a large part of the long-lived radioactive elements from waste that might have to be permanently stored.

This might be the place to point out that the deregulation crusade moved into high gear when, in the United States, a number of important persons, with the support of the business press, came to the conclusion that the demand for power had ceased to expand, and instead of building more and/or larger power plants, a change in the structure of the electric industry was in order. Implicitly, that change meant an end to the construction of nuclear installations.

At the same time that I advance the above opinions, let me assure all readers that I know — just as they would know if they thought about it — that the opposition to nuclear energy by many members of the anti-nuclear brigades has nothing to do with nuclear safety. What it involves is an almost pathological opposition to scientific and industrial progress, because — many of these people feel — this progress has had or will have a negative influence on their lives. There is a similar attitude toward globalization by many of the same individuals — which I happen to share — but I find it difficult to justify the anti-nuclear scenario. Bringing into existence the kind of alternative, high-quality society that many anti-nuclearites might find attractive could require more rather than less energy. Large amounts of electricity will almost certainly be required for such things as the optimal employment of computers, robots that will improve the quality of manufactured goods, faster and more efficient electric trains, and other means of transport that will increase the attractiveness of ground-level collective travel arrangements, etc. And something that everyone seems to have overlooked is that enormous quantities of dependable power may be necessary to transform biological and other resources to motor fuels, to include providing the electricity needed to produce hydrogen (from, e.g., electrolysis) for use in, e.g., fuel-cell and other applications.

In my lectures I sometimes cite a few examples about things like nuclear and electric deregulation. This might be unnecessary, however, because these examples are everywhere, and it is hardly possible to avoid them. If we take for instance Progress Energy Florida (PEF) at the present time, they have calculated that each megawatt (MW) of power serves 615 homes, and so increasing the gross output of their nuclear facility from 900 MW to 1080 MW will allow an additional 110,700 homes to be served. In addition, they claim that nuclear is now the most cost-effective way to generate electricity, and this increase in capacity is the best way to manage rising fuel costs. The project is expected to cost $382 million, which includes potential transmission-system improvements.

By way of contrast, in Texas the operators of the power grid are proposing to deal with a lack of capacity by a service-interruption system for commercial users. In that state, increased gas prices have caused the utility industry to stop building new gas-fired plant, and instead much more coal will be used. Wind is also very popular in Texas, and as a result we constantly hear about the miracles that will be forthcoming from wind-generated electric facilities. This sounds good, but it happens that together with a stagnation in total investment, this ongoing change in the pattern of generation should ensure that Texas consumers in all categories face higher electricity prices. So much for another purported electric deregulation success story.

8. Kyoto and Its Discontents

According to David Victor (2001), the Kyoto Protocol was 10 years in the making and has become a symbol of the world's resolve to address the problem of global warming (or, as it is sometimes called, the greenhouse effect). It was signed for the United States by Vice President Al Gore in 1997, but only three years later the new president, George W. Bush, decided that the United States could not implement the protocol as it stood because it might place too great an economic burden on his country. The US Senate went along with this by voting 95–0 against having to consider a treaty that ostensibly could damage the US economy. President Bush also had some reservations about becoming a party to an agreement that exempted 80% of the world from compliance for economic reasons. As pointed out earlier, he has been forced to recant to a certain extent, because his rich allies are visibly annoyed about being informed that what may turn out to be the greatest threat to Earth's physical stability in human history should be played down unless the poorest countries in the world also picked up a part of the bill for doing something about it. Note the phrasing here: "what *may* turn out to be the greatest threat …". In other words, it is not completely certain, and this lack of certainty has led to some bad feeling and animosity in the scientific community, as well as elsewhere.

The greenhouse effect has to do with the trapping of heat by certain gases in the atmosphere — often referred to as "greenhouse gases" — and this phenomenon is not, in itself, a dangerous thing. On the contrary, this process is essential for most life on earth, since the trapped heat keeps the earth's temperature warmer than it would be otherwise. What may be happening, however, is that the amount of heat being trapped is excessive, and at the bottom of this unfavorable development we find human (or *anthropogenic*) activities instead of some climatic pattern that is independent of what is, or has been, taking place on earth.

According to the Inter-governmental Panel on Climate Change (IPCC), which includes most of the world's leading climate scientists, it has been suggested that during the present century the earth could warm up by between 1.4°C and 5.8°C, with the median rise working out to an alarming 2.5°C. Almost all of the living Nobel laureates who commit themselves on this matter accept these figures to one extent or another, although a small group of "experts" — most of whom are self-appointed — dispute whether the earth has warmed at all and, if so, whether human activities are responsible.

Let me say here, however, that it should not make the slightest difference whether these figures are correct or not, nor whether these Nobel laureates were sober or tipsy when they expressed their belief in anthropogenic-based global warming (or AGW as it is sometimes called in the literature). Nobel laureates and the cream of climatologists are preferable to the crank chorus working the other side of the street.

These opponents of global warming will not find it easy to promote their convictions, because almost all the leading business periodicals in the world have now published long articles emphasizing that the greenhouse effect is very likely a great deal more than upscale science fiction. In addition, in the United States, the Pew Center on Global Climate Change has a large and growing number of corporate members on its rolls at the present time, to include important firms like DuPont, IBM and United Technologies, and in the US Congress bipartisan bills have been introduced in both the Senate and the House to regulate CO_2 — even if these ladies and gentlemen have come to the conclusion that the Kyoto Protocol, in its present condition, is not worthy of their full attention. "Congress is not going to sit back, if you will, and fiddle while the planet warms", Senator Lieberman informed his president. I think that we can rely on this, especially since sitting back could cost many hardworking congressmen and congresswomen the votes that they might need to continue their political careers. Even the president got that message in a relatively short time, and it is useful to note that his father, when occupying the same office, signed the Framework Convention on Climate Change, which was the treaty that launched the process that led to Kyoto.

An unpopular opinion I occasionally express is that the US government has always been a key player in formulating a global agenda for curbing global warming, and remains one at the present time. This makes sense to me because if something does go wrong, the rich have more to lose than the poor. The people who have caused the trouble are not the hard-line anti-warming legislators in Congress, or business persons, or employees of some of the conservative "think-tanks", but various jet-setting environmentalists and pseudo-environmentalists whose principal concern is not with global warming but with what, for lack of a more appropriate euphemism, I will call their careers. During my long "tour" at the Palais des Nations (in Geneva, Switzerland) I encountered a large number of these careerists, and it is in remembering their various professional defects that I became convinced that it is only through inter-governmental cooperation at the very highest level that the threat of global warming can be adequately dealt with.

But until the time when the leaders of the most important nations meet annually for the specific purpose of examining the state of the global environment, much more is going to be required from Washington than upholding, rejecting or becoming embroiled in senseless debates over controversial policy overtures. First and foremost, a systematic attempt should be made to appreciate the inadequacy of the main proposals forwarded at Kyoto and related palavers, and then putting together and advertising widely some "obviously" superior propositions. What we saw at the elephantine talk shops like Kyoto and Rio were what President Bill Clinton called "the world's most serious environmental problem" disposed of in an abstract (though upbeat) manner that might have been appropriate for dealing with an increased growth of tumbleweed near the Bay of Fundy, but did not really have much to do with ugly events that might cause countless trillions of dollars of economic damage before the new year's eve parties begin in 2099.

In the light of all the misevaluations of the Kyoto exercise, I regard the short article by Victor mentioned previously an important exposition, and the same is true of a later paper by Ruth G. Bell (2006). After perusing the work of Dr Bell on emissions trading, I immediately remembered a communication from an economist working on global warming. According to him, emissions trading has been shown to be viable both theoretically and empirically. In reality, of course, this is not a correct statement. Most high-level conferences are distinguished by the absence of claims to this effect, because economists who say that they have crafted believable arguments as to the efficacy of emissions trading generally have no desire to confront a competent audience with their pseudo-scientific conclusions.

Most of the opponents of global warming believe that there is no trouble ahead, and so they will not — as in the great Fred Astaire song from *The Fleet's In* — have to "face the music and dance"; but even those people are capable of understanding that if things should go wrong, non-linear and self-reinforcing processes could be set off whose complex mechanisms would make it impossible to avoid some extremely distasteful outcomes — even if the output of all greenhouse gases were immediately eliminated. This might also be the place to mention what I call The Tyranny of Small Differences: the fact that many extremely bad things happen so slowly that they cannot be detected, but even so might eventually add up to deep trouble for a large number of unlucky citizens who find themselves in the wrong place when the water starts rising or hot-spells increase in both average length *and* intensity.

In my article in *Energy Sources* (2000), I attempted to point out that the problem with global warming involves stocks rather than flows: specifically, the growing stock of CO_2 in the atmosphere. *The Economist* (7 April 2001) has drawn the conclusion that because most greenhouse gases are long-lived, can remain in the atmosphere for a century or longer, and regardless of their origin can make their combined effect felt around the globe, restrictions — or "strict caps" — make little sense in the short-term since they involve flows.

Since there is a simple algebraic relationship between stocks and flows, it might be argued that, at the alpine heights of pure theory (where annoyances like long time horizons and political considerations are ignored), "caps" make all the sense in the world. However, *The Economist* (and what they call "like-minded boffins") are correct in suggesting that Kyoto should be amended to ensure that — since reducing the stock of pollution is a very long-term project — the economic burden of compliance is both stable and supportable in the long as well as the short run, in that the sacrifices that are made at any given point in time in reducing (or mitigating the increase in) the *total* stock of pollution are not in vain because later some newly elected, near-sighted governments, decide that sacrifices made by previous governments were a waste of time. And, in fact, they might appear to be a waste of time to even far-sighted governments, because locally — due to the non-linear dynamics of greenhouse gases — very precise measurements taken over a fairly long period might unexpectedly give the impression that the worst possible outcomes of global warming are progressively decreasing in likelihood. Personally, I cannot see how this dilemma can be handled unless those persons who genuinely want something done about global warming are prepared to be more rational about nuclear energy.

By selectively expanding — rather than contracting — the global nuclear sector; and by taking greater advantage of government cooperation in the research and development activities of the transportation industries, where greatly increased fuel efficiencies are now almost within reach, time could be bought which conceivably could eventually allow greenhouse gas emissions to be reduced by the balanced introduction of superior technologies, with an emphasis on renewables. In addition, it might be possible to get precise answers to some of the questions that have been raised by climate warming sceptics, which apparently include some very heavy players in Washington, DC.

Let me add that jamborees such as those held at Rio and Kyoto detract from the challenge posed by financing and organizing these measures, because they give the impression that significant progress is, or will soon be, made in reducing environmental hazards if they can get the right signatures on this-or-that document. Hardly anywhere do we see the opinion of observers like the past chairman of the IPCC that if we do not go far beyond what was achieved at Kyoto, atmospheric greenhouse gases will continue to increase in the next decade exactly as they have in the past 20 years. I am tempted to say that this is something we want to avoid at all costs, but I will refrain because I doubt whether the people who are organizing the next environmental talk shop are really interested in hearing how little they have achieved in the past.

At the Kyoto meeting, it was decided that emissions trading was to be the core of the pollutions suppression system. In the paper by Victor referred to previously, he says that an emissions trading system is like a unicycle with rusty bearings. It is worse than that, because it opens the door for the same kind of greed and incompetence that preceded rolling blackouts in California. Apparently, the United Nations Conference on Trade and Development (UNCTAD) was scheduled to set up a unit for the formulation of an international emissions trading scheme, and its director once declared that the details of a practical trading mechanism will be easy to work out. I was glad to hear that, but when I was informed that he expressed confidence that the scheme will be operative by 2008, I knew that this project was hopeless.

The thing to remember here is that although in theory — and perhaps in practice — tradable emission permits might be the best method for dealing with *domestic* atmospheric pollution; this may not be true if we are think-ing in terms of the real *international* world, where psychopathic greed, corruption and incompetence are commonplace. I personally see no reason for establishing a cross-border program for dealing with global warming in which these highly undesirable qualities are given a new outlet. Before tens of billions of dollars in highly *fungible* vouchers are passed out, I would like to be certain that they will not be misused. (An asset is said to be fungible when it is freely changeable into another asset. Money is most fungible.)

9. "The Financialization of Energy"

"The financialization of energy" is an expression employed by *Business Week* (12 February 2001) in a long and surprisingly non-partisan article whose purpose was to review the adventures of the Enron Corporation in the great world of electricity deregulation, as well as that firm's involvement with a few less controversial activities. Enron, which was once the seventh largest firm in the United States, has been a persistent and loud cheerleader in the deregulation sweepstakes (for the usual self-serving financial rea-sons); however, it did *not* pioneer the financialization of energy, as claimed by *Business Week*. This was mostly done by establishments such as the New York Mercantile Exchange (NYMEX) who were responsible for organiz-ing "the best game in town", as the trading of oil futures and options was once called. Readers of this book will find a long elementary exposition of futures and options in Chapter 8, but unfortunately that topic is too out of the ordinary and too important to be introduced at this time, even though it is not intrinsically difficult.

One of the main reasons why I like *Business Week's* presentation is their citing a statement by Mr Douglas Heller, consumer advocate with the Foundation for Taxpayer and Consumer Rights in Santa Monica, California. According to Mr Heller, "Electricity is not a commodity fit for the compet-itive marketplace. Private investors do not have public safety in mind". He is not the only one whose thoughts move along those lines. Loic Caperan of EdF once remarked: "Electricity is a national asset as well as a right, and is strongly linked to human development and well-being". Please note that the basic issue here is not ownership but abundance: it is providing consumers with the electricity they require at prices they can afford.

Mr Heller's statement is not completely accurate, but it is a good beginning of a necessary debate. That gentleman also advocated a referendum which would result in the government of California buying enough of the California power-system to prevent a repetition of the kind of bizarre energy dilemma to which Californians found themselves exposed several years ago. I favor such a referendum too, and if it took place I might be tempted to move to California once again in order to give my modest support to any and all legislation aimed at liquidating those deregulation remnants that might have survived the great meltdown.

A distinguished foolishness put into widespread circulation was that the form of ownership of a firm was *always* crucial in determining its efficiency, and private enterprise was *always* superior to public enterprise. For instance, according to Jeffrey K. Skilling, when he became one of the kingpins at Enron, the (electric and gas) utilities were "incredibly expensive and provided horrible service to their customers". This was undoubtedly true in a number of cases, but absolutely and totally false in many others. Accordingly, if we employ the logic of neo-classical economics, we can immediately suggest that even in a world of ironbound regulation, it is possible for the managers of utilities to be as smart and effective as the ladies and gentlemen commanded by Mr Skilling, and possibly as *gung ho* as Mr Skilling himself.

Incidentally, most unbiased observers are of the opinion that, on the whole, the electric sector in the United States has generally provided excellent service at a reasonable price. A good example here would be the Southern Company, which is the largest US investor-owned regulated utility, and which dominates electricity supply in Georgia and Alabama as well as owning facilities in Mississippi and Florida, and appears to be on its way to becoming a major player outside the United States. When this was being written, Southern's customers paid 20% less for their power than the US average, and this highly innovative and profitable company regularly finds itself in the top five in the country in customer satisfaction surveys. On the other hand, William Pfaff (in the *Herald Tribune*, 22 February 2001) maintained that "the privatization of public utilities can be a disaster" (i.e., could *turn out* to be a disaster). It may certainly be a misfortune for persons buying electricity from Southern, because as the chairman of the Georgia Public Service Commission, Mr Stan Wise, has pointed out, "Any potential national benefit of deregulation would come at a cost to states such as ours".

This discussion could go on indefinitely, but I think it useful to note that a high-ranking insider in the UK academic world, Professor John Kay, has concluded that the case for renationalizing British Rail (which became *Railtrack*) is "compelling", because in his opinion the competence of the deregulated management was less than gratifying. In addition, after mulling over some economic theory, the bad news from California and New Zealand and the collapse of Enron, he suggests that deregulated electric sectors should be at least partially re-regulated. This is worth noticing because being an insider, he must know that thanks to Enron's presence in energy trading, the UK's electric distribution firms could have experienced a California-like shock. According to Will Hutton in the *Observer* (13 January 2002), it took some arm-twisting by the regulatory body OFGEM to keep the UK lights on. Hutton also says that "smart and effective regulation is the handmaiden of well-run markets that serve the public interest", by which he means markets for *necessities*.

One of the things that I tried to do in my international finance textbook (2001) was to convince readers that financial economics is a fascinating and important subject. "The physics of economics" is my favorite way of describing it, although finance is much easier to understand than physics — despite the grotesque attempts of some finance teachers to convince students of the opposite.

When the UK government passed the Electricity Act in 1989, its three stated goals were to introduce full competition, reduce prices, and open up price and risk management opportunities. The risk management scene, they hoped, would eventually be dominated by exchange traded *futures contracts*, since these could (in theory) generate the visible *scarcity* or *efficiency* prices that we present to our students as being the key to obtaining an optimal allocation of resources in a market economy. The same goals were adopted in Norway. The problem with this ivory-tower vision of the electric market is that when storage is impossible, something called *basis risk* [which causes physical and/or paper (i.e., *futures*) prices to move in an undesirable direction] could be enormous. Thus, unlike the situation with many other commodities and financial assets, transactors can never be sure that futures will provide a "low cost" reliable hedge against price risk most of the time. (Note: *most*, and not *always*.)

At the *Scuola Enrico Mattei*'s Forum on deregulation, I insisted that electric futures trading has been a huge disappointment, despite what sponsors of this trading claim. (The main source of difficulty is a shortage of liquidity. Transactors are constantly disadvantaged in this market, and in the long run they take their money and naiveté elsewhere.) NYMEX is easily the most important commodity exchange in the world, but even so their recent failures include a "natural gas basis contract" and — according to the *Financial Times* (13 July 2001), — "the much hyped electric contract". Much hyped and later delisted to be exact, but almost certain destined to return in one form or another, and if not at NYMEX then at one of its clones somewhere in the world. As a certain, Mr Meyer Lansky pointed out that when he was involved with the operation of dice tables and roulette wheels from Las Vegas to Havana; "The winners are those who control the game. The professionals. All the rest are losers". This being the case, there will always be establishments where the winners roll out lush red carpets for potential losers, and in terms of the financial turnover per employee, those casinos where electricity is traded are beautiful examples.

"Much hyped" is a good expression. It has been noted that on the German exchanges paper contracts are only 2–3% of physical transactions, while on NordPool that figure is 25%. This is supposed to mean that NordPool is a success. However, if we look at a really successful futures contract, such as oil futures in New York or London, we see that paper transactions can amount to as much as four or five times physical transactions. It is only when we have multiples on this order that we can be reasonably certain there is sufficient trading on an exchange to generate the kind of liquidity that is necessary to provide efficient hedging (= price insurance).

Similarly, the very high volatility that is an important cause of excessive basis risk for futures would mean very expensive options. (This contention can be immediately verified by readers who are familiar with the Black–Scholes option pricing formula.) That leaves us with contracts for differences (CFDs) — which are analogous to swaps. CFDs are ubiquitous, and possibly the most important component of the financial side of the electricity scene in the United Kingdom and elsewhere, but they do not provide the price transparency so fondly spoken of by many teachers of economics and finance. In addition, there have been suggestions that the price benchmarks used to settle many contracts can be manipulated. I think that a version of Murphy's Law might be appropriate here: if they *can* be manipulated, they *will* be manipulated. The upshot of all this is that without a fully credible and flexible (financial) mechanism for hedging highly volatile prices, the efficacy of electric deregulation has not even been established on the most elementary theoretical level, and the expression financialization is to some extent a misnomer if applied to the electric market.

The wonders that financial instruments are supposed to work with electricity, but in reality have not worked, are occasionally mentioned in regard to "global warming" or the "greenhouse effect", where the large-scale trading of emission permits — the major market-based alternative to taxes — has been envisaged as having a key role to play in the strategy to reduce the output of CO_2 to acceptable levels. As already mentioned, researchers like Bell and Victor do not believe that these devices are useful in an international setting. Neither did one of the advisors to President Vladimir Putin of Russia. His comment was that emissions trading was about money and not the environment. This impression cannot be examined in detail here, but discussions of the future trading possibilities of these permits are constantly turning up in the more down-to-earth financial literature (e.g., *Risk* magazine), with most of these discussions focusing on the short-run financial gains that emissions trading should make possible for brokers, traders and various "intermediaries".

In my paper "The Kyoto Negotiations on Climate Change: An Economic Perspective" (*Energy Sources*, July 2000), I offer the following assessment: "Measurement and verification problems would be virtually insuperable, although even legally binding goals cannot be attained if implementation is unverifiable. There will also be information shortages that will prevent the formation of the 'scarcity' (i.e., efficiency or competitive) prices that certain theoreticians believe will allow pollution to be shifted back and forth like pizzas in a neoclassical pasta emporium, where management always stands ready to repurchase the piece of crust that you did not eat, in order to sell it to some less fortunate customer". I can add that there would be high transactions costs, biased price signals, and worst of all, cheating and irrational behavior by rogue polluters/states that cannot be easily held accountable for their bad conduct, etc.

A number of economists have worked on issues associated with emissions trading for many years, and they have achieved exactly nothing: most of the work that they have published in the theoretical journals does not apply to the real world. One reason for this abysmal showing is that something like mathematical physics is child's play as compared to obtaining the kind of answers that the Kyoto grandees mistakenly thought that even neophyte economists could provide with a year or two of serious effort. On the basis of the theoretical work that has already appeared and is due to appear in various unread journals, even a century of round-the-clock exertion by a regiment of investigators is unlikely to provide us with a fraction of the information and techniques that we should possess in order to make this scheme work.

Before ending this section, I want to cite what the *Financial Times* (17 May 2006) says about emissions trading: "EU finds carbon emissions trade impossible". This is interesting, because I found it not only impossible but absurd the first time that I heard of it. According to the editor of that publication, "governments are to blame, not the basic market design". I agree wholeheartedly in that governments should never have bought this cockamamie scheme. It is strictly something for those many unread learned journals gathering dust in our university libraries.

Figures released by the European Commission showed that most member states have given their industries too many carbon credits, which undermines the program to reduce CO_2 emissions. What we have to understand here is that when governments have to choose between the profitability of and employment in domestic industries and a harebrained setup that may or may not cut emissions, it is a no-brainer. The thinking here by most individual governments is that some other country can carry the burden. Besides, most politicians and civil servants now realize that the best way to reduce emissions is with a greater resort to nuclear power, along with restrictions on industries that are heavy emitters. These restrictions would be balanced by subsidies and tax reductions that encourage investment in more environmentally suitable facilities.

The director of one large power producer (RWE npower) has pronounced the EU emissions trading scheme as the best approach to getting results in the momentous task of reducing CO_2 output. According to that concerned observer, the program involves 25 member state governments, a host of different industries reporting on emissions from 9400 separate factories and power stations, and last but not least, the (administrative) machinery of the EU itself. Since the machinery of the EU has mangled almost everything it has touched, some question must be asked as to why it should be allowed to get near something as important as environmental legislation.

Just now, many scientists take issue with President George W. Bush's somewhat passive approach to global warming. Faced with the many uncertainties associated with this issue, it might be wise to think of the way that Neumann and Morgenstern might react. Although I have been told that the following is uncouthly expressed, I think that it deserves some attention by sophisticated readers: *global warming is not the same thing as a global tour by some rap artist that you can avoid by simply not buying a ticket. If global warming comes to town, you get a ticket whether you want one or not, and even worse, you have to use it.* Therefore, a modicum of precautions should be taken in order to make sure that it does not appear at an embarrassing moment.

10.   More Deregulation Blues

Before concluding, a few more comments on the far-reaching and contentious subject of deregulation can be offered.

Included in the earlier "research" efforts of some of the academics mentioned in this chapter were attempts to revoke the concept of "increasing returns to scale" (or "decreasing costs" as it is often called with reference to the falling portion of U-shaped cost curves). Interestingly enough, increasing returns to scale may be one part of mainstream economics that is a part of the cosmic rulebook — the way the real world works. As long ago as 1848, in his *Principles of Political Economy*, John Stuart Mill wrote that "The laws and conditions of production partake of the character of physical truths. There is nothing arbitrary about them". To this could be added a recent conclusion of perhaps the leading deregulation scholar, Professor Alfred Kahn. He says: "I am worried about the uniqueness of the electricity markets. I've always been uncertain about eliminating vertical integration . . . It may be one industry in which it works reasonably well".

In these circumstances, I prefer to continue thinking that both your world and mine would be a better place if electric deregulation had stayed at the debating stage for another few decades, or best of all, completely forgotten. The changes proposed by the dreamy functionaries of Brussels should be considered an affront rather than an example to the world at large: they are not a part of the natural evolution of an industrial society, where ideally science, technology, economic theory, journalism and the media, in alliance with the common sense of voters, should focus on such things as increasing employment opportunities and social security, and improving the quality of life rather than indulging flashy bunkum hypocritically introduced in order to widen income differences.

I find it difficult to predict at the present time the bottom line in these deregulation melodramatics, but I am not at all certain that the EU Commission will succeed in making their case in the long run. For instance, General Charles DeGaulle unambiguously said that "the great common sources of wealth", by which on that occasion he meant natural gas, "belong to the nation and would not be used for individual profit making". It was unnecessary for him to refer to electricity, because in conjunction with the Conseil de la Resistance, the general had already made it perfectly clear that French industry and households were not to be denied the electricity they needed, and it was to be made available at modest prices.

This does not mean that French electricity and/or generating assets cannot be sold to foreign purchasers, nor should free markets nor the price system be subverted, but it so happens that in a world in which nuclear energy may be on the verge of making a comeback, the present French nuclear facilities and — much more importantly — the next (technological) generation of these installations may turn out to be extremely valuable assets. In these circumstances, I doubt whether any French government will be able to trivialize these assets in the manner that the present Swedish government is succeeding in trivializing what may still be the most efficient energy economy in the world in order to curry favor with high-flown EU elitists who neither understand nor are interested in understanding even the simplest concepts in energy economics.

A recent German chancellor declared himself unsympathetic to the attitude of the French government, as well he should. If all Europeans have the right to choose their suppliers of electricity (and gas), then many Germans would attempt to utilize this opportunity to purchase relatively inexpensive French energy (although their demand could make that energy more expensive). This could create problems for German utilities, and since deregulation commenced with perhaps 70,000 employees in the German electric sector being turned out of their jobs, it could increase social tensions throughout the country. Moreover, if the price of electricity reacts the way that it has in Sweden, Norway and Finland — first decreasing and then increasing — then electric deregulation can be held at least partially responsible for many other economic torments, such as the movement of important firms to countries where energy prices are lower.

Professor Stephen Littlechild, the considerably-less-than-impressive former UK energy regulator, believes that liberalization will continue because energy consumers want greater choice and freedom. What we really want, of course, is lower prices and a continued high level of reliability. Some of these consumers will probably obtain a taste of the good things advertised by Professor Littlechild, although a majority will find themselves having to settle for considerably less. The calculation in Brussels is that members of the latter group will keep their cool and continue to pay their energy bills on time.

Brussels and the EU governments have put much effort into attempts to find a common EU framework for resolving the liberalization enigma, although up to now the results are paltry. Mr Paul Hennemeyer, a director of Enron (Europe) in those days when it served as a role model for the international energy producing and trading community, strongly disliked the failure of the French government to open its energy market to competition, and he also had misgivings about the German authorities. In fact, he and his associates lived in a bubble for so long that he felt it appropriate to announce that if he were their teacher, he would make the entire EU "stay after school for extra lessons".

Enron was then an imposing firm with a sound business concept, but the sermon that Mr Hennemeyer wanted to preach soon lost its appeal after Enron's shares collapsed and the behavior of that firm's leadership made them candidates for an extended visit to a federal detention facility. On the other hand, the day may come when the EU High Commission in Brussels finds it opportune to utilize Mr Hennemeyer's pedagogical talents, because many voters have gotten in the habit of ignoring their long-term self-interest, and thus might provide him with the audience which he feels he richly deserves. One thing though is certain: he will not get much empathy from the thousands of unhappy Enron employees who not only lost their jobs, but also lost well over a billion dollars of their pension savings due to the fall of that corporation.

11. Final Remarks and Conclusions

> *"Even a tiny bit of genuine knowledge goes a very long way"*
> — *Paul Ormerod (2006)*

This is a very long chapter, and the reason for its length is that it is intended as a preview of the main topics in this textbook. Some readers will find a few things in this chapter — and in this book — controversial; however, I do not think that I will have to answer to the charge of misrepresenting anything. One of the papers presented at the international conference of the IAEE in Berlin in 2006 was called "Why has the Nordic electricity market worked so well?" If you examine this chapter you would be tempted to draw the conclusion that it has not worked well at all, and you would be perfectly correct. In fact, the day that I received a copy of that paper, the front page of the most important business publication in Sweden (*Dagens Industri*) showed a graph of the Swedish electricity price, and it was not a sight for sore eyes. Not only is the spot price on the Nordic electricity exchange (NordPool) more than 70% higher than it was at the same time the previous year, but the electricity-intensive Swedish industry is taking a severe beating.

Interestingly enough, spokespersons for those industries are now asking for an end to deregulation, while several academic economists recently blamed the problems of Swedish industry on a shortage of electric capacity instead of deregulation. As to be expected, those "scholars" were unable to comprehend that the lack of capacity in this country is due to deregulation.

Possible sources of controversy in this book are of course renewables and nuclear energy. According to *Business Week* (6 March 2006), President Bush has become a poster boy for renewables, and specifically plant-based (or grain-based) ethanol, wind power and photovoltaics. As a result of my evaluation of the small amount of evidence to which I have access, I am still unable to muster an overwhelming enthusiasm for ethanol and photovoltaics. Ethanol was mentioned in the president's 2006 State of the Union address, and there seems to be little doubt that it is destined to become an extremely valuable item; but according to the argument in this chapter, it has certain important disadvantages. I certainly see no reason to believe that it will exert a significant downward pressure on the price of motor fuel unless much larger volumes are produced than are planned at present. What it could do, however, is to put a pressure on the price of grain and therefore add significantly to world hunger.

According to Alan Jenkins in *EnergyPulse* (2006), biofuels have been "oversold", and in a comment on that paper, Jim Beyer argues that "ethanol makes sense as a fuel additive, but the economics are much less favorable as a significant fuel component itself". Let us put it this way: biofuels, wind power, solar, tar sand oil and other unconventional energy sources are useful and/or promising, but not as useful and promising as we are often led to believe. The real advantage from ethanol will probably appear when the underlying fuel is cellulose-based (e.g., switchgrass and wood) instead of grain- or plant-based (e.g., corn), which means that many more years will pass before it is possible to accumulate enough ethanol refineries to change the global energy picture.

At the same time, it should be recognized that in environmental matters, *social profit* is probably as important as *private profit*, and so measures like production tax credits for ethanol and similar initiatives should be resorted to without hesitation in the battle to reduce the dependency on fossil fuels. It might also be useful if governments consider functioning as buyers for some of the new products, as the US government did with microchips: they provided a market that encouraged producers to move rapidly up the learning curve in order to lower costs (and raise profits) by exploiting economies of scale.

Wind was discussed at some length in this chapter, and it is rewarding to note that in the United States, its use increased by 35% in 2005, which amounted to 2500 MW of additional power. The United States is a very large country and wind resources are considerable, but having noticed the deceleration in the growth of wind-based power in Northern Europe — and especially Scandinavia and Northern Germany — I have to infer that it is not the nostrum that some observers believe it to be. The maximum rating of a wind turbine is not a very good indication of how much energy can be obtained, since its capacity factor might only be 25% or lower. (The capacity factor indicates what percent of rated power is available on average.)

Under no circumstances, though, should the further development and eventual large-scale utilization of unconventional/renewable energy sources be obstructed. However once again, there is no place in the world where governments and voters are friendlier to renewable energy than in Scandinavia, and in addition, technological know-how in these countries is world-class, but even so there is a visible stagnation in the rate at which renewable energy is entering the energy mainstream. For instance, the 1600 MW of new generating capacity that will be installed in Finland could possibly have been provided by wind, but hardly at a price that Finnish voters would have been glad to pay, given the alternatives.

As noted in an editorial in *Science* (30 July 1999), "Affordable energy is the lifeblood of modern society. Without it, the network of transportation, agriculture, healthcare, manufacturing, and commerce deemed essential by many of the world's inhabitants, would not be possible".

Not mentioned in this resumé was entertainment and various other forms of relaxation. When these extremely important activities are ushered onto the scene, then it is quite clear that many of our fellow citizens are not particularly enthusiastic about adjusting their behavior in such a way as to reduce the growth of energy use, nor adopting lifestyles that would facilitate materially reducing discharges of CO_2 into the atmosphere. Changing this situation in the short run is unlikely, although the technological means are now available that will eventually bring this about, and hopefully they will soon be applied.

The governments of many countries have confronted the very (politically) sensitive private transportation issue by engaging in half-hearted attempts to convince motorists that it is in the interests of themselves and their descendants to make sacrifices that might be necessary in order to enable the provisions of the (very overrated) Kyoto Protocol to be realized, but inevitably their entreaties are tuned out as quickly as possible. After all, it would be difficult — to say the least — for a number of politicians to portray themselves as icons of self-denial. This has certainly become true in Sweden, and in particular applies to those politicians dreaming night and day of highly paid non-jobs in Brussels.

According to Michael Farrell, director of the program for global environmental studies at the Oak Ridge National Laboratory (Tennessee, USA), the (average) estimated increase in the global temperature will be 2.5°F for the present century, while even if the provisions of the Kyoto Protocol are fully carried out, the increase will be only slightly less. In addition, Sidney Borowitz (1999) — a New York University physicist — calculated several years ago that the atmospheric concentration of CO_2 was 358 ppmv (volume parts per million), and increasing at a rate of 1.5 ppmv. He considered this to be without precedent over the past 160,000 years. If these assessments are reasonable, or nearly reasonable for that matter, then it might be a good thing if many of the lovelorn references to the Kyoto Protocol should be toned down as much as possible, and a new program for reducing climate warming set into motion by some influential and charismatic person.

The thing to always keep in mind when dealing with this subject is that we are not talking about blackouts or brownouts, or the possibility of irksome increases in motor fuel prices because a pipeline somewhere got in the way of some rockets, but disasters that in earthquake terminology belong at or above the top of the Richter scale. The present President Bush has been awarded the bad-guy role in this drama, but it might be a good idea to remember that although his father once had a similar attitude toward ozone depreciation and acid rain, when the very conservative UK Prime Minister Margaret Thatcher insisted that something be done to diminish this hazard, he felt compelled to go along. Perhaps the new President Bush should also listen to her, or for that matter listen to a group of experts that he recently appointed who argued that anthropocentric-based global warming is the real deal. Moreover, in a fairly recent speech to the Royal Society, Baroness Thatcher said that "We may have unwittingly begun a massive experiment with the system of the planet itself".

In a lecture that I once gave in Italy, I showed perhaps an excessive amount of intolerance for the fairly low degree of honesty that we find on the part of many people dealing with deregulation. This was regarded as "attitude" by one of the academic deregulation insiders. However, as US Congressman Peter De Fazio remarked at the beginning of the deregulation escapades on the US West Coast, "Why do we need to go through such a radical, risk taking experiment? The answer is that there are people who are going to make millions or billions". (The academic gentleman to whom I am referring will make a great deal less, but as they once said in the United Kingdom: In for a pound, in for a penny.)

Some of Congressman De Fazio's potential millionaires and billionaires still believe that there is a place for them on the deregulation gravy train, while many of those already on board want to upgrade their tickets. I have no problem with this. My problem is with the so-called energy experts in California and elsewhere who failed to see that when regulated utilities are replaced by unregulated oligopolies, the exploitation of market power by these oligopolies is exactly what their textbooks told them would take place.

Oil and gas play a very large part in this book, both in chapters on these commodities and in the long chapter called "Energy and Money", where I examine some of the mechanics of derivative markets. It might be a good idea, however, to refer to a recent article in the *Financial Times* by Carola Hoyos, with the title "Mideast oil to play bigger role in global growth" (22 January 2006). Several of the points touched upon by Ms Hoyos were considered by me 15 or 20 years ago, and here I am talking about the possible shifting of the center of gravity of world oil refining to the Middle East. I also included petrochemicals, and unless I am mistaken, so did Professor Morris Adelman. It is always possible to say that certain people who should have received Nobel Prizes were deprived of them for one reason or another, but where quantitative development economics is concerned, I have no doubt at all that the late Hollis Chenery was the champion. Unfortunately, his use of linear programming and input–output analysis did not go over too well with the rank-and-file engaged in teaching and studying development economics, but for those of us who taught from his articles and the book that he wrote with Paul Clark (1962), it was clear that the big oil producers of the Middle East should not be eager to ship their oil in unprocessed form.

It has been noted by several observers that the unique feature of recent oil market developments is the near-term capacity constraints existing in some parts of the petroleum industry — e.g., refining in the United States — and the gradual decrease in excess sustainable crude oil production capacity in virtually every major oil-producing country except, perhaps, Saudi Arabia. ("Perhaps" because in both Saudi Arabia and Iraq, things like water flooding have reportedly led to an increase in the natural decline of deposits.) The complacency displayed toward this ominous situation is nothing less than remarkable, although behind the scenes I am sure that the heads of any number of central banks are informing their principals that they should do everything possible to prevent the kind of "anomalous" event (such as a serious political flare-up in or near an oil-producing country) that would remove a few million barrels of oil (per day) from the market, because that is all that it would take to send the oil price to a level where ugly macroeconomic and/or political consequences could follow. In addition, at the present time, the oil price is much more volatile than it was in the recent past, largely because the low investment of the past few years has kept storage and transport facilities from expanding as fast as output, and as a result, increased the possibility of the kind of bottlenecks that lead to wild price swings.

I close this chapter by noting that I still gain some consolation for my earlier and future forecasting failures, to include perhaps some in this book, when I recall that one of the most brilliant and influential physicists of the 20th century, Niels Bohr, once said that "true expertise comes only after making all possible mistakes". At the same time, I think it wise for most of us to accept that it would not be a good thing if we take too lightly the mistakes that are possible concerning the availability of oil and natural gas.

There is also some bad news that might someday be connected with global warming, since together with oil any expertise that we gain might have to be demonstrated in a world with a new and disagreeable economic and political structure — a structure that is not particularly responsive to the application of traditional know-how and procedures, and which features very loud noises and the rather distinctive sound of assault rifles and gunships.

All this and more should be taken note of by those persons who have become receptive to the arguments of the small but strident group of academic dissidents and deregulation buffs who regard global warming as a hoax, and to an amazing extent have a similar opinion of the peaking of the global oil supply, while never missing an opportunity to insist that their own quirky point of view deserves the same respect as that of the large majority of outstanding researchers who say that we cannot afford to be careless in these matters.

Appendix: Observations on the Main Text — Units and Equivalencies

There are two parts to this appendix. The first (A1) attempts to clarify several simple misunderstandings having to do with popular presentations of energy topics. This is an essential part of any energy economics course that I teach, however I am prepared to accept that this departure is not essential for the general reader at the present stage of the game. What is essential though is A2, which consists of the materials on units and equivalencies referred to on several occasions in the chapter and in the rest of the book. Here I can say that regardless of appearances, anyone who has made any calculations having to do with the changing of currencies in their local FOREX or airport, or for that matter on a quiet street corner in Gifu or Schwabisch Gmund, will have no difficulty following this discussion.

Appendix A1: Observations on the main text

(1) The nominal (or current or money) price of a good — e.g., oil — is its market price on a given day. The real price, however, takes into consideration the rate of inflation from some previous date. With this topic we generally limit attention to the real price of the good for a single country, although we could put together some kind of approximation for a group of countries.

In order to calculate the often cited real price of oil (P_r) at time t, we use the relationship $P_r = [\text{CPI}_z/\text{CPI}_t] \cdot P_t$, where the calculation is made with respect to the consumer price index (CPI) at a time z, which may or may not be the base year (b). But for our purposes we will make $\text{CPI}_z = \text{CPI}_b = 100$, and as is usually the case, the base year is the year of the first "oil price shock", or 1973. Thus, it turns out that after 1973 we see as expected an increasing CPI_t (i.e., $\text{CPI}_t > 100$), but P_r moves up and down, depending on what happens with P_t. We can sum up what we have thus far with the equation $P_r = P_t/C_t$, where $C_t = \text{CPI}_t/100$.

According to the good Josh on the television serial "The West Wing", the maximum P_r for the United States over the period 1973–2005 was in 1981. This probably makes sense, since the Iranian Revolution took place around that time, and the oil price surged.

Unfortunately, however, Mr Josh's observation was not particularly useful. In the United States as in Sweden, what we see is a flattening of personal income (or wages and salaries) for a large part of the population over the past quarter of a century. This flattening usually commences at about the age of 50. Thus, the recent oil price escalation is definitely bad news for persons in that age category, as well as many others, because this impacts on them both directly and indirectly: indirectly because of the influence of the oil price on the aggregate inflation rate, and directly because of what it means for things like the price of motor fuel and the cost of heating their homes. In the United States, the latter item mostly involves natural gas, but as pointed out in my natural gas book (1987), the price of gas is often indexed to that of oil. For instance, a simple indexing formula might be Gas Price = (Average price of five crudes/P_{ob}) · P_{gb}. In this expression P_{ob} is the price of oil in the base year (b), and P_{gb} is the price of gas in the base year.

The conclusion must therefore be that individuals who feel that their standard of living is threatened by rising oil or energy prices are correct, and Mr Josh should reserve his opinions about the real price of oil to conversations with his colleagues in the White House, and especially his boss. Needless to say, Mr Josh will probably never be in a position where rising oil prices interfere with the use of his late model automobile.

It can also be pointed out that a total differentiation of $P_r = P_t/C_t$ would give $g_r = g_t - g_{ct}$, where g signifies the growth rate. The claim of Mr Josh thus seems to be that $g_{ct} > g_t$, and so to his way of thinking g_r is in reality descending at the present time — which is definitely not the case.

(2) It was stated in the main text that economics places a limit on the amount (q) that we should remove from an oil (or gas) deposit of R during a given period. We can accordingly write $\Delta R/R \leq \lambda^*$, however $\Delta R = q$, and so we obtain $q/R \leq \lambda^*$. In the next chapter careful attention will be paid to the inversion of this relationship, or $R/q \geq 1/\lambda^* = \theta^*$, because the general discussion of oil shortages usually involves the reserve–production (R/q) ratio.

Incidentally, we often have to entertain strange tales about the R/q ratio in the context of which the expression "dynamic" is used to claim that reserves are adequate. However, if we start at the present date and ask about the development of this ratio, we can write $Re^{\alpha t}/qe^{\beta t}$, and since it is very clear that β is larger than α, the dynamics do not seem to work in favor of the oil optimists. At the same time, readers should remember that the key thing where this topic is concerned is the date at which the global q peaks because, as pointed out on numerous occasions, when that happens the lifestyles of a good many citizens might be in significant danger. In continuing, examine Table 1.1 for some commonly used prefixes.

Table 1.1.   Commonly Used Prefixes, with Examples

Prefix	Symbol	Power	Meaning	Example
Kilo	K(k)	10^3	thousand	kW (kilowatt)
Mega	M(m)	10^6	million	MW (megawatt)
Giga	G	10^9	billion	GJ (gigajoules)
Tera	T	10^{12}	trillion	TJ (terajoule)
Peta	P	10^{15}	thousand-trillion	PJ (petajoule)
Exa	E	10^{18}	million-trillion	EJ (exajoule)

Appendix A2: Units and equivalencies

Next, it should be noted that 1 t is the designation of one metric ton, or 1 tonne, which equals 2204 pounds (lbs). We also have a short ton, which in most countries is simply called a ton. One short ton (ton) = 2000 lbs; and l t = 1.103 tons. Finally, there is a long ton, which is 2240 lbs. As most readers know, 1 mile = 1609 m = 5280 ft, and so 1 m is approximately 3.28 ft = 39.37 ins, giving us 1 in = 2.54 cm. Furthermore, 1 kg is approximately 2.2 pounds (lbs), and if we have to convert Centigrade to Fahrenheit we use the formula {Fahrenheit = (9/5)Celsius + 32}, remembering that Celsius now seems to be used instead of Centigrade.

When working with energy we are often interested in heat, which is usually measured in British thermal units (Btu) and joules. 1 Btu is the amount of heat needed to increase the temperature of 1 lb of water by 1 degree (= 1°) Fahrenheit. One metric ton (1 t) of bituminous coal has an energy content (on the average) of 27,700,000 Btu, and the reader can convert this to joules using Table 1.2. 1 t of crude oil has an average energy content of 42,514,000 Btu, and one thousand cubic feet (= 1 kcf = 1 kft^3) of natural gas has an average energy content slightly in excess of 1,000,000 Btu. (The exact figure is given below.)

It was often said that Btu would be completely replaced by joules (J), but this is not certain. It would not seem natural at the present time to quote natural gas prices in dollars per joule instead of dollars/Btu, although joule

Table 1.2. Conversions: Joules — kWh — Btu

	Joules (J)	Kilowatt-hours (kWh)	Btu
1 joule	1	0.278×10^{-6}	0.948×10^{-3}
1 kWh	3.6×10^{6}	1	3.412×10^{3}
1 Btu	1.055×10^{3}	0.293×10^{-3}	1

is a member of the international system of units (SI units). The kWh and MWh are very popular and well-known units, and readers should get used to working with them. A short table of equivalencies can now be given.

It is worth remembering that 1 million tonnes of oil equivalent ($=$ 1 mtoe) can be converted to Btu, should this unit be relevant to the discussion. Handy transformations are 1 barrel of oil ($=$ 1 b) = 5,800,000 Btu. We also have 7.33 b (on the average) enclosing 1 t of oil. The most popular unit for measuring the consumption and production of oil is barrels per day ($=$ b/d). For example, the output of the OPEC countries at the present time is about 27 mb/d, and this can be turned into another popular unit — millions of tonnes per year (mt/y) — by multiplying by 50. Thus, 25 mb/d = 1350 mt/y. Where this 50 is concerned, we get it from a simple dimensional analysis: 1 (b/d) $\times$ 365 (d/y) $\times$ (1/7.33)(t/b) $=$ 50 (t/y), and thus 1 mb/d = 50 mt/y.

Power is defined as the rate of doing work. The best-known units for measuring power are the watt (W), which is equal to one joule (J) per second, and the horsepower (hp). These units will be looked at more closely in the chapter on electricity. However, just now, the following table seems useful:

Table 1.3. Conversions: Watts — hp — Btu/h

	Watts (W)	Horsepower (hp)	Btu/Hour (Btu/h)
1 W	1	1.341×10^{-3}	3.41
1 hp	0.746×10^{3}	1	2.54×10^{3}
1 Btu/h	0.293	0.393×10^{-3}	1

One of the most interesting things about Table 1.3 is the introduction of time into the picture. For example, we go from watts — which is a measure of power — to Btu/h. There is no point in making a big thing of this at the present time; however, if we start with a pile of coal, it contains a certain number of Btu, and these are transformed into the brightness in your kitchen via the bulbs in that room. The larger the bulbs, the faster the coal pile is depleted. I could perform the relevant calculations now, and you would have no problem understanding them, but it is probably best to wait until the chapter on electricity.

Finally, in summary form, some useful equivalencies are:

(1) 1 barrel of crude oil $= 42$ US gallons, and weighs 0.136 metric tons (t).
(2) 1000 cubic feet $(= 1000\,ft^3)$ of natural gas $= 28.3$ m^3, where $1\,m^3 = 35.33\,ft^3$.
(3) 1 kWh of electricity $= 3413$ Btu $= 860$ kilocalories (kcals).
(4) 1 t bituminous coal $= 27,700,000\ (= 27.7 \times 10^6)$ Btu (on average).
(5) $1000\,ft^3$ of natural gas $= 1.035 \times 10^6$ Btu $= 2.61 \times 10^8$ calories.
(6) 1 t of hard coal $= 4.9$ barrels of crude oil (on average).
(7) $1000\,ft^3$ of natural gas $= 0.178$ barrels of crude oil (on average).
(8) 1000 kWh of electricity $= 0.588$ barrels of oil (on average).

Key Concepts

API number	primary recovery ratio
base load and peak load	reserve–production ratio
decline rate	reserves
derivatives	retail and wholesale prices for
EROI	electricity
hedging	secondary recovery
LNG	spot prices
M. King Hubbert and peaking	tar sands
money and real prices	tertiary recovery
oil-in-place	

Questions for Discussion

1. What do you think about my version of Murphy's Law: "Any financial system that can be manipulated will be manipulated!" Do you think that Gordon Gekko would agree?

2. Explain: The peaking of the oil supply in the United States can be explained by economics. Geology is a constraint! "Hubbert's Peak" was mentioned in an episode of the "West Wing". Pretend that you are President (and professor of economics and Nobel Prize winner) Jed Bartlet, and explain it to your admiring subordinates.
3. There seems to be plenty of natural gas in Alaska and Northern Canada. Why is there a growing gas deficiency in the "lower 48" of the United States?
4. What are the arguments for and against an expansion of nuclear energy? What are the arguments for and against a rapid expansion of renewables.
5. How do you think Neumann and Morgenstern would handle this matter of global warming, given the approach to uncertainty in their book *The Theory of Games and Economic Behavior*.
6. LNG is not as popular as some people think that it should be. Explain!
7. As far as I am concerned, electricity deregulation has failed. Discuss in detail.
8. Do you think that the oil-rich countries of the Middle East will provide us with all the oil that we think that we need, at prices that we think are reasonable?
9. Emissions trading seems to have worked in the United States for SO_2, but important researchers like David Victor and Ruth Greenspan Bell do not have much faith in it on the international level. Why is this?
10. What are the objections of President George W. Bush and his government to the Kyoto Protocol? What appears to be the objections of the writer of this book? How do you feel about this? What was the former prime minister of the United Kingdom Margaret Thatcher's comment on this topic?
11. Former Governor Gray Davis of California used the expression "Out of state criminals" when discussing the deregulation meltdown in his state. Discuss the background to this unusual terminology.
12. Enron was a brilliant firm that ran into some problems a few years ago. Explain. Not too long ago the price of natural gas in the United States averaged $14.5/mBtu. What is the oil equivalent price? Often in this book I use the expressions "spiked" and "sustained". Discuss and give some examples.

Bibliography

Adams, Rod (2006). "Comment on Dixon 'Wind Generation's performance during the July 2006 California heat storm' ". *EnergyPulse* (www.energypulse.net).

Al-Fattah, S.M. and R.A. Startzman (2000). "Forecasting world natural gas supply". *Journal of Petroleum Technology*, May: 62–72.

Banks, Ferdinand E. (2001a). *Global Finance and Financial Markets: A Modern Introduction*. London, New York and Singapore: World Scientific.

—— (2001b). "A disobliging lecture on gas and electric deregulation". Lecture presented to a forum at the Scuola Enrico Mattei, Milan, Italy, 9 June 2001.

—— (2000a). *Energy Economics: A Modern Introduction*. Boston and Dordrecht: Kluwer Academic.

—— (2000b). "The Kyoto negotiations on climate change". *Energy Sources*, 22: 481–496.

—— (1996). "Electricity deregulation and privatization: an introductory survey". *Energy: The International Journal*, 33: 1–13.

—— (1987). *The Political Economy of Natural Gas*. London: Croom-Helm.

Bell, Ruth Greenspan (2006). "The Kyoto placebo". *Issues in Science and Technology, Resources for the Future*.

Beyer, Jim (2007). "Comment on 'How do we get off fossil fuels?' " *EnergyPulse*.

Beyer, Jim (2006). "Comment on 'Let biofuel investors beware' ". *EnergyPulse*.

Borowitz, Sidney (1999). *Farewell Fossil Fuels: Reviewing America's Energy Policy*. New York: Plenum Publishing Corporation.

Brown, Lester (2006). "Appetite for destruction". *Fortune*, 4 September.

Cairns, Robert D. and Graham A. Davis (2001). "Adelman's rule and the Petroleum firm". *The Energy Journal*, 22(3): 31–54.

Chenery, Hollis B. and Paul Clark (1962). *Interindustry Economics*. New York: John Wiley and Sons.

Coppens, Francois and David Vivet (2004). "Liberalization of network industries: is electricity an exception to the rule?" *National Bank of Belgium Working Paper No. 59*.

Davis, Morton (1974). *Game Theory*. New York: Basic Books.

Dixon, David (2006). "Wind generation's performance during the July 2006 California heat storm". *EnergyPulse* (www.energypulse.net).

Dorfman, Robert, Paul Samuelson and Robert Solow (1958). *Linear Programming and Economic Analysis*. New York: McGraw Hill.

Flower, Andrew (1978). "World oil production". *Scientific American*, 283(3): 41–49.

Franssen, Herman (2005). "The age of peak oil: old myth or new reality". *Petroleum Intelligence Weekly*, September.

Freeman, Marsha (2001). "It's not supply and demand". *21st Century Science and Technology*, Spring.

Funk, C. (1991). *Wettbewerb im erdgassmarkt*. Stencil: University of Bergen.

Giegler, Don (2007). "Comment on 'How do we get off fossil fuels?'" *Energy Pulse*.

Gould, Len (2006). "Comment on Dixon 'Wind generation's performance during the July 2006 California heat storm'". *EnergyPulse* (www.energypulse.net).

Haas, Reinhard and Hans Auer (2001). "The relevance of excess capacities for European electricity markets". Paper presented at the 24th IAEE Conference, Houston, Texas, 25–27 April.

Hatamian, Hamid (1998). "Natural gas supply and demand problems". *Journal of Petroleum Technology*, January: 58–63.

Herbert, John H. and Erik Krell (1996). "US natural gas markets: how efficient are they?" *Energy Policy*, 24: 1–5.

Hopf, James (2007). "Comment on 'How do we get off fossil fuels?'" *Energy Pulse*.

Hotelling, Harold (1931). "The economics of exhaustible resources". *Journal of Political Economy*, 39: 137–175.

Hunt, Tam (2007). "How do we get off fossil fuels?" *Energy Pulse* (26 February 2007).

Hunt, Tam (2006). "We don't need LNG in California". *EnergyPulse* (www.energypulse.net).

Jenkins, Alan (2006). "Let biofuel investors beware". *EnergyPulse* (1 June 2006).

Kok, Kenneth (2007). "Comment on 'How do we get off fossil fuels?'" *Energy Pulse*.

McKibben, Bill (2001). "Some like it hot". *The New York Review*, XLVIII(11): 35–38.

Neumann, John von and Oscar Morgenstern (1944). *Theory of Games and Economic Behavior*. Princeton: Princeton University Press.

Ormerod, Paul (2006). *Why Most Things Fail*. New York and London: Pantheon.

Percebois, Jacques (1989). *Economie de L'energie*. Paris: Economica.

Salameh, Mamdouh G. (2001). "The quest for Middle East Oil: The US versus the Asia-Pacific Region". *Energy Policy*, 31(11): 1085–1091.

Saunders, Harry D. (1984). "On the inevitable return of higher oil prices". *Energy Policy*, 12(33): 310–320.

Sharma, Deepak (2001). "The multidimensionality of electricity reform — an Australian perspective". *Energy Policy*, 31(11): 1093–1102.

Slesser, Malcolm (1978). *Energy in the Economy*. London: The Macmillan Press.

Tanguy, Pierre (1997). *Nucleaire: Pas de Panique*. Paris: Editions Nucléon.

Teitelbaum, R. (1995). "Your last big play in oil". *Fortune*, 30 October.

Victor, David G. (2001). "Climate of doubt". *The Sciences*, 41(2): 18–23.

Walters, David (2007). "Comment on 'How do we get off fossil fuels?'" *Energy Pulse*.

Woo, Chi-Keung, Debra Lloyd and Asher Tishler (2001). "Electric market reform failures: UK, Norway, Alberta, and California". *Energy Policy*, 31(11): 1103–1115.

CHAPTER 2

ECONOMIC THEORY AND WORLD OIL: A SURVEY

"Oil is a magnet for conflict"
— Richard G. Lugar and R. James Woolsey (1999)

I believe that where matters of oil and conflict are concerned, we should not hesitate to treat with considerable respect the opinions of (US) Senator Lugar, and the former director of Central Intelligence, R. James Woolsey. It might be useful to add however that oil is also a magnet for gross misunderstandings, some of which could cost the major oil importing countries dearly in the not too remote future.

The world oil market is a very different thing today from what it was just a decade ago. The strength of global demand for oil has surprised just about everybody, while at the same time it has become clear that there is insufficient investment in additional production capacity. The core issue here is that it is becoming increasingly difficult to locate additional large deposits of oil, and as a result, the major oil companies consider it financially unwise to look as hard as they did in the past. The executives of these firms have a comprehensive insight into the costs and risks that are associated with exploring and trying to produce in marginal regions, and as a result, they are paying more attention to the preferences of their shareholders. Among other things, this means increased dividends and share buy-backs instead of spending on exploration and production.

It pays to be careful about what we believe when dealing with this topic. According to Professor Khartukov (2004) — perhaps the leading energy economist in Russia — "Russia can easily produce up to 30 million barrels per day (= 30 mb/d) of oil and condensate for many years to come". He was, probably referring to the Former Soviet Union (FSU), although it really does not make any difference: neither Russia nor the totality of the nations comprising the FSU can produce 30 mb/d, now or in the future. Similarly, Guy Caruso (2001) — director of the US Energy Information Agency — has written that with "more than 260 billion barrels of proven reserves, Saudi Arabian resources would appear to be adequate to reach a 20 mb/d rate of production, and would leave a reasonably comfortable reserves to production ratio". (Saudi Arabia has the largest proven reserves in the world, and in addition this statement implies the acceptance by that country of a long-term *plateau* production of 20 mb/d. This matter was touched on earlier and will be examined in more detail in the next chapter.)

With all due respect, I find it impossible to agree with both of these observers. Production peaked in "Russia" (i.e., the FSU) about 15 years ago at almost 13 mb/d, and a recovery to 30 mb/d is almost completely out of the question. It may be conceivable that with reserves close to 80 billion barrels, production in the FSU might grow for a while if the necessary investment can be financed, but reaching the previous peak would only make economic sense if there was an enormous and durable escalation in the oil price. (A recent paper in the important *Geopolitics of Energy* by Lee (2004) examines this topic in considerable detail, to include two scenarios for future Russian oil production.) On the other hand, *sustained* production at the previous peak is completely out of the question unless the oil price reached astronomic levels. Let me also note that if Russia manages to pull itself out of the macroeconomic doldrums on a countrywide basis, which in theory should be possible given present trends, then there will be much less Russian oil available for export than observers have come to believe.

As for Saudi Arabia, the International Energy Agency (IEA) has estimated that a Saudi production of 20 mb/d is possible, but as I argue in the next chapter of this book, the Saudi government ruled out that possibility at least 30 years ago. Recently, a high ranking Saudi official said that a production of 15 mb/d can be attained, and there has been some talk of an output of 12.5 mb/d in 2009, however as noted in the previous chapter, my contention is that 12–12.5 mb/d over a not particularly long time horizon is the best that can be hoped for. (It might eventually be possible to get capacity higher for a short period of time, but *surge* capacity and *sustainable* capacity are two quite different things, and readers should make sure that they understand the difference.) Interestingly enough, Caruso has supplied the reason why: "The Saudis have shown some sensitivity in the past with respect to resource depletion issues, and are concerned that peak (i.e., plateau) production would be short lived. Diversification of the Saudi economy would be challenged by even greater dependence on oil exports".

This is an extremely important observation when considering the oil future of Iraq, which to my way of counting has the second largest oil reserves in the world. These reserves come to approximately 115 billion barrels, while Saudi Arabia has an estimated 260 billion barrels. (In other words, I am ignoring the attempt to "negotiate" up Canadian reserves from a trivial 5 billion barrels to 180 billion barrels by a reclassification of tar-sand resources.) Before the beginning of the war with Iran, Iraq was well on its way to a prosperity that could have been compared with all the countries in the region except, possibly, the smaller oil states. Moreover, as is not adequately appreciated, this prosperity was not just based on oil but on an ambitious and intelligent population whose expanding educational level was setting its course toward a European standard of living. As Cassidy (2003) makes clear, when produced with other than short-term considerations having to do with collecting oil revenues in mind, resources like oil and gas are capable of financing a great deal of *development.*

Assuming that Iraq eventually conforms to President George W. Bush's dreams, that country would contribute almost 6 mb/d of oil exports to the satisfaction of a global demand that the United States Department of Energy (USDE), as well as the International Energy Agency (IEA), believes will reach 120 mb/d in period 2025–2030. As it happens, whatever contribution Iraq makes from what Salameh (2004) calls "the last great oil prize" will almost certainly be inadequate for bridging the global gap between demand and supply that (given present trends) seems almost certain to appear at some point in the next decade. It has begun to seem likely that only very large *demand-suppressing* price rises can do that, and contrary to the sort of thing that the financial press often tells us at the present time, these could leave havoc in their wake.

Another much talked about region that will not be pulling the oil chestnuts of importing countries out of the fire is the Caspian basin and its immediate surroundings. The major strikes that everyone was expecting in that region have not materialized, with the possible exception of the Kashagan field in Kazakstan. I use the word "possible" because production may not start until the end of this decade, and there is still some doubt about the total amount of oil that is involved. One thing though is certain: with, e.g., US imports steadily increasing, and domestic output steadily declining, Kashagan will only be of minor importance — if that.

In addition, since oil firms in the FSU have been in the habit of maintaining that deposits that *might* possibly be developed, but have not yet been discovered, and should be treated as *bona-fide* assets for everything except tax purposes, it could happen that somebody at some negotiating table might find themselves believing things that they would be better off ignoring and making deals that they could ultimately come to regret. If you examine the ratios of estimated undiscovered reserves to identified reserves, you will find that these are quite modest everywhere except for the FSU. The average estimated value for regions outside the FSU is 2. For the FSU (as a whole) it is about 4, and for the Caspian Basin it appears to be as high as 10.

Some years ago the Baker Institute (in Texas) issued a report which said that "Oil production in Central Asia and the Caucasus will never match the Persian Gulf. Many of the countries of the Caspian Basin have limited, if any, oil potential. In short, the Caspian Basin is not going to be an "ace in the hole" for international energy security". This appraisal is not certain though, because in the great world of oil nothing is certain, however, it is interesting to note that one of the persons now taking the position that the capacity of the Caspian is less than generally believed is Professor Maureen Crandall of the United States National Defence University.

When I wrote my intermediate energy economics textbook, one of my intentions was to help fill most of the gaps in the existing literature. This was not done to my satisfaction, and it may not be possible in the present book to the extent that I would like, but several topics have been taken up in this contribution (and this chapter) that deserve attention because of recent developments on the energy front. It was impossible to avoid the use of a small amount of mathematics, but for the most part this does not involve anything more demanding than secondary school algebra. As for the diagram in this chapter that is a key explanatory device for short-run price movements, neither this diagram nor the small amount of algebra associated with it has ever shown signs of being an obstacle to any of my first year students in economics or finance.

Readers of this chapter may have encountered or will encounter similar information in other chapters; however, there is no real harm in this. As I found out in teaching economics and especially finance, anything that is important is worth repeating. I can also note that this chapter's appendix contains some non-elementary mathematics.

1. Some Absolutely Essential Background

"Never underestimate the power of oil", was a suggestion once offered by *The Economist* (13 April 2002). Despite rumors to the contrary, this has not been done for a number of years, especially by enterprises who might be thinking of applying for membership in the billionaires club and who for one reason or another picked up the scent of a coming escalation in oil prices.

Fesharaki (2004) sums up the latest happenings on the oil market by noting that "everyone is making money in every part of the business...*This is unprecedented in history*". "Everyone" now apparently includes the perennially hard-luck refining sector. Finally, he adds: "If you are clever you can make a lot of money. If you are not, you can still make a lot of money".

One prerequisite for cleverness is abandoning the amazing amount of wishful thinking that is still in circulation. At the international meeting of the International Association for Energy Economics (IAEE) in Rome, in 1999, many delegates were informed once again that it was only a matter of time before a large new oil province was discovered — probably in the FSU; even if this were not true, the worldwide recovery rate for oil would eventually reach 40%, which would mean an addition to reserves that was roughly equivalent to the discovery of another East Texas oil province. For some reason Lord Browne of Madingly, CEO of BP, went even higher than that, but once he began talking about the price of oil falling to between 20 and 30 dollars per barrel, everybody who was anybody stopped listening.

As pointed out in the previous chapter, the first thing to do in appraising this kind of wisdom is to distinguish between *oil-in-place* and recoverable reserves. The first time I taught in Australia the global recovery rate was believed to average about 32%, while at the present time it is somewhere around 35%. Accordingly, this fraction has increased about 3% in 27 years, which is not an earthshaking change. Technological improvements will almost certainly raise this, but hardly at a more rapid rate, and considering the very low recovery rate of unconventional oil, if these resources play a more prominent role in the oil melodrama, 40% will be very difficult to reach.

In addition, an increasing fraction of any increases will probably be canceled out by "natural depreciation" — i.e., a fall in the reserves from individual deposits that is the result of pressures in a reservoir decreasing as hydrocarbons are extracted. This is a greatly underrated phenomenon by various observers, especially academic economists, and this decline cannot always be easily compensated for in the production program by, e.g., injecting water from a contiguous acquifer, or drilling new wells.

As for making new discoveries, Flower (1978) said that it was unlikely that genuinely new discoveries will be made even at the modest rates that had been achieved over the five years prior to the appearance of his seminal article. This is exactly what happened. Furthermore, the upward adjustment of reserves that routinely takes place in fields already discovered appears to be diminishing. (A good example here is probably the UK North Sea, where some years ago an associate director of the Cambridge Energy Research Associates reacted to rumors of a higher oil by remarking that "OPEC's fate is not in its own hands". What he should have said was that the United Kingdom's energy fate was probably no longer in its own hands due to the possibility of a growing dependence on ever more distant sources of oil and gas, as well as the bizarre electricity and gas deregulation being devised in Brussels.

But suppose that none of this was true, and a giant or super-giant field was uncovered. If this happened in an OPEC country, it would almost certainly change very little, because the governments of most of these countries have discovered, are discovering, or will discover the immense social, political, and economic value of having access to a sizable oil income over a very long time horizon. On the other hand, if it took place elsewhere, it would also be of only marginal significance: the Kashagan strike mentioned earlier has hardly been noticed.

What all of the above will mean for a continuation of our present way of life is not easy to say, although I happen to be convinced that a measure of pessimism is more appropriate than irrational optimism where this topic is concerned, unless concentrated efforts are made to reduce the dependence on conventional crude oil. By way of contrast, Fesharaki injects a resounding buoyancy into his inquiry. "There will be no oil shortage or collapse in the world economy! Higher prices will reduce demand and encourage alternatives as economic theory tells us". In a recent issue of the important review *Hydrocarbon Asia* (January–February 2006), one of Mr Fesharaki's colleagues claims that after 2010 technological advances will keep prices in check!

I am afraid that this does not characterize the economic theory that I teach. The theory presented in my classrooms always pointed out that these reductions or increases, and/or appearance of alternatives, require time — and sometimes a great deal of time. This might also be the place to note that in the United States alone, in 2004, many thousands of oil and gas companies spent 58 billion dollars in their search for local resources, but this only brought about a 0.4% increase in reserves during that year. These researchers fail to understand that any reduction in China's demand will be compensated for by increases in the demand by India, and for the time being at least, an increase in production from Canadian tar sands will almost be balanced by a decrease in oil production from other sources.

Lawrence Goldstein, the long-time president of the Petroleum Industry Research Fundation in New York, once said that the increased demand for oil up to year 2000 will largely be met by increased non-OPEC supplies. He was probably thinking of something like a recent large "strike" in the Gulf of Mexico. As for OPEC, they will find themselves "in a stagnant volume environment at best". This kind of guesswork is not of great value when considering the oil future, although the source of the difficulty may be that Mr Goldstein was too great a great believer in the utility of the unadulterated Reserve–Production (R/q) ratio for estimating the length of time that the oil buying world will enjoy adequate supplies of oil. (The units here are barrels for R, and barrels/year for q.) With that ratio equal to 40, he and his associates and many other influential observers were quick to point out that, as one of them put it, "With all the reserves in place now, we have a 40 year supply of oil even if we do not find another drop".

The R/q ratio is indeed important, but not when used in this manner, and so I will resort to an example that I used in the first lecture that I gave on oil. If the R/q ratio falls below a certain level — probably somewhere between 10 and 15 — then the deposit is being "damaged" in the same manner that sucking too hard on a straw will damage an ice-cream soda. This particular R/q ratio can be designated the *critical R/q ratio*, or θ^*, and for simplicity I always take it as 10 — although Flower (1978) prefers the higher figure (for reasons spelled out with some simple algebra in my coal book (1985), and also mentioned in my previous textbook). The damage will be manifested by a reduction in the total amount of oil that can ultimately be removed from the deposit.

Now for the important point. *When the $R/q(=\theta)$ ratio reaches the critical value, the critical value will determine production in the sense that production should adjust in such a way as to hold the critical value approximately constant.* (*Note*: *should* and not *will*, because there might be valid economic reasons for hastening depletion. Moreover this is a theoretical point in economics rather than physics, and so from time to time it may be possible to see large exceptions. We do not expect any exceptions to the first law of thermodynamics.)

An example is useful here. Assume that we have a field with 225 units ($= R$) of oil reserves, and we desire to lift 15 units per year, and our critical R/q ratio (θ^*) is 10. Using the logic expressed in the previous paragraph, it is obvious that we can have an output of 15 units/year for five years. During this period the R/q ratio falls from 14 (at the end of the first year) to 10 at the end of the fifth year, while reserves fall to 150 units. After that, however, if we continue to remove $q = 15$ units/year, we are violating our constraint: the R/q ratio will fall under 10. For instance, if we remove 15 more units ($q = 15$), then reserves would fall to 135, and R/q decreases to $135/15 = 9$.

To keep this ratio at 10 ($= \theta^*$), production in the sixth year should not be larger than 13.64. (Thus, $R/q = (150 - 13.64)/13.64 = 10$.) Continuing, in the seventh year production cannot be larger than 12.4. Readers should be able to get these results by simple trial and error; however, this exercise may be generalized to show that $10 \leq R_t/q_t \leq (R_{t-1} - q_t)/q_t$. In turn, this expression may be solved to give $q_t \leq R_{t-1}/11$ (or, more generally, $q_t \leq R_{t-1}/(1 + \theta^*)$. As noted in Appendix A1 of the previous chapter, this operation is merely another way of saying that in any (e.g.) year, the percentage of reserves extracted should be less than or equal to 10%.

The above is an important example, and after making sure that they understand it perfectly, readers should confirm that there is a large amount of oil in the ground when output turned down. Moreover, when we look at the production profiles of *actual* major oil or gas regions like the United States, what we see is that when peaking takes place (and production sooner or later begins to decline), there is still a huge amount of the resource in the ground, and in addition much of this is immediately extractable. The interpretation here is as follows: *the peak is explained by economics and not geology. More is not extracted — and the peak delayed — because in the interests of profit maximization, the optimal behavior is to extract it later!* As explained in Banks (2004, 2000), geology essentially functions as a constraint. This is a crucial point that everyone reading this chapter should make every effort to understand.

Now for some elementary oil geology. The production of conventional oil involves reservoir fluids flowing under pressure out of the reservoir rock into a production well (or borehole). Initial production tends to be constant for a period ranging from several days to several years. Then, as the pressure drops and the oil has to move a greater distance through the reservoir rocks to reach a given borehole, the output will tend to decline — *ceteris paribus*. One of the things that will reduce the pressure is a too rapid depletion. This can result in the deposit being damaged, which in turn makes the oil more difficult to extract (for the same effort), as well as decreasing the recovery factor. Now we see why the R/q ratio is so important: by operating below the *critical* R/q ratio ($= 10$ in the above discussion) we reduce the ultimate (i.e., total) flow of oil from the asset. This immediately suggests that the R/q ratio can serve as a proxy for some important geological information. For example, the decline of the R/q ratio under the critical R/q ratio might be the forerunner of a larger than normal reduction in deposit pressure.

As shown in my previous textbook, the production profile for many oil fields — where a field is a group of reservoirs in the same general area — exhibits rising production, a plateau, and then falling production. Obtaining this profile calls for drilling (over time) a number of production wells. Initially the flow from new wells exceeds the depletion of those already drilled, and so we start out with a rising production pattern. Then, new drilling is usually programmed at a pace that is designed to keep output more or less constant, because managers and engineers believe that this will maximize intertemporal profits; finally, drilling slows because as the amount of oil remaining in the field declines, the cost of extra wells is high compared to the additional amount of oil obtained. The downturn in drilling accounts for the declining portion of the profile. This pattern also applies to gas. When the development of a given quantity of reserves is initiated, a large investment can result in a large initial output, but as alluded to both above and later in this exposition, the trade-off is a more rapid depletion as reserves are "used-up" and "down-hole" pressure falls.

The fundamental law of decline applies *everywhere*. Additional wells must constantly be put in place, and/or processes introduced for maintaining pressure by such things as water or gas injection; even then natural depletion can cause a sizable annual reduction in exploitable reserves that later will be reflected in larger (per barrel) production costs. Accordingly, inadequate investment during the last decade could mean that a country such as Iraq might experience difficulty in quickly raising production to its reported target level of 6 mb/d, even though the embargo on Iraqi oil has been lifted, a heavy injection of foreign capital is possible, and installations may not find themselves the targets of various projectiles. Similarly, it has been said that low investment combined with aging oil fields and a high rate of growth of domestic consumption will cause Iranian production to plateau earlier than expected.

If a reservoir is tapped by drilling a well, and the pressure in the well-hole is considerably less than that in the reservoir, there can be a "natural" flow of oil to the surface, and into a pipeline. This category of production is termed *natural drive*, and it tends to prevail for a relatively long time in the richest oil fields. Eventually, this pressure will fall, and some category of artificial lift must be introduced, and/or other wells drilled. Thus, what started out as a pure "one shot" investment problem of the "point-input-continuous-output" type leads unavoidably to an intertemporal consideration of investment that might be described as a "continuous-input continuous-output" (or *repeated* point-input-point-output) process.

On several occasions I was pointedly told that when the R/q ratio in the UK North Sea was closer to 5 than to 10, the output continued to rise. Even if true, this does not vitiate the above discussion. What it probably meant is that even in medium-deep water, production costs (to include taxes) were so high that, given the existing and expected situation with prices and reserves, maximizing (discounted) profits entailed an increased rate of "consuming" some of the remainder of the deposit in order to speed up the recovery of the capital that was invested in the deposit so that hopefully it could be invested in higher-value projects. And this capital was almost certainly needed. More than 60% of the new oil being discovered is offshore, and drilling a deepwater well can cost a great deal more than performing the same operation onshore. Moreover, risks can be enormous. As an example take ChevronTexaco's Toledo prospect in the Gulf of Mexico's Alaminos Canyon area. Despite the availability of space-age technology, which led management to estimate that the property contained 200 million barrels of oil, it turned out to be an expensive dry hole. It is also not certain that the latest new discovery in the Gulf will be as well endowed as advertised.

If you consider the above discussion in the light of the materials in your favorite microeconomics textbook, what is being done is choosing outputs (over time) that maximize the present value of profits from a deposit or field. If, for example, prices (and profits) were rising, and expectations were that they would continue to do so, then efforts would be made to extract the largest total *physical* amount possible (*over time*) from the asset. Accordingly, both economic *and* geological considerations would lead to the adjusting (i.e., moderating) of production rates (= outputs per time period) so as to preserve the asset.

As Craft and Hawkins (1959) clarified, many reservoirs are *rate sensitive*, and a too rapid production of oil may reduce reservoir pressure and cause a permanent loss of the resource. What is a "too rapid" production of oil? The simplest way to describe is it is a production level which pushes the R/q ratio below what was earlier defined as the critical R/q ratio; but in addition it should be appreciated that if, e.g., 10 mb of oil is to be extracted over a five-year period, an extraction program that lifts 2 mb/year for five years could have a different effect on the ultimately recoverable amount of this resource than a program that removes 5 mb the first year and 1.25 mb in each of the remaining four years.

2. More of the Same

"...in order to keep prices up the Arabs would have to curtail their output by ever larger amounts. But even if they cut their output to zero, they could not for long keep the world price of crude at $10.00 per barrel. Well before that point the cartel would collapse... World oil prices are weakening. They will soon tumble". Or so Professor Milton Friedman thought. (*Newsweek*, 4 March 1974).

Whenever the economics section of the Nobel Academy has an important "function" an invitation is likely to be speeded to Professor Milton Friedman. The reason is politics rather than economics, because that gentleman has a long history of being aggressively wrong where subjects like energy are concerned, although that shortcoming has not harmed his popularity in certain academic and business circles. Even more important, as Marshalla and Nesbitt (1986) point out, is that attempting to forecast the (future) oil price is not something to be taken lightly, because the cost of systematic miscalculations can turn out to be very many billions of dollars.

At the same time it is useful to note that just as Mr Friedman had his sights set too low, many knowledgeable observers have erred in the other direction. I still remember a survey published in the Swedish business publication "*Dagens Industri*" in which a large group of energy students and professionals anticipated a century-end price that averaged 75 dollars per barrel (= $75/b), while according to Resource Planning Associates (cited by Marshalla and Nesbitt), probabilistic estimates of end-of-century prices by 28 independent experts were in the range $70–$110 per barrel for 25 of these experts. (For example, Occidental Oil's controversial boss Armand Hammar, and Exxon's forecasters came to the conclusion that oil would sell for $100/b by 2000.) These, incidentally, were supposed to be sustainable prices, because in 2005 the price spiked to and above $70/b.

The reader can judge these estimates in whatever light he or she feels is appropriate; however, I would like to stress that in forecasting exercises of the kind that I prefer, the emphasis is usually on getting the economics right; *getting the economics right is not always a prelude to getting the forecast right — especially in the oil market!* What does this mean? It means that such things as irrational behavior and corruption by various buyers and/or sellers can occasionally cause oil markets to exhibit the kind of price movements that most reputable economics textbooks tend to classify as unreasonable.

Getting the economics right means emphasizing again and again that the world oil market is *drastically* different today from what it was 25 years ago. So different that it would be gross carelessness if our political leaders accepted half-baked theories that have their origin in *ad hoc* junk economics. "We keep looking for more oil, and finding more oil", one well-known observer has told his clients, forgetting that the quantity of oil discovered is on a falling trend, and this trend is visible to all who take the trouble to look.

More emphasis might be useful here. Early in 2005, huge oil "major" Shell admitted that over the previous year it had only found enough new reserves to replace at most 25% of the production during that period. About the same time Chevron — the second largest energy group in the United States — announced that its reserves replacement had declined to 18%. ExxonMobil, the largest oil company in the world, announced reserves replacement of only 83%, while BP was a star of sorts, although they were well under 100%. They were somewhat less than a star in another respect, however, because their director, Lord Browne, confessed that in the future BP will become more "profit" than "volume" oriented, which means that they will not be going after elephants (i.e., super-giant deposits) any more because, I assume, they — and equally as important their better informed shareholders — have come to the conclusion that there are no more ele-phants. This situation can probably be summed up best by mentioning that according to a leading oil consultancy, IHS Energy, over the last decade the annual global consumption of oil has averaged 26 billion barrels, while the average amount of new oil reserves found each year has been 7.5 billion barrels.

It also needs to be appreciated that even if it is true that technology is "overwhelming natural depletion" and reducing costs all along the line, without an increase in the amount of oil discovered, preferably in the form of very large deposits, production cannot continue to rise. This can conve-niently be derived from the work of M. King Hubbert that was discussed in the previous chapter. Some observers have called Hubbert's success in predicting the production in the "lower 48" of the United States a fluke, but what is not a fluke is the fact that with the exception of the temporary increase caused by Prudhoe Bay coming on line, output in the United States has been trending down ever since.

One scholar who developed a serious set of issues with Hubbert's work is Ryan (1966). He wrote that "There is no fundamental law of physics ensuring that cumulative discoveries or cumulative production will follow a logistic pattern in the future. The logistic equation is not the logical con-sequence of physical concepts such as the laws of conservation of mass or energy. Nor is it a reasonable projection of the consequences of the future economic, political, or technological developments that will largely determine future discovery rates". (In this discussion a logistic pattern is roughly equivalent to a bell-shaped or normal curve.)

I can certainly sympathize with much of his evaluation, but Ryan's opinion was rendered a long time ago, and unfortunately the subsequent evidence does not work in his favor. Al-Jarri and Startzman (1997) found that Hubbert's geometry gave the best explanation of production in the 67 countries that they scrutinized, and in the lower 48 states of the United States, onshore production followed — as Hubbert specified — a rough bell-like curve, peaking in 1970, and falling to less than half the peak output at the present time. (It is the inflection point on the logistic curve referred to by Ryan that corresponds to the peak of the bell curve. In addition, the area under the curve represents the ultimate availability of the resource.)

The oil that is necessary to keep the global production peak in the distance depends on the large discoveries that were made in the past: this was the fundamental insight of Dr. Hubbert, and what it comes down to is that to an approximate extent the production peak will be a mirror image of the peak of discoveries. The term "mirror image" might be too precise for this discussion; however, it would be difficult to derive a theory of oil (or gas) production that is capable of casting aspersions on this approach. Discovery in the United States peaked in 1930, and 40 years later production peaked. By the same token, discovery in the UK North Sea peaked in 1974, and comparatively high rates of production brought about an output peak in 2000. Norway's oil has suffered the same fate, and of (Western) Europe's indigenous energy supply, only Norway's natural gas appears to be going strong. Whether it is going strong enough is quite another matter, because it is estimated that the demand for gas by EU countries will increase by at least 70% in the next 25 years. The upshot of all this is that the energy dependence by Western Europe on foreign resources is going to increase by a very large amount in the not too distant future.

World oil discovery peaked in 1964, and since 1981 much less oil has been found than consumed. This suggests that a global peak is unlikely to be delayed much past 2010. Of course, some people suggest that the mere idea of a global peak is nonsense, but, as argued in the previous chapter, this kind of thinking is difficult to understand. If oil production peaked in North America, the North Sea, China, Russia, Algeria, Indonesia, etc., mathematical induction would seem to indicate that a *global* peak is not only possible but certain.

Some observers say that Mexico is close to its production peak, which sounds reasonable now that Mexico's state oil company, Petroleos Mexicanos, recently announced that the world's second-largest oil producing field (Cantarell, in the shallow waters of the Campeche Bay), with an output of 2.2 mb/d, was moving into decline. Since Cantarell produces more oil than all the installations in Kuwait, that particular piece of news must concentrate a number of minds in Washington, DC, where previous overestimates of future oil supplies have begun to encounter hard realities. The same applies in other parts of the world. For instance, some years ago an important Swedish journalist once assured his readers that by one means or another the pop group ABBA was going to obtain a large slice of the oil that Sweden requires. Misunderstandings of this kind are one of the reasons why Sweden lost its position as one of the richest countries in the world.

We can proceed by using a simple approximation to say something about another Hubbert result. Ideally his geometric production curve takes the shape of a normal (bell-shaped) curve, but the approximation that I will employ is a *triangle* that has a base of $2H$, which is intersected at its mid-point (H) by a straight line of height H. If vertical distances in this figure represent production, and horizontal distances time, then the area of this triangle — which is H^2 — shows total (i.e., ultimate) reserves $(= \bar{R})$. This triangle has for a dimension (output/time-period) $\times$ (time-periods), or output, and so we must have $\bar{R} \equiv \Sigma q_t$ (from $t = 1$ to $t = \infty$).

Now double these reserves — i.e., make them $2H^2$ — and see what happens to the mid-point of the base! This increases by only 41%. Continue by increasing reserves once more by the same amount (H^2) to $3H^2$. The mid-point now increases by 31%, etc. *Large reserve additions are not reflected by corresponding increases in the time to the new peak production!* Remember though, that in reality, percentage increases in global reserves are no longer anywhere near these amounts. Even the discovery of impressive deposits (such as *Crazy Horse* in the Gulf of Mexico) can only delay the arrival of the peak by a comparatively short period of time. In fact, still using the (perhaps inappropriate) approximation of a triangle for a normal curve, and sticking to the Hubbert conception of a decline in output after one-half of the ultimate reserves is exhausted, we find ourselves having to consider the possibility of a comparatively early peak in world oil production if economics rather than politics determine the outcome.

3. Some Further Aspects of Oil Production

Between 75% and 80% of today's oil output originates in fields that were discovered more than a quarter of a century ago, and since almost all of these fields are in full decline, this is another case in which upbeat expectations should be carefully examined and justified before our political leaders and their experts use them to make pivotal decisions.

The spurious argument on which oil optimists construct their case almost certainly has its origin in the theorizing of Professor M.A. Adelman, and what it begins with is a (correct) hypothesis that the amount of oil that can be removed from a typical deposit almost always exceeds the original estimates. Exploration only discloses pools of unknown magnitude (and likely profitability). It is when these pools are turned into producing properties that we can judge their various attributes, to include getting an accurate — or nearly accurate — idea of the reserves that are present. Many researchers use the United States as an example. Unfortunately, this is the wrong example, because regardless of the technological prodigies that are ostensibly being performed on or planned for deposits in that country, *aggregate production* will continue to decline (to an expected 5.5 mb/d by 2020, although the *total* US energy demand is expected to increase by a large amount). Accordingly, imports of crude will continue to expand, perhaps at an increasing rate.

This is not a particularly attractive prospect for a country where a shortage of oil is often pictured as a direct threat to national security and economic well-being; however, there is not very much that they can do about it. The US oil sector is on the falling portion of its depletion curve, and a durable reversal of this situation is almost unthinkable — and by that I mean almost unthinkable if every square inch of onshore and offshore US territory, to include the Arctic National Wildlife Refuge (ANWR), were immediately thrown open to exploration and production, regardless of the environmental costs.

At the same time it deserves to be noted that certain aspects of the above analysis raise questions that might be worth a modicum of consideration. The continuous increase in *proven* reserves that Adelman alludes to during what might be called "the act of production" could, *ceteris paribus*, tend to eliminate the "scarcity rent" that forms an important part of the (theoretical) explanation as to why, when we have an exhaustible resource, firms could choose to produce at a point where price greatly exceeds the marginal cost — as contrasted to the *price = marginal cost* stipulation that economics textbooks prescribe as the profit maximization output when we do not have an exhaustible resource, and the market in question has a competitive-like delineation. Thus, with reserves being continuously adjusted upwards, in a *competitive* situation the market price of oil could remain in the vicinity of the marginal cost. An oil price that deviated from the marginal cost of extraction might thus be interpreted as being due to some form of "monopoly" rather than to a shortage of reserves.

There are still people in important positions who are partial to this kind of reasoning; however, in terms of *economics* (and not geology), and taking the possible development of the world population into account, as well as macroeconomic growth in Asia, I consider it advisable to believe that oil is scarce *now*, given the potential demand for it in the not so distant future. At the present time, in the light of the manner in which our civilization is tied to this most valuable of all commodities, it is hardly rational for political and industrial leaders to think in terms of a future characterized by a surfeit of low-cost oil, even if (ex-post) this turns out to be the case!

A few statistics can be added to the above discussion. The conventional oil already produced is (about) 900 billion barrels (= 900 Gb). The consensus figure for *proven reserves* available now is somewhat less. The (estimated) amount that will still be found is 300–500 Gb, and a reasonable estimate of *ultimate* reserves might be 2000–2200 Gb. Optimists, however, say that ultimate reserves are 3000 Gb, and pessimists say less than 2000 Gb. A few years ago the forecasts of the IEA for world crude oil demand in 2010 were 95 mb/d, and in 2020 the estimate was 115 mb/d. Taking ultimate reserves as 2000–2200, and thinking in terms of Hubbert's rule, the peak production year would in these circumstances be no later than 2010, with the production of conventional oil somewhat greater than 95 mb/d (as compared to about 85 mb/d just now). Four or five adjustments were made on these figures, and eventually it was concluded that production around 2030 would reach 121 mb/d. To my way of thinking, this figure does not make sense.

4. Some Algebraic Aspects of Production and Pricing

We have now reached a point where some algebra might be useful. The really important part of this analysis, however, is to be found in the diagram (Fig. 2.1), and the discussion associated with that diagram. The present algebra is incidental though, and the serious mathematics is in the appendix, where serious in this case does *not* mean essential. Whether teaching economics or finance I insist that persons in my courses are capable of explaining in detail Fig. 2.1, and I assure all students that it will be on the final examination. I do not remember a single student failing to get the message, although a few might not have gotten it to the degree that I wished.

But before we look at that figure, I want to present some algebra that extends an earlier discussion, although it is not nearly so important. What we will be dealing with here are increases in reserves and consumption employing simple functions such as $R_t = R_0(1 + y)^t$ and $q_t = q_0(1 + x)^t$. Accordingly, we can continue with some uncomplicated manipulations, which lead to an interesting conclusion about the R/q ratio. Let us start out with the expression $R_{t+1} = R_t - q_t + y R_t$. By using the expression $\theta = R/q$ for the appropriate periods (i.e., "t" and "$t+1$"), and introducing x as the growth rate (in decimal form) for output q_t [and so $q_{t+1} = q_t(1+x)$],

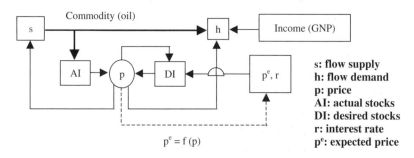

Figure 2.1.   A Stock-Flow Model of the Oil Market

we write

$$\theta_t + y\theta_t - 1 = \theta_{t+1}(1 + x) \text{ or } \theta_t(1 + y) - 1 = \theta_{t+1}(1 + x). \quad (1)$$

The next step is to write $\theta_{t+1} = \theta_t + \Delta\theta_t$. If this is put in (3), and we assume a sufficiently small $\Delta\theta$ so that $x\Delta\theta_t \rightarrow 0$, we get after a small amount of manipulation

$$\Delta\theta = \theta_t(y - x) - 1. \quad (2)$$

We can now ask what is required for $\Delta\theta$ to be greater than zero, which signifies reserves growth relative to output. The answer from (2) is that we must have $(y - x) > 1/\theta_t$. The best way to explain what this means is to use some of the numbers from the previous numerical example. For the fifth period we had $\theta_t = 10$, $q_t = 15$, and $R_t = 150$. In addition I will take $x = 0$, but $y = 5\%(= 0.05)$. With reserves growing, but production constant ($x = 0$), we might conclude that θ is growing (or is constant); but this is not true. Using these figures we get $R_{t+1} = 150 + 7.5 - 15 = 142.5$, where 7.5 is the increase in reserves during period "t". But if q remains at 15, we end up with $\theta_t = 9.5$.

Using Eq. (2) we find that in order to have reserve growth relative to output we must have $\theta > 1/(y - x) = 1/(0.05 - 0) = 20$. Put another way, if $\theta = 10$ at the time we begin our scrutiny ($= 150/15$), then for θ to increase, reserves must grow by more than 10%. That is, we must have $10 > 1/(g - 0)$ or $g > 1/10(= 0.10 = 10\%)$.

Here I would like to reiterate that a full comprehension of the oil story does not require any mathematics beyond that made available in the first two years of a secondary school — even the kind of secondary school that I attended on the great South Side of Chicago: recent "pieces" in the *Financial Times* provide the full story.

That brings us to the volatility of oil prices, and the use of Fig. 2.1. This volatility is often so extreme that it leads to a mistaken evaluation of what is actually taking place in the oil market. Many mistakes are made about where this market is going, because the flow models that are studied in price theory and microeconomics courses are completely unfit for discussing the stock-flow model that is required for a knowledgeable discussion of oil pricing. For example, it needs to be made explicit that the change in demand or supply, and subsequent price changes, might greatly influence expectations about future demand. This in turn is capable of impacting on prices in such a way as to generate a high level of instability.

The model below, which was originally developed to examine pricing in non-fuel minerals markets, is analogous to what is known in electrical engineering as a servomechanism, and its feedback mechanism can, in some cases, lead to extreme instability. The key point is that *equilibrium* in stock-flow models is defined as a situation where the demand for inventories (or stocks), DI, is equal to actual inventories, AI. This will be written as DI = AI. On the other hand, in your introductory and intermediary courses in economics, equilibrium was defined by (flow) supply, s, being equal to (flow) demand, h, or $s = h$. (*Note*: h is being used in the present exercise instead of the customary d!) The thing to appreciate is that we can have a flow equilibrium without having a stock equilibrium, but without a stock equilibrium (DI = AI) we cannot claim to have a full equilibrium. Readers should take note of the units that are involved if we are talking about oil: flow production (s) is in barrels/year, while stocks (R) are in barrels. We can now turn to Fig. 2.1.

Now we can initiate an informal discussion of some mechanics of price formation. As usual we begin with a full equilibrium, or DI = AI, and $s = h$. Then, let us assume that many inventory holders decide that they are in possession of excessive stocks. (They may come to this conclusion because they expect oil prices to fall, and so if they use or sell the stocks that they are holding, they can rebuild their inventory positions later at a low cost.) The reasoning that takes us from one full equilibrium (where the values of the variables of interest are constant) to another full equilibrium could go as follows:

The demand for stocks falls, or DI < AI. AI cannot drop at once, since at a given point in time they are determined by physics and not economics.

For AI to decrease, the price must fall from a point where we have $s = h$. This fall causes current (i.e., flow) production to fall, and/or current consumption to rise. Thus, with $h > s$, some of the existing stocks are consumed in current consumption and/or production activities.

The fall in the price might also influence price expectations, which are of crucial importance. If expectations are formed adaptively, inventory holders might come to believe that the price will continue to fall, and it is pointless to hold more than a minimum amount of stocks. Accordingly, they would be reduced (i.e., sold) as soon as possible in order to recoup their cost, *and* to make room for new stocks that can be bought later at the lower prices that are expected.

We make the usual assumption that flow supply (s) and demand (h) are functions of price, or $s = s(p)$ and $h = h(p)$, and a flow equilibrium takes place when $h(p^*) = s(p^*)$, where p^* is the equilibrium price. As long as AI > DI, $p < p^*$, for reasons given above, and it is only when AI = DI that once again we get $p = p^*$ and our equilibrium: the system is at rest, and s, h, AI, and DI are not changing. The crucial element in the analysis was the stock equilibrium, which implies the flow equilibrium! The opposite, however, is not true. Readers who are interested in a slightly more abstract discussion can see Banks (1994), and incidentally, I use h instead of d for demand because I need d to designate "derivative".

A simple (but useful) exercise for the reader is to begin with DI = AI, and after assuming DI > AI, discuss how a new equilibrium is reached. As for discussing the volatility of price movements, this is something for the reader with an interest in difference and/or differential equations, and so it will be bypassed in this book.

5. A Few Comments on OPEC

Unfortunately, these comments include some mathematics, but for readers who can handle symbols there are a few points here that it might pay to remember in the coming years. I can also mention that the next chapter of this book pays particular attention to Saudi Arabia, which is the most important OPEC country.

During the last 20 years, a great deal of effort has gone into an attempt (by the main oil importing countries) to reduce the importance of OPEC in world oil. At one time or another considerable attention was directed toward the energy assets of Latin America, Northern Europé, the South China Sea, etc., just as now the Caspian region is regarded by some so-called experts as the region that is most capable of preventing OPEC from "dictating" the world oil price by an adroit manipulation of its production. Recently US Vice President Cheney has been in the Caspian region, where he has attempted to convince the locals that they have everything to win and little to lose if they increase their production as rapidly as possible.

Some years ago Alhajji and Huettner (2000), among others, had strong reservations about the reputed strength of OPEC. To their way of thinking at that time, any success that OPEC might enjoy was due to the "political, natural, and technical" limitations foisted on those members who desire to "cheat" on their quotas. They did not go so far as to suggest that if nature were free to take its course, a barrel of oil would be sold for the price of a can or two of Coca Cola, but the implication was clearly that if potential rogue members of that organization were provided with the wherewithal to upgrade their facilities and market their output, then oil buyers will be spared more oil price escalations. (When going through their paper, I found myself remembering Ernest Hemingway's contention that everyone would behave badly if given the opportunity.) Before proceeding let me note that I doubt whether these gentlemen still support that illusion. Professor Alhajji has become one of the most astute and frequently cited observers of the global oil scene, and I doubt whether this would have been possible unless he recognized the position of OPEC in a world that is increasingly characterized by a scarcity of oil.

My position was and is quite simple where OPEC is concerned: why *give* something to basically unsympathetic outsiders that they are willing to pay top dollar for? I think that it is also time to get rid of some dangerous myths. Roger Anderson, director of the Energy Research Center at Columbia's Lamont-Doherty Earth Conservatory, came to the remarkable conclusion that the oil problem is not worth losing any sleep over because "if you pay smart people enough money, they'll figure out all sorts of ways to get the oil that you need". Putting himself in the shoes of one of the smart people that he has so much confidence in, he claimed that the total expense of producing a barrel of fuel (i.e., oil) from natural gas has been reduced to $20. He then said that "That will effectively put a ceiling on the price that anyone can charge for a barrel of oil — which is something that has never existed in history. The moment anyone tries to charge above this amount, people will switch to fuels derived from natural gas" (*Discover*, June 1999, p. 85).

The very "*moment*" this scholar claims! Statements like this give smart people a bad name, because nobody is going to sell a barrel of oil for $20 that can be sold for more. When the first barrels are rolled out from the lucky plant that produces this cut-rate oil, shareholders in that enterprise will most likely jump for joy, because it should be possible to sell them for a price that is well over twice as much. Admittedly, if enough of these plants are constructed, the first course in economics tells us that their output could eventually press the market price of oil down to the vicinity of $20, particularly if the major oil producers switch their brains into an every-man-for-himself mode. But even so, it might be a good idea for Mr Anderson to take note of something a former official at the Saudi Petroleum Ministry told *Newsweek* (8/15, April 2002): "You want alternatives? That's just so much sweet talk. Suppose you target the cost of alternative energy at so many dollars per Btu — and then we lower the cost of oil below that. All your investment goes down the drain".

As Winston Churchill pointed out, coalition warfare has always been a tricky business, but he understood perfectly that when push came to shove, the United States invariably got its way. The same kind of thing might apply here. OPEC has gradually evolved so that the dominance of Saudi Arabia has greatly increased, but at the same time they and the other producers are finally learning how to work together. In theory — and perhaps in fact — that organization should soon be in a position to create a situation where the oil price develops in a manner that is consistent with the economics and finance that I teach, and for the most part believe in.

If approached in terms of mainstream economic theory, this price should move in such a way as to accurately reflect the (likely) increasing scarcity of oil, as well as to provide the oil producing countries with the physical, financial, and human resources they will require when their oil eras approach the final curtain. At the same time, this price increase should not greatly inconvenience or disillusion those consumers who have purchased expensive energy-intensive durable goods (such as vehicles) because they believed that the real price of oil was destined to continue to fall, nor would it decrease the attractiveness of oil in, e.g., the rapidly expanding Asian market, nor would it attenuate efforts to find substitutes for conventional oil. This is asking for a great deal, and there is more, to include some political constraints that must be taken into consideration. For example, many oil sellers live in a world where ostensibly they could require both the political and military support of oil buyers in Europe and the United States.

Alhajji and Huettner have provided some empirical work to support their hypothesis about OPEC's impotence. I prefer to overlook most of this, because *in economics* not only should common sense be put on the same level as formalism, but as Professor Karl Vind once said "in economics empirical work (i.e., econometrics) can never take the place of theory". On the other hand, some aspects of the theory behind their empiricism might be applicable because they bring OPEC's market share into the picture, and this is something that tends to be overlooked in theoretical expositions. Their final result is not in a form to my liking; however, something close to it can be obtained as follows. Take $Q_o = Q_m - Q_n$, where Q_o is the demand for OPEC oil, Q_m, the market demand, Q_n, the non-OPEC supply, and P is the market price of oil. Differentiation gives $dQ_o = dQ_m - dQ_m$, and dividing both sides by Q_o, we get

$$\frac{dQ_o}{Q_o} = \frac{dQ_m}{Q_m - Q_n} - \frac{dQ_n}{Q_m - Q_n}$$

$$= \frac{Q_m}{Q_m - Q_n}\left(\frac{dQ_m}{Q_m}\right) - \frac{Q_n}{Q_m - Q_n}\left(\frac{dQ_n}{Q_n}\right). \tag{3}$$

Some elasticities can be formed if we divide both sides by dP/P. On the left-hand side of (13) we have E_o, or the elasticity of the derived demand for OPEC's oil. On the right-hand side we have β, the market elasticity of demand for oil, and δ, the elasticity of supply of non-OPEC sellers. A further simplification is to define as positive the elasticity of demand — which is naturally negative — and to work with market shares instead of quantities — i.e., "deflate" the Qs with Q_m. Q_o/Q_m is then simply called Q_o. This turns the above expression into

$$E_o = \frac{1}{Q_o}\beta + \frac{(1 - Q_o)}{Q_o}\delta. \tag{4}$$

The first term, β/Q_o, shows why the demand for OPEC's oil could be very elastic (i.e., price sensitive), although the overall demand for oil might be fairly inelastic. If, e.g., OPEC has 25% of the market for oil (i.e., $Q_o = 0.25$), then just considering that term, the elasticity of demand for its output would be four times that existing on the overall market. Assuming that OPEC decided that it wanted a higher price, then (*ceteris paribus*) it could find itself absorbing virtually the entire reduction in the export output needed to support the higher price, and the smaller their share (Q_o), the greater the burden. Export revenue could conceivably implode.

As for $(1 - Q_o)\, \delta/Q_o$, this can reinforce the first component in the expression. If OPEC's market share is small, and the non-OPEC supply elasticity is large, then an even greater reduction in OPEC export volume is necessary to maintain the target price. What this equation and its interpretation indicates is that to make itself highly effective, OPEC requires a sizable market share and, in addition, must face fairly low non-OPEC supply elasticities. Since I make a point of ignoring most of the elasticities that one finds in the econometric literature, I will confine myself to reminding readers that OPEC's market share is increasing all the time, just as the supply elasticities of non-OPEC producers are very likely falling. I therefore do not find it easy to accept the (earlier held) contention of the above authors that OPEC's previous success was transitory.

Before leaving the present discussion, readers should be aware that a peculiar variety of irrationality is entering the discussion about what OPEC should and should not do. In many respects it reminds this observer of the recent Enron scandal, in that a determined attempt is being to sell a vision of the oil producing world that may be completely invalid. On many occasions I have been grandly informed by purported oil experts that without extensive foreign investments, the OPEC countries were riding for a fall. I can understand this kind of thinking, because if the OPEC countries open their energy sectors to the major oil companies and give them the return on investment to which these enterprises feel that they are entitled, then it would amount to a major business triumph for such tender-hearted guardians of human rights as ExxonMobil and Royal/Dutch Shell. These organizations are pouring billions into non-OPEC zones such as the Caspian basin, the Gulf of Mexico, and Angola, but where they would really like to see these billions go is into the Middle East. In these circumstances, the opinion here is that given the technical skill available to the OPEC countries both domestically and from some of the major consuming countries, they should think twice before rolling out the red carpet to those international oil companies who, behind the scenes, have expressed a preference for dealing with corrupt governments and officials, even if they control far smaller reserves.

Sarkis (2003) has published a paper in the journal *Medenergie* called "Les prévisions et les fictions", in which he questions the willingness or the ability of OPEC countries to sweeten the dreams of the oil importing world.

Dr Sarkis knows — as I and many of you know — that regardless of the good will that the governments of the OPEC countries have, or say that they have, for their largest clients, they might find themselves subjected to considerable economic and/or political discomfort if they become involved in trying to make the impossible possible. Everyone, of course, does not agree with this appraisal, where by "everyone" I am thinking in particular of the IEA and the USDE. The question then becomes, "why would the highly educated experts of these organizations go off the deep end with their theorizing about the availability of oil"? The answer here is obvious: the people who pay their salaries have told them — directly or indirectly — that it would be best for all concerned if they did not allow themselves to be led astray by reality.

On the basis of the projected oil demand in 2020, and non-OPEC and OPEC intended or likely supply, Sarkis detects an ex-ante gap of about 15 mb/d. The implication here is clear: since an ex-post gap is impossible, OPEC will have to do better, because on this score, the others are hopeless. As already noted, within the foreseeable future, heavy oil and/or tar sands are not going to provide us with a bonanza on the order of Saudi Arabia's potential output, despite what we are constantly told. A similar story applies to Russia: output in that country is increasing at the present time, and with more investment it can continue to grow for a while, but a theory has been offered by analysts at Sanford Bernstein (and elsewhere) that this upswing can only last until 2007/2008. If so, then it is likely that neither Russia nor the Caspian region can live up to expectations!

Without going into figures and dates, a similar hypothesis has been put forward by the CEO of the large French oil group "Total" — Mr Thierry Desmarest — who makes it clear that for oil supply to meet growing demand, OPEC must "open its doors", and open them very wide for investment in exploration and new production. (The *Financial Times*, 13 September 2004). Total has recently paid a billion dollars for some Russian energy properties, but unless I am badly mistaken, the purpose of this investment is to obtain oil from existing facilities to sell at the high prices that Mr Desmarest and his colleagues expect to prevail in the future. Only a minor amount of that billion is likely to be earmarked for an increase in output.

6. The Refining Gap

The expression "refining gap" may remind some readers of the expression "mineshaft gap" in Stanley Kubrick's brilliant film "Doctor Strangelove". The difference though is that the latter is fiction, while the former is quite real. So real that in some countries high ranking politicians have gone to local oil refiners with their hats in their hand and kindly asked them to build more capacity.

Not too long ago OPEC's president Sheikh Ahmad Fahad Al-Ahmad Al-Fahad Al-Sabah informed one of his critics in the oil importing countries that despite appearances, OPEC was "offering everything in our pocket"; and furthermore, if it were really and truly desired, "I would be happy to sell it to him". Everything in his pocket was refuted to be 2 mb/d of spare capacity, but some of us are not so sure that this figure is relevant, because it almost certainly applies to surge (i.e., temporary) as compared to the sustained output.

No price was mentioned, but perhaps a detail of this nature was unnecessary: it was clear that his offer could not be taken up due to the shortage of capacity for refining the proffered oil into the desired end products, the most important of which were motor fuel and jet fuel. This is one of the main reasons why the price of gasoline in the promised land of motoring (the United States) spiked to record heights, and not just because of the high price of crude. (In May of 2006, crude oil accounted for 55% of the cost of each unit (e.g., gallon) of gasoline, refining 22%, taxes for 19%, and distribution and marketing for 4%.) Moreover, according to the *Financial Times* (29 September 2005), it may take a decade to remedy the refining shortage. This is because the profit uncertainties associated with refining have made investors ultra careful.

Refining is a topic that is mostly ignored in the scholarly literature, and so perhaps the best way to begin these comments is by noting that a refinery is an installation for turning crude oil into a *slate* of various products. By convention, these products are divided into three cuts or fractions: light products such as gas, naptha, and gasoline, middle distillates such as kerosene and light gas oil, and residual and heavy products such as fuel oil and heavy gas oil. If there is such a thing as a typical or average barrel of oil, then 20% would be the basis for light products, 25% middle distillates, and while most of the rest would be heavy products and residue. Unfortunately, however, this mix does not conform to typical consumption patterns. Traditionally, the most valuable end of the barrel is the top end, which provides so-called white products, although naptha, which is important for the improvement of gasoline quality and is virtually an essential feedstock for petrochemical production, can be extracted from both the light and middle ranges of distillate cuts.

In one sense or another, refiners buy crude and sell refined products. What they want is a low price for crude and a high price for their refined products — i.e., what is called a large "refinery margin" (or sometimes a "crack spread"). One unusual characteristic of this industry is that much of the time they are badly disappointed. For instance, if the price of crude rises while prices for motor and jet fuel sags (as, e.g., after 9/11), then margins shrink.

The basic production process functions as follows. Crude oil is pumped into a tall distillation tower that is pressurized and is hotter at the bottom than at the top. The various oil products have different boiling points, with those that are the lightest having the lowest. When the crude enters the tower, the heaviest part remains in liquid form and falls to the bottom. In a sense it is the part left over after "cracking" and distillation. The rest is vaporized, but the various constituent products are transformed into a usable liquid form as they reach the lower temperatures higher up the column. As a result they can be piped away.

Sophisticated products such as aviation gasoline and diesel oil can be produced from basic products such as naphtha and kerosene. The proportion of these products derived from a barrel of oil depends on whether the oil is relatively heavy or light: a light oil produces a larger proportion of light products, while a heavy oil results in proportionally more heavy products. In addition, the heavier the crude, the larger the percent of carbon, and *ceteris paribus* the lower the quality.

Oil is graded according to an American Petroleum Institute (API) number, and the higher the number, the lighter the barrel. Another important determinant of quality is the sulfur content: oil with a high sulfur content is called a sour crude, and oil with a very low — e.g., under 1% — sulfur content is designated a sweet crude. It should also be appreciated that oils of different weights are generally located in different places. Venezuelan and

Mexican oil tend, *on the average*, to be heavy, which in view of the usual market preference for light products causes them to be sold at a discount to the lighter oils that are found in a country such as Libya. As for the oil super power Saudi Arabia, they possess substantial quantities of both light and heavy oils, and probably still retain a considerable choice as to the mix of these that will be produced. West African oil is also light.

Now we see the main refinery problem. The intrinsic mix of products from a barrel of oil may not correspond in a satisfactory way to the desires of consumers unless expensive processing takes place. Inevitably, a larger percentage of white products are desired than can be obtained from the simple refining activity described above (and in addition environmental regulation may call for "cleaner" products). The way this is usually handled is to introduce more complex refining procedures in "simple" installations, and in certain situations to build new refineries with the kind of equipment that will provide a maximum amount of high-value white products. A fairly common approach is to install "cokers" and "hydrocrackers" that can transform heavy products to items like motor fuel and petrochemical inputs. The basic chemical process here involves converting large molecules into smaller ones.

Operations of this kind are not, however, something for amateurs to indulge in, as the economic history of this sector makes clear. As a result it appears that large oil companies possessing both "upstream" (finding and producing oil) *and* "downstream" (refining and perhaps petrochemicals) activities have an advantage over "independent" refiners. Large integrated firms tend to have sufficient non-refining projects (usually in the form of wellhead operations) to tide them over in periods when refining losses are particular heavy (particularly for firms that are exclusively refiners), although it has happened on a number of occasions that these large firms also felt it wise to cut their refining losses. Fire sales, merger-related divestments, expensive price wars and general consolidations have at times put so many old refineries on the block that striking opportunities were created for the best managed — and the luckiest — enterprises.

One of these at the present time is the brilliant concern, Valero Energy. They were able to take advantage of the bad business strategy (or bad luck) of other firms to become the largest refiner in North America, where the others include the "big four": ExxonMobil, BP, Royal Dutch Shell, and

Chevron Texaco. Valero purchased the facilities of many firms whose margins were inadequate, and perhaps could not afford to upgrade their refineries, and reconfigured them to transform heavy sour oils into the lighter and cleaner products preferred by both customers and regulators. The key thing though is that they possessed the flexibility to upgrade at the right time, and to make sure that they made the right choices where both feedstocks and product slates were concerned.

Interestingly enough, Valero has also made mistakes. In 1980, they bought what they thought was the right facility for processing residual fuel into gasoline. What happened though was that the price spread between the two decreased from $12/b to $5/b, which left them with income enough only to cover operating (i.e., variable) costs. Fortunately, when their creditors came knocking on the door for their debt payments, Valero's pockets were deep enough for them to stay in business. By a similar token, the Fortune Five-Hundred perennial Exxon built what was in 1977 the world's largest upgrading facility for turning high sulfur residual oil into a more marketable low sulfur grade, but the markets shifted in such a way as to reward their daring with multi-million dollar losses. As good luck would have it though, they had no real problem waiting until the markets came into balance, while at about the same time a few dozen "teakettle" independents ended up in bankruptcy courts or became the property of scrap dealers.

One of the more interesting things about ExxonMobile is that it refines more oil than the very large amount it pumps, and ostensibly has never had any trouble buying crude for its refineries. One of the reasons is that until recently oil was inexpensive, and refining capacity was scarce. Accordingly, ExxonMobile enjoyed a nice position as a monopsony — much nicer than pictured in mainstream textbooks because of certain "dynamic" considerations (such as being able to purchase oil on long-term contracts).

It is hardly a secret that refiners in Europe have had serious problems, but some of us think that their troubles are far from over. The Middle Eastern countries with serious development ambitions are finally learning that refining and petrochemical installations that can be provided as an input of the most inexpensive energy (local natural gas) and feedstocks (local oil) in the world can make a great deal of sense. In fact, in the courses on development economics that I once taught I attempted to sell the idea that in the long run these countries would be better off by shipping a smaller amount of crude oil, and instead paying much more attention to exporting refined products and petrochemicals. This is not necessarily true any longer with the oil price at its present level, but clearly if these countries are worried about a return of low oil prices, they would do well to greatly increase their downstream commitments. Some observers view the growth in Asia-Pacific refining capacity as a threat to new capacity in the Middle East, but this is a delusion that can probably be explained by a transfer of cash to these observers from persons or organizations who want to see this outcome.

In India a new oil refinery (the Jamnager) has been constructed which is now the world's third-largest refinery, and can sell aviation fuel and motor fuel for several dollars less than its closest Asian rivals. Plans also exist to turn this refinery into the world's largest, capable of processing more than 60 million tons of crude oil per year. This is interesting, because although much of this output will go to export, much will feed a growing domestic population of vehicles. Just now all eyes are turned toward the Chinese consumption of crude and refined products, but in due course a very large Indian demand will also have to be accommodated. Of course, the place for the world's largest refinery is in the Middle East, and eventually it will probably be there.

Things might also work internationally as they worked domestically in the United States many years ago. New refineries with the latest technology and efficient management can offer their products to existing markets at prices that cannot possibly be matched by traditional suppliers. This is why expressions like "blood-bath" and "reign of terror" were frequently used in this industry, because when the market shifted or expensive hardware failed to deliver, losses were not just "large" but enormous. The way that was handled was to stop building refineries, and instead to upgrade existing installations.

7. Ancillary Issues

Not long ago a researcher with a good insight into the oil market wrote and congratulated me on my long survey paper "*Beautiful and not so beautiful minds: an introductory essay on economics and the supply of oil*" (2004). At the same time, though, he was not too happy with my treatment of

Harold Hotelling's model of resource depletion (1931). That construction was undoubtedly a fundamental ingredient of his training in resource economics, and he had probably passed it on to his students as holy writ. In addition, if Professor Hotelling's mathematics are interpreted in a certain way, it is easy to draw the conclusion that claims about the shortage of oil are exaggerated. For instance, if it is possible to accept Professor Morris Adelman's frequently expressed belief that oil will be bought and sold thousands of years from now, which sounds correct to me, then it is also possible to show with Hotelling-type dialectics that the *scarcity price* of oil (at the wellhead) might be less than $20/b. (As for the scarcity *rent* — i.e., the amount that has to be added to this price in order to account for forthcoming depletion — this is zero in the case being discussed.)

While I occasionally brood in the silence of my lonely room over the many flaws encountered in academic economics, I have spent well over a decade loudly denigrating the application of Hotelling's work to the real world, and fortunately its shortcomings can no longer be concealed from, e.g., thoughtful undergraduates. The most favorable thing that can be said about the Hotelling model is that it is utterly devoid of any scientific value: it pertains to a nonexistent world. It is particularly irrelevant to the oil market *since in a genuinely scientific presentation, scarcity would be concerned with the peaking of the world oil production instead of, e.g., lifting the last drop of that resource from "Iceberg Alley" or similar locales off the coast of Northern Canada, or in the Barents Sea.*

Until recently Hotelling's model was found in almost every microeconomics textbook, but this seems to be changing. Recent editions of these texts no longer choose to insult the intelligence of their readers by suggesting that they accept a narrative about the movement of oil prices that has no relation at all to anything that they might intuit or read in the business press. Unfortunately though, when Mr and Ms economics teacher find it necessary to discuss the pricing of natural resources (such as oil) with curious students, many will turn immediately to a Hotelling song-and-dance or spinoff.

Here it might be useful to mention Albert Einstein's "equivalence" principle, which in one version or another applies just about everywhere: *if two phenomena produce equivalent effects, they must be manifestations of the same fundamental law.* Since the world being described in Hotelling's model, and the real world have almost nothing in common, it follows that they possess a dissimilar logical structure. It happens to be an especially ugly fact of life that many academic resource economists often employ Hotelling's valuation principle (which is an extension of his well-known $\Delta p / p = r$, relating the growth rate of price to the real rate of interest) to estimate what the market value of oil should be in an ideal (or text-book) setting, and what they think it would be were it not for the presence of OPEC or the lack of imagination of oil companies and governments. The reason this is done is to promulgate the (erroneous) impression that it should still be possible to purchase oil at bargain basement prices. Even the late Merton Miller — whom I regarded as the leading academic financial economist in the world — became involved with an empirical exercise of this nature, but to my way of thinking he obtained theoretical market values for reserves and output that characterize the Himalayan heights of wishful thinking.

Of late we hear a great deal about a comprehensive energy plan that the US government is in the process of launching, but the reason that it is derided by high level insiders like Lee Raymond, the former CEO of ExxonMobil, is that the only energy plan that makes sense in the short run is the one promoting the deployment of more nuclear installations, as well as a sensible explanation of how the United States and other high oil consuming countries are going to be able to gain access to — in the near as opposed to the distant future — the huge amounts of conventional oil that are absolutely necessary for the international macroeconomy to function in a relatively satisfactory manner, although occasionally he and his colleagues like to pretend that this will not prove to be a problem. Things like oil from tar sands, as well as biofuels, will help, but much more will be needed in the near as opposed to the distant future.

8.   Comments on Oil Derivatives and the War Against Risk

I believe that I provided the essential oil derivatives story in my energy economics textbook (2000), but the general knowledge about these assets is still insufficient, and very often we encounter situations where deriva-tive markets do not live up to expectations. This calls for a consider-able amount of attention to be paid this issue, and in the sequel an entire chapter will be used to examine derivatives on a level that is only mildly technical. But some comments seem justified at this point in the exposition.

If he had thought of it, one of the ancient Greeks might have written a play with the title "The war against risk cannot be won — except, sometimes, by the very smart or the very lucky, who at the same time are workaholics". One reason is that risk in one form or another is almost always one of the more unpleasant facts of life. (Not "always" because there are occasions when the opportunity to assume a relatively small amount of risk opens the possibility of great gain.) But at the same time, in the modern world, risk averse persons can sometimes mitigate some of its worst effects by the intelligent use of various forms of insurance. This is what derivatives (futures, options, and swaps) are supposed to do for buyers and sellers of energy who do not want excessive exposure to risk/uncertainty, but unavoidably find themselves in its way. Some authors also put *forwards* in the same category as futures, but these very simple assets will only be mentioned en passant below.

One thing however must be emphasized. Arranging to insure your SUV or private jet is a fairly straightforward matter (even if for one reason or another you find the expense distasteful). This is often not the case with derivatives, and as a result, it is easy to find examples of multi-million dollar blunders that have been made by skilled professional risk managers. In the finance literature, risk management is often presented as a science, but it is probably more of an art: the kind where it can be a costly mistake to rely too much on mathematics and statistics rather than history, common sense, and long hours of very hard work.

At the international meeting of the IAEE in Washington, DC, in 1996, Mary Lindahl of the University of Alaska noted that Alaska gained or lost 120 million dollars (= $120m) in annual state revenue with each dollar per barrel change in oil prices. At that time the consensus forecast was still for a declining oil price, and as a result, the state government was investigating the opportunities for hedging a considerable part of its exposure employing derivatives (i.e., futures and options, and/or swaps). The role model for Alaska was thought to be Texas, where an apparently successful pilot hedging program had been put into operation in 1991, and expanded in 1993.

Had a finance expert like Professor Henrik Houthakker of Harvard University been consulted, no hesitation would have taken place, because a few years ago when asked for an opinion on the future of oil, he assured anyone who would listen that derivative markets — and in particular futures and options — could always hedge buyers and sellers against price risk, and in some mysterious way even provide a remedy against physical depletion.

All of this happens to be completely wrong, because commodity markets in many respects are different from the purely financial markets that Professor Houthakker specialized in. One of the basic differences is the lack of enough liquidity in even highly successful commodity derivatives markets to handle exceptionally large transactions. Lindahl (1996) concluded that if major oil firms and sovereign producers could hedge their output, so could Alaska, but in point of fact these players are only minor participants in the derivatives game.

Now let us take a brief look at the three main hedging tools. These are examined in considerable detail in my international finance textbook (2001) and later in this book.

Futures: The oil futures markets are superbly organized, especially the New York Mercantile Exchange (NYMEX) and the International Petroleum Exchange (IPE) in London, and they have adequate liquidity for short-term transactions. A key item here is liquidity: being able to buy or sell at "listed" prices, without large differences between buy and sell prices, and without large changes in prices over fairly short period of time. Locking in the present spot price of physical oil (i.e., hedging), or betting on the future price of "paper oil" (i.e., speculating), is a comparatively simple matter that will be discussed at length later. A recurring fantasy is that eventually *long-term* futures transactions for energy resources will make sense, which is highly dubious — e.g., if the present price of oil is $65/b, and as a buyer of oil you are afraid that it will go to $100/b, then according to this fantasy you can contact a futures market and arrange to lock in a price of $65/b for several years in the future. In reality there is low liquidity for transactions of more six months, and at the present time perhaps three months. Accordingly, it is best to limit hedging ambitions to a few months. At the Washington meeting mentioned above the discussion was often in terms of futures contracts with maturities of three to six years, however this was a play for the gallery. A big advantage for futures is price transparency, since they are traded on organized exchanges (which also means that credit risk is "organized away").

Lindahl cites *basis risk* as a major disadvantage, which in certain situations might be true: when the price of one type of oil (e.g., Alaska North Slope oil) is hedged using price quotations for another (e.g., West Texas International), the correlation of these prices might be so weak that the hedge is unsatisfactory. But, a large part of the time this may not be the case. Basis risk is explained in considerable detail later in this book.

Options: Buying an option gives you the right but not the obligation to buy or sell an asset. You pay for this right with something called a *premium*, which is also the maximum loss that you can suffer. The person who sold the option to you hopes to pocket the premium, but if things go wrong could suffer a very large loss. The options that we are interested in come in two varieties — *put* (sell) and *call* (buy), so note the terminology: you can buy a sell option! The two important terms associated with these are *premium* (i.e., price of the option) and *exercise* (or *strike*) price. Suppose that I am a seller of oil and am very afraid that the price of oil will be less than $50/b. Then — if I am lucky — I might be able to buy a put (i.e., sell) option on oil for a premium of, e.g., three dollars a barrel and an exercise (strike) price of, e.g., 50 dollars. If the price of oil does fall below $50/b I exercise the option (i.e., sell for $50/b). If it does not, then I simply discard the option, having lost $3/b. Roughly speaking, an option functions somewhat like an insurance policy. Like futures, options are traded by hedgers (insurers) and speculators (gamblers). This type of asset will also be discussed in some detail later.

Swaps: When my previous energy book was being written, I perceived swaps as a major derivatives tool. This is still the case; however, many observers — particularly in the academic world — find them uninteresting because they are traded over-the-counter (OTC) rather than in an exchange. (In some sense a swaps market is like a futures market without speculators.) Swaps are based on a very simple concept: if you are afraid of a price rise, and I am afraid of a price fall, then (via an intermediate) we enter into an arrangement where if the price rises I pay you, and if the price falls you pay me. The mechanics, of course, might be much more complicated. Although exchanges have steadily gained in status, it may be true that many market participants favor opaque OTC markets where the lack of transparency often permits excess trading profits. An advantage with swaps is that there is no basis risk, and, in addition, very long maturities are possible (since in a smooth functioning swaps market, liquidity considerations do not enter the picture, and the *swap arranger* guarantees payment). There is some talk that the volume of transactions in swaps may be larger than the total for futures and options on NYMEX *and* the IPE. NYMEX has introduced (or intends to introduce) a facility for the trading of swaps.

9. Final Remarks and Conclusions

> *"Experience is an expensive school, but the only*
> *one in which fools can learn"*
> — *Benjamin Franklin*

The study of energy economics seems to be moving in the right direction at last, although it may still be true that the business press provides a more useful insight into the oil market than the analyses that we encounter in some of the most learned of the "learned journals". However now that we are gradually removing Harold Hotelling's model of exhaustible resources from the textbooks, and so-called "blue-sky" (or unrealistic) deregulation discourse is being expunged from many economics and business periodicals, it should only be a matter of time before we obtain the high level but realistic analyses that students of energy economics like you and I deserve.

It has also been postulated that the volatility of oil prices is failing to incite the same unease as was once the case (*Financial Times*, 4 September 2004). I am afraid that it may be a little too early to draw this conclusion. Andrew Oswald of Warwick University has shown on a number of occasions that almost all the oil price escalations since 1973 have brought bad macroeconomic news in their wake, and there is still plenty of time for this kind of thing to be repeated.

The evidence clearly indicates that in almost all countries in which production has peaked, the output pattern for a typical oil field or province follows roughly a bell-shaped curve, and an overwhelming amount of empirical evidence shows that the peak comes when between 40% and 60% of the oil has been extracted. But even before that point, the rate of growth in the output (*ceteris paribus*) has started to decline due to a fall in pressure in the deposit, and a given flow can only be maintained by increasingly costly investment.

At the present time only one barrel of oil is being discovered for about every three or four produced. The last time as much oil was discovered as was being produced was in 1980–1981. There is also this matter of quality. Light oil is at a premium, and once again nature strongly favored the oil producers of the Middle East.

Although economics is supposed to be a non-experimental science, experiments are taking place all the time. We just had one in the UK North Sea where production quietly peaked. Prior to this event, certain researchers as well as the business press assured us that miraculous changes were taking place in that oil province due to new technology and "deals" of various sorts. All of this was nonsense, however the remarkable thing is the failure to notice the rapid decline in the number of deals, as well as the sudden interest by producing firms in immediate profitability as compared to the purchase of an additional property. These were sure signs that a new day had arrived.

This new day could have serious consequences for Europe, since when the United Kingdom was producing at close to its maximum output, with a widespread belief that a decline was not in sight, it helped to reduce the overall uncertainties that were endemic to the international oil market — which in money terms probably removed a few dollars from the oil price. Now, of course, the oil importing world must accept that Norway is also unable to continue to produce at its fairly high maximum level, and this is hardly a cause for celebration.

Some time ago it was pointed out in *Fortune* that the Pentagon was making a study of the political turmoil that could result if the extreme physical consequences of global warming suddenly appeared on the scene. It was suggested that someday countries with sizable military assets might be tempted to maintain their prosperity by imposing on weaker states with considerable natural resources.

As far as I am aware, no one has investigated in detail what a peaking of global oil production might mean from a military point of view; however, shortly after the first oil price shock (in 1973 or 1974) a US congressional document appeared showing landing zones in the Gulf for military forces from the United States, or for that matter a coalition of concerned Cadillac owners. Professor Douglas Reynolds of the University of Alaska is also familiar with publications discussing a possible seizing of oil producing assets by force, although it is not impossible that all of these documents/publications are part of an activity that in game theory is known as *screening*. This includes helping to concentrate the minds of rivals or potential rivals by circulating misleading information about your intentions. (According to Reynolds, *Time Magazine* carried an interview with Dr Henry Kissinger in which the military option was ventilated. The legendary "Red" Adair — the oil industry's favorite fire fighter — was constantly referred to during that period, since a hypothesis had been broached that the oil fields would be set ablaze in the event of an effort to seize them.)

In any event, some question must be asked as to whether the motorists of North America and Europe would, in the event of an oil price approaching or exceeding \$100/b, be willing to garage their Volvos and SUVs, and calmly wait until a technology appears which permits an economical exploitation of assorted unconventional resources, or for that matter items such as conventional oil from The Chaco or Iceberg Alley. (I am assuming that if it is possible to obtain such a technology, it will take a very long time, although a peaking of world oil production might result in a Manhattan Project type effort that considerably speeds things up.) The thing to be aware of here is that in much of North America, as well as, e.g., the Northern part of Scandinavia, the economy cannot function without a large input of motor transport. I am also curious about the willingness of the politicians and bureaucrats of, e.g., "peace loving" Sweden to cancel their precious junkets to the restaurants and cafes of Brussels and Strasbourg because of a shortage of jet fuel.

In a recent issue of *New Scientist* (2004), Bob Holmes and Nicola Jones offer the following: "If production rates fall while demand continues to rise, oil prices are likely to spike or fluctuate wildly, raising the prospect of economic chaos, problems with transporting food and other supplies, and even war as countries fight over what little oil is available". This is not a new idea, and I can recall it being mentioned several years ago by a Japanese researcher who was arguing in favor of an expansion of nuclear based electricity, since the energy content of uranium and thorium is much greater than that of fossil fuel reserves. Unfortunately, I do not know in what room in the Pentagon questions of this nature are being treated, but I

certainly hope that it is not the one in which I had the good luck to fail my
first officers' candidate board.

Appendix: Some Quantitative Matters

Although the above analysis insinuates that we could wake up one morning
to the tune of a very serious oil price shock, a few words must be said about
the volatility of oil prices. This volatility is often so extreme that it leads
to a mistaken evaluation of what is actually taking place in the oil market.
Experts from the great world of journalism constantly make mistakes about
where the oil market is going because the flow models that they studied in
their university courses were completely unfit for discussing the stock-flow
model that is required for a knowledgeable discussion of oil pricing. My
previous energy economics textbook explains the stock-flow construction
in some detail, but a few things deserve to be emphasized. The stock-flow
model that is presented in this chapter, which I developed many years earlier
to examine pricing in non-fuel minerals markets, is analogous to what is
known in electrical engineering as a servomechanism, and its feedback
mechanism can, in some cases, lead to extreme instability.

The key point is that *equilibrium* in stock-flow models is defined as
a situation where the demand for inventories (or stocks), DI, is equal to
actual inventories, AI. This will be written as DI = AI. On the other hand,
in your introductory and intermediary courses in economics, equilibrium
was defined by (flow) supply, s, being equal to (flow) demand, h, or $s = h$.
(*Note*: h is being used in the present exercise instead of the customary d!)
The thing to appreciate is that we can have a flow equilibrium without
having a stock equilibrium, but without a stock equilibrium (DI = AI) we
cannot claim to have a full equilibrium. If you listen to the economics news
on television, or read the financial/economic press, then when discussions
of the oil price take place, inventories are very often mentioned. (See also
Banks (1994).)

I have already presented an informal discussion of some mechanics of
price formation, but I will repeat that discussion here before presenting
some mathematics. As usual we begin with a full equilibrium, or DI =
AI, *and* $s = h$ (where h is flow demand). Then let us assume that many
inventory holders decide that they are in possession of excessive stocks.

(They may come to this conclusion because they expect oil prices to fall, and so if they use the stocks that they are holding, they can rebuild their inventory positions later at a low cost.) The reasoning that takes us from one full equilibrium (where the values of the variables of interest are constant) to another full equilibrium could go as follows:

The demand for stocks falls, or DI < AI. AI cannot drop at once, since at a given point in time they are determined by physics and not economics. For AI to decrease, the price must fall from a point where we have $s = h$. This fall causes current (i.e., flow) production to fall, and/or current consumption to rise. Thus, with $h > s$, some of the existing stocks are consumed in current consumption and/or production activities.

The fall in the price might also influence price expectations, which are of crucial importance. If expectations are formed adaptively, inventory holders might come to believe that the price will continue to fall, and it is pointless to hold more than a minimum amount of stocks. Accordingly, they would be "consumed" or sold as soon as possible in order to recoup their cost, *and* to make room for new stocks that can be bought later at the lower prices that are expected.

We make the usual assumption that flow supply and demand are functions of price, or $s = s(p)$ and $h = h(p)$, and a flow equilibrium takes place when $h(p^*) = s(p^*)$, where p^* is the equilibrium price. As long as AI > DI, $p < p^*$, for reasons given above, and it is only when AI = DI that once again we get $p = p^*$ and our equilibrium: the system is at rest, and s, h, AI, and DI are not changing. The crucial element in the analysis was the stock equilibrium, which implies the flow equilibrium. The opposite, however, is not true. (See Banks (1994).)

A simple (but useful) exercise for the reader is to begin with DI > AI, and discuss movements to equilibrium. Thus far nothing has been said about the volatility of price movements, but anything meaningful requires some mathematics. What will be done here is to give readers some idea of the *kind* of equations that will be required for a comprehensive discussion of matters dealing with volatility. (This is a good place for readers who are uninterested in algebra to tune out, and go to the next chapter!) With I as inventories, I^* a given level, and λ a constant, a simple beginning might be to think in terms of equations such as $p_t = p_{t-1} - (\Delta I_{t-1})$ or $p_t = p_{t-1} - \lambda(I_{t-1} - I^*)$. Similarly, taking I_0 as inventories at time "0", we construct an equation for the time derivative of price that is based on the difference between actual inventories (at time t) and desired inventories. This is

$$\frac{dp}{dt} = \Psi \left[I_0 + \int_0^t (s - h)dt - DI \right], \quad \Psi < 0. \tag{A.1}$$

If AI (which is the sum of the first two terms in the bracket) is greater than desired inventories, the price falls. In this case $d > s$, and the integral works in such a way as to reduce stocks below their their initial level, I_0. This process continues until we get

$$DI = I_0 + \int_0^t (s - h)dt = AI \quad \text{and} \quad s = h. \tag{A.2}$$

The first equation (A.1) has to do with a stock equilibrium: it indicates that if desired inventories are not equal to actual inventories, then a flow equilibrium cannot exist, and $s \neq h$. This flow disequilibrium persists until $DI = AI$. The role of the price should also be considered. When the equilibrium conditions (4) are satisfied, $dp/dt = 0$. By way of contrast, if the stock equilibrium is disturbed, then $s \neq h$, and $dp/dt \neq 0$. Equation (A.2) provides the differential equation of the system, and some simplifying assumptions will be made here to keep from overstressing the reader. The first step is to differentiate (A.1) with respect to time, while assuming that desired inventories are a fixed amount at any given time. We thus obtain

$$\frac{d^2 p}{dt^2} = -\Psi \frac{d(AI)}{dt} = -\Psi(s - h). \tag{A.3}$$

Taking linear flow supply and flow demand functions (e.g., $s = b + ep$ and $h = a + fp$), we obtain the following simple differential equation:

$$\frac{d^2 p}{dt^2} + \Psi(e - f)p - \Psi(a - b) = 0. \tag{A.4}$$

The equilibrium (i.e., steady-state) solution of this expression is

$$p^* = \frac{a - b}{e - f}. \tag{A.5}$$

It is a simple matter to verify that (A.5) describes a flow equilibrium, with $s = h$; but since it also involves $dp/dt = 0$, we immediately perceive that we have a stock equilibrium — and thus a full equilibrium. It is not certain, however, that we will achieve this equilibrium. By solving (A.4) we get the path of p over time. One way of writing this is

$$p = p^* + X \cos(\psi t - Y). \qquad (A.6)$$

In this expression, X and Y are constants that are determined from the initial conditions, while ψ is a "structural" constant that we get from solving (A.6). It is easy to check that values of X, Y, and ψ can be specified so that we get a smooth convergence to equilibrium, or an oscillatory convergence, *or* oscillations around equilibrium. On the other hand, if, e.g., desired inventories had been made a function of expectations, and expectations were formed, e.g., "adaptively", then explosive price behavior would have been possible.

It has been clear for a number of years that inventory changes are a key destabilizing factor in many markets, and inventory behavior is very strongly influenced by changes in expectations. As was observed during, e.g., the first Gulf crisis, futures markets encourage a frequent revision of expectations, because prices on futures markets are often taken to be the best estimate of spot prices in the future — which may or may not be true. It has been (irresponsibly) suggested that a high price volatility should not be considered too important by participants in physical markets, since the availability of futures markets means that price risk can be hedged; but as will be explained in a later chapter, high volatility could mean ruinous margin calls for transactors in the futures markets (and, for participants in the options market, extremely high premiums).

It seems to be the case that in considering the cost of obtaining oil, some economists have recently discovered that this cost should be taken as a function of the amount extracted to date as well as current production. This idea is to be found in the discussion above, although it is not spelled out in detail. However, as it happens, I emphasized a volume effect in my book on natural gas (1987). The mathematics of this arrangement could not be included in my energy economics textbook, because calculus was not employed in that work; however, a shortened version might fit in here.

Once again, though, let me suggest that readers who are uninterested in this kind of presentation should simply move to the next section.

We can start by considering a situation in which we have two production factors, a single output and no taxes or depletion allowances. The (intertemporal) expression for the cost of a continuous-input, continuous-output scheme might then be

$$C = \left[C_0(q) - \frac{C_T(q,T)}{e^{rT}} \right] + \int_0^T wX(q)e^{-rt}dt. \qquad (A.7)$$

C is the present value of cost over the time horizon T. Similarly, $C_0(q)$ is the investment at time $t = 0$ for a facility with an annual output of q. C_T is the salvage value of the installation at time T, while r is a discount rate, which is taken as constant over the time horizon T. $X(q) = X(q(t))$ represents the amount of the variable factor employed at time t, in association with production $q(t)$, while "w" is the (constant) unit cost of the variable factor. It is also important to be aware that this single (present value) cost C for an annual output q over a time horizon T can be turned into an annual cost (designated as A for each time period over T) by annuitizing C. There are essentially two ways to write this expression for A, where the continuous one is simply $A = 1/(1 - e^{-rT})$. The marginal cost can be obtained from 9 by evaluating the integral and then making a straightforward differentiation. We then get

$$\frac{dC}{dq} = \frac{\partial C_0}{\partial q} + w\frac{\partial X}{\partial q}\left[\frac{1 - e^{-rT}}{r} \right]. \qquad (A.8)$$

This expression is unambiguously positive, but unfortunately the effect of volume (V) is not readily apparent. Volume is introduced via the manipulations shown directly below:

$$w\frac{\partial X}{\partial q}\left[\frac{1 - e^{-rT}}{r} \right] \approx w\frac{\Delta X}{\Delta V}\left[\frac{1 - e^{-rT}}{r} \right]\frac{\Delta V}{\Delta q} = \frac{\Delta C}{\Delta V}\frac{\Delta V}{\Delta q} \approx \frac{\partial C}{\partial V}\frac{\partial V}{\partial q}. \qquad (A.9)$$

The question that can now be asked is where did we get the $\partial C/\partial V$. The answer is that when the change in the variable cost (for each period) that is associated with a change in the volume [$= w(\Delta X/\Delta V)$] is taken as the value of an annuity payment, and multiplied by the expression in the large parentheses, we get the present value of these changes (over period T).

Equation (A.9) then becomes

$$\frac{dC}{dq} = \frac{\partial C}{\partial q} + \frac{\partial C}{\partial V}\frac{\partial V}{\partial q}. \tag{A.10}$$

This is obviously a more complicated expression than the usual equation for marginal cost. In case the reader has some problem with the sign of (A.10), it should be remembered that on the basis of the previous discussion, the cost goes up when the volume goes down, while the volume (from a given deposit) goes down when q goes up.

Key Concepts

artificial lift
Canterell oil field
critical R/q ratio
light products
M. King Hubbert
natural depletion
natural lift
normal curve
oil refinery
OPEC
options

peak
plateau production
Red Adair
reserves; resources
stock-flow model
surge production
sustained production
swaps
sweet crude

Questions for Discussion

1. What do you think about the work of M. King Hubbert?
2. Where do you think oil refineries should be constructed?
3. Suppose that there are excess inventories. Using a stock-flow model explain how this matter is handled.
4. Do you think that there will be a global peaking of oil production?
5. The disadvantages of oil from tar sands, and heavy oil, were also discussed in the previous chapter. Review this discussion. What do you know about shale oil?
6. Do you think that it is easier or more difficult for OPEC countries to agree now than it was 10 or 15 years ago?
7. How worried should OPEC countries be about the introduction of synthetic motor fuel?

8. Explain in detail the use of the critical R/q ratio. Note — in detail!

Bibliography

Alhajji, A.F. and David Huettner (2000). "OPEC and other commodity cartels: a comparision". *Energy Policy*, 28: 1151–1164.

Allen, R.G.D. (1960). *Mathematical Economics.* London: Macmillan.

Banks, Ferdinand E. (2005). "Economic theory and some aspects of Saudi Arabian oil". *Dialogue* (of the US Association for Energy Economics).

—— (2004). "Beautiful and not so beautiful minds: an introductory essay on economic theory and the supply of oil". *The OPEC Review*, 28(1): 27–62.

—— (2001). *Global Finance and Financial Markets.* Singapore and London: World Scientific Publishing Company.

—— (2000). *Energy Economics: A Modern Introduction.* Boston and Dordrecht: Kluwer.

—— (1994). "Oil stocks and oil prices". *The OPEC Review*, 23: 173–184.

—— (1991). "Paper oil, real oil, and the price of oil". *Energy Policy*, July–August.

—— (1972). "An econometric model of the world tin economy". *Econometrica*, 40: 749–752.

Bushaw, Donald and Robert Clower (1957). *Mathematical Economics.* New York: Irwin Publishing.

Cairns, Robert D. and Graham A. Davis (2001). "Adelman's rule and the petroleum firm". *Energy Journal*, 22–23: 31–54.

Caruso, Guy (2001). "Energy to 2020". *Oxford Energy Forum*, May: 11–12.

Cassidy, John (2003). "Beneath the sand". *The New Yorker*, 14 & 21 July.

Clo, A. (2000). *Oil Economics and Policy.* Boston, Dordrecht, and London: Kluwer Academic Press.

Craft, B.C. and M.F. Hawkins (1959). *Applied Petroleum Reservoir Engineering.* Englewood Cliffs, New Jersey: Kenwood Press.

Crandall, Maureen (2005). "Realism on Caspian energy: over-hyped and under-risked". *IAEE Newsletter* (Second Quarter).

Deffeyes, K.S. (2003). *Hubberts Peak: The Impending World Oil.* Princeton: Princeton University Press.

Dorfman, R., P. Samuelson and R. Solow (1958). *Linear Programming and Economic Analysis.* New York and London: McGraw Hill.

Duffin, Murray (2004). "The energy challenge 2004 — petroleum". *EnergyPulse* (www.energypulse.net).

Fesharaki, Fereidun (2004). "The global oil market: have we reached a new plateau or just another cycle?" *The IAEE Newsletter* (Fourth Quarter).

Flower, A. (1978). "World oil production". *Scientific American*, 283(3): 41–49.

Franssen, Herman (2006). "The end of cheap oil visited". Paper delivered at Conference in Abu Dhabi, 1 May.

Hall, C., P. Tharakan, J. Hallock, C. Cleveland and M. Jefferson (2003). "Hydrocarbons and the evolution of human culture". *Nature*, November: 318–322.

Hanke, Steve H. (2004). "Take $10 off the price of oil". *Forbes*, 29 November.

Hawkins, David and Herbert Simon (1949). "Note: some conditions of macroeconomic stability". *Econometrica*, July–October: 245–248.

Holmes, Bob and Nicola Jones (2004). "Brace yourself for the end of cheap oil". *New Scientist*, 2 August.

Hotelling, Harold (1931). "The economics of exhaustible resources". *Journal of Political Economy*, 39(2): 137–175.

Hoyos, Carola (2004). "Tough choices for oil companies in the quest to head off a global capacity crunch". *The Financial Times*, 22 September.

Khadduri, W. (2004). "The Iraqi oil industry: a look ahead". *Geopolitics of Energy*, December.

Khartukov, Eugene M. (2004). "Russian production can grow". *PetroMin*, July.

Kiely, J. (1980). "World energy in the 21st century". The Fourth Wilson Campbell Memorial Lecture.

Kubursi, A.A. (1985). "Industrialisation in the Arab States of the Gulf". In Tim Niblock and Richard Lawless (eds.), *Prospects for the World Oil Economy*. London, Sydney, and New Hampshire: Croom Helm.

Lee, J. (2004). "Waking the bear: the outlook for Russian oil production". *Geopolitics of Energy*, October.

Lindahl, Mary (1996). "A hedging strategy for Alaska: learning from the Texas experience". *Journal of Energy Finance and Development*, 1(1).

Lugar, Richard G. and R. James Woolsey (1999). "The new petroleum". *Foreign Affairs*, 78(1): 88–102.

Marshalla, R.A. and D.M. Nesbitt (1986). "Future world oil prices and production levels: an economic analysis". *The Energy Journal*, 7(1): 1–22.

Pashley, C. (1999). "Crude oil price volatility". *PetroMin*, February.

Reynolds, Douglas R. (2005). "The economics of oil definitions". *OPEC Review*, 29(1): 51–73.

—— (2000). "The case for conserving oil resources: the fundamentals of supply and demand". *OPEC Review*, 24(2): 71–86.

Ryan, J.M. (1966). "Limitations of statistical methods for predicting petroleum and natural gas availability". *Journal of Petroleum Technology*, March: 281–284.

Salameh, Mamdouh G. (2004). *Over a Barrel*. Beirut: Joseph D. Raidy.

Samuelson, R.J. (2004). "The dawn of a new oil era?" *Newsweek*, 4 April.

Sarkis, N. (2003). "Les prévisions et les fictions". *Medenergie*, No. 5.

Smil, Vaclav (2002). "Energy resources and uses". *Current History*, March: 126–132.

Tempest, Paul (1996). "Defining and overcoming risk — some global and Middle East factors". *IAEE Newsletter* (Spring).

CHAPTER 3

OIL AND SAUDI ARABIA, RUSSIA AND AFRICA

Everything that you need to know about the future of Saudi Arabian oil production can be found in a staff report to the subcommittee on international economic policy of the committee on foreign relations of the United States Senate (1979). Regardless of what you may or may not have heard on that increasingly relevant subject, between 1979 and now hardly anything has changed, although the question must still be asked why this and similar documents were — and still are — overlooked by many energy professionals.

The purpose of this chapter is to add a few observations on the structure of the global oil market to the work on this subject in previous chapters. Geology and supply–demand mechanics are still of crucial importance, but more attention has been paid to what might be called certain game-theoretical insinuations. Some very useful background to the present exposition is provided in an article by Murray Duffin (2004), which can be found with a number of other papers on oil (and gas) topics in the leading energy forum EnergyPulse (www.energypulse.net). There are also a great deal of valuable information in the comments that are published directly under Duffin's paper.

As strange as it seems, what many observers have missed is that according to the logic of mainstream development economics, the countries of the Middle East are not going to exhaust their supplies of irreplaceable energy resources in order to pull the chestnuts of American and European motorists out of the fire, even if they assure every government and television station in the world that they prepared to do so — and even if, as Humphrey Bogart remarked in the film "Sahara", they adore chestnuts. There is also a widespread tendency to overlook or misinterpret certain extremely important macroeconomic themes having to do with oil, and which need repeating as often as possible.

Recently President George W. Bush promised to help break the "addiction" to oil of his country. This sounds good, and whatever program he comes up with should be encouraged; however, it is more or less certain that it will take time. The managers of Saudi oil, having made mistakes in the past, now seem convinced that they fully comprehend the mathematics and economics that will put them on the road to the kind of economic future that is compatible with their social and cultural aspirations. They probably also comprehend that while the geological upside of their Gulf colleagues Iran and Iraq is enormous, these countries may have serious difficulties with their plans to raise or maintain production.

1. Introduction

According to journalist Max Rodenbeck, the United States became a net importer of crude oil for the first time in 1976, and in 2000 imports accounted for more than half of the US consumption of this commodity. At the present time imports are about 11 million barrels per day (= 11 mb/d). These observations by Mr Rodenbeck — who "covers" the Middle East for the *Economist* — have enough validity to be useful to many of the readers of that publication, even if most of his other comments principally serve as a reminder that the present state of knowledge about the most important raw material in the world is far from what it should and could be. For instance, he is in error about the way that real world oil markets work, and he does not have an adequate acquaintance with the basic scarcity of oil — a scarcity that turns on the inelastic demand for that commodity over the foreseeable future. Moreover, his reference to the "vast and conveniently located reserves of oil shale" in Canada is the kind of mistake that I *always* advised my students to never make if they wanted to survive the first five minutes of an employment interview. (The relevant non-conventional resource in Canada is oil from tar sands, and while vast it is far from convenient. A key hypothesis in this book is that while it may change the global *reserve* picture, it will mean far less for the *production* picture.)

Both my previous energy economics textbook (2000) and my book on oil (1980) failed to give adequate recognition to the crucial role that Saudi Arabia occupies on the world oil scene and, more important, is expected to occupy in the future. But now is the time to correct this oversight, because in my opinion the plans of the Saudi Arabian government are very different from those attributed them by many journalists, as well as persons from academia; very different in fact from their own optimistic and accommodating pronouncements. Moreover, these intentions have not changed over the past 30 years or so. Let me add that an attempt to make a comprehensive estimate of the present goals of the leadership of the most important oil producer on the face of the earth, as well as some knowledge of the intentions of other governments and firms toward that producer, may turn out to be the key to introducing some energy economics wisdom into the lives of certain influential observers who still expect that the oil future will resemble the oil past.

As alluded to in the sequel, the general feeling today is in the direction of pessimism where both oil production and investment in new capacity are concerned. This makes a great deal of sense. There are still, however, a few observers of the flat-earth variety who do not share this attitude. In their world, physical investment is capable of finding oil that the geologists say is not there — or, to put this another way, they think that "market solutions" and technological innovation can overwhelm the laws of physics. Steve Forbes, owner/editor of the business periodical *Forbes*, apparently sees the interplay of supply and demand eventually reducing the price of oil to under \$40/b, and even more grotesque, the CEO of British Petroleum, Lord Browne, believes that it can decline to the \$20–30 range. Martin Vander Weyer — financial commentator of *The Spectator* (UK) — believes that technology will provide a hundred more years of oil. Actually it will provide thousands; however, once global production has peaked, it hardly makes any difference what the actual figure turns out to be.

For what it is worth, the *Petroleum Economist* (October 2004) stated flatly that investment no longer keeps pace with high oil prices, which is a sure sign that in the executive suites of major oil companies, the general belief is that there are no longer investment opportunities capable of matching those of the past. Regardless of the upbeat bulletins and rumors emerging from those venerable premises, this should always be kept in mind, because even investment in OPEC countries (by local and/or foreign "players") has slumped badly, and if this trend continues the production forecasts of the International Energy Agency (IEA) and US Department of Energy cannot possibly be fulfilled. One prominent consulting organization, PFC Energy, has stated that by 2020 at the latest, OPEC will not be able to make up the difference between non-OPEC supply and global demand. This is not a very welcome prophecy, but even so I am at a loss to explain why it is not more widely discussed.

2.   A Few General Observations

Before attempting to put the supply of Saudi energy resources into perspective, a few general remarks about oil are essential. The theory is now frequently advanced that high oil prices no longer threaten the stability of the global macroeconomy, but as far as I am concerned this is a serious misunderstanding. It is a misunderstanding that is largely based on hero-worship of the former Chairman of the US Federal Reserve System (i.e., central bank), Alan Greenspan. What observers do not realize, however, is that Dr Greenspan's undeniable success was mainly due to the huge debts that, luckily for him, could be accumulated by households in the United States, as well as by the US government, and in addition over the past few years there has been a level of capital investment by large corporations that was sufficiently moderate to restrain interest rates. An arrangement of this sort is untenable in the long run, as readers of the financial press are constantly informed in unambiguous language.

Private consumption in the United States is still at a record high. It has been raised to a much greater than normal extent by increases in the price of real estate (i.e., a wealth effect), as well as the continued availability of inexpensive credit. At the same time there is under-consumption in most of the rest of the world, particularly in Europe and China. According to the chief economist of (the investment bank) Morgan Stanley, Mr Stephen Roach, the deficit in the US balance of payments is now close to 7.5% of the gross national product, while at the same time the US accounts for 70% of the total global balance of payments deficits. (He could have added that a large fraction of the US current account deficit can be attributed to imports of energy, and in particular oil.) Roach regards this as unnatural, which it is, and he predicts a "crisis". Moreover, he pictures that crisis reaching every part of the world because of the cross-border linkages created by globalization. As it happens though, regardless of the curse of globalization, these linkages have always existed for reasons shown in every book dealing in any way with international economics, to include my elementary international finance textbook (2001).

The exact circumstances that would initiate a macroeconomic crisis are often unclear, but one avenue would be via a sharp (upward) interest rate adjustment, either directly because of a decrease in the saving of foreigners, or indirectly because of another sustained increase in the oil price boosting the macroeconomic price level. The wealth effect referred to above would then move in the opposite direction, and the impact effect of the resulting decrease in spending could have serious consequences for both physical and financial markets everywhere. Note the expression "impact effect", because (*ceteris paribus*) eventually a decrease in spending in the United States would have to take place in order to obtain what they called an "equilibrium" in your macroeconomics courses.

This might also be a good place to mention the "yield curve" (which is a plot of the interest rates (or yields) for a particular type of bond, against different maturities for that asset). As explained in Chapter 6 of my finance book, a flattening (or inversion) of this curve — which took place when this was first written — could lead to a very bad macroeconomic scene. The reason for this inversion turns on rising short-term interest rates, along with an increased demand for long-term paper.

Unfortunately, Alan Greenspan entertained a few illusions where the yield curve is concerned, saying that an inversion no longer implies a recession, as was often the case earlier. It may turn out that he is correct, however the financial history of the last 50 years or so suggests that an inverted yield curve is not a desirable state of affairs. By way of contrast though, the chairman never ceased trying to make it clear that very high oil and gas prices are capable of badly damaging the US economy. He undoubtedly remembers the recessions that followed previous oil price escalations, and more importantly, he understood that while the laws of economics — unlike those of physics — can be rescinded temporarily, they cannot be abolished. For example, the macroeconomic and financial markets expansions of the 1990s almost certainly would have been impossible if the *nominal* (i.e., money) price of oil in that period had been anywhere close to where they are at the present time. (The *real* — i.e., inflation adjusted — price of oil is still lower than it was 20 years ago, using the 1973 oil price as a base, but I get the impression that attention is usually called to the real price by persons who want to claim that oil costing $70/b or more is not particularly expensive.)

The International Energy Agency (IEA) has postulated an increase in the world oil demand from the present 85 to 121 mb/d in 2030. Normally, I would express some curiosity as to the scientific background for that estimate; however, I propose to use it to make another preliminary remark about the supply capabilities of Saudi Arabia. At the time when this 121 mb/d is supposed to be produced, OPEC is pictured as being responsible for about one-half (as compared to approximately 35% just now). This suggests an expected OPEC production of approximately 60 mb/d. At the present time Saudi Arabia supplies almost a third of OPEC oil, and given their reserve situation relative to the other OPEC (and non-OPEC) countries, this fraction will hardly decrease. (Saudi Arabia apparently has proven reserves of about 260 billion barrels, while second place Iraq has 120 billion barrels.) Accordingly, it seems that IEA experts believe that Saudi Arabia will supply at least 20 mb/d in 2030.

One of the main purposes of this book is to convince readers that Saudi Arabia is not going to willingly supply 20 mb/d in 2030, or at any other time in the near or distant future, regardless of what you may hear on the grapevine. A high-ranking Saudi official once stated that 15 mb/d should be possible, and if this amount is attained, he appeared certain that it could be maintained indefinitely. This kind of assurance undoubtedly sounds lovely to the world's motorists, but the economics that I teach informs me that 15 mb/d is a goal that will not be easy for Saudi Arabia to reach, while the game theory that I have taught tells me that this kind of talk should be taken with a grain of salt. Furthermore, and more important, even if that production level was realizable, it would not be maintained for more than a comparatively short period — unless the Saudi government had come to the conclusion that less money was preferable to more.

The situation in Saudi Arabia should be easy to understand. Most of the oil in that country originates in four or five large deposits that were discovered from 40 to 50 years ago. In order to keep production at the present level, huge amounts of water must be pumped into the deposits, and if the input of water (per period) is raised considerably above the present level in order to obtain more oil, it will simply mean that it becomes increasingly difficult (i.e., costly) to obtain this oil. Some question must also be raised as to what effect the use of this additional water and perhaps other secondary procedures will have on the ultimate quantity of oil extracted.

What I do not question however is that the government of that country will do everything possible to approximately double its share of the global petrochemical output from its present 7% share over the next five years. The reason I accept this is because from an economic point of view, a greatly increased petrochemical (and refining) output in the near future is a more reasonable economic goal than attaining a crude oil production of more than 12 mb/d at any time. According to the Saudi government, foreigners are welcome to invest/participate in the production of petrochemicals and refined products in that country, but I suspect that the reason for this generosity is the desire to use the influence of large energy companies to facilitate the access to foreign markets of Saudi Arabia's petrochemical and refined output.

There is also some question as to what OPEC as a whole will be able to achieve. A report from the consulting firm PFC Energy (as mentioned in the *Petroleum Economist*, October 2004) indicates that OPEC is producing much more oil every year than it has been finding. This situation has been pictured as changing if, e.g., Libya and Iraq intensify their exploration activities; however, even under the best of conditions I find it impossible to believe that this will be of other than marginal significance for the IEA targets mentioned above.

Of late we have been hearing a great deal about oil from tar sands (in the Athabasca region of Canada), and the heavy oil of the Orinco region in Venezuela. As it happens, if a large expansion takes place in the output of these unconventional resources, then those observers who feel that the resources of the Middle East are overrated might be correct, because in those circumstances it is conceivable that the 9–10 mb/d output of Saudi Arabia could be matched or overmatched.

As suggested by Crandall (2005) and Reynolds (2005), the total output of unconventional oil from these two regions will not reach anywhere near 9–10 mb/d in the near or medium future, and by the time it does the global production of conventional oil might have turned down. Accordingly, we would still be faced with an oil price that is capable of devastating the international macroeconomy, as well as creating social/political chaos in the large importing countries. The CEO of one of the major oil companies has sworn what almost amounts to a sacred oath that his enterprise is prepared to assume the responsibility for developing the kind of technology needed to make unconventional oil economically attractive, but this sounds like the kind of pledge that is delivered late at night after the cognac has gone around the table a couple of times.

Herman Franssen is one of the leading oil consultants in the world, and president of International Energy Associates, Inc. According to him tar sands will provide about 2 mb/d in 1010, and 3.5 by 2020. The Non-OPEC oil producing world will plateau soon after 2010, while the Middle-East OPEC, which is the core of OPEC, desires at least a three decade long plateau. He also views the scope of gas-to-liquids with considerably less enthusiasm than many observers, concluding that global output will only be 0.5 mb/d by 2020. His most recent survey paper was delivered at the Middle East Petroleum and Gas Conference in Abu Dhabi, 1 May 2006.

3. The Annoying Truth about Saudi Arabia and Oil

> *"They think that it's running out. It's running out and ninety percent of what's left is in the Middle East."*
> — *Matt Damon in "Syriana"*

Well, Matt, it is not really 90%, but since the gentlemen who wrote and produced that film are not quite clear on the difference between Hollywood truth and the real deal, I do not think that it is worth going to war over — which is what the next line in that quotation suggested.

It has already been explained that the typical production profile for oil exhibits rising production, a plateau, and then falling production. As an example we can consider the Khurays field in Saudi Arabia, where expansion may already be under way. It is estimated that altogether 400 wells will be required over a period of three years in order to obtain a total of 1.2 mb/d. What happens after those three years is uncertain; however, I have heard it suggested that the field will be in full decline, although to some extent this sounds like an exaggeration. It will also need 2 mb/d of water injection, facilities to process the water, and pipelines, and according to an article in *Business Week* (10 October 2005), natural depletion in Saudia Arabia now amounts to between 400,000 and 500,000 barrels per year. (I have heard it said that this estimate is too small, however I have no way to determine the true figure.) In hearing this kind of thing, a natural question might be the one put by Mr Rockefeller when he launched his money-making activities: "why bother with upstream activities" (i.e., production of crude oil). As noted later, investment money destined for deployment in Saudi Arabia might be optimally spent on increasing petrochemical and/or refining capacity.

Just before I began to study energy economics, which was around the time of the first oil price "shock", the Saudi Arabian oil economy was being programmed by its foreign "owners" (which included Exxon, Texaco, Standard Oil of California, and Mobil) to produce 20 mb/d of oil. Exactly how that figure was reached is unknown to myself; however, given the extremely low cost of producing oil in Saudi Arabia at the time, certain academic economists had no difficulty accepting that in the light of the existing and the expected price, 20 mb/d was an appropriate profit maximizing quantity for the government of that country. (Interestingly enough, that figure was recently used by an academic petroleum engineer as the amount that he could obtain if, presumably, he were given the office of chief decision maker in that country.)

But despite the unsolicited scholarly expertise at his disposal, as pointed out in the staff report mentioned above, Crown Prince Fahd stated that "Saudi Arabia has worked and is working sincerely and earnestly to provide an appropriate level of oil and gas production as an expression of its feeling of shared responsibility in the international community, but our feelings of responsibility toward future generations in Saudi Arabia also claim careful consideration and the establishment of a calculated balance between the present and the future".

This kind of thinking is too reasonable to be commensurate with an output of 20 mb/d. The more oil used today, the less will be available tomorrow; and thus the monetary return from the present output should take into consideration the amount of profits and/or consumer satisfaction that might have to be sacrificed later. Put another way, the cost that we should be dealing with at each moment of time should include a *scarcity rent* or *scarcity royalty* that is related to the using up of an exhaustible resource. This is not an easy thing to calculate, although it might be suggested that the scarcity royalty on the Saudi Arabian oil is considerably larger than that of the off-shore oil produced by Denmark, largely for macroeconomic reasons that cannot be gone into here.

In any event, the proposed production — and specifically the *plateau rate* — of 20 mb/d mentioned above was soon scaled down to 16 mb/d, and from there to 12, and subsequently to less than 10. At the same time it appears that investments were undertaken to provide for a *surge capacity* of about 10.5 mb/d. (Surge capacity represents the output that can be provided for a short period of time — perhaps several weeks or longer — without damaging the reservoir.) A great deal is now being made of that capac-ity — which today might be as high as 12 mb/d — because theoretically it represents a particularly valuable piece of insurance for the oil consuming world.

In addition, Crown Prince Fahd informed the large oil importing coun-tries that their best strategy was to moderate their consumption of oil, while introducing as rapidly as possible alternative sources of energy. (Someone else who feels this way is Mr Red Cavaney, president of the American Petroleum Institute, who has started singing the praises of conservation as compared to increased exploration and drilling.) Since he also emphasized the need to preserve his country's petroleum wealth for future generations, it seems likely that, unlike certain prominent academics, Crown Price Fahd did not view the oil reserves of his country as inexhaustible.

Now let us go back to the figure given above as the possible or desired production of Saudi Arabia in the early 1980s — i.e., 20 mb/d. Fortunately for all of us (i.e., both producers and consumers) this economically insane program was canceled after the nationalizations that took place as a result of the 1973 war in the Middle East. The main reason given by the new owners — the Saudi Arabian government — was that an output of 20 mb/d entailed mismanaging a national asset. Every person of normal intelligence who is responsible for managing the economic future of themselves or their family should intuitively agree with this, even if they are oblivious of some of the technical details that play an important role in programming the flow from petroleum reservoirs. The crucial observation in this case is that an output of 20 mb/d could only be maintained for a relatively short period of time without badly damaging reservoirs and reducing future output. In addition, after ramping production up to 20 mb/d, the billions of dollars spent for fixed investment to produce and distribute that amount of oil could be lost due to the inevitable decline in output (and, once again, if this decline were delayed, then when it took place it would be steeper).

Some citizens of Middle East countries — to include Saudi Arabia — were quite vocal about the economic and social inadvisability of producing too much oil. According to an article in *The Economist*, (29 May 2004), Mr bin Laden was one of them, but when I recently gave a lecture on energy economics I limited myself to referring to the last Shah of Iran, who often stated that petroleum was too valuable to be "burned up in the air". When I used that expression at the international meeting of the International Association of Energy Economics (IAEE) in Copenhagen, in 1991, it caused some annoyance, but I cannot really understand why, since as I later found out many persons from that part of the world were thinking along the same line.

The Middle East has an enormous competitive advantage in petrochemicals, and perhaps also in refining. Moreover, remembering my talk in Copenhagen, I have some difficulty understanding why half of the new capacity that is planned for the coming decade is not already on line. According to the *Financial Times* (21 September 2005), one of the problems facing Saudi Arabia is that it is not a member of the World Trade Organisation, which means that it is "fair game for protectionist measures". Personally, I have a difficult time imagining any government initiating protectionist measures against the global oil superpower, particularly since that superpower is ostensibly "looking at scenarios to bolster production to even 15 mb/d" (*Business Week*, 10 October 2005). I do not spend as much time studying game theory as I once did, but what they are probably looking at are scenarios that would help them to convince the rest of the world that they can or will produce 15 mb/d, and in addition produce this amount over a long period. The first "might" happen, but the last is completely out of the question, and should be recognized as such.

I can add that if a country like South Korea could build a viable petrochemical export industry although it lacks domestic petrochemical feedstocks, or inexpensive energy for running these facilities, then a country like Saudi Arabia has an indisputable advantage over any and all competitors, to include competitors in North America and Europe.

Before concluding this part of the discussion, I would like to cite the opinion of the Houston investment banker, Matthew R. Simmons, who has attracted a great deal of attention with his book *"Twilight in the Desert"*, in which he says that Saudi production may be peaking. Peaking in this case probably means that while it will not increase, it may not decline by a palpable amount in the near future. Simmons undoubtedly is a strong believer in this prospect, because he had bet a New York journalist and the widow of economics professor Julian Simon $5000 that the price of oil is on its way to $200/b. Five thousand dollars is hardly more than walking-around-money for Mr Simmons, but in any case he is certain to lose that bet, because assuming that the oil price continues to rise at the rate experienced over the past three years, long before it reaches $200/b we will have to deal with a new world depression — *observe, depression, and not recession* — and perhaps a great deal of military activity whose aim is to secure oil.

4.   Some Aspects of Russian Oil

Russian oil is a topic that was not scheduled for an appearance in this textbook, but after recently being assured that steadily increasing amounts of this commodity will flow in the direction of both the major and minor oil importing countries, I thought that a few extra words to the professedly wise might be in order. One reason is that "minor" in this case means the Kingdom of Sweden, and if it is true that oil will continue to arrive in sufficient quantities, it would facilitate my access to the sport and people-watching associated with this country's superb beaches and ski areas.

In a decade Russia together with the adjacent former members of the Soviet Union will probably be the only region outside the Middle East with a reasonably large exportable surplus of oil, "probably" for two reasons. First, some surprises may eventually turn up in the interior or offshore districts of Africa and South America, although a question must be raised as to whether they are the kind of surprises that we might be desperately in need of at that time. There is also this matter of exactly how that Russian surplus may develop.

Russia is now the second largest oil exporter after Saudi Arabia, and recently its exports spiked to a higher level. One *difference* between the two countries is that production in Saudi Arabia may not have peaked as yet, while for all practical purposes a peak arrived in the Russian (i.e., the former Soviet Union) output at a level close to 13 mb/d about 1990. It could happen of course that production in the former Soviet Union (FSU) could spike above this level; however, I do not believe that any great significance should be applied to an event of this nature should it occur. A *similarity*, however, is that important observers in both countries have announced production goals that are almost certainly out of reach, and with this in mind, I have decided to reemphasize that estimates by the IEA and United States Department of Energy (USDE) of a global supply of 120 mb/d of oil in 2030 are also virtually impossible to attain — assuming that the movers-and-shakers in these two countries have things like profit maximization and the overall welfare of their citizens in mind.

The oil minister of Saudi Arabia once said that his country could raise output to 15 mb/d, and keep it there indefinitely. As emphasized above, at no point in the past 33 years have the decision makers in that country indicated that Saudi production would exceed 12 mb/d, although recently someone somewhere alluded to a production of 12.5 mb/d by the end of 2009. If it were technically and economically conceivable, it might certainly be true that Saudi Arabia would like to make a marginally larger contribution to averting an oil price explosion, because the present global oil price scene is close to wish fulfilment for many of the OPEC countries, and it is not in their interest to disturb this equilibrium — if it is an equilibrium — in order to make the dreams of amateur energy experts in their customer countries come true.

A year or so ago the leading oil economist in Russia published a note in the important review *PetrominAsia* in which he stated that oil production in his country could reach 30 mb/d. Unlike Mr Oil Minister, he did not provide an estimate of how long this bonanza could be maintained, although it hardly makes a difference. Output in the FSU is not going to come anywhere near 30 mb/d, just as a production in present day Russia of more than 10 mb/d could hardly be sustained for more than a few years. The large oil firms outside Russia are perfectly aware of this fact, and as a result they are not prepared to invest billions and billions in that country in order to pursue this mirage.

An interesting observation here might be that there are almost certainly a large number of highly profitable projects that could and will be made in Russia over the coming decade, and these will be greatly appreciated by managers and equity owners in the investing enterprises, but in terms of size these ventures should probably be described as unexceptional, and will not even partially mitigate the all-inclusive requirements of the main oil importing countries. More important, although conveniently forgotten by most researchers, about the time I published my oil book (1980), the CIA was predicting that Russia was on its way to becoming an oil importer. The assumption then was that the Russian economy would eventually be patched up to an extent where it could attain a standard of living about on the level of Italy. This did not happen, but whether it happens or not at some point in the future, some question must be put as to whether energy rich Russia would find itself reduced to buying large quantities of expensive foreign oil.

Before continuing with the main topic, I would like to add a short comment to the previous discussion. Global oil consumption just now is about 85 mb/d, but practically the only spare production capacity is in OPEC countries, and altogether *may* amount to about 2 mb/d. Saudi Arabia has most of this, and a total production of almost 10 mb/d. These numbers suggest that at best there is only a small margin available in the oil exporting countries with which to counter a drastic supply disruption, which is probably why Daniel Yergin has said that the world is experiencing a slow-motion oil price shock. This is not a good thing, although it is better than the alternative, which with a high probability would include an ugly macroeconomic and/or financial market adjustment.

5.   A Beautiful Myth

The oil story in every country has certain similarities — finding oil, and then exposing it to the right kind of management and technology. The "right" management, of course, is eminently capable of locating the right employees and any finance that might be necessary. As Rhett Butler told Scarlet O'Hara in "Gone with the Wind", there are few things in this old world of ours that money will not buy, and at present prices oil discovered in the most primitive countries imaginable can easily be brought to the surface, and without too much trouble can be dispatched to the far corners of the globe.

That brings us to a beautiful myth: Russia is desperately in need of outside assistance to enable it to realize its oil production potential. I first commented on this in my oil book, and my thinking went as follows: "That the Soviet oil industry is in trouble is well known, but various sectors of the Soviet economy are always in trouble. The point is that time and time again the Soviets have shown that when they concentrate their efforts, they have a remarkable capacity to break bottlenecks and get results. The quantity and quality of Soviet military hardware should make this abundantly clear". Here I was thinking in particular of the quantity and quality of the hardware in what was then East Germany, and which definitely matched the assets at our disposal in the Western part of that country. On the basis of what we knew about their training, the same was almost certainly true of their infantry and armor personnel.

Two Russian gentlemen who are not buying any of this are Vladimir Kvint, who was/is a frequent contributor to one of the best business publications in the world, *Forbes*, and Vladimir Milov, president of the Institute of Energy Policy in Moscow. Writing in 1990, Mr Kvint informed us that "If the capital and expertise of companies like Exxon, Shell and BP could be turned loose on the region (East Siberia), there is no telling how high production could go". Maybe he could not tell, nor could I at that time, since the Soviet empire was imploding, but I am very definitely capable of carrying out that assignment today. It will not go much higher than when he was vigorously trying to peddle this bizarre misunderstanding to his admirers in the financial districts of London and New York.

The second Vladimir wants no less than a repudiation of the "desire" to limit foreign investments in Russia's energy sector. To his way of thinking "we need strategic foreign investors in Russia to ensure development of our new oil and gas fields". The truth happens to be that just as these investors are not wanted by the Russian government, they are not needed. President Putin has openly and explicitly called for a limitation of foreign investment in what he calls "strategic sectors" of the economy, because he understands that foreign investors do not necessarily have the best interests of ordinary Russians at heart; and if he does not understand this, a majority of his countrymen may choose to inform him or his successor in very crude language some day. As bad luck would have it, the television audiences in

Sweden and America are a bit vague on this topic, but it may happen that future events will bring them to their senses.

At the same time that he does not want foreigners tooling about in Siberia and elsewhere in his country, Mr Putin has expressed an interest in equity positions in foreign enterprises in western Europe. To obtain this, he apparently is prepared to use the oil weapon — i.e., to say, reduce the availability of oil to large importers of Russian oil. There are probably some illusions of grandeur which led him to take this position, because in a rational world he would discern that there is a tremendous amount of work that needs to be done within the boundaries of his own realm, and it is unlikely that this would be expedited by giving some of his best Russian managerial talent the opportunity to purchase their electronics and underwear at the more exclusive outlets in London or Paris.

Since Russia is an extremely large country, it is easy to perpetuate the delusion that enormous amounts of exploitable oil and gas will be located in the not too distant future, particularly in Eastern Siberia or the Barents Sea. Observe: "enormous" as compared to merely large! This is the kind of eccentric idea that certain professors in the United Kingdom have attempted to foist on the unwary for years, despite the fact that they know — or should know — that in the executive suites of the oil majors mentioned by Kvint, contrary beliefs have been in circulation for a number of years. If we look at North America, for instance, we see that the best technology in the world never uncovered any supergiant deposits of conventional oil in Canada, which is a country about as large as Eastern Siberia; nor has it been able to reverse the US peak, although almost all of the oil produced in that country in the last century has been extracted from only a miniscule portion of the total surface area of the lower 48 and Alaska.

Milov also wants "Moscow" to repudiate what he calls the "gas supply blackmail" now being practiced by his government. He could have called it the "oil supply blackmail", given the direction in which a new large Russian oil pipeline will ostensibly run: a 1.6 mb/d installation from the Irkutsk region to somewhere on the Pacific coast opposite Japan. However let me emphasize that while that scholar may call it "blackmail", in the MBA lectures at Harvard and Stanford it is called *business*, and what it amounts to is making it clear to potential customers that if they cannot match the offers of other buyers, they will have to obtain their requirements elsewhere.

According to the chief of the Russian pipeline "Transneft", Russia should cut supplies to "overfed" Europe, because according to him "economics manuals" clearly indicate that "excessive supplies depress prices". Low oil prices apparently have no place in his latest five year plan. The part about supply and demand is correct, but unfortunately he and his colleagues should have examined, in the late 1990s, the Russian equivalent of Econ 101. According to the kind of reasoning in that and similar volumes, he might have been able to deduce the theoretically correct conclusion that his country was producing too much oil. Not only would a higher price have provided Russia with a larger export income, but it would have sent a valuable signal to oil users that there was probably less of that commodity in the crust of the earth than they were being led to believe.

With all due respect, I think that it might be an excellent idea if our political masters and their advisors attempt to understand exactly what Russia and adjacent states will or will not be able to offer when, or if, oil demand suddenly lunges ahead of oil supply, and the gap might have to be closed by some traumatic price escalations. What I do not suggest though is that extra attention should be given a recent "Special Report" on oil in the *Economist* (22 April 2006). Among other things this half-baked contribution contains a quote by the "boss" of a prominent consultancy, who tells his clients not to worry because, e.g., "Kuwait has 50 years of production left at current rates". He apparently is still blissfully oblivious of the widely known fact that almost every intelligent person with other than a superficial interest in oil realizes that the crucial issue is identifying when the production of a country like Kuwait peaks. At the current output, that will be well under 50 years, and it will not be good news for the oil importing world.

More important for any neophyte "masters of the universe" reading the present discussion, that issue of the *Economist* also quoted Professor Kenneth Rogoff of Harvard University — formerly chief economist of the International Monetary Fund (IMF) — who calls our attention to "long-dated futures going out five to seven years", which therefore might make it possible to lock in present oil prices until 2012 or thereabouts. In making this ridiculous claim he is more optimistic than Professor Henrik Houthakker of the same institution, who some years ago cited oil futures with maturities of three years as being available to hedge price risk, and at the same time referred to oil options.

In dealing with this kind of bunkum, think about what it means to be a large transactor on the short side of a futures transaction when talk is in the air about the likelihood of the oil price rising from in the vicinity of its present $70/b to between $90/b and $100/b, and more alarming the Houston investment banker Matt Simmons continues to predict an oil price of several hundred dollars a barrel in a few years. If the price zoomed up, margin calls on short positions could be ruinous. By the same token, long hedgers would be facing intolerably high premiums, regardless of what the actual price turned out to be. Here it should be appreciated that liquidity shortages in a long-dated market of the kind posited by Rogoff could severely punish transactors who succeeded in opening a position anywhere in the vicinity of one of the longer maturities mentioned by Professor Rogoff. Something else to focus on is that in reality it would be difficult to find a long-dated contract that "went out" more than five to seven months, if that. I can note that in New York, 1,420,734 futures contracts were traded in one day in the middle of April 2006, thereby exceeding the previous record of 1,383,616. There was a great deal of nervousness behind these figures, and average maturities were probably in weeks rather than months.

6.   Near and Far

If Vladimir Milov is a mite hazy on the mechanics of capitalistic business mechanics, he apparently knows enough about oil production to suggest that Russia should not be producing more than 7.8 mb/d of this commodity instead of 9.5 mb/d that was recently announced. The latter figure implies that in order to maintain this production, serious long-term damage is being inflicted on reservoirs. In an easily read article in the important *"Geopolitics of Energy"* (2006), Julian Lee of the Centre for Global Energy Studies adds that Russian oil production hit a post-Soviet high in November 2005, of 9.6 mb/d.

Professors Sadek Boussena and Catherine Locatelli (2005) of Grenoble University have also examined this subject, noting that forecasts of Russian output in 2010 range from 6 to 12 mb/d, while in 2020 the range is between 5 and 11 mb/d. I think we can say that these are the kind of numbers that are being bandied about in the executive suites of the oil majors, although they might not be made available for general viewing. I also suspect that figures like these would prevent much credence given to forecasts by the IEA and USDE of a global oil output in 2030 of 121 mb/d, with perhaps OPEC supplying 60–65 mb/d and Saudi Arabia 20–23 mb/d. These numbers are intended for the unthinking portion of the TV audience, because they are almost certainly impossible, as is the estimate by the POLE model (mentioned by Boussena and Locatelli) of an OPEC supply of crude of 40 mb/d in 2010, as compared to slightly less than 30 mb/d at the present time. The upshot of all this is that the world oil supply situation leaves a great deal to be desired by those of us on the buy side of the market, and reinforces the predictions and analyses of the Association for the Study of Peak Oil (ASPO or ODAC).

The Barents Sea did not play much of a role in the above expositions, but according to the Norwegian foreign minister Jonas Gahe Store (2006), it is "Ett hav av möjligheter" (A sea of possibilities). This may be true, even though that gentleman hardly has the background to discuss this issue with a knowledgeable audience. An outstanding discussion of this region, however, is that of de Zardain (2005), which helps to substantiate my belief that Russia is in a similar situation to that existing in the United States: a huge area but with access to much less oil than was taken for granted only a short time ago. He also emphasizes the complicated oil politics in Russia; however, I see no reason to spend time examining these because the bottom line is the above figures, which indicate that regardless of how things work out, and who gets or loses what job, Russia is not going to be able to deliver anywhere near the amount of oil that we would like for them to deliver.

It has also been mooted that there is a possibility that Russia is in possession of large oil deposits that were overlooked in earlier "sweeps". In considering Iraq and Saudi Arabia, it appears that some oil experts in the Bush administration have strongly recommended the extensive use of advanced seismic technology; but I would like to inform them that during the past two decades, seismic technology has revealed the *absence* of new large fields. Moreover, since a number of existing and potential producing countries are as interested in investment dollars as they are in income from actual production, they would hardly appreciate having their lack of productive capabilities revealed by seismic or other means. It is also the case that the petroleum engineers of Saudi Arabia, Iraq, and Russia hardly require any advice from Washington.

That brings us to the Caspian — or what some observers have come to believe is the richer part of the FSU in regard to oil!

The Caspian was referred to as the next oil frontier in a long article in *Business Week* (27 May 2002). The most interesting item in that exposition was a notice that by 2010 the Caspian could claim 3% of global oil output. The well-known oil economist and consultant Mamdouh G. Salameh (2004) outlined his reservations about that part of the world in his important book, *Over a Barrel*, although like other researchers he likens this region to the North Sea in terms of reserves and output potential. This means a great deal of oil, but unfortunately not enough, because the production build-up in that part of the world may not exceed by much the increasingly rapid decline in the North Sea.

Professor Maureen Crandall (2005) of the US National Defence University calls the Caspian "overhyped", and I am sure that she is correct. Salameh uses the expression "The Great Game" in his article, which has overtones from the work of Rudyard Kipling, but which now refers to who owns Caspian oil and controls pipelines in that part of the world instead of the high-jinks on the Northwest Frontier of India that featured Victorian England and Tsarist Russia. To me the "Great Game" might refer to certain aspects of the course in game theory that I am preparing, and in particular the part involving threats, insinuations, ignorance (or more politely "lack of information"), and of course blatant as well as unobtrusive lies.

In the *Business Week* article referred to above, a US Assistant Secretary of State for European and Eurasian Affairs tied the US commitment in the Caspian to the goal of eliminating terrorism. I prefer to believe that the goal is helping to get rid of the threat or actuality of a sudden lack of oil. In this case "American soldiers, oil men, and diplomats" — to use the lingo of the article — are probably in the wrong place, although identifying the right place is unfortunately beyond the capacity of this teacher of economics and finance.

Crandall provides some estimates for production in this region for 2010 and 2015. These are 3.25 mb/d and 3.6 mb/d, respectively. This is not a great deal, but unlike the situation in Russia, domestic consumption may not place an excessive burden on export possibilities. It will, though, place more of a burden than in most oil producing countries along the west coast of Africa, where diplomats do not have to be on hand to explain to well over 90% of the local population that they should not get their hopes up that they will share in any oil income that might befall their homelands.

An interesting feature of the present Russian scene was the establishment of a so-called energy fund in 2004 whose ostensible purpose was to cushion the federal budget from a slump in oil prices. This fund apparently invests most of its receipts in high-grade fixed-income securities (i.e., bonds). Some economists have claimed that this fund should follow the lead of Norway, and be put in the hands of external asset managers to invest in potentially high yielding shares and bonds, and also currencies. The fund now has about 61 billion dollars, which makes it very attractive to many professional asset managers because of the potential management fees.

The opinion here is that a large part of this capital should be invested in technical and health-care education for secondary school students, and others, which might enable Russians to fully realize the gains associated with the conscientious application of modern technology, that the excellent Russian engineers and scientists have no difficulty in mastering and introducing into their country. According to the World Bank's chief economist for Russia, the fund could reach 2.3 trillion dollars if properly invested in financial assets and left untouched. "Properly invested" is the key phrase here, but given my knowledge about the smarts of World Bank busybodies, I doubt whether they are the right people to become involved with this or any project.

Mr Chief Economist and others should also be aware that Norway has a huge fund that every year yields the Norwegian government a great deal of money. I have heard it said though that with reference to health-care, this money has not been deployed efficiently. For example, a question has been asked by one of the extremist parties in Norway as to why such an obviously rich country does not have better equipped hospitals.

The Russian oil economy is not easy to figure out, as is evident from the timely and well-known research of Jennifer Considine and William Kerr. I am not sure, however, that I need to spend any time here on its qualitative aspects, because the key issue is and will continue to be how much oil that country and the other former members of the Soviet Union will produce and/or export in the future. The conclusion in this book is that it will not be enough, regardless of the actual figure.

I have also noted that the widely quoted figures for oil production in 2030 by the International Energy Agency and the United States Department of Energy are not credible, which implies that there will be a global oil output peak before that time — unless somebody decides to take some oil at gunpoint.

Everyone does not share this belief, to include Ronald Bailey, the science correspondent of *Reason Online*. Let us see if we can straighten him out. Oil production peaked in the United States, in Russia, in the United Kingdom and Norwegian North Sea, in Indonesia, etc. It has flattened in China and India, where consumption is leaping ahead, and macroeconomic growth rates are the highest in the world. It had also flattened in Canada until it was decided to add tar sends to conventional reserves and production, but this is all right because as with several other regions of great hope, such as the Caspian and Mexico, the upper boundary on production is clearly visible. It may also be relevant to note that only about one barrel of oil (or perhaps less) is being discovered for every three consumed. That we can get these peaks and plateaux everywhere, but in the light of the global rate of increase of consumption, global output will not peak, suggests to me that when discussing oil, *Reason Online* should be renamed *Unreasonable Online*.

7.   African Skies

A "theory" has started making the rounds that eventually enough oil will be found in Africa to compensate for any shortfalls from the Middle East. In fact, someone recently notified me that everywhere they look in Africa they find oil. When I hear this kind of guesswork I think of one of the most popular songs in Senegal when I was teaching mathematical economics there. Its title was *African Skies*, and I think the lesson it contained was that under those skies your dreams could come true — though not the dream in oil importing countries of reducing the price of a barrel of oil to that of a barrel of Coca Cola as a result of the rich bounty to be found in Africa.

The oil of Africa is not evenly distributed. The Sirte basin in Libya is estimated to have about 66 Gb of Africa's estimated reserve total of 300 Gb.

As I have been aggressively informed by Ms Maria Kielmas, there could be more, because the technology at the disposal of oil exploration is so imperfect that huge deposits are missed by a matter of "feet". (I chose to call information of this type an expression of contempt for modern science and technology.) The rest is mostly found in Nigeria, Angola, and Algeria — and perhaps Sudan and Egypt. Lesser amounts have been located in the Cameroons, San Tomé, Gabon, Equatorial Guinea, Chad, etc. The point is though that with the oil price where it is today, every barrel counts. Nigeria also has a palpable share of the world's LNG capacity, and one of the most famous natural gas pipelines in the world is the conduit between Algeria and Italy.

At the present time (June 2006), Africa produces about 9 mb/d of oil, with West African nations accounting for between 4 and 5 mb/d. There is some talk of production in the latter rising to 9 mb/d by 2030. According to the International Monetary Fund (IMF), the fastest growing economies in Africa are the oil exporting nations of Angola, Mauretania, and Sudan. Africa provides about 18% of the US oil imports, and that continent has 8% of the known reserves of natural gas.

Moreover, much of Africa's oil is considered "safe", hassle-free oil that is also of a high quality. The endemic corruption that characterizes many of the countries in that part of the world is now seen as an attraction rather than a curse by many foreign firms anxious to find some way to take advantage of what remains of the age of oil. The exact identity of the owners of much of this bounty is — to paraphrase Winston Churchill — a mystery within a mystery; however, almost all of the oil majors are on hand: BP, Shell, ExxonMobil, Total, and Chevron, and they are not there on a charity mission. China and India are also available to join in the bidding for whatever is on offer, and their deep pockets are welcome. China, for instance, bought a 45% stake in Nigeria's Akpo field for a reputed 2.3 billion dollars.

Interestingly enough, ExxonMobil (or Exxon as it was at that time) made several large investments in Africa when the oil price was in the doldrums. This may well have had something to do with what I interpret as the investment philosophy of the Exxon leadership, which is that the key thing is to gain access to sizable deposits of oil, and not worry too much about the price of the day. According to Mr Rex Tillerson, the present CEO of ExxonMobil, oil fields take so long to develop, and are in production for such a long time that the oil price on any given date is "almost entirely irrelevant" to investment decisions. This can be put another way: if the oil price is low, the field can be developed slowly, and if market conditions change (upwards), development can be hastened. Given the likely long-run movement in the oil price, this strikes me as a win–win strategy, because in an emergency the firm will have the option of selling the property for a profit. It was a strategy of this nature that increased the market capitalization of Exxon by almost 400 billion dollars in about 13 years.

According to Carola Hoyos of the *Financial Times*, the US government is involved in training the military in some "strategically" located African states in order to "help ensure that oil has a free path through which to reach international markets". It is possible — though not certain — that this information reached Ms Hoyos via an unpublished paper of mine that I circulated widely, and in which I noted that at least one of these states enjoyed the presence of a US Marine Corps training detachment that was specifically tasked with teaching some of the military of that country how to keep terrorists, troublemakers, and other "bad guys" away from existing or potential pipelines. Nothing was mentioned about the bad guys in the government of that and other countries who spend a large part of what they acquire from the sale of oil on plane tickets and weapons.

Students of oil economics have a very different picture of the situation in Africa from students of development economics. In the past it was characteristic to paint Libya as a rogue state; however, the opinion here is that the situation in that country could develop very favorably for its residents, and particularly now that friendly relations have been established with potential customers. The Mediterranean coast of Libya could be turned into a facsimile of, e.g., Dubai, where oil money has created a picture-perfect haven of luxury accommodations and touristy ease. Libya has a more favorable location though, and perhaps could tie into the European economy as more than a supplier of unprocessed oil.

US firms such as Amerada Hess, ConocoPhillips, and Marathon Oil have returned to Libya after being informed in the 1980s that their presence was no longer desired. The simple fact of the matter is that Libya is a very large country, and may contain any number of pleasant surprises. After all, a new and supposedly large field was just found in Kuwait, which is a very small country. This suggests that even the most modern technology can sometimes overlook prizes, which is certainly more possible in Libya than in Kuwait. (Whether they could overlook them by "feet", however, is quite another matter.) Of course the question must be asked if this new field was actually overlooked, or if in reality is a fairly small asset whose extent is being exaggerated in order to attract some of the billions of dollars that are available to invest in what oil hungry countries and firms judge to be promising ventures.

A country that has suddenly made a big splash on the oil scene is Sudan, whose reserves were listed in the latest BP statistical review as 6.3 billion barrels (= 6.3 Gb), while production is 500,000 mb/d, and apparently on its way to about 700,000 mb/d. Carola Hoyos compares this with the remaining reserves of the United Kingdom of 4.5 Gb, without noting that if there is such a thing as the "self-sustaining economic growth" that we once studied and taught and thought so much of in courses on development economics, then this oil has provided Sudan with a golden opportunity to launch a serious development effort. Whether they utilize this opportunity remains to be seen, since a human rights disaster has apparently unfolded in the province of Darfur.

One of the most notable things here is the relatively late date on which the exploitation of Sudan oil commenced. There is a light panic spreading throughout the oil importing world as a result of fears as to the future availability of this commodity, and the price rises that have resulted have sent oil companies scurrying to places that they previously ignored. Twenty-five years ago I was told that the east coast of Africa was more favorably regarded than the west coast; however, eventually the east coast was dropped from the plans of the oil majors. Now some of the world's largest companies are exploring for oil and gas from Kenya and Tanzania down to Mozambique, and there is even talk of offshore East Africa becoming the next North Sea.

We certainly can hope that this is not wishful thinking, because in many parts of Africa onshore oil could turn out to be as big a bone of contention as illegal liquor was in the United States during Prohibition, although many times as deadly. An example of what I am talking about here is the Niger Delta of Nigeria, where well-armed clans might eventually be able to severely damage oil production.

According to Ms Hoyos, the ostensible odds are one to five against making a "big discovery", but one of the reasons for the tempo at which drilling is taking place in that part of Africa is that only a very small fraction of the wells that have been drilled in Africa were drilled in east Africa. This approach may sound right to some people, but in truth logic of this sort is basically meaningless where oil is concerned.

If the availability of oil was an uncomplicated function of the availability of explorable territory, South Africa would be even better situated than they are at present. That large country may have a very small amount of gas, and it possesses huge coal deposits, but intensive onshore and offshore exploration over many years, assisted by world-class technology, has failed to discover any oil.

As has been clear since the Second World War, the full spectrum of refined hydrocarbon products can be produced from synthetic oil derived from, e.g., coal. These products include aviation and motor fuel, diesel and heating oil, etc. The products produced in Germany during WWII from synthetic oil employing the Fischer–Tropsch process were inferior to the "real thing" in several respects, but this technology was eventually upgraded in South Africa by Sasol, the largest producer in the world of synthetic fuel (having a coal or gas base).

A Sasol gas-to-liquids plant is about to open in Kuwait, and other gas-to-liquids operations sponsored by that firm have been proposed for Nigeria, Iran, Algeria, and Australia. Coal-to-liquids processes are of particular interest in Australia, China, and the United States. A problem here might be the greenhouse gas emissions associated with this procedure; however, claims have been advanced that this shortcoming can eventually be remedied at an acceptable cost.

8. Some Conclusions

According to Professor Vaclav Smil (2002), "Most discussions of the earth's energy resources and their use by modern societies betray a widespread lack of scientific literacy and abound in misinformation, biases, and proffers of dubious solutions driven by various special-interest agendas".

Unfortunately, however, this magnificently perceptive observation is blemished by that scholar calling oil pessimists "Cassandras", and in the course of his presentation making heavy weather of such things as the latest evaluation of global reserves by the United States Geological Survey (USGS), which estimates that the amount of *undiscovered* conventional oil is actually 20% higher than that agency's previous assessment. (As the reader hopefully recalls, in Greek mythology, Cassandra, the daughter of Priam, actually possessed the gift of prophecy, but it was her fate never to be believed. For some strange reason, her name has come to mean someone who predicts misfortune.) There is also a cheerful reference to the value of the unconventional oil that is "locked" in tar sands and oil shales, and it is duly noted that these resources are already being exploited in Canada and Venezuela.

The last observation immediately convinced this humble teacher of economics and finance that, in one sense or another, Mr Smil has knowingly or unknowningly latched on to one of those very special agendas that he deplores, because anyone with his extensive background in energy matters should know by this late date that if we have to depend on unconventional resources to keep the oil wolf away from the door, then somebody is running the risk of being in deep trouble before the end of the present decade. And, incidentally, by "oil shales" he probably means heavy oil, although for the purposes of the present discussion, neither heavy oil nor shale — and *especially* shale — will be capable of coming close to replacing conventional (crude) oil as a viable energy alternative for a very long time. Their present "exploitation" hardly deserves to be called trivial.

It would be nice to think that the oil market is so easy to understand that our political masters understand it perfectly; however, this is far from the case. In reality they are trusting to luck to get them through a world in which the sudden absence of a very small percentage of oil production is quite sufficient to ruin the economic prospects of millions of people.

The government of Saudi Arabia has more or less announced that they plan to raise sustainable oil production to 12 mb/d as a prelude to later raising, i.e., to 15 mb/d. I consider 15 mb/d to be completely out of the question, which among other things means that production estimates for 2030 by the IEA and the US Department of Energy are difficult — or impossible — to accept. Of course, it may happen that (ex-post) they are right on the mark; however, turning once again at the work of John von

Neumann and Oscar Morgenstern, it make no difference at the present time what they are. In the light of evidence that is presently available, the correct procedure is to ignore those IEA and USDE estimates and to do everything possible to reduce the growth in consumption of oil as much as possible. According to the economics and finance that I teach, this would improve things for everyone — to include the oil exporting countries — because a reduction in consumption growth need not mean a reduction in price, and what income is lost could be regained from a larger production of oil products.

And things may turn out this way. Bill Farren-Price, deputy editor of the influential Middle East Economic Survey, recently noted that Algeria has now achieved a satisfactory level of oil revenue, and "the emphasis must now be on conservation". The same is probably true for most of the Middle East oil suppliers and, moreover, they know it. As pointed out in this chapter, Saudi Arabia has known this for decades, and now they are in position to do something about it.

Key Concepts

a beautiful myth	real price
advanced seismic technology	scarcity rent (royalty)
Cassandra	South African oil
"chestnuts"	spare production capacity
energy fund	surge capacity
gas and oil supply "blackmail"	tar sands
long dated futures	upstream (vs downstream)
nominal price	wealth effect
oil production profile	yield curve

Questions for Discussion

1. Comment on the IEA forecast of 121 mb/d of oil in 2030.
2. What do researchers like Douglas Reynolds and Maureen Crandall have to say about oil? What about Herman Franssen?
3. Why should the scarcity rent (or royalty) on Saudi Arabian oil be larger than that on Danish or Norwegian oil?

4. Do you have any thoughts about using long dated futures to hedge against
   a rise or fall in the oil price? If not, keep this question in mind when you
   come to Chapter 8 in this book.
5. What was Cassandra's problem?
6. Why would the executives of certain large oil producers depart from the
   truth in discussing their oil production plans, and their beliefs about the
   future oil price?
7. Discuss the prospects for petrochemicals and refined products for the
   major Middle East oil producers.

Bibliography

Aleklett, Kjell (2002). "Vakna – oljan sinar!" *Svenska Dagbladet*, 5 Augusti.

Banks, Ferdinand E. (2000). *Energy Economics: A Modern Introduction*. Boston/Dordrecht/London: Kluwer Academic.

—— (1980). *The Political Economy of Oil*. Lexington MA: D.C. Heath & Company.

Boussena, Sadek and Catherine Locatelli (2005). "Towards a more coherent oil policy in Russia". *OPEC Review*, 29(2): 85–105.

Crandall, Maureen (2005). "Realism on Caspian Energy: over-hyped and under-risked". *IAEE Newsletter* (Second Quarter).

De Zardain, Paul (2005)."The Barents Sea: strategic options for oil exports to Russia's Northwest". *IAEE Newsletter* (Third Quarter).

Duffin, Murray (2004). "The energy challenge 2004 — petroleum". *EnergyPulse* (www.energypulse.net).

Hoyos, Carola (2004). "Tough choices for oil companies in the quest to head off a global capacity crunch". *The Financial Times*, 22 September.

Khadduri, W. (2004). "The Iraqi oil industry: a look ahead". *Geopolitics of Energy*, December.

Kiely, J. (1980). "World energy in the 21st century". The Fourth Wilson Campbell Memorial Lecture.

Kubursi, A.A. (1985). "Industrialisation in the Arab States of the Gulf". In Tim Niblock and Richard Lawless (eds.), *Prospects for the World Oil Economy*. London, Sydney, and New Hampshire: Croom Helm.

Landrot, Antoine (2002). "Les Russes: rois du petrole". *Le Nouvel Economiste*, 5 Avril.

Lee, Julian (2006). "Has Russia's oil production growth come to an end?" *Geopolitics of Energy*, January.

Pashley, C. (1999). "Crude oil price volatility". *PetroMin*, February.

Pauwels, J.P. and C. Swartenbroekx (2002). "La politique pétroliére Russe: entre le G8 et l'Arabie Saoudite". *Revue de l'Energie*, numero 537, June.

Reynolds, Douglas R. (2005). "The economics of oil definitions". *OPEC Review*, 29(1): 51–73.

—— (2000). "The case for conserving oil resources: the fundamentals of supply and demand". *OPEC Review*, 24(2): 71–86.

Salameh, M.G. (2004). *Over a Barrel*. Beirut: Joseph D. Raidy.

Samuelson, R.J. (2004). "The dawn of a new oil era?" *Newsweek*, 4 April.

Sarkis, N. (2003). "Les prévisions et les fictions". *Medenergie*, No. 5.

Smil, Vaclav (2002). "Energy resources and uses". *Current History*, March: 126–132.

Store, Jonas Gahe (2006). "Ett hav av möjligheter". *Svenska Dagbladet*, April.

Tempest, Paul (1996). "Defining and overcoming risk — some global and Middle East factors". *IAEE Newsletter* (Spring).

United States Government Printing Office (1979). "The future of Saudi Arabian oil production". 96th Congress, 1st Session.

CHAPTER 4

AN INTRODUCTION TO NATURAL GAS ECONOMICS

This chapter is an up-to-date, but only moderately technical survey of the natural gas market. Supply, demand, and pricing are discussed, and in the light of the electric deregulation experiment in California, where the expression "dangerous failure" has been repeatedly used to describe the extensive losses suffered by final consumers and utilities (or retailers), there are some unfriendly comments on the deregulation of natural gas. Some microeconomics of the natural gas market are presented at a more elementary level than in my previous energy economics textbook (2000), or my book *The Political Economy of Natural Gas* (1987), and I make an attempt to avoid bringing the misleading Hotelling model (of exhaustible resources) into the exposition.

I am also anxious to leave the impression that, in the long run, natural gas is unlikely to replace nuclear energy in electric power generation. For example, the global production of natural gas could peak in 20 or 30 years, while nuclear facilities (with a "life" of more than 60 years) are unlikely to experience any shortage of fuels in the foreseeable future. In 2006 a large gas discovery in the South China Sea was thought to be the largest offshore gas discovery ever made in China, or about fifteen billion cubic feet ($= 15\,\text{Gcf} = 15\,\text{Gft}^3$). But when compared to the Shtokman field in Russia, which is 20 times as large, or the North Field/South Pars in Iran, which is 200 times as large, it is difficult to become enthusiastic. It is also far from encouraging to realize that world gas consumption is now accelerating.

Finally, there are sections dealing with the very important subject of Russian gas and some comments on risk management. The latter topic however is considered at a much greater length in the chapter called "Energy and Money", which can be read at any time.

Natural gas has not been adequately treated in the economics literature. Many misunderstandings about the characteristics and future of this valuable resource have not been properly addressed, largely due to the inability of some academics to distinguish between the important and the trivial (and this, incidentally, was one of the more useful observations of John Nash that was *not* featured in the Hollywood travesty *"A Beautiful Mind"*) . For example, the failures of electric deregulation have not been adequately outlined, and as a result a deregulation of gas and electricity has commenced in the European Union (EU) that could be bad news for most consumers and producers — most, but definitely not all, since the deregulation of these items in Europe (and probably elsewhere) was promoted by and designed to benefit a small group of market actors (e.g., Enron) as well as unenlightened politicians and civil servants. I am happy to report, however, that some spectacular disappointments have been experienced by this select group of self-appointed winners.

Earlier versions of this chapter did not contain any algebra, which failed to please seminar participants in various countries, and so this oversight has been partially remedied. At the same time the algebra has been kept to a minimum, and has been placed so that individuals who are not impressed by simple equations can ignore them. After all, on 18 March 2006 Sir Digby Jones said that the United Kingdom was as close as that country could possibly be to a "natural gas emergency", and it would be counterproductive to approach that kind of situation with the help of equations: common sense is more appropriate.

Just about everything in the chapter is self-explanatory, however it might be useful if readers review the information on units (i.e., dimensions) in the first chapter.

1. Introduction

The chapter on natural gas is the longest in my previous energy economics textbook for a very simple reason: natural gas has become the energy medium of choice for many governments and environmental groups throughout the world. For example, in one of the most coal intensive of all countries, India, the growth rate of gas consumption during the last decade has been about four times that of coal, and the only thing that interrupted the continuation of this trend were some spectacular doubts about the capabilities of the Enron Corporation to help supply the next large increment of gas. In California, new power generation capacity has been almost entirely gas-based; while in China the intention is for gas to supply about 8% of energy needs by 2010, and perhaps more later on. In that country, future projects include a 4000 km gas pipeline from the west of the country to Shanghai (the West–East Pipeline), an increased utilization of pipeline-transported Russian gas and oil, and the provision of enough liquefied natural gas (LNG) import facilities to make China this decade's fastest growing LNG market. In fact, an Australian consortium recently signed a contract involving 25 billion Australian dollars (= A$25 bn) to supply LNG to China from Australia's offshore North West Shelf gas fields, and it is believed that British Petroleum (BP) will eventually provide a great deal of gas to Fujian province (in China) from its proposed Tangguh project in Indonesia.

But on the other hand, as economists are always saying, the Chinese may end up constructing as much new nuclear capacity as is planned for the entire rest of the world. They know, even if their competitors in world markets do not, the kind of advantage provided by plentiful low cost electricity. (They will also probably construct a large number of coal-based installations. Exactly how clean this coal will turn out to be is not certain, however from an environmental point of view this is not something to look forward to.)

Japan has joined in the movement to gas by striking an extremely large natural gas deal with Iran and Qatar. The amount of money involved is about $2.7 bn. According to a Japanese minister of economics, trade, and industry, "In comparison with oil and coal, natural gas is an advantageous energy, generating less carbon dioxide". He had also come to the conclusion that, unlike oil, very large deposits of natural gas can be found in many parts of the world. This, of course, is very interesting, although there is a considerable likelihood that for Japan, nuclear energy will be preferred when the political (and technological) situation allows. Certainly, when examining the figures for the percentage of electric generating capacity that will be gas fired in that country, there is no indication of a far-ranging resort to gas.

The International Energy Agency (IEA) has come to the conclusion that natural gas resources are abundant, and can easily meet the massive ongoing shift to gas, however whether this is an unambiguously wise choice for all countries remains to be seen. For instance, it should not be overlooked that in late 2000 in the United States — which together with Canada was consuming close to 25 trillion cubic feet of gas a year (= 25 Tcf/y) — the price of gas at the wellhead (i.e., the production source) suddenly spiked to a completely unexpected 5.15 dollars per million BTU (= $5.15/mBtu) as compared to $1.75/mBtu a year earlier, and there were occasions when, on the New York Mercantile Exchange (NYMEX), gas prices were almost double this amount. Remember too that the share of transportation in total supply costs will increase as supply chains lengthen, which will necessitate huge investment costs for production facilities and infrastructure in order to transport gas to market. Even so, the IEA apparently continues to believe that the transport of natural gas (by pipeline and ship) is more cost-effective than building long-distance electric transmission lines, however this is another case in which the IEA is probably drastically wrong where a few regions are concerned. In North America, for example, the opinions of that organization on most energy matters strike this humble observer as completely unrealistic.

Although drilling in the United States and Canada now averages a very healthy 25,000 new wells a year, there has not been any significant increases in the supply of gas in these two very energy-intensive countries, while in some of these new wells, decline rates (which will be explained once again just below) that are as high as 40% have been experienced in the first year of production. One way of approaching this situation is to take note of the (monetary) yields on gas investments outside North America. On average they seem to be about 25% higher than in North America, and energy companies have reacted in the traditional manner: they have made it clear that they are not going to invest billions of dollars in a "mature" gas producing basin (i.e., region) such as North America in order to sell at bargain-basement prices whatever gas that might be obtained. This kind of attitude led to the US Senate voting in favor of a plan to offer tax incentives to producers of Arctic gas if gas prices drop below $3.25 per thousand cubic feet (≈ $3.25/mBtu), while if the price of this gas rises above $4.85/mBtu, then producers would have to repay any tax credits that they may have received. As of the present date, producers are not tempted by these incentives, and it is very unlikely that such will ever be the case again. Very likely they have come to realize that if gas consumption in North America is really going to increase as much as is being forecast, then they do not have to enter into arrangements in which they have to repay anything.

As things stand at present on the energy front, it seems very likely that some sort of pipeline must be built to carry gas from Northern Canada or Alaska to the United States. A (mostly underground) pipeline to carry gas 3640 miles from the North Slope of Alaska to the US Midwest would be a huge construction project. It has been estimated that it would require up to 6 million tons of steel, 236 large bulldozers, a motor pool of 1600 trucks and buses, etc. The construction time has been estimated to be three years, and total cost between 20 and 22 billion dollars, however cost overruns are not only likely but certain for this kind of venture. Gas serves 6 out of 10 American households, or roughly 62 million homes. Expectations are that at plateau production this pipeline could supply 10% of US gas requirements, but the length of this plateau might cause some problem: the North Slope has 36 trillion cubic feet ($= 36\,\text{Tcf}$) of proved reserves now, but it has been suggested that at least 53 Tcf would be necessary to make this project viable. Of course, it might be possible to make Canadian reserves a part of this scheme.

This very important matter of decline rates will be briefly scrutinized again, and readers with a serious interest in the present topic should make sure that they understand it. *The decline rate, or natural decline (or natural depletion) rate, is the fall in the production capacity of a gas (or oil) deposit (or field or even well) that is mostly caused by past and present production. Clearly, a decline in deposit pressure is a key factor here.* Accordingly, in the case of, e.g., Canada, whose estimated gas potential is to a large extent in the form of shallow "pools", high decline rates can be observed very early in the exploitation of these deposits. One of the conclusions that we can draw from this phenomenon is that the "life" of global gas (or oil) reserves, or the reserves in a particular region, as expressed in the media or by amateur energy economists using the simple ratio of reserves to output — the reserve–production (R/q) ratio — is essentially meaningless from a scientific point of view. Instead, as emphasized earlier, we need to think in terms of a *critical* reserve/production ratio for a deposit, since this tells us something about the rate at which the deposit can be depleted if *ultimate* production from that deposit is such that total profits are maximized. Put another way, if production in a given period is carried to a point where the actual R/q ratio is lower than this critical reserve/production ratio, there will be a significant reduction in the (economical) ultimate resource recovery. (As was noted in Chapter 2, the R/q ratio also ties in with the decline rate and reservoir pressure, though not in an easily derivable manner.)

Although various observers are making heavy weather of the fact that the ratio of proved gas reserves to production now stands at 60:1, for both geological and economic reasons, world gas production could peak in around 20 years. According to scenarios developed by the global business environment department of Shell in 2002, "gas resource uncertainty is significant". The problem, according to Shell and various other observers, is whether "there can be timely development of the infrastructure to transport remote gas economically".

The world's largest gas field — North Dome in Iran — is at present only producing 10% of its intended plateau production. Production from several other giant fields in the world also appear to be on hold, apparently waiting to sign up customers on what the owners of these fields consider favorable terms. The world's largest oil field, Ghawar, still apparently contains 86 billion barrels of oil ($= 86\,\mathrm{Gb}$), while in energy equivalent terms, North Dome contains $233\,\mathrm{Gb}$. Both in quantitative terms and taking into consideration the resources in other large fields, North Dome is in a class by itself.

An interesting situation here is that of the top gas fields, only about half possess a sufficient estimate of their reserves, and are thus qualified to become objects of optimal (i.e., large-scale) investments. The problem is that without an adequate production history, there is no empirical basis for estimating certain crucial production criteria (e.g., the decline curve), which in turn means that a satisfactory estimate of the value of the asset is lacking. Needless to say, this is especially true for offshore deposits. In considering the situation in the Barents Sea, north of Norway and Russia, rewards might turn out to be enormous, but so are risks, and it has become impossible to conceal this disadvantage from potential investors. As a result, most of them are not in the mood to finance new prospects without the kind of price guarantees that deregulation efforts by the European Union (EU) are designed to exclude.

The average (global) price of gas has increased dramatically over the past year, but the record amount of drilling that is taking place in, e.g., the United States and Canada, has not markedly increased availability in North America. In fact, the rapid expansion of the liquefied natural gas (LNG) sector indicates the lack of reality in earlier forecasts that somehow pictured the gas price falling to the vicinity of $2.00–2.50/mBtu: LNG is a comparatively expensive commodity because of the huge investments that it requires, and it is difficult to imagine a situation in which profit maximizing gas suppliers would be generous enough to sign contracts again that specify prices anywhere near this range. One of the things that should be noted here is the considerable amount of energy that is used (i.e., consumed) in the liquefaction and deliquefaction activities, which may result in the efficiency of this process being less than 80%.

Before continuing it needs to be noted again that Btu means British thermal units, and has to do with the energy (or heat) content of a fuel. Dimensionally we are taking $1\,mBtu \approx 1000$ cubic feet of gas $= 1000\,ft^3 = 28$ cubic meters, and thus a price in dollars per thousand cubic feet can be immediately translated to dollars per million Btu. (The actual figure though is $1\,ft^3 = 1035\,Btu$, instead of $1\,ft^3 = 1000\,Btu$.) Since the average barrel (b) of oil contains 5,800,000 Btu, then in terms of heating value the price mentioned above of $5.15/mBtu is the (oil) equivalent of $5.15 \times 5.8 \approx \$29/b$. At the present time, this would be considered a low price, even if gas is *not* as flexible a resource as oil. This is one of the reasons why fairly expensive investments in fuel-switching capacity have once again become attractive for producers of petrochemicals and other energy-intensive activities. (Fuel-switching means having the kind of physical capacity available that will permit the use of several different varieties of inputs: e.g., gas, oil, and coal.) Although it was not generally discussed outside of executive suites in the United States, gas that was priced in the range $4–5/mBtu was regarded as very bad news by some industrial purchasers. Now, with the price well above that level, the directors of many gas-intensive industries are thinking about saying goodbye to North America.

Large amounts of natural gas have been produced for decades, and its qualities are known and appreciated by both gas consumers and energy professionals. Pipelines can distribute natural gas with almost the same efficiency and flexibility as national and local grids can distribute electricity, and in many countries gas and electricity are regarded as competitors in certain usages. In addition, unlike solid fuels (but like oil), gas can be delivered at a precise rate to households and industries. Natural gas in the form of LNG can be transported in huge amounts between continents by specially designed ships, although often at a considerably higher cost (per-unit of energy) than oil; and according to Bahgat (2001), about one-quarter of internationally traded gas takes the form of LNG. Once again I would like to point out that the rapid expansion of the LNG trade that is inevitable could not take place if market "insiders" did not expect a much higher average price for *all* gas in the coming years.

A particularly vexing problem is that we are not really sure of the availability of gas to those regions where consumption is high, and still growing rapidly, although it has been claimed that gas' share of global primary energy consumption could increase to an extent that in 2020 it reaches almost 30%. For example, on a number of occasions in 2000, several prestigious financial analysts informed their clients in the United States that they should be careful about putting their money into goods, services, and financial assets that could be negatively influenced by increases in the price of natural gas; and in June 2001, the chief of the Dallas (Texas) Federal Reserve Bank, Robert McTeer, stated that the rise in gas prices in the United States was a greater threat to the economy than the relatively high and unstable oil price because of the rapidly expanding use of gas in electricity generation. One of the reasons that the rise in gas prices was so annoying was because, to a certain extent, it could undermine various highly advertised advantages that were supposed to result from the high combustion efficiencies and relatively favorable environmental qualities that characterize gas-burning, combined-cycle technologies. Furthermore, the theory that any rise in US prices due to a shortage of domestic supplies could eventually be reversed by drawing on the supposedly plentiful gas reserves of Canada and Mexico turned out to be considerably less than accurate. In January 2001, the price of a great deal of Mexican gas was almost double that in the United States (which had unpleasant consequences for several important Mexican industries), and although there was excess pipeline capacity from Western Canada for at least a year, there was no significant production growth in that region during that period, nor exports of gas to the United States.

As I emphasized at great length in my previous energy economics textbook, up-to-date surveys are invaluable because in economics, unlike, e.g., engineering, it does not always pay to rely too heavily on wisdom derived from the mainstream technical literature. For example, in their book *The Emerging New Order in Natural Gas*, DeVany and Walls (1995) say that "Because power pools, wheeling, and energy trading have a long history in the electricity industry, the necessary institutions and practices are in place for a smoother transition to markets than natural gas had".

This is not a correct statement! In many parts of the world, what these authors call "the transition to markets" has been anything but smooth for electricity *or* gas. Ironically, in California, the legislator who sponsored electricity deregulation wasted no time in "deserting" to the anti-deregulation forces when, on a number of occasions, the (wholesale) price of electricity exploded upward, and there was a vigorous pressure originating with deregulation enthusiasts to increase the retail price. (The *wholesale* price is the price paid by distributors to generators, while the price at which electricity is sold by distributors to final consumers (e.g., households) is the *retail* price.) Perhaps the most important thing to keep in mind when reading the remainder of this book is that in both gas and electricity markets, the increase in uncertainty caused by emphasizing *spot* markets as opposed to traditional long-term arrangements will likely lead to a socially undesirable decrease in physical investment (that *cannot* be compensated for by a more extensive resort to mergers and acquisitions by firms). *Ceteris paribus*, this decrease could lead to considerably higher energy prices in the future, as well as greater price instability.

In the case of the California electric sector, the absence of sufficient generating capacity has been singled out by both the former governor (Gray Davis) and the international business press as the key contributor to a state of affairs that advocates of deregulation claimed would be impossible once deregulation began. With regard to both electricity and gas, the observed decrease in physical investment means that a transition from regulated monopoly to unregulated oligopoly is going to be a major source of irritation for many businesses and households. We have a good example here in the activities of the El Paso Pipeline Company, the biggest pipeline enterprise in North America. Together with two of their affiliates they have been accused of reducing the supply of natural gas to California for 121 days in order to raise prices. In addition to the $9 b that the California government wanted from electric generators (who, they say, have charged "unjust and unreasonable wholesale electricity prices"), they have gone to court and asked for a refund of $3.6 bn from gas suppliers. Although it appears that various judges agree that some compensation is due, it may cause potential investors in new gas and electric projects to look for a less uncertain placement for their money. According to one observer, the state of California may have to do its own construction if it wants to keep the lights burning during those long, sensual California nights.

As the then head of British Gas (Robert Evans) said a decade ago, if gas firms are broken up in the manner described by mainstream deregulators, they may not be able to gain access to the resources needed to restructure into efficient organizations, and this is particularly true if long-term contractual pricing is abandoned or marginalized. He then gratuitously added that the "half-baked fracturing" of companies to bring about competition was not likely to be successful. Although not often discussed, I feel reasonably certain that Mr Evans was directing his remarks at the UK gas "regulator" (OFGAS), which together with the Office of Fair Trading (OFT) and the Monopolies and Mergers Commission (MMC) had embarked on a crusade to increase competition in the contract gas market. Exactly how they intended to go about this curious project when there is a disquieting shortage of energy economists on the UK scene has never been explained, however on the basis of an important paper by Dixon and Easaw (1999), it appeared that what economics knowledge is available is characterized by serious flaws.

In the United States, approximately 16% of electric generators use gas at the present time (and about 50% coal), but according to *Forbes* (13 November 2000), 88% of 250 "new" power plants were scheduled to be gas-fueled. Taking into consideration what has happened with gas prices, 88% is almost certainly too high an estimate, but even so it seemed certain to me that, in these circumstances, gas prices had to find a higher equilibrium.

2. Simple Geology and Economics

Natural gas from a well consists of methane (on the average 85%), heavier hydrocarbons collectively known as natural gas liquids (NGL, and composed of ethane, propane, butane, pentane, and some heavier fractions), water, carbon dioxide (CO_2), nitrogen, and some other hydrocarbons. (And, note here, that gas is *not* free of CO_2. It merely has less than oil and coal.) Before dry natural gas can be distributed to consumers, some undesirable components must be removed and, by decreasing the share of heavier hydrocarbons, a uniform quality is attained.

The last-mentioned operation takes place either at or near the gas well itself or in special installations farther away. It is at this point that the NGL can be separated out. (NGL should not be confused with LNG, which to a considerable extent consists of methane and ethane.) The most important constituents of NGL are butane and propane, and in liquid form these are called liquefied petroleum gas (LPG). In many countries, LPG is sold under the name gasol or bottled gas, and in Australia at the present time the government wants an increased use of LPG.

Because of its importance, LNG will be taken up later in this chapter, but a few words are appropriate at the present time, because the demand for energy in the world has meant an enormous boost in the demand for LNG. The first thing to stress is that the demand for natural gas is, for the most part, very far away from where the gas is obtained. For instance, China and India have become very large consumers of energy, and their demand for gas is such that it is more economical to satisfy this demand by a resort to LNG as compared to pipeline gas. Gas is "frozen" in the country of origin, and transported on very expensive and technologically sophisticated LNG carriers to terminals in or near consuming countries where it is re-gassed. For instance, gas originating in Russia might be shipped to Mexico (i.e., Lower California), and from there transported by pipeline to the United States. At the present time Indonesia, Algeria, Malaysia, Nigeria, and Australia are the world's largest producers of LNG, but in the long run it is expected that the "Big Five" will be Qatar, Nigeria, Indonesia, Russia, and Iran.

Figure 4.1 sums up the previous discussion, and should be given careful attention.

The principal disadvantages of gas are probably associated with the huge investments required to produce, process, and transport this resource. As a result, long-term commitments — sometimes involving contracts with a running time of more than 20 years — are essential before the exploitation of

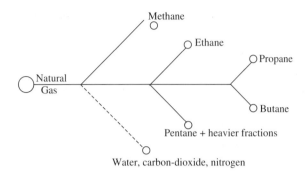

Liquified at   Definitions
Butane (normal)-   0.5°C   NGL: Natural gas liquids
Butane (Iso) - 12.0°C   LPG: Liquified petroleum
Propane - 42.0°C   LNG: Liquified natural gas
Ethane - 88.0°C   SNG: Synthetic (substitute) natural gas
Methane - 161.0°C

Note: Natural gas = methane + NGL + (water, nitrogen, CO2).

NGL = ethane + LPG + (pentane and heavier fractions).

LPG = propane + butane + mixtures of propane and butane

Figure 4.1.   Natural Gas Components

even rich gas fields can commence. This observation is especially true when projects involving LNG are under consideration. The total capital costs for a fairly large LNG project (involving liquefaction facilities, tankers, terminals at both ends of the chain, and possibly considerable pipeline capacity leading away from the import terminal) could easily reach 15 to 20 billion US dollars, which indicates that the cost of transporting gas by ship is much higher than transporting oil by ship.

At this point we can identify four components of a mature natural gas industry. These are production, transmission (or transportation), storage, and distribution, where the distribution networks are developed around the main transmission line. For instance, after being collected from wells in a gas field in Siberia, gas might be transported in a very large (transmission) pipeline to some sort of terminal or hub (with storage) in Germany, where eventually it is transferred to smaller pipelines, and then distributed to final consumers — e.g., firms and households — who use the gas to generate electricity, to heat water and "space", and for cooking. Here the Russians act as wholesalers, and the German distributors as retailers. Under the "old" system these four components could be integrated or independent, but under deregulation the intention is to make them as independent as possible, with sales being made as much as possible on a spot rather than a long-term basis, and with as much "free marketing" as possible being practiced. (For example, pipelines could not refuse business in order to give one customer an advantage over another.) What about the risk that this involves? In theory this would be handled by some sort of derivatives market — ideally the buying and selling of "futures contracts" in an auction type market (such as NYMEX), with all prices visible, and enough liquidity (i.e., buying and selling) to dampen price volatility. This was also the ambition with the electric market in California, and what happened was that spot transactions were soon reduced to a minimum, although long before that point was reached, hedging the price with futures contracts was recognized as a lost cause. In fact, as I predicted in a lecture in Hong Kong, NYMEX delisted all its electric contracts and at least one of its natural gas contracts. (You can also examine my non-technical paper *"Futures markets that may be without a future"* (2000).) As an aside, at least one prominent business person has noted that physical gas cannot always be replaced by "paper" gas — i.e., gas on a futures contract.

The key relationship in all this is between retailers and wholesalers. There are a number of possible arrangements, but typically a retailer might contract for a large increment of gas to be delivered on a monthly basis. This particular increment would be an amount *estimated* by the retailer as the quantity that would likely be purchased by the households and businesses with whom he has some contact. Since it is highly unlikely that this estimate would be free of error, some kind of provision would have to be made for *swing gas*. The amount and price for this relatively small "slice" could conceivably be set every morning for gas to be delivered the following day. Finally, a still smaller component would be designated *spot gas*, which is gas that, e.g., is bought in the morning for delivery later the same day. Quite naturally, fanatic deregulation buffs would like to see everything bought on a spot basis, and in California — at the beginning of its deregulation adventure — it was proposed that long-term transactions should be prohibited by law. Eventually this kind of irrational thinking had to be discarded, particularly when retailers found themselves in debt to the tune of billions of dollars to wholesalers that the governor of California chose to give the quaint designation of "out-of-the-state criminals".

As explained in my previous energy economics textbook, a well-known practice consists of the indexing of the gas price to the price of oil. German natural gas import prices are often tied to the price of gas oil and heavy fuel oil in that country. German import contracts also exhibit take-or-pay clauses that, according to Morten Frisch (1997), cover 90% of the contracted amount. At the same time though, buyers have the right to ask for 110% of the contracted amount at agreed upon prices. This particular arrangement would be called a "90/110" contract.

3. Supply and Demand

According to a recent publication of the IEA, the global natural gas demand (and supply) is expected to grow at an average annual rate of 2.6% in the period 1995–2020. By way of comparison, oil demand growth should hover around the 1.5%/year ($= 1.5\%/y$) mark over the same period. Much of this growth in gas demand has been due to a steady upward trend in fossil fuel switching (e.g., from coal to gas) in the residential, commercial, public, and industrial sectors, that is caused by the attractiveness of combined-cycle power generation technology, and the supposedly favorable environmental qualities of gas. It should not be forgotten, however, that combined-cycle coal-burning equipment is also available, and in the very long run, it should not be expected that gas will push coal out of the picture: there is simply too much coal available, and in a world in which population is still expanding, the energy in this coal cannot be ignored.

Let us look at this situation in a slightly more dramatic light. No reputable economist would attempt to predict the source and price of gas in 2020, nor for that matter a few years earlier or later; but there is not a high probability that the real (i.e., the inflation-adjusted) price of coal at that time will be much higher than it is when you read this paper. As a result, it may well happen that there is going to be an enormous temptation to use very large quantities of coal, regardless of environmental considerations. Of course, by that time technological advances might have made it possible to burn coal in an environmentally acceptable manner, though at a higher cost. There are claims that the gasification of coal using the most up-to-date techniques will already provide us with a means for solving the environmental problems associated with coal.

As mentioned earlier, at the present time gas accounts for about 22% of global primary and secondary energy consumption, where primary energy means energy obtained from the *direct* burning of coal, gas, oil, etc., as well as electricity having a hydro or nuclear origin. (Electricity obtained from, e.g., burning gas is a secondary energy source.) When I was writing my book on natural gas, every effort was being made to reduce the employment of natural gas in power generation, but what has happened since then is that gas has been widely proclaimed as the fuel of the future, and the increase in the use of gas to generate electricity has been forecast by the IEA to eventually attain (on the average) the relatively high level of 4.5%/y. In the United Kingdom, gas-fueled power stations account for about 30% of all generation, while 10 years ago this kind of installation supplied something in the neighborhood of 1%.

Since the so-called "life" ($= R/q$) of worldwide gas reserves is approximately 60 years at the present time, it seems unlikely that there will be a shortage of gas in the next 20 years or so — where "shortage" here means that (for economic and/or technical reasons) world gas production cannot continue to expand; but as pointed out by Dispenza (1995) and Commichau (1994), a difficulty could be raised by the geographical distribution of gas resources relative to the markets in which there is a large and growing demand for gas. There will be an increasing call on the vast resources of the Middle East — Iran, Qatar, Abu Dhabi, and Saudi Arabia — and very likely also Russia and Central Asia, and the expenditures associated with the production, transport, storing, and distribution of the anticipated quantities of "additional" gas will be enormous. Whether this call will be answered in a way commensurate with the wishes of consumers depends on a number of factors. As indicated above, several more or less inflexible "contractual" conditions guaranteeing the reception of and compensation for this gas will have to be established in order to initiate the large investments that are necessary to ensure that this gas flows at the most cost-efficient levels, which in turn would mean reasonable prices for final consumers. Personally, I suspect that a gas market with more "competition" on the demand side, but strong oligopolies on the supply side (as will be the case in, e.g., Europe) will not be an especially favorable arrangement for final consumers, however I am not certain that I have the knowledge, personality or vocabulary needed to convince the decision-makers that such is the case.

Although it is not easy to estimate supply and demand trends, there seems to be considerable confidence in the various estimates of gas reserves. The IEA lists total ultimate reserves of 11,448 trillion cubic feet ($= 11,448\,\text{Tcf}$), where ultimate reserves in this context are defined as cumulative production + remaining recoverable reserves + undiscovered reserves. The most important areas are East Europe and the Middle East, but it is interesting to note that while North America still possesses substantial reserves, the R/q ratio of that region has slumped to 8, and there is considerable pessimism about gas supply prospects. For reasons spelled out in my previous textbook, given the inflexibility of demand in that region, and the prospects for LNG trading, what happens in North America could greatly influence the gas price in every part of the world. The implication here once again is that the R/q ratio is a misleading guide in determining the long-term availability of a resource such as gas (or oil), and particularly when no attention is paid to the global distribution of that resource. Furthermore, the US Geological Service has gone to a great deal of trouble to estimate the amount of undiscovered gas, and what it comes down to is that the great hope that once existed that this undiscovered gas would surface in North America or the North Sea should be discarded for the time being.

Before changing the subject, it can be noted that BP-Amoco estimates that 13.3% of existing gas reserves are in the OECD (with most of these in North America), while 33.8% are in the Middle East and North Africa, 38.7% in the Former Soviet Union (FSU), and 18.4% in the rest of the world.

Since gas production in the OECD is almost flat at the present time, and expectations are that it will begin to decline in less than 15 years, the importance of imports cannot be overstressed. For Western Europe, pipeline supplies from the FSU are already essential, but over a longer time period, the Middle East is going to assume a vital importance. The IEA expects a major rise in the trading of LNG, which is not unthinkable, and also intimates that an LNG spot market will eventually be organized — which probably makes little or no sense. Also, according to the IEA, worldwide gas production is not expected to peak until well after 2020. There are many energy supply scenarios in which the year 2020 seems to have a special significance, and so it might be useful for interested observers to begin to consider what the world energy situation could be about that time, since if the output of gas is close to peaking, and oil production has already peaked, which seems increasingly likely, then much of the world could be vulnerable to severe macroeconomic shocks that might bring a series of very unappetizing political shocks in its wake.

As was pointed out earlier, there are many observers who have expressed an opinion that more attention should be paid on the markets for natural gas, since a too rapid price escalation in those markets could mean considerable macroeconomic distress.

4. Gas and Microeconomics

Perhaps the best way to begin this section is to reconsider a gas reservoir or field. Following confirmation of an adequate amount of gas, investments take place in drilling (and perhaps processing) equipment, as well as pro- duction platforms if the deposit is offshore. Pipelines and compressors (i.e., pumping equipment) are then put in place, and in time the gas will start flowing, gradually building up to a peak or "plateau". During the period of plateau production and afterward, costs are mostly for pipeline and com- pressor maintenance, as well as the gas that is used as the energy source for the compressors. Something that needs to be appreciated here is that in theo- retical work (in economics) the unit cost of gas should be taken as a *negative* function of the size of the deposit: very large deposits permit the optimal employment of pipelines and pumping equipment, which *ceteris paribus* reduces capital costs, and in my natural gas book I introduce the influence of (deposit) volume on the marginal cost of production. (At the same time, remember that output from wells can decline precipitously. According to *Forbes* 22 January 2001), in the Gulf of Mexico, which supplies 20% of US demand, output from some of the wells drilled in the 1990s is declining by 50%/y. In other words, every year 50% of the capacity existing at the beginning of the year is lost.) What this implies in, e.g., North America is that annually, for economic reasons having to do with current production and natural decline, billions of cubic feet of new supplies must be found just in order for existing reserve levels to be maintained, apart from the decrease in reserves that is due to current production.

The quantity of gas that is considered recoverable is the amount that can be directed from a reservoir into pipelines. (On the average, about 60% of the gas in reservoirs is recoverable, as compared to approximately 35% in oil deposit at the present time.) Some of this movement is made possible by the pressure difference between the gas reservoir (or "trap" as it is sometimes called) and the pipeline entrance, and in some cases it can happen that this pressure difference is large enough to "propel" the gas a considerable distance through the pipeline without the assistance of pumping equipment.

The usual arrangement, however, is for external energy (via compressors) to enter the transmission picture, with these compressors transferring energy from a motor to the gas that is to be transported. Since the main source of energy loss in pipelines is due to friction — i.e., "wall friction" — and this loss (in terms of the quantity being transported) is a decreasing function of pipe size, there is a trade-off between pipe size and compressor size: the greater the pipe diameter, the smaller the compressor capacity required to pump a given amount of gas a specific distance — although this relationship is nonlinear, and for economic reasons almost certainly breaks down after a certain point. As shown in my previous textbook, a production function of the form $F(q, X_1, X_2) = 0$ is usually specified to describe this concept, where q is output, and the Xs represent pipeline capacity and compressor capacity, respectively. Units can be chosen so that q is net of the gas consumed as fuel for the compressors, since this gas is an intermediate input. Pipe thicknesses can also be of importance for determining the optimal dimensions of the system, although it is not easy to introduce this item into an elementary economic analysis, nor is it essential, but a comprehensive production function would perhaps take note of reservoir dimensions and decline.

Next we should ask which of the inputs should be taken as the variable factor. According to Howard Chenery (1952), this function is taken by the compressors. His reasoning is that (ex-post) the pipe is an indivisible factor, and much more costly than pumping costs. Consequently, as in conventional microeconomic theory, this determines the size of the "plant". Rough empiricism would seem to support this logic. There is a 900 million (Australian) dollar pipeline taking gas almost 1000 km from Western Australia's Northwest Shelf to Perth, however there are only five compressor stations, each costing several million dollars. Another interesting example is the proposed Yamal pipeline project running from Siberia to Germany, with gas expected to flow at some point after 2010. Here, there would be three 56-inch ($= 56''$) pipelines running from Yamal to Torzhok, north of Moscow, and then two $56''$ pipelines from Torzhok to Frankfurt-am-Oder (on the Polish–German border). The interesting thing with this proposal is that although production at the Yamal end will be approximately 83 Gcm/y, about 10 Gcm/y will be consumed as compressor fuel. It might be conceivable then to think of compressor fuel as a variable factor in this discussion.

As in elementary production theory, adding compressors to the system — i.e., increasing the quantity of compression — will raise output (q), and it has happened that by adding enough compression (the variable factor), the maximum output has been raised by several times the initial (or planned) output. At the same time though we should understand that this procedure can entail a rising cost per unit of output obtained. Thus, at some point it will be economical to increase pipeline capacity rather than to add compression. Chenery refers simply to a duplication of the pipeline, however unfortunately this description is inadequate. In engineering, as opposed to economics, this particular activity is approached as a problem in *looping*.

By supercharging the existing compressors, and/or adding compressors, it can become economical to add parallel sections to the existing pipeline. Note that this does not strictly mean duplication, since the cost–output relationship turns on the amount of supercharging or additional compression, the diameter of the pipe used for looping, and the construction expenses associated with the looped section. An interesting looping exercise was carried out on the Roma–Brisbane pipeline in Southern Queensland (Australia). Sections of 16-inch pipe were laid parallel to the main 10.75-inch line, with a separation of 4–8 m. In this way capacity was doubled, although the price of the gas being delivered increased. Of course, this price increase was necessary in order to justify initiating this particular looping project.

In theory, output expansion via looping can mean constant, increasing, or decreasing unit costs. Without going too deeply into the matter, it should be noted that if there are increasing returns to scale in compression and transmission, which is likely over a wide range of outputs, then neo-classical economics suggests that optimal behavior calls for initiating (and in some cases completing) projects well ahead of the demand for new capacity. Among other things, if this is done it might be possible to avoid any (per unit) increasing costs associated with looping if it turns out that sizable increases in capacity are necessary at a later date.

If this is realistic, then why are we witnessing a tendency to resist building ahead of demand? The answer here is that before the arrival of deregulation, and in its early stages, if the demand for gas did not match expectations within a given time period, then pipeline firms in countries like the United States were allowed to increase their tariffs (or rates) to cover their costs — which also suggests that over a longer time horizon, if demand increases, then rates could be regulated down. But with deregulation, regardless of the specific arrangements (which vary from country to country), pipeline companies might find themselves in a position where they have to accept additional risk. In neo-classical theory — and the real world — more risk translates into less investment. (Real options theory can obtain the opposite result, but as far as I am concerned, this is the kind of situation where, when investment pertains to non-financial assets, real options theory is wrong.) Once again it is useful to be aware of what has happened in the electric sector, where it is clear that the volatility of prices is often a direct result of inadequate investment and, by the same token, inadequate investment is the result of the volatility of prices. What we have here is a "vicious circle".

An important topic that is considered in some detail in my previous textbook is third-party access — i.e., the right of other than designated producers and consumers to use a facility. In some situations, third-party access can be thought of as a substitute for new transmission, since it definitely improves the flexibility of some transactors by making it possible for them to avoid building expensive new pipelines, or increasing pipeline capacity by looping. This is clearly a good thing, as long as it is understood that third-party access can only substitute for new transmission up to a certain point (and that new players do not overly inconvenience existing enterprises). Beyond that point — e.g., as demand increases — inefficiencies might be introduced into a system that lead to such things as higher retail prices, higher volatilities, coordination problems, and a sharp decrease in the security of supply.

In practice it turns out that third-party access almost always reduces to "open access" or "common carriage". Common carriage requires the pipeline to provide capacity for all requests. If the pipeline is operating at full capacity, then users' volume should be reduced on a pro-rata basis until new capacity is available. As for open access, capacity is supplied on a first-come, first-served basis up to the full capacity of the pipeline. Interestingly enough though, by applying some principles from game theory, we find that the often used *postage-stamp* system of allocating costs for pipelines has extensive shortcomings. (A postage-stamp system is one in which users pay the same amount per unit of capacity, regardless of distances. A letter from Uppsala to Stockholm costs the same as a letter from Uppsala to the far Northern ski resort of Riksgränsen.)

A final observation about LNG might be useful. As I explained in my book on natural gas, and also in a lecture that I gave at Cambridge University dealing with the attempted boycott of Soviet gas by President Ronald Reagan, it should never be forgotten that the economics of natural gas projects are such that initiating and operating them at less than optimal scale are not to be recommended. I was particularly anxious to show that with Soviet pipeline gas available, a heavy resort by European buyers to LNG originating in West Africa or South America would necessitate paying a very large subsidy in both direct and indirect costs. As is usually the case, my honesty was not appreciated by the decision-makers, however we seem to be reaching a point on the energy front where it might be best for all concerned if our political masters and their experts do not underestimate the costs that are associated with allowing sentimentality to interfere with good business practices. In terms of the same amount of energy, the overland costs for gas are between three and five times greater than for oil, while for maritime transportation they can be much more. If we consider large gas using areas such as the United States and OECD Europe, local sources of gas are unlikely to be augmented by new discoveries or new technologies, and these regions seem destined to become more dependent on distant sources that, until recently, were not considered competitive.

Just now, Canada is expected to contribute 70% of North American production growth by 2010, and at one time it was believed that much of this will come from the Western Canada Sedimentary Basin (WCSB), which has been the most important production area in that country for the last 50 years; but most of the new supplies from this region originate in shallow pools of the type mentioned earlier. In these circumstances it might be a good idea to accept that Western Canada may be grossly overvalued in terms of its growth potential, and more attention will have to be paid to the Canadian Arctic and to offshore East Canada, where the cost structure for exploration and production is very different from what they have been in the WCSB.

I conclude this section by noting that one of the reasons for not going into detail where pipelines are concerned is that the reader should be familiar with a few basic concepts from thermodynamics or fluid mechanics, such as gas viscosity and compressibility, gas molecular weight, etc; however if we use the old academic economics trick of assuming these away, we can approach the determining of the diameter of a (transmission) pipeline by considering the following implicit relationships:

$$V = f(Q, D, P), \qquad (1)$$

$$F = g(D, V), \qquad (2)$$

$$\Delta P = h(F, L, Q, P, D). \qquad (3)$$

V is the gas velocity, Q is the gas flow rate, P is the operating pressure, D is the inside pipe diameter, F is the friction factor, ΔP is the pressure drop, and L is the length (of pipe between compressor stations). The big question is how are we going to use these expressions, and particularly the last, and the answer is that we must add the following condition: Maximum Allowable Pressure Drop ($= M$) must be greater than or equal to ΔP, or $M \geq \Delta P$. M is then specified on the basis of figures determined by optimal engineering conventions, and computer programs are available which allow us to obtain (via what amounts to trial-and-error procedures) the value of D required to transmit a given Q.

The algebraic approach to distribution (as opposed to transmission) is along the same lines as the above, although it is necessary to stress that pipe size is a function of the maximum daily demand, and compression plays little or no part in the analysis. As clarified by Jean-Thomas Bernard *et al.* (2002), the total estimated maximum daily demand is computed by adding estimated or contracted maximum daily demand over all consumer classes, taking into consideration — if possible — the response to natural gas rates. As usual, I prefer theory to empiricism in economics as well as finance, however their observation that in Quebec (Canada) the average annual load factor of approximately 35% is important: it suggests that the introduction of some innovative pricing might be able to greatly increase the efficiency of the system (by increasing the load factor), which should be reflected in reduced costs for producers and reduced prices for final consumers. (The *load factor* is usually defined as the ratio of the average output to the peak output for a given period, in this case a year. Sometimes it is confused with the *capacity factor* which, in this case, might be the total deliveries of gas during the year in relation to the maximum amount that could be delivered for the same period.)

5. Storage, Hubs and Market Centers

To reiterate somewhat, the gas production–consumption process begins with the lifting of gas, and proceeds from there to a transmission or "merchant" (large diameter) pipeline, with perhaps some gas removed from this conduit for storage, further processing, or sale to very large consumers such as industries and electric generators. (Large industries might also buy gas from wellhead producers and/or distribution companies, particularly in a deregulated system.) It then goes into a local distribution system where pipes are smaller, and eventually to the homes and/or commercial establishments that are usually called final consumers. In Germany, in 1995, there were 18 transmission firms that also fulfilled a merchant function (*ferngasgesellschaften*). These provided gas to about 675 regional and local distribution companies (LDC), and also to, e.g., some large industrial consumers. For that country, with almost no domestic gas, the producing (i.e., wholesale) function is largely carried out by Holland, Norway, and Russia.

Storage is another of those topics which submits to an interesting theoretical/mathematical treatment, although for this survey, the exposition will be non-technical. Strangely enough, storage is an issue that is almost completely ignored in microeconomics textbooks, despite its importance. Gas in storage is a carefully watched statistic, particularly in the run-up to winter. For example, low storage levels mean that any shortages of gas that may appear during the coming months could put an upward pressure on gas prices, as well as the availability (and price) of other fuels, such as heating oil.

Just as transport involves moving a commodity through space, storage performs a similar function with respect to time. "Similar" but not identical, because time runs in only one direction. By putting goods into inventory we move them from the present to the future at finite cost, but returning them to the present — and also recreating the background existing when the decision to store was made — is conceptually a much more difficult operation, and for the most part impossible. This suggests that we have a *consistency* problem: at time "t" we make a plan for $t + 1, t + 2, \ldots, t + x, \ldots, t + T$, but at, e.g., $t + x$ we may perceive that the decision taken at "t" was sub-optimal. A new plan can then be put into practice but, apparently, we would have been happier if we had gotten things right in the first place, or formulated a strategy that would have taken into consideration the possibility of making mistakes. Depending upon the overall situation, this strategy might have turned on storing more or less of the commodity, and relying more heavily on such things as futures and forward markets.

A concept that is unique for storage is the convenience yield. This (negative cost) is explained in some detail in my previous textbook and also to a lesser extent in Chapter 8 below, but roughly it is the yield (i.e., gain) associated with greater flexibility (and less inconvenience), that devolves on the owners of inventories. For example, the availability of inventories (i.e., stocks) permits output to be increased without incurring the expenses that are often unavoidable when the managers of a production activity have to resort to spot purchases. The theory here is straightforward: an additional unit put into inventory can provide a large *marginal* convenience yield if inventories are small, while with very large inventories, the marginal convenience yield (associated with adding another unit) might be zero — although the convenience yield would still be positive, and could be very large. Marginal convenience yield is an extremely useful concept, and it should not be treated lightly, because it can be invaluable for theoretical work. In the simplest of cases, inventory accumulation would continue until the cost of a marginal unit outweighed its marginal (convenience) yield.

In the United States, there are more than 400 underground storage sites, and the general understanding is that (gas) storage is supposed to function the way that inventories theoretically function in a market for some metals and foodstuffs. They are held so that when the price of the good escalates, the inventories are sold (which might help to moderate upward price movements), while when the price declines, it usually makes sense to augment inventories, in which case this buying could help function as a price support.

Accordingly, it should be self-evident that inventories can function as an excellent *hedge* against price *and* volume uncertainty. With natural gas — as with electricity — a key issue is peak demand. If a storage option is available, the exposition just above indicates that gas is stored during off-peak periods, and if peak demand jeopardizes the ability to deliver large quantities to final consumers, then gas is removed from storage. (Of course, electricity producers cannot function in this manner since electricity is for the most part non-storable, and this non-storability is the main reason why the volatility of electric prices is so high.)

Something worth remembering here is that under a system in which large amounts of traded gas are covered by long-term or medium-term contracts, with gas suppliers obligated to make the deliveries specified on these contracts, transactors who are uncertain about the availability of pipeline space would be inclined to pay a great deal of attention to storage. On the other hand, when deregulation enters the picture, spot arrangements are supposed to increase in importance, along with the *derivatives* (futures, options, and swaps) that are required to hedge the increased risk associated with short-term transactions. In such a situation, storage was thought to become of less concern to transactors — which turned out to be another of the myths associated with deregulation. Once again, as bad luck would have it, paper assets (e.g., futures contracts) cannot substitute for physical gas, and it is quite evident to alert observers that the development of spot and futures markets for natural gas was incapable of eliminating the need for bilateral contracts in order to insure that sufficient quantities of pipeline gas would always be obtainable.

In most circumstances, storage leads to a higher overall satisfaction because it optimizes the utilization of off-peak capacity. Another way of putting this is to say that having access to a large amount of storage encourages the transfer of consumption from periods in which its value is low to those periods when it is higher (e.g., peak periods). If a firm is in position to store gas throughout the year, and is capable of withdrawing large amounts rapidly when this is required, then that enterprise's commercial/bargaining position could be greatly strengthened. In a recent paper, Hawdon and Stevens (1999) show that overall utility is increased when auctions for storage can be held, since these may be capable of revealing which players on the supply side are able to make the best use of the existing storage capacity.

The Netherlands has often been regarded as a swing producer for the Western European gas market, and it still aspires to that role, although its Groningen gas field is declining due to a rapid fall in well pressure; however the presence of a large storage capacity with a high withdrawal capacity (in cubic feet/day) would mean that it could still fulfill a swing function — which is to supply gas, at appropriate prices, when it is unavailable from other sources. (Saudi Arabia is generally regarded as the swing producer for oil, while the United States appears to have performed this service for coal during the last decade.) The ambition to provide more than 150 Gcf of gas storage, as well as 6 Gcf/d of fast withdrawal capacity is an expensive proposition, although it has been argued that it makes more sense than installing compression (or additional compression) at Groningen, or storing gas in depleted reservoirs that take a long time to fill and empty. (Remember that the "G" in these numbers means "*giga*", which in scientific usage represents billions.)

It appears that one of the reasons for a large increase in storage is the need for *peak shaving* facilities. This is another of those expressions that usually bring a frown to the faces of energy economics students, but what it means in the present context is the release of stored gas into the pipeline system during periods of maximum demand (i.e., peak periods). Possessing the capability to supply the peak load from storage might, in some situations, make investment in additional producing or transmission facilities unnecessary.

Hubs are physical transfer points that are sometimes called pipeline interchanges. They make it possible to redirect gas from one pipeline into another, however at the present time I prefer not to accept a recent report which claimed that spot prices at Henry Hub, which is one of the largest and best-known gas-market hubs in the world (and is close to the Lake Charles (Louisiana) LNG terminal), have assumed the role of international reference prices. This kind of contention is sometimes tied to the belief that a large expansion of the trade in LNG will eventually lead to an international market that is capable of replacing regional markets in LNG; and in the very long run this hypothetical international gas market would comprise — via uniform net prices — both pipeline gas and LNG. A short survey is not the place to speculate on a setup of this nature, although if the demand for gas in North America, and particularly the United States, reaches the levels predicted by the US Energy Information Administration, then the movement of LNG toward North America will increase to a point where there will be an upward pressure on gas prices in every market, although this does not necessarily mean that these prices (net of transportation costs) will converge, since the unavoidable use of long-term contracts will assure a diversity of prices.

In theory it should be desirable to combine hubs with *market centers*, where either of these might provide facilities that permit the buying and selling of services such as storage, brokering, insurance, and *wheeling* (where wheeling means the provision of pure transportation services between external transactors). For pedagogical reasons hubs are often portrayed as displaying a radial pattern of spokes (i.e., pipelines), and conceivably these spokes could be joined by adding short links.

Market centers are supposed to be able to operate independently of facilities for producing, transporting, or storing the physical product, but even so they should be able to provide a locale where shippers, traders, etc. can buy and sell transportation, gas, etc. To a certain extent the layout of these establishments could remind observers of trading facilities in brokerages and investment banks. If there are imbalances anywhere, then an "ideal" market center will provide a mechanism where they can be rectified, which includes access to tradable pipeline space and storage capacity, with (perhaps) a large amount of the latter available in the vicinity of the facility. In the United States, for instance, market centers have direct access to almost 50% of *working gas* storage capacity, and in general enjoy a special relationship with many of the high deliverability storage establishments. (Working gas is the amount of gas in an underground storage facility in excess of the "cushion" or "base" gas that is needed to maintain facility pressure and deliverability rates.) Regardless of the actual configuration, it is hard to avoid the conclusion that market centers will tend to form at or in the vicinity of hubs, and that the number of arbitrage paths (for obtaining uniform prices in a system) are expanded due to the proliferation of hubs, market centers, and storage facilities.

As Corzine (1999) points out, expanding transcontinental pipeline systems that connect remote natural gas reserves to industrial and population centers several thousand kilometers away will increase the desirability of gas relative to other energy media, especially since environmentally acceptable combined-cycle equipment is fairly inexpensive to install, and perhaps to operate. This is all very well, however fuel costs are more than 60% of the total cost of electricity from gas-fired power plants, and when — as, e.g., in Mexico last year — the price of gas increases by a large amount, it leads to some very unpleasant surprises for those producers and consumers who were assured that the increased use of gas would make their lives more comfortable. At the same time it is not completely correct to maintain that making gas and coal more easy to trade by creating "consistent, open liquid markets" will result in these resources becoming more appealing in the long run: this prescription could just as easily lead to greater price volatility, which in turn could hinder investment, and thus eventually bring about higher electric and heating prices. According to the president and chief operating officer of Enron North America, which is — or at least was — a major player in the risk management business, it is possible that the swings in natural gas prices can be close to 100%, and while the swings in coal prices do not move by nearly as much, the changes that are taking place in energy markets mean that "the price is going to be much more volatile". (*Financial Times*, Thursday, 23 September 1999.)

As we saw above, volatility is usually expressed in percentage terms, and so a volatility of, e.g., 50% for a given time period means that the percentage change in the gas price can run 50% higher or lower for that time period. As for the cause of a volatility of this magnitude, it is not advisable to overlook or ignore inadequate pipeline capacity; sudden changes in supply or demand; coordination and scheduling problems of the kind that often make an appearance after embarking on a badly thought out-market liberalization, and "gaming": i.e., when certain transactors have superior access to important market information, and can use this advantage to exploit their oligopolistic position — as happened with electricity wholesalers in California after deregulation.

For a number of reasons, it is illuminating to consider the situation in Brazil, where a near-chronic energy shortage recently escalated because of the adoption of a poorly constructed deregulation policy — a policy that, at one point, led to a desperate government calling for more prayer. Brazil expects a new gas pipeline from Bolivia to help reduce its energy shortages, but with gas priced in dollars, the variability in the dollar-*real* exchange rate introduces enormous uncertainty into the Brazilian gas price. A ceiling on retail gas tariffs in Brazil would keep a gas price flare-up from being passed to final consumers in that country, but an increased amount of loose talk about this kind of remedy has caused a large part of the investment that was once thought to be forthcoming from private sources to vanish. Is there a solution to this dilemma? One solution is to forget about gas, and to build more nuclear facilities. What about forgetting a ceiling for retail gas prices, and accepting market imposed prices? For political reasons that I discuss elsewhere, both of these remedies are almost impossible, although in the United States output from existing nuclear facilities is steadily increasing (due to higher load and capacity factors raising efficiencies), while the price of nuclear fuel (uranium) is almost stationary.

Brazil is a country that, in terms of natural resources, is extremely rich, while Ecuador is comparatively poor; but recently the Energy Development Corporation (EDC) — a US oil and gas exploration and production company — opened an electricity generation plant in Ecuador as part of a $300 million natural gas project. Ecuador is even more dependent than Brazil on hydroelectric generation, and since this project is capable of providing 5%–10% of the Andean nation's installed capacity, the state-run electricity sector has taken an important step to avoid having to call for more prayer if the lights should go out. Quite simply, the Brazilian government should have sponsored investments that would have helped to avoid or mitigate power outages during drought months, and where prices were determined domestically instead in another country.

The government of Ecuador would also like to enter the privatization sweepstakes, but thus far political and trade union opposition has made this impossible. According to "analysts", more privatization would help to increase efficiency and reduce corruption, however the owner of EDC — Samedan Oil Corporation, which has platforms drilling for oil and gas in areas such as the Gulf of Mexico, the North Sea and China — has a contract with the government of Ecuador that offers the state a 20% share of gas production on top of taxes. A comment here might be that AES, an American owned power company in Brazil, suspects that deregulation might create more problems than it solves, and EDC has similar misgivings.

As referred to earlier, one of the attractions of natural gas has to do with its effect on the environment: on the average, it emits about one-half the CO_2 of coal when employed to produce electricity, and in some modern gas-based installations, that figure is about one-third. Of course, if the consumption of gas actually grows by the predicted amount, then the amount of CO_2 produced could still be too much to satisfy the Kyoto stipulations. It also happens that methane — the largest constituent of natural gas — is not an environment-friendly substance.

6. Some Economic Aspects of the Russian Gas Puzzle

The story of Russian gas is to a certain extent beautiful, somewhat like the soap-opera about the perennially rejected suitor who ends up as the object of everyone's affection. And that was not the only rejection I had in mind while preparing this section. Professor Jonathan Stern took issue with my book on natural gas because I insisted that the more Soviet gas purchased, the better for everyone on the buy side of the market. He liked however my claim that the only conceivable attack by Soviet citizens on Western properties during the later stages of the Cold War, would have been an attack on the duty-free gin and whiskey so prominently displayed at various diplomatic and commercial receptions.

In any event, the kingpins of the EU have held a meeting at which the availability of Russian natural gas and oil was discussed at length, and none other than the *Financial Times* (23 March 2006) suggested that the sale of Russian gas to China and Japan might have a negative effect on the energy prospects of Western Europe. By extension, in the long run, this also means North America, because the global gas scene has begun to take on some of the features of a mainstream textbook market. Of course, it could never take on all the attributes because — as pointed out in the later chapters of your favorite volume on price theory — a "natural" oligopoly or monopoly in natural gas has too many special features to end up with a perfectly competitive configuration.

I have no way of knowing exactly what took place in the energy discussions of the aforementioned Brussels conclave, but undoubtedly the gas price and reliability of delivery were somewhere in the picture. As far as I can tell though, the year 2015 kept entering the deliberations like a pop-up version of the Ghost of Christmas Past — to be specific, the one associated with the first and second oil price shocks. Both the IEA and the United States Department of Energy (USDOE) have assured us that we can forget about our oil anxieties until 2030, which implies that we do not need to worry about gas until an even later date, however this is the kind of assurance that in theory no intelligent person would entertain for a fraction of a second, although for assorted reasons (mostly connected with money), many do, and also attempt to impose on others.

Even if those technological miracles appear that energy corporations have started to promise us in the millions of dollars worth of advertisements they have plastered over full pages in almost every Sunday supplement in the civilized world, it is impossible to avoid suspecting that some very ugly energy news could appear at any time as an integral part of CNN or Fox News infotainment. The problem here is simple and reduces to numbers rather than economics. The IEA estimates that gas currently supplies about 21% of the global energy supply, and is on its way to 24% of a much larger amount. The latter observation is conveniently played down by that organization because it places a very large question mark next to their earlier (informal) predictions about future energy prices. Note, energy and not just gas prices!

According to Claude Mandil, executive director of the IEA, gas import dependence for the 25 EU members will eventually grow from just under 50% to 80% (which says something about the expected decline of output in the North Sea), while in North America, the present small level of imports will reach 14% (*Financial Times*, 23 March). Mandil also confirms that the import reliance of Japan and Korea will remain very high, while China and India will emerge as "big gas importers". How big? This he does not reveal, although I feel sure that his experts have provided him with some guidelines. In case they provided him with the wrong ones, let me suggest that the effective demand of these two giants is potentially large enough to cut the ground out from under the international macroeconomy. (By "effective" I mean that they can pay for any purchases they make with hard currency.) Anyone doubting this should schedule a heart-to-heart with Alan Greenspan before he loses interest in these matters.

One of the items in my gas book that apparently kept it from a prominent position on the favorite bookshelf of Mr Stern was my contention that while the United States and most of the states of Western Europe were political allies, they were also economic rivals: they have always been, and they always will be — and this is more the case now than ever. One person who had some difficulty with this concept was former US president Ronald Reagan, whose experts informed him that instead of buying gas from the Soviet Union, his European comrades-in-arms should make some effort to obtain the supplies they required from, e.g., Africa and Argentina. The reason the chief executive was told this was because he was constitutionally unable to accept the logical option, which was to contract for the largest possible quantities that could be obtained from the Soviet Union.

I also took the liberty of claiming that the energy rivalry between Europe and the United States would be increasingly intense because Japan and other rapidly developing Asian countries would become major players in the great gas game. Now it appears that the chicken have come home to roost. Mr Stern could not possibly have gotten this correct however, because as he enjoyed proclaiming at the energy conferences where he was an honored guest, he had no background in economics or engineering, and thus could not possibly understand the complex cost-benefit issues that form the basis of a scientific inquiry into this subject.

When I wrote my gas book the ideological commitment of the Soviet Politburo was ostensibly to Marx and Lenin, although I was assured by some very serious persons that it was equally to dollars and deutschmarks, which made executives in the Soviet gas industry prone to discharge their business obligations. If we can assume that there is no change in this posture, then it might be useful to examine the proposals of Claude Mandil to prevent what he views as a potential supply gap whose closing will take "money and time".

Given that he estimates that it will require only $11 bn/y if sufficient investment takes place so that Russian production and export goals can be met, the key issue appears to be time, because it should be possible to obtain the cash involved by just passing the hat at an ad-hoc photo-op arranged for the most presentable billionaires in a recent *Forbes* listing (27 March 2006).

My assumption is that this 11 billion would actually go to the production and transportation of gas, rather than things like junkets to wonderful Courchevel or gorgeous "Kitz" at the height of the skiing season, as Mr Mandil indirectly implied. Personally, I believe that the Russian firm Gazprom was correct in showing offence at this aspersion. They would also be correct in ignoring Mr Mandil's suggestion that the Russians should provide "real third-party access" to gas pipelines, since by third-party he probably means foreigners interfering with matters whose interior logic they are incapable of understanding.

It has been suggested by some of the Norwegian colleagues that for Russia to live up to expectations about supply, high gas prices will be necessary if investments are to be financed. How high? My teaching of game theory leads me to believe that the same low-level, half-baked analysis is being resorted to on this topic that was utilized in the electric and gas deregulation farces. The key issue is clearly production capacity, and so the optimal strategy is probably for the EU — and perhaps others — to lend Russia the money they need to expand capacity, with the provision that repayment would be in gas. The repayment schedule would be designed not to interfere with privately arranged transactions, and if possible the gas would, e.g., be sold to private consumers and firms.

More and more the question is being raised as to how we are going to make sure that we will never be painted into an energy corner. As I see things, there is an excessive reliance on natural gas, and not enough reliance on nuclear. I would therefore like to see a number of things carefully investigated and discussed. For instance, the reasons why Finland choose nuclear instead of gas and/or renewables when they decided to increase their electric capacity by 1600 MW should be pointed out in detail to the anti-nuclear booster clubs.

In the conference of EU movers-and-shakers referred to above, it was proposed that the EU countries should formulate a joint strategy for dealing with their energy vulnerabilities.

I can sympathize with this to a certain extent, although I fail to see how a suggestion of this nature ties in with the deregulation nonsense that was launched by the EU Energy Directorate. I can also note that while Hannibal was the commander of a multi-national army that defeated many foes, these outcomes might have been different if the same army had been commanded by his wine steward.

Let me put this another way. The commander of the EU Energy Army is a man who believes that "peak oil" is only a theory, and even worse, has announced that electric and gas deregulation makes good sense. Accordingly, I think that we would all be better off if we pretend that this high-flown and dispensable conference with its bogus deliberations never took place, and future calls for a joint energy strategy are either pointedly ignored or ridiculed.

7. Liquefied Natural Gas (LNG)

The only complaint that I remember receiving about my natural gas book (1987) had to do with the scarcity of materials dealing with LNG. At that time however, I felt that the LNG market had not really "taken off", but even so I did make a few observations that I considered useful and interesting. One of them was to remind readers that LNG markets can be quite complicated in that when gas is shipped by sea it must first be liquefied, and after reaching a terminal that might be thousands of kilometers away deliquefied. On the other hand, items such as crude oil and oil products can be pumped directly into a tanker, and at the terminal end pumped out in what amounts to a relatively uncomplicated procedure. As a result, capital investment in a typical LNG "chain" is necessarily very expensive. Annual LNG production at the present time amounts to almost 150 million tonnes per year ($= 150$ mt/y), and if all planned projects are realized, this could increase by upward of 100 mt/y in the next 10 to 15 years, and eventually to more than 400 mt/y, but it must be recognized that there is considerable opposition to increasing the import of natural gas in several very gas-intensive countries. One of these is the United States, where there are increasing objections to a very large dependence on foreign energy.

It is hardly a surprise that for short to medium distances, pipelines are more economical than LNG chains. In my gas book I suggested that the cross-over point for an LNG chain relative to an onshore pipeline appeared to be around 4000 km, after which economics tends to favor LNG, but for a submarine pipeline in very deep water it might be about 1500 km, and without the deep water stipulation about 3500 km. These figures are strictly approximate, but even so they imply that it is only with high existing or expected gas prices that LNG chains are profitable (i.e., prices that are high with respect to historical prices).

It seems clear though that if expected supply and demand continue to develop as at present, then gas prices will remain high, and here we need to remember that one reason for elevated gas prices is that these prices are often coupled (or indexed) to the price of oil. Gas is the fastest growing form of primary energy, and the former director of the Oxford Institute for Energy Studies, Robert Skinner, puts the expected annual growth rate at 2.7%–3.0%/y (2005). (Electricity is the fastest growing energy medium in final consumption at 2.5%/y, or more.) In these circumstances the low gas prices that characterized the last decade of the 20th century are unlikely to be seen again.

Although natural gas is found in many parts of the world, LNG projects should be based on comparatively large amounts of reserves in the vicinity of the exporting point. For these projects to be profitable, facilities should exist for the processing and transporting of a great deal of gas, and so it is very discouraging if the gas runs out while very expensive facilities for liquefying gas have a great deal of their operational life left, or even if capacity is greatly underutilized. Not only must adequate reserves be present, but it usually makes commercial sense for buyers and sellers to be willing to commit themselves, via long-term contracts, to deliveries and acceptance of a certain amount of gas at prices within a fairly rigid framework, although some variation in the price might be acceptable on the basis of a formula that is agreed upon by both buyers and sellers.

Many years ago I was told by a colleague, Professor Marian Radetzki, that technological change would make the cost structure of the LNG industry much more attractive. This had not happened by the time I published my gas book, but it appears that genuine changes are now taking place. Robert Skinner believes that LNG costs have decreased by at least 30% since the early nineties, with this result being largely attributable to the development of larger and more efficient equipment for the liquefaction stage of the train. New tankers also cost less, *ceteris paribus*, and moreover both tanker and train sizes have increased. Increasing returns to scale and the rapid growth of gas demand are probably the most important explanatory factors here.

It also happens that transactors will adopt an arrangement that allows price negotiations every few years for existing contracts, and there has been a great deal of talk about a greater utilization of spot pricing for LNG. As yet though this is mostly talk, although some very short-term contracts have been entered into when there is considerable spare plant and shipping capacity available. In his important paper, Skinner asks whether there will be a *global* gas market, and given the rapid growth in supply and the (theoretical) possibility for arbitrage within and between "basins" (i.e., markets) due to price differences, it seems clear that the amount could increase over time; but on the other hand, in considering, e.g., an LNG chain based on arctic gas at the supply end, the very great cost of the investments that are involved in producing this gas gives me the impression that suppliers are not likely to be enthusiastic about trusting their future to the appearance of favorable spot prices.

It can be added that LNG is still more expensive in the Far East (Korea, Taiwan and Japan especially) than in Europe or the US. Suppliers have noticed this, and given the large gas reserves in that part of the world, it dominates the LNG trade. On the other hand, while China is set to greatly increase its reception of LNG, it has access to a great deal of pipeline gas, and more seems to be on the way from Russia.

There are four distinct phases in an LNG project: 1. gas production, treatment, and transportation to a liquefying plant; 2. liquefaction, storage, and loading onto a ship; 3. shipping the LNG in special cryogenic tankers to the reception terminal; and 4. receiving and unloading the LNG, followed by storing and regasifying. These operations can be examined individually.

The gas that is at the entrance of an LNG supply chain is basically identical to that which flows through a pipeline. At the same time more attention should be paid to the quantity (and quality) of this gas, because for economic reasons a liquefaction plant should operate as close to full capacity as possible at all times. The gas is carefully processed, and most impurities removed, and if it happens that the gas contains an unusually high percentage of carbon dioxide, hydrogen sulphide, nitrogen, and/or particles that could disrupt the production process, a very intensive treatment is required before initiating the liquefaction activity.

Liquefaction involves cooling methane to about $-161°C$, and reducing its volume to about 1/600 of gaseous methane. As already noted, the liquefaction plant is usually a very expensive link in the LNG chain, and the most expensive components of this activity are the steam and power generating facilities. Increasing economies of scale (i.e., declining unit costs) prevail for liquefaction plants up to a very large capacity, and it appears that operating (i.e., maintenance + labor) costs are only a very small percentage of total costs. When considering operating costs, the energy required to operate the liquefaction plant should be included. This averages roughly

10% of the gas input if gas is used as the source of energy for running the plant.

When examining transportation, distance is very important. In my natural gas book I cited an arrangement involving an LNG project for North Africa–Europe in which a fleet of five ships was needed to maintain an input at the consuming end of 500 mcf/d. This relationship is almost certainly more favorable at the present time, and in addition the boil-off (which is the gas that is vaporized by heat leakage in the LNG tanks) has been greatly reduced in the most modern cryogenic tankers.

Finally, at the terminal end of the chain a suitable harbor and regasification facility must be available. Very large capital costs are involved here, although fortunately operating costs tend to be quite modest. A not often mentioned cost has to do with possible suboptimal locations for LNG terminals due to a fear by many voters of negative environmental impact and "fireballs"; this is particularly true for the eastern seashore of the United States, but also for the west coast: for example, the citizens of Long Beach (California) have made it very clear that they do not want any LNG facilities in the neighborhood. There are already five large LNG import terminals on the Gulf Coast, with one of these offshore, and that part of the country has generally been rated as LNG-friendly, but after the Sandia National Laboratories in New Mexico circulated a report saying that an accident at a $300,000\,m^3$ storage and regasification facility could melt steel at a distance of a half mile, and if a vapor cloud formed there would be severe casualties out to a distance of four miles, the enthusiasm for LNG seems to have moderated considerably in the Gulf States.

Regardless of the difficulties that keep materializing, there is clearly a great deal of natural gas in the future of energy consumers in the United States and elsewhere. In 2005 it was announced that energy companies were set to spend more than $50 bn on LNG facilities in Qatar alone. ExxonMobil and Chevron accounted for 18 billion of this investment. Forty LNG terminals have been proposed for the United States, however from an economic and political point of view it is difficult to regard this as a serious figure.

LNG plants can often produce at more than 15% above the rated capacity, and what this means is that an expansion may require only a small amount of additional investment, as compared to the complexity and expense required to bring a "greenfield" facility into operation. Of course, there are persons in both Europe and the United States who feel that it is all for the better if LNG never came into the picture. One of these is Hunt (2006). The most important thing about this article are some of the superb comments on it by Giegler (2006), Reid (2006), Gould (2006) and others.

8.   Some Unpleasant Gas Market Vibrations in the United States

We often hear that economics is a non-experimental science, however in truth decisive informal "experiments" occasionally take place. Probably the best examples concern oil and gas in the United States. For oil, the quantities added to reserves by exploration peaked long before production peaked in the early 1970s. A similar sequence was observed for gas. Today, in the United States, the consumption of oil and gas steadily increases, while the domestic production of both items steadily decreases: much more oil and gas is consumed every year than is found during the same period, and a significant fraction of the huge US trade deficit takes the form of payment for energy imports. Despite the scepticism of various influential optimists, the same production patterns should eventually be experienced on a global scale, although it is impossible to say exactly when the peaks will arrive, and what the levels of production will be at that time.

Fortunately, the majority of energy professionals no longer believe that oil and gas are so plentiful that technology and an ivory-tower price system will always guarantee their availability at prices that we think are affordable. For all practical purposes, the writing is on the wall, and it is meaningful to everyone who approaches this topic with an open mind. The explosive energy demand in China, added to present trends in the remainder of the world, means that global oil demand could become close to 95 mb/d before the end of 2010, as compared to 85 mb/d at the present time. A demand of this size should ensure that the era of bargain-basement oil is over forever, which in turn will add to other pressures on the gas price since, if only because the price of gas is often indexed to that of oil. (The most interesting indexing formula is reviewed by Asche *et al.* (2001). This is $P_t = P_0 + \Sigma \alpha_{jt}(P_{jt} - P_{j0})E\lambda_j$, for all values of "$j$". The reference price is P_0, α_j is the weight of a given substitute "j" (e.g., oil), with $\Sigma \alpha_j = 1$; $(P_{jt} - P_{j0})$ is the price change for substitute "j" from the base period "0" to the reference period "t", E is an "energy equivalent", while λ_j is an "impact factor" for changes in the price of substitute "j". This is also a kind of weight, and possibly we should have $\Sigma \lambda_j = 1$.) One of the causes of the present high gas price is an oil price of that is expected to remain in or over the range $65–75/b over the indefinite future. This provides some indication as to where gas prices might be heading, and perhaps more important, where they will not be heading.

Several years ago the price of gas seemed frozen in the $1.75–2.50 mBtu range, but unexpectedly it suddenly jumped to almost $4/mBtu. Just now the average world gas price is between $6.00/mBtu and $7.00/mBtu, but has often spiked to values that — if experienced on the oil market — could result in a panic or despair among both buyers and politicians. For example, it has happened on at least one occasion that the gas price moved to a level on spot markets that corresponds to an oil price of $100/b, or greater. Equally noticeable is the fact that recently in the comparatively gas-rich United Kingdom, in January 2004, the gas price is the same as in gas-poor Japan, or about $5.0 mBtu — which in oil terms would be $29/b. The question also needs to be put as to what will happen in the near future in the United Kingdom as gas imports (rather than exports) become the new reality. Many observers still fail to comprehend that the UK North Sea is on the downward slope of its production profile, and as in the United States, a reversal is unthinkable.

The $4/mBtu figure mentioned above corresponds to an oil price of $23/b, which by itself was hardly sufficient for former US Energy Secretary Spencer Abraham to convene a National Gas Summit (on 26 June 2003), or for the former Federal Reserve Chairman Alan Greenspan to tell the US Congress that an energy fiasco was imminent unless major changes took place in the gas market. Since Greenspan's personal political philosophy would hardly allow him to suggest interfering with consumer choice, it was obvious that he was referring to the overall availability of gas in US gas markets (and here it should be appreciated that the chairman did *not* claim, as various politicians have done, that the problem could be solved if his government opened more public land and offshore areas to private gas developers). Some estimates indicate that the demand for gas for power generation may increase by more than 6%/y up to 2010, while environmental and other considerations seem to have resulted in over 75% of new power plants in that country being gas-based. A large percentage of these lack fuel-switching capacity, which was supposed to be the case, and with older plants that are capable of fuel switching tending to be less efficient, the entire system may have become less versatile.

Both Greenspan and other important observers have occasionally suggested that a serious gas shortage would be a greater danger to the US macroeconomy than an interruption in the oil supply, largely because many gas-burning households and industries cannot substitute for their energy source in the short run. Greenspan goes so far as to say that eventually high gas prices might force some industries (such as chemicals) to move to countries where gas prices are lower. One of these countries might be Trinidad-Tobago, where expected prices are still relatively low. Former Energy Secretary Abraham expanded on this theme, noting that in cold climates, persons on fixed incomes might have to choose between heating and groceries. This may have turned out to be more than idle speculation, because the evolving gas shortage stabilized prices in the vicinity of $5–6/mBtu.

The basic problem is that the United States is a mature production area, and the only direction that output in the "lower" 48 can go is down. Just as unfortunate, the relief that was once expected from Canada or Mexico or a mass drilling assault on "public lands" is still off the table for physical (and not political) reasons. *Natural depreciation* in Mexico's gas fields is extremely high — so high in fact that in conjunction with increasing consumption, Mexico will be transformed to an importer of gas. A similar phenomenon is visible in Canada, where for the most part gas is found in shallow pools that are characterized by a high natural depreciation. Alaska and the very far northern districts of Canada may still possess enough gas to provide appreciable exports to the United States, but in order to have access to these resources several extremely expensive pipelines must be constructed, and even if these projects were to commence today, it would take years before this gas reaches US markets. Of course, no major pipeline projects seem likely in Canada, the United States, *or* Europe unless the decision-makers recognize that low gas prices are unacceptable to gas producers and the financial institutions that finance their activities; and in addition there is a place in the scheme of things for very long-term, very inflexible "take or pay" contracts, regardless of the irritation they cause deregulators. *This is another way of saying that one of the major tenets of deregulation — establishing or expanding spot markets for buying and selling gas — does not have much of a future in the real world!*

There is also a revival of the unrealistic desire to establish — in the short run — an international market in natural gas by greatly increasing the amount of liquefied natural gas (LNG) moving across the oceans and seas. In the United States preparations are being made to take terminals for receiving LNG out of "mothballs", and there is talk of building a large number of ships for carrying this commodity. The cost that is relevant for present projections is probably well in excess of 100 billion US dollars, which is one of the factors ensuring that the gas price of a few years ago is history.

One of the arguments for deregulation in the United States turned on the belief that more "competition" — to include a greater resort to derivatives markets — could substitute for the unavoidable depletion of physical resources. As pointed out in the aggressively free-market business periodical *Forbes* (22 January 2001), deregulation has meant greater "efficiency", but unfortunately this not-very-easily-defined property has led to increased gas prices and lower reliability. This is even more pertinent for electricity deregulation, where neither consumers nor businesses voted in favor of deregulation because they lusted after increased "efficiency". What they wanted — and were promised — is lower electricity prices with unchanged reliability, and in addition more certainty in regard to future prices.

For several years I was convinced that DeVany and Walls (1995) were mistaken when they suggested that the deregulation of electricity would be easier to bring about than that of gas — where the latter was something they saw as being well under way, but not completed because of the opposition to deregulation by "socialist" politicians and theoreticians. But now I understand that they were correct: electricity deregulation is for the most part a lost cause, while the deregulation of natural gas almost completely lacks any scientific justification. As suggested in the appendix to this chapter, the place to take notice of this is Europe.

9. Some Aspects of Risk Management

This book contains an entire chapter dealing with some aspects of risk management, going from the very simple to the not so simple, but it might be a good idea to introduce certain concepts here. If the reader should run into difficulty, then he or she can proceed to that chapter without delay.

But first let us look at several basic topics. One of these is efficiency, and in discussing the natural gas market, the term efficiency is not used in the same way as in your elementary or intermediate microeconomics text. Herbert and Kreil (1996) prefer to speak of informational efficiency, but for the purpose of this discussion, it is probably just as well to cite the work of DeVany and Walls, who have (incorrectly) pronounced the US natural gas market efficient because of the presumed efficient functioning of the natural gas futures market — which is not a true picture of the state of that market; and because they believe that enough arbitrage will come about to confirm the "law of one price", taking into consideration transportation costs. Eventually, this latter stipulation may turn out to be correct, and since memories are short, the ongoing and/or proposed fragmentation of gas markets might at that time be declared a roaring success by certain unsophisticated observers; but as with the proposed "re-engineering" of the electric market, it would be a success purchased at an uneconomical price — i.e., the price of the investment in additional transmission capacity and other facilities that are required to eventually bring about the "ideal" level of arbitrage — if such a level actually exists when the high cost of achieving it is taken into consideration.

The futures market will always surface in discussions of this nature, because as pointed out on several occasions above, once long-term arrangements are abandoned or scaled down, a great deal of risk will be encountered, and conventionally strenuous efforts will be made to hedge this risk. In both this book and my previous textbook I devote a chapter to "non-exotic" derivatives (i.e., conventional futures and options), but it does not take an intensive scrutiny of the non-academic literature to realize that this topic is seldom given the attention that it deserves. A few general remarks might be useful before we turn to specifics.

Uncertainty means that we do not know what will happen in the future, although we know what *might* happen; and if we can attach a probability to the latter, we usually call it *risk*. To keep things simple though, what we perhaps should call "uncertainty aversion" in finance and elsewhere, we almost always call risk aversion: among other things, it sounds better.

A *state of the world* is the background in which an event can or cannot take place. For example, a revolution in Monaco or Luxembourg might mean that less natural gas is purchased by the citizens of those very rich communities, but at the same time there is a high likelihood that they would not reduce their demand, particularly if the shooting started in winter. After a state of the world is revealed — revolution, or no revolution — many market "actors" (or agents) will discover that their expectations — gas price rise, fall, or no change — were mistaken, and wish that they had bought or sold various physical or financial assets. The availability of a *full set* of derivative markets will, in theory, enable some of us to eliminate some of the disappointments often associated with time and uncertainty, since these markets can function in a similar manner to an insurance market. Unfortunately though, a *full* set of derivative markets is the kind of arrangement that is only available in the class and seminar rooms where reality is strictly *persona non grata* a large part of the time. I can also remind the reader that an asset can be defined as anything that has value.

At the center of (real-world) futures markets we have the futures contract, which can be considered a highly standardized forward contract. (In the pure forward market delivery always takes place, and while the futures contract is also a forward contract in that usually delivery *can* take place, the structure of the market is such that delivery does not have to take place.) We usually say that a forward contract is used in the "physical" market, while a futures contract is traded in the "paper" market.

In any event, against a background of speculators "betting" on the direction and size of price movements by buying and selling futures contracts, it is possible for producers, consumers, inventory holders, and other traders in physical products to reduce (and sometimes to eliminate) undesired price risk by also buying and selling these contracts. More specifically, traders in a physical commodity can employ futures markets to reduce price risk if other traders and/or speculators are willing to assume this risk. The social gain from futures trading derives from the voluntary redistribution of risk between speculators and risk averse transactors in physical (or financial) assets. The management of futures markets are prone to insist that these institutions exist only to provide price insurance for transactors in physical products, but a futures market without a heavy dose of speculation (i.e., gambling) is probably without a bright future.

Now let us look at some details. If a speculator (who is someone who does not handle the physical item) believes that the price of a commodity is going to rise, he or she opens a position by buying futures contracts for that commodity. Traditional futures contracts are also forward contracts, since delivery conditions are specified on them relating to a specific amount of a commodity, delivered during a certain period to one or more specified locations; but it is possible to avoid taking delivery if, at any time before the contract matures, an offsetting (i.e., reversing) sale is made of a contract for the same amount of the commodity, referred to the same delivery period. This is called "closing a position". (In some cases the matter of delivery is superfluous, since in the 1980s contracts with cash settlement (instead of delivery) were introduced.) In the United States the New York Mercantile Exchange (NYMEX) has for many years provided a highly effective market for the large-scale trading of natural gas futures contracts, while the Henry Hub is the designated delivery point for its contracts. Readers should note that the theoretical aspects of this discussion will be examined more thoroughly in the chapter called "Energy and Money".

Offsetting — or closing an *open* position before or at the *maturity (or expiry) date* of the contract — is always possible in a viable futures market. Here it should be *very carefully noted* that a viable market is one with a high degree of liquidity that is brought about by the presence of a large number of active transactors, both hedgers and speculators, where transactions can be carried out very soon after buy or sell orders are given, and at a price that is close to that of the most recent quoted price. (Emphasis was placed on "very carefully noted" because although in the United States, futures trading is considered a key component of an efficiently functioning natural gas market, liquidity has occasionally been inadequate, and this is unquestionably one of the reasons why natural gas is second only to electricity in the volatility of futures prices.) If, as in this simple example, a futures contract is bought and sold later at a higher price, then the (*long*) speculator has made a profit. Similarly, if a speculator thinks the price is going to fall, then he or she opens the position by selling a contract (i.e., going *short*), hoping to make a profit by closing the position at a lower price.

Going short! There is a lot of unnecessary mystery associated with this expression. For instance, you might begin your day by picking up your telephone and calling your broker, and telling him or her to *sell* a futures contract for 1000 barrels of oil. Then you put your telephone down and start eating your breakfast. If things go well, or badly for that matter, later that day or week you will pick up your telephone again, call your broker, and tell him or her to *buy* a futures contract for 1000 barrels of oil. If things have gone well — that is, the price of oil has declined — then you have made a profit equal to the difference between the sell and the buy price, minus brokerage fees. *Note*: you have not seen any oil! The transaction was initiated because you had a certain feeling about what will happen to the oil price.

We have all heard of speculators who have lost a great deal of money, but in theory — on the average — speculators as a group should gain the risk premium that risk-averse hedgers are willing to pay to avoid very large losses.

Hedgers — i.e., persons who buy and sell physical items such as oil and natural gas — also buy or sell futures contracts, depending upon whether they want to guard against price rises or price falls. Essentially, hedgers want to insure against price risk. They want to lock in a price, and under ideal circumstances the price that is locked in is that on the futures contract at the time the "paper" transaction is initiated, assuming that all goes well. This will be explained in the chapter, Energy and Money.

Continuing with this example, only switching to gas from oil, if the spot price of the gas rises, then the gas *buyer* who is hedging her forthcoming purchase of (physical) gas by buying futures, will face a "loss" on the physical transaction, but — as is shown below — since the price of the futures contract should also rise, a compensating gain should be made on the offsetting sale of futures. Consider, for example, a situation where the price of physical gas is $4/Mcf on the first day of January, while a futures contract with a maturity of 30 days, and for a certain number of cubic feet, is bought for $4.01/Mcf on the same day. Now imagine the price of *physical* gas increasing by 1 cent every day, and so it is $4.30 on January 30. Assuming that the buyer could not arrange or was not interested in a forward transaction to buy the gas at a lower price, then a nominal loss of 30 cents has been registered (= 4.30 − 4.00) over the maturity period on the physical transaction. But if the price of physicals and futures converge on that date, then this "loss" on the physical transaction of 30 cents is almost balanced by the gain of 29 cents (= 4.30 − 4.01) that is made by selling the futures contract! Note something else in this example: the hedger pays $4.01/Mcf for the gas (= 4.30 − 0.29). As will be shown in the chapter "Energy and Money", if the futures and physical prices converge, then the hedger locks in or almost locks in the price of a physical good by using a futures contract.

Observe the expression "if all goes well" above. In textbook markets, where the commodity on the futures contract is identical to that being traded in the physical market, liquidity is always adequate, and a few other minor conditions are satisfied, all will go beautifully in the great majority of cases. But in real world natural gas markets, because of *basis risk* — which involves the non-convergence of physical and paper prices — attempting to hedge price risk with futures can occasionally turn out to be a losing proposition. (John Herbert even goes so far as to mention hedging programs that "derailed into disaster".)

If a firm is selling gas, and is afraid of a price fall, then hedging involves opening a position by selling futures contracts — i.e., going short in futures. If the price of the physical gas does fall, then the price of futures contracts should also fall, and a compensating gain for the loss on the physical transaction will be registered by way of a (offsetting) purchase of futures contracts at a price that is lower than the price at which the position was opened. The hedge being described here is a short hedge — i.e., short in futures. Using the discussion in this section, some readers might already be able to formulate a simple numerical example of the type constructed above to show how a seller of gas can use futures to reduce exposure to price risk, and perhaps even show that the price locked in by the hedger is the futures price, assuming a convergence of paper and physical prices.

We have now arrived at a crucial subject: the means for obtaining the convergence of the futures price and the spot price of a commodity. It is only when these converge that a futures market can provide hedgers with the certainty of avoiding price risk. (Otherwise there could be a loss.) In principle this involves a market where we have the same "underlying" (as the physical item is often called) as the commodity specified on the futures contract, where the seller of a futures contract has the right and ability to make delivery on the contract, and where the buyer can hold open a contract, and thus obtain delivery — assuming that delivery can indeed be made. This last stipulation is pivotal in the present discussion, because the problem with natural gas is often that delivery facilities are inadequate.

In truth, even if these facilities were greatly expanded, delivery by or to some transactors during peak periods might be impossible due to a lack of pipeline and/or storage capacity.

I will present next a very simple algebraic discussion that will be repeated in the chapter "Energy and Money", but which some readers might like to examine already if they are curious about price convergence. If, for example, the price of a commodity on the spot market (S) is higher than the price of the commodity on a futures contract (F) at the *maturity* (or *expiry*) date of the contract, then speculators who had bought a futures contract would not make an offsetting sale of the contract. Instead, they would accept delivery of the item and immediately sell it on the spot market. This very elementary type of arbitrage, if it can take place, should eliminate the price discrepancy.

We can take another approach. The shorts would not deliver anything that could be sold at a higher price in the spot market, and so, as the delivery date approaches, if S turns out to be greater than F (i.e., $S > F$), they would offset their contracts. This amounts to an increase in the demand for futures contracts that raises their price, and thus drives F closer to S. Similarly, the longs would not want to take delivery of anything that they could buy more cheaply elsewhere. Thus, if $F > S$ as the delivery date approaches, they will offset their contracts. In this case we have what amounts to an increase in the supply of futures, which tends to depress F, while their demand for the underlying raises its price: S increases.

Even in highly successful commodity futures markets, transactions costs that are associated, among other things, with the inconvenience of delivery will almost always keep a full convergence of S and F from taking place; but in the case of natural gas, insufficient pipeline capacity and/or insufficient storage capacity, as well as geographical differences between markets, etc., will occasionally not only lead to prices not converging, but cause them to move in opposite directions.

The problem of non-converging prices is called *basis risk*. In this discussion basis risk considers only the situation at the maturity date of the contract, however there can be an equally important basis risk that describes the financial discomforts that could be associated with a diverging spot and futures price during the "running time" or maturity of a futures contract, and as a result of which very large "maintenance margin" charges will be incurred. (Futures transactions take place at an exchange, and margin is a "security deposit" that must be paid the exchange at the opening of a futures transaction and which, if the price of a futures contract moves in the wrong direction — down for a long, and up for a short — must be "topped up". To reiterate, in an ideal market the complete convergence of physical and paper prices at the maturity date will yield a perfect (or near-perfect) hedge; while in real markets complete price convergence may not take place, but even so transactors will regard the situation as preferable to not having access to this kind of market.

It needs to be carefully noted though that basis risk could bring about devastating margin calls during the running time of a contract, because the exchange is not in the business of accepting losses. They are also not in the business of making profits — where profits are revenues in excess of costs — and so, if during the running time of a contract gains accrue to the holder of a contract, these can be obtained almost immediately.

The mention of losses that are caused by various shortcomings mentioned above will inevitably start certain persons thinking of correcting the above situation by building more pipelines, storage facilities, hubs, etc., in order to facilitate arbitrage. This is almost certainly taking place now, although to my way of thinking a better strategy would be to leave things the way they were before it was decided to introduce competition for the sake of competition, and thus make it possible for firms of the Enron variety to compensate for their many blunders by increasing their energy trading profits by a few billions of dollars.

It can also be noted that in addition to a futures contract associated with the Henry Hub, there is an options contract. The mechanics of option trading is taken up at some length in my previous textbook, and will be reviewed in this book in the chapter, "Energy and Money". Eventually however some readers will come to the correct conclusion that managing risk is a very tricky business where in many cases long-term agreements should be resorted to instead of things like exchange-based futures and options contracts.

10.   Final Observations and Concluding Statement

At the Copenhagen meeting of the International Association for Energy Economics, in 1991, I gave a talk in which I predicted that the Middle East could be on its way to becoming a superpower in the production of petro-chemicals before very long. My approach to this turned on the availability of inexpensive oil being used as the main petroleum feedstock, with the energy input for heat and power being provided by inexpensive natural gas. As things have developed, gas has also become a key feedstock, and in particular for ethylene production. By the end of this decade, according to a forecast in the *Financial Times* (Monday, 14 October 2002), the Saudi Basic Industries Corporation (Sabic) should be well on its way to becoming one of the top five global ethylene producers.

Iran also has ambitions along this line, since its gas resources are even larger than those of Saudi Arabia. It needs to be appreciated that given the huge global demand for petrochemicals, and thus the growth in demand for core petrochemical products (e.g., resins, plastics, and synthetics), and the ability of countries without a genuine "competitive advantage" in petro-chemicals (such as South Korea) to build and profitably expand export-oriented petrochemical facilities, it is extremely likely that as the "stock" of state-of-the-art technology and management skills available to the gas-rich countries of the Middle East increases, the need of these countries to worry about the oil age coming to a (for them) premature end should decrease considerably. The "starter" materials in the petrochemical indus-tries are methane, ethane, propane, and benzene — all obtained from natural gas or the distillation of crude oil — as well as benzene, toluene, and xylene produced by the catalytic cracking of crude oil, and since the main thing driving investment location decisions is a substantial feedstock advantage, countries like Iran and Saudi Arabia should eventually have an unbeatable price advantage over their competitors, whoever and wherever they are.

Something that has not been given sufficient emphasis in this paper is the price inelasticity of supply of natural gas (and also oil). In the mid-dle of the 1970s, with only half as much natural gas being found in the United States as was consumed, the situation had reached a point where in California drilling was taking place in the decomposed garbage in land-fills. The situation brightened somewhat in the next quarter of a century, but not because of increased in gas prices. What happened was increased exploration and production in the Gulf of Mexico, although at the present time, as noted earlier, the future of that source is uncertain. More impor-tant, in 1975, the world-class energy economists Paul MacAvoy and Robert

Pindyck used one of their elegant econometric models to forecast that if gas prices were "freed up" (i.e., deregulated), gas production would reach an unprecedented (for that time) 34 Tcf/y. This distinguished example of econometric overkill was an embarrassment to everyone with the slightest knowledge of real-world gas markets, but it did serve to alert a few decision-makers of the difference between geological truth and econometric truth, to the detriment of the latter.

A question that I remember asking on an examination was what happens to the supply and price of natural gas when the price of oil rises. Since in some geological formations (associated) gas is automatically produced with oil, when the price of oil displays what is considered a durable increase, the supply of oil *might* also increase, and if it does, then the supply of gas increases. *Ceteris paribus*, this should reduce the price of gas — assuming that the gas market functions the way that they say it functions in your favorite microeconomics text, which is not always the case.

Some countries that produce a great deal of associated gas, such as Nigeria, cannot get this gas to market, and so it is *flared* (i.e., burned up in the air). Occasionally this gas is referred to as "stranded gas", and regarded as an ideal input for the so-called natural gas refinery, where gas is converted into synthetic liquid fuels that are especially attractive from an environmental point of view. It has long been obvious that enterprises in South Africa that have a comprehensive expertise in Fisher-Tropsch chemistry are planning to build GTS (gas-to-liquids) refineries in other parts of Africa (probably Angola and Nigeria), and also in the Middle East.

This sounds quite reasonable as long as we are talking about stranded gas with a relatively low cost; but as is apparently not often realized, the capital and operating costs of these refineries is considerably higher than for conventional installations using crude oil as a feedstock, and so the economics of this new technology is not particularly impressive when it has to use gas priced at "normal" prices. At the same time it must be admitted that the environmental bonus provided by these facilities might provide a high level of "social" utility.

A number of very strange things are taking place in the natural gas markets at the present time. One of them is a methodical attempt on the part of many "players" to misrepresent the supply–demand situation, as well as the efficiency of deregulation — although, admittedly, this could simply be carelessness on the part of these ladies and gentlemen, and particularly on the part of our political masters (and their advisors) who have unfortunately been put in a position where they are forced to address concepts and situations that they are simply unable to understand, even if they wanted to.

However, regardless of what has gone wrong, as a resident of Sweden, I am supremely unimpressed. The simple truth is that in countries like Sweden, a monumental self-deception about energy and other matters on the part of the television audience has contributed — and continues to contribute — to a slow but apparently irreversible social decline in the sense that, for perhaps the first time in modern history, certain components of the Swedish society are going to slide down the economic ladder. Accordingly, rising energy prices are going to contribute both directly and indirectly to an erosion in the quality of life, where the latter will be at least partially caused by an increased awareness of the incompetence of government in these and similar matters. Surely, Dr Pangloss would have been tempted to call this situation the worst of all possible worlds, although, with due respect to Voltaire, it is no joking matter. When a country that was first rate in all regards begins to lose its shine, it is a loss for the entire civilized world.

Appendix: The Deregulation of Natural Gas

As compared to physics and mathematics, economics is an easy subject — "an easy subject that is difficult", as John Maynard (Lord) Keynes emphasized. This can be put another way: "Economics is easy but subtle", to paraphrase the physicist Paul Ehrenfest.

Much of the difficulty, subtlety, and/or other annoyances is the result of attempting to replace common sense, mainstream logic and economic history with an overdose of mathematics, statistical game playing, and wishful thinking. Electricity deregulation (or *restructuring*, as it is more correctly called) has failed, is failing, or eventually will fail for a very understandable reason: deregulation increases uncertainty, and this uncertainty has a provably negative effect on physical investment. As I was careful to point out in both my book on natural gas (1987), and my previous energy economics textbook (2000), natural gas faces exactly the same dilemma.

The principal item that needs to be understood by all categories of readers is that when proposals were initially made concerning deregulation in gas and electricity markets, it was recognized by all concerned that this meant an increase in price *risk* — or more correctly, price *uncertainty* (which can be interpreted as risk without being able to assign probabilities to outcomes). What was not understood, however, was that in these markets, conventional derivatives (such as futures and options) are often incapable of providing satisfactory insurance against unfavorable outcomes. The reason for this is the exceptionally high volatility of *physical* gas (and electricity) prices, which is reflected in a high volatility for the price of *paper* gas (and electricity) — i.e., derivatives. Thus, unlike the situation with derivatives for oil, oil products, and financial assets, attempting to hedge the price risk encountered with gas (and electricity) by using futures and options has very often turned out to be a lottery. (The reason for placing such an excessive faith in futures and options, rather than swaps, was a desire for the kind of price *transparency* experienced in, e.g., share markets.)

The failure to understand this point has caused numerous would-be *hedgers* (i.e., insurers against price risk), and also speculators, to reach for the aspirin, although many of these players smartened up when their careers and net-worth threatened to move south. This "smartening up" has generally contributed to inadequate *liquidity* for exchange-traded electricity and gas futures contracts, which inevitably led to higher volatilities in both the paper and physical markets — which in turn resulted in unacceptable *basis risk* for these assets. (Basis risk means prices moving in the wrong direction for individual transactors, and thus invoking a monetary cost in the form of *margin calls*.) In addition, it was inadequately understood that even in the best of situations, the conventional lack of liquidity for long-dated futures and options prevents these assets from providing adequate long-term protection against undesirable price movements.

In trying to make the impossible possible, the blunder known as European natural gas deregulation has gathered momentum. What we have here is a situation where in an ideal or perfect world, it would be impossible to find a single intelligent person with even a mild social conscience who would countenance tinkering with the EU gas supply in order to make a Ronald Reagan–Milton Friedman fantasy of perfect competition come true.

This kind of language is often unacceptable in academic circles, however I cannot imagine a situation in which I would be sympathetic to policies that favored the very few over the very many. For a dozen years, and in many dozens of lectures, I have attempted to make it clear that deregulatory uncertainty and short-term contracts are the enemy of gas-consuming households and businesses, and by the same token some major producers and intermediaries in the natural gas sector. When the irrational gas deregulation proposals of the EU Commission first surfaced, they contained the absurd specification that purchase and sale contracts were *not* to exceed one year, which provides me with a wonderful opportunity to repeat a brilliant line from Graham Greene's *The Quiet American*: "*such naiveté is a form of madness*". Longer contracts are apparently now acceptable, but as yet we do not know to what extent. It is easy to guess however what the Executive Director of the IEA meant when he said that "The great news therefore — and which some will find disappointing — is that liberalization does not reduce government intervention . . . but it changes its nature". In more coherent terms, it does not reduce regulation, but because of the gross shortcomings of deregulation — as revealed in electricity markets — regulation of one type or another might have to be increased.

What some observers seem to have missed, and this includes important energy economists like David Walls (1993), is that the natural gas industry is inherently less flexible than, e.g., the electricity industry (although on the whole it may be true that it is more efficient to transport gas than to transport electricity from power plants sited very close to coalfields). Because the electricity sector is subject to Kirchoff's laws, many students of deregulation think that it is easier to control flows in the gas sector, and thus bring about the amount of network price equalization (i.e., arbitrage) required to obtain the utopian results promised by the deregulators. But contrary to this gratuitous fiction, spot prices at widely separated points in large gas networks have not followed each other so closely that it is possible to claim that they are in one market. This is largely due to coordination problems that are almost unavoidable due to erratic shifts in the demand for gas. With the present market structure, time lags are unavoidable in scheduling deliveries, which results in a suboptimal use of storage and transmission capacity that is further distinguished by the frequent appearance of transactional bottlenecks. Even the electricity market is more accommodating when it comes to avoiding "glitches" of this nature.

When Professor David Teece (1990) talks about the "chaotic" arrangements for delivery that often overwhelms pipeline transport controllers, and which often leads to congestion and imbalances, he is in essence referring to long lasting and as yet traumatic coordination problems. For what it is worth, he is informing the deregulation enthusiasts in Europe that restructuring in the United States has "jeopardized long-term supply securities and created certain inefficiencies".

He also has a message to deliver that every European "stakeholder" — as gas burning households and especially industrial users were called at the EU's "Gas Summit" in October, 2003 — should make it their business to ponder:

> "While more flexible, a series of end-to-end short-term contracts are not a substitute for vertical integration, since the incentives of the parties are different, and contract terms can be renegotiated at the time of contract renewal. There is, therefore, no guarantee that specialized irreversible investments can be efficiently and competitively utilized."

To this can be added his observation that "*Basically, whenever an industry has large investments in specialized, non-deployable assets, an integrated structure has great virtues that benefit owners and consumers*". Something that many energy buyers (and sellers) are coming to understand in this era of market liberalization is that frequent renegotiation can produce some very nasty surprises.

In the case of Europe, one of these great "virtues" afforded by integration is that large European firms can negotiate with the same authority as monopolistic or oligopolistic external suppliers — to include the kind of suppliers that former Governor Gray Davis of California occasionally labeled "out-of-the-state criminals". One hopes that the present governor of California is capable of such insights, although it is possible that he prefers the so-called wisdom of Mr Joe Roeber, who in an almost hysterical article in the *Energy Journal* (1996), told his readers that "... big gas interests in continental Europe ... will do their best to stop it happening ... and you may be sure that they will fail". By "it" he means spot or short-term markets becoming the centerpiece of European gas markets, and thus the possible replication of a California electricity-market situation where, as Professor Darwin Hall informed me in a private communication, four new governmental agencies had to be established, and the State's budget was ruined. Exactly what the ruining of a State budget means in the United States is a mystery to this humble teacher of economics and finance, but in Sweden it would simply be another step on the road to a world where things like high-quality health care and personal security continue their Brussels-sponsored journey into the welfare sunset.

In selling electricity and gas deregulation to the voters, among the pseudo-scientific arguments first employed were that increasing returns to scale were passé. A competent teacher of economics or engineering should be capable of exposing this myth in a half-hour by employing some secondary-school algebra or "soup-bowl" type cost diagrams to interpret the relationship between the expected growth rates of gas and electricity consumption, and the incentive to take advantage of scale economies (or *sub-additivity*) of the relevant cost functions. Unfortunately, however, competent teachers are seldom listed on the dance cards of the deregulation booster club: they generally turn to another class of "partner". Accordingly, one way in which this matter was approached was to complicate it by claiming that sub-additivity was absent in these industries, and thus introducing into the discussion technical matters that most readers took considerable pains to avoid.

As it happens though, the relevant materials on sub-additivity (or increasing returns to scale) are easy to access. The best approach to its theoretical aspects can be found in the intermediate textbook of Schotter (2003), while a valuable empirical application to natural gas pipelines was recently published by D.V. Gordon *et al.* (2003). On the basic theoretical level this concept works as follows.

If there is a firm that produces an output "q" at a cost $C(q)$, and there are "n" other levels of output $q_1, q_2, \ldots, q_n$, with each smaller than q, and at the same time we have $\Sigma q_i = q$, then if $C(q) < \Sigma C(q_i)$, for all levels of q (and with $\Sigma q_i = q$), we have a sub-additive cost function. In this case the (returns-to-scale) conditions for natural monopoly are satisfied, and as Gordon *et al.* note, when the issue is pipelines, any benefits that *might* be gained due to competition could be lost because of the forfeiture of scale economies, with the emphasis on "might".

Key Concepts

90/110 contract	Enron
arbitrage	Fisher-Tropsch chemistry
effective demand	flaring

"going short"	out-of-state-criminals
hubs	peak shaving
LNG	storage
market centers	stranded gas
methane	third-party access
North Dome	wheeling
open access	working gas

Questions for Discussion

1. Discuss Professor David Teece's observations on restructuring!
2. What are some of the objections toward LNG?
3. Why are economists always saying "on the other hand"?
4. What is the importance of the R/q ratio for the supply of gas? The present R/q ratio is about 60 years. What does this mean, and what it does not mean? What is natural depletion?
5. Iran is not exporting as large an amount of gas as you might expect, given their reserves. What does this mean?
6. The average price of gas today is about \$6.5/MBtu. What is the oil equivalent price? Comment!
7. What are hubs and market centers? Are inventories important for the price of gas? What is the marginal convenience yield?
8. Discuss the economics of gas pipelines, making sure that you mention compressors and looping!

Bibliography

Asche, F., P. Osmundsen and R. Tveterås (2001). "Market integration for natural gas in Europé". *International Journal of Global Energy Issues*, 16(4): 300–312.

Bahgat, Gawdat (2001). "The geopolitics of natural gas in Asia". *The OPEC Review*, 25(3): 273–290.

Banks, F.E. (2003). "An introduction to the economics of natural gas". *OPEC Review*, 27(1): 25–63.

—— (2001). *Global Finance and Financial Markets*. Singapore, New York and London: World Scientific.

—— (2000). *Energy Economics: A Modern Introduction*. Boston, Dordrecht and London: Kluwer Academic.

—— (1987). *The Political Economy of Natural Gas*. London and New York: Croom Helm.

Bernard, Jean-Thomas, Denis Bolduc and Annie Hardy (2002). "The costs of natural gas pipelines: the case of SCGM, Quebec". *Energy Economics*, 24(5): 425–438.

Bushaw, D.W. and R.W. Clower (1957). *Introduction to Mathematical Economics*. New York and Newark: Irwin Publishing.

Chenery, Hollis B. (1952). "Overcapacity and the acceleration principle". *Econometrica*, 20(1): 1–28.

Commichau, Axel (1994). "Natural gas supply options for Europé — are distant supplies affordable?" *The Opec Bulletin*, May: 8–12.

Corzine, Robert (1999). "Battle with gas gets underway". *The Financial Times*, 23 September.

Cremer, H., F. Gasmi and J.-J. Laffont (2003). "Access to pipelines in competitive gas markets". *Journal of Regulatory Economics*, 24(1): 5–33.

DeVany, A.S. and W.D. Walls (1995). *The Emerging New Order in Natural Gas*. Westport Connecticut: Quorum Books.

Dispenza, Domenico (1995). "Europé's need for gas imports destined to grow". *Oil and Gas Journal*, 13 March.

Dixon, Huw D. and Josby Z. Easaw (1999). "Regulatory policy and competitive processes in the UK contract gas market". Paper presented at the 21st International Meeting of the IAEE, Rome, Italy, June 1999.

Esnault, B. (2003). "The need for regulation of gas storage: the case of France". *Energy Policy*, 31: 167–174.

Frisch, Morten (1997). "West European gas supply/demand balance". *IAEE Newsletter* (Spring).

Giegler, Don (2006). "Comment on Hunt 'Does California need liquefied natural gas?' " *EnergyPulse* (www.energypulse.net).

Gordon, D.V., K. Gunsch and C.V. Pawluk (2003). "A natural monopoly in natural gas transmission". *Energy Economics*, 25: 473–485.

Gould, Len (2006). "Comment on Hunt 'Does California need liquefied natural gas?' " *EnergyPulse* (www.energypulse.net).

Green, R. (2003). "Failing electricity markets: should we shoot the pools?" *Utilities Policy*, 11: 155–167.

Hawdon, David and Nicola Stevens (1999). "Regulatory reform in the UK gas market — the storage auction". Surrey Energy Economics Centre.

Herbert, John H. (2001). "Natural gas hedging". *Public Utilities Fortnightly*, 1 October.

—— and Erik Kreil (1996). "US Natural gas markets: how efficient are they?" *Energy Policy*, 24(1): 1–5.

Hopper, R. (1994). "Open access in Europe". *The Financial Times Energy Economist*, 147–151.

Hotelling, H. (1931). "The economics of exhaustible resources". *Journal of Political Economy*, 39(2): 137–175.

Hunt, Tam (2006). "Does California need liquefied natural gas?" *EnergyPulse* (www.energypulse.net).

Majed, G. (1996). "A survey of financial derivatives utilised within the petroleum industry". *OPEC Review*, 20(1): 87–115.

Radetzki, Marion (1995). *Tjugo År Efter Oljekrisen*. Stockholm: SNS Förlag.

Read, Edward A. (2006). "Comment on Hunt 'Does California need liquefied natural gas?' " *EnergyPulse* (www.energypulse.net).

Roeber, J. (1996). "The natural gas spot market". *Energy Journal*, 17: 1–12.

Samuelson, P.A. (1958). *Foundations of Economic Analysis*. Cambridge: Harvard University Press.

Schotter, A. (2003). *Microeconomics: A Modern Approach*. New York: Harper Collins.

Skinner, Robert (2005). "LNG: filling gaps and flying kites — toward a global gas market?" (Stencil — presentation at a Deloitte seminar.)

Späth, Franz (1983). "Die preisbildung für Erdgas". *Zeitschrift für Energiewirtschaft*, 4(3): 99–101.

Teece, D. (1990). "Natural gas in Germany and the United States". *Energy Journal*, 11: 1–18.

Walls, W.D. (1993). "A note on natural gas futures". *The Pacific and Asian Journal of Economics*, 3(2): 221–228.

CHAPTER 5

COAL AND ITS DISCONTENTS

An examination of the energy economics literature makes it clear that this is an important chapter. In the last 15 years coal tended to become a minor topic, with the possible exception of the attention paid to its environmental shortcomings; but even so the consumption of that resource continues to grow at a rapid pace, and for a good reason: there is an enormous amount of coal in the crust of the earth, and for a long time it has been comparatively inexpensive. In addition, large or fairly large deposits are found on six continents and in 50 countries, and this "geographic balance" helps to solve a certain bothersome political issue. Global coal consumption jumped by 25% between 1994 and 2006, and now amounts to approximately 5 billion tonnes ($= 5\,Gt$).

Needless to say, some environmental matters will have to be commented on, since coal emits twice as much carbon dioxide (CO_2) as natural gas; however, I am more interested in a few economics issues that have been overlooked in the pedagogical energy economics literature, but are of considerable significance. For instance, there are fewer regions in which coal has been more thoroughly deemphasized (verbally) than the United Kingdom, but even so coal still provides about 32% of that country's energy.

I want to underscore at this point, however, that the really terrible thing about *excessive* global warming, if it is taking place, may turn out to be that it is NOT man-made. The problem then would be that we could be faced with situations that are economically and socially devastating regardless of the precautions that are taken. In fact, if an extreme range of unpleasantness seemed imminent, the lights in the Pentagon and similar establishments will burn very late at night, as Bruce Willis types in Armani military creations plot to keep the home-folks from occupying cheap seats in the losers club. (The same thing could happen with the wrong kind of oil-supply scene.)

A sort of caveat may be appropriate here. The physical destruction inflicted on New Orleans by Hurricane Katrina was clearly worse than that suffered by some German cities that had been subjected to repeated bombing during World War II. But by the end of the Korean War (in 1953), regardless of the amount or type of damage that individual communities had experienced, most of them functioned satisfactorily. On the contrary, there is talk of it taking 20 years to rebuild New Orleans, assuming that the project is undertaken. The interesting thing in this case, however, is that if the probabilities had been correctly calculated, and a modest amount of investment undertaken over the years, the kind of sophisticated engineering that has been practiced for decades in, e.g., the United States and Holland could have turned Katrina into no more than a soggy happening.

I also want to use this chance to bring up to date several topics in my earlier energy economics textbook (2000) and my book on coal (1985). Interestingly enough, I wrote another coal book but never published it because I thought that hardly anyone would bother to read it; however, once the production of oil has peaked, or shows signs of peaking, and the future availability of natural gas is correctly appraised, a new coal book might find the readership it deserves — though hardly before. It might also be a good idea if, before examining this chapter, readers examine a short, non-technical article by Murray Duffin (2004) in www.energypulse.net, and also the incisive comments on his work that are published at the end of the article. Zach Allen (2005) was also useful on this topic.

There are a few equations in this chapter that many readers would prefer not to encounter; however, they can be easily skipped. The point being made in Eqs. (1)–(4) is that although from a static point of view there might be, with present production, 260 years of coal left, once we take into consideration the rate of growth of coal production or consumption, this figure becomes much smaller.

1. Some Background

Coal is formed from the remains of trees that have been preserved for millions of years under special non-oxidizing conditions where, after falling, they either did not rot or rotted very slowly. Top-grade coal requires a gestation period of tens of millions of years, and scientists have calculated that the average time required to accumulate enough vegetable-like matter to eventually form 1 m of coal is about 1.6 million years. Similarly, a 1 m thick coal seam might have been compacted originally from a 120-m layer of plant remains.

A good example of what this is all about is the coal rich state of Wyoming, in the western United States. It has been estimated that the basis of coal seams in that region was formed tens of millions of years ago, and the dead vegetation was positioned in such a way that it did not rot or dry out. Perhaps 60 million years ($= 60$ my) of this arrangement led to the thickest coal seams ever found — up to 60 m thick in some places — with a low sulfur content. High-value resources such as this provided a strong incentive for further exploration: the United States has the world's largest coal reserves, and is the second largest hard coal producer after China. The US coal industry is also on average the most productive (as measured in output/man-years), even though "eastern coal" — from east of the Mississippi River — is largely from underground mines. (Western coal production is generally an open-pit (or opencast) activity, where productivity is about 2.5 times as large as in underground installations.) About 72,000 persons are employed in the US coal industry, and coal has an important role in millions of US homes, largely after being initially transformed to electricity.

It is possible to distinguish a spectrum of coals, ranging from peat through anthracite. Peat, which is brown, porous, has a very high moisture content, and often contains visible plant remains, is the lowest class of coal, with an average energy content of 8.4 GJ/ton. (Here G signifies *giga*, which is a billion, and J signifies the basic energy unit *joule*. Thus, $1\,GJ = 1,000,000,000$ joules. The matter of energy units and equivalents will be taken up again at some length in this chapter.) Next we come to lignite, which can be regarded as the transition link to hard coal ($=$ bituminous $+$ anthracite coal). Lignite also contains a great deal of water, and its average heat content is 14.7 GJ/ton. Bituminous coals, on the other hand, are characterized by a low moisture content, while the moisture content of anthracite coal is extremely low. Where energy values are concerned we distinguish between sub-bituminous coal, with an average energy value of 25 GJ/ton, and bituminous coal, with an average energy value of

29.5 GJ/ton. Anthracite coal, which is jet black and difficult to ignite, has an average energy value of 33.5 GJ/ton. (Note here that thus far the short ton (= ton = 2000 pounds) is being used instead of the more common metric ton (or *tonne* or "t" = 2205 pounds), and so 1 t = 1.1025 tons.)

According to Brendow (2004), coal accounted for 37% of global electricity generation in 2000, and it will reach 45% in 2030. The power plants in which this coal will be used will, on average, be technologically superior to those in use today, but from an engineering point of view they will remain relatively simple affairs. Coal is burned in a boiler, and hot steam under high pressure is produced. This goes to a steam turbine, whose mechanical work output takes the form of a rotational movement of generator shafts, which makes it possible to produce electricity. Students of thermodynamics and engineering dynamics know that energy losses cannot be avoided in this activity, but with a "combined cycle" arrangement, some of the heat that might have been lost can be used to generate more electricity, which can sizably boost the overall efficiency of the installation. Brendow believes that by 2030 more than 70% of coal-based power generation will take place, employing advanced coal combustion technologies. Obviously, for this prediction to hold, some gigantic financing problems will have to be solved.

In examining the energy literature on any level, we are constantly encountering the word "primary". Primary energy is energy obtained from the direct heating of coal, gas, oil, etc., as well as electricity having a hydro or nuclear origin. Electricity obtained from the burning of substances such as coal is a secondary energy source. Something that should be appreciated is that the energy content of the coal used to, e.g., generate electricity is inevitably greater than the energy content of the electricity itself, because the coal burning equipment does not possess an efficiency of 100%.

In some countries it is common to categorize coal as soft coal or hard coal. Soft coal consists of brown coals and lignite, whereas hard coal is bituminous coal and anthracite. In this system, peat is regarded as a fuel type in itself, and is not particularly desirable any longer from a commercial point of view. Still another system divides coal into two classifications: brown coal and black coal. Brown coal is geologically young and high in water content, while black coal is considerably lower in water content, and contains much more carbon. Black coal ranges from sub-bituminous coals (which are usually dull black and waxy in appearance) to anthracite, and is divided into two general categories: coking or metallurgical coal, and thermal or steaming coal. (Coking coal will only appear en passant in this book.) Brown coal is usually "consumed" fairly close to where it is mined, while steam coal for exports are exclusively high energy value coals.

The demand for coal (= hard coal + brown coal + lignite) grew by 62% over the 30 years before 2003, and the International Energy Agency (IEA) expects it to grow from that year by another 53% up to 2030. These figures make it very clear that coal is *not* on its way out — as many believe and/or hope. In addition, in 2030, one prediction has it that, globally, power plants will absorb some 74% of coal supplies as compared to 38% in 2000. The world might be a better place if we learned how to use less coal, but in some respects the electricity generating sector is not a bad place for growth to take place: that sector probably has more experience in suppressing deleterious emissions than any other, and is better financed to make the necessary investments.

It might also be useful to note that the average global power generation efficiency is approximately 33%, while state-of-the-art efficiency is almost 45%. Considering that most of the existing power plants will be scrapped or upgraded by 2030, the aggregate efficiency in that sector should reach at least 40%. This will greatly favor coal as an alternative to nuclear energy, although by my calculations, in a carbon-conscious world, nuclear energy will be a more economical source of electricity. On the other hand, on strictly private economical grounds, coal should be clearly preferable to gas at that time as a result of the greatly decreased availability of gas (due to depletion).

With regard to the efficiencies mentioned above, these are the so-called "first-law efficiencies", after the First Law of Thermodynamics. Calling this efficiency E_1 we can write E_1 = (energy transfer achieved by system)/(energy input to the system). It would not be easy to challenge this definition on intuitive grounds; however, moving from a verbal assertion of the First Law to E_1 is too complicated to be done here. It can be mentioned, though, that the First Law is the well-known Conservation of Energy, which is usually stated as energy cannot be created or destroyed, and thus the total energy of the universe is constant.

It needs to be added that the icing on the thermodynamic cake is the Second Law of Thermodynamics, which happens to be a work of genius first proposed by the French artillery officer Sadi Carnot. It can only be referred to on this occasion, but one of the things it tells us is that there is an upper thermodynamic limit to efficiency, and technological progress involves no more or less than gradually raising the actual efficiency to that limit. It is difficult to say exactly what this limit will be for coal-based generating equipment, but Janssens and Cosack (2004), and others, indicate that 60% is the best that can be hoped for, although this will not be realized in the near future.

The most important exporting countries for hard coal are Australia, China, South Africa, and Indonesia. The exports of these countries total about 75% of seaborne hard coal, however the United States is still regarded as the global swing producer/exporter of coal, occupying the same position with that energy resource as Saudi Arabia does with oil. Japan is the most important importing country, and it is forecast that Japan will account for 25% of world imports in 2020. Coal consumption has declined in Europe because of environmental stipulations that favor gas, which at present is available in large amounts from the Norwegian North Sea, Russia, and North Africa — and perhaps eventually by pipeline from Central Asia via the Former Soviet Union.

Steam coal trade in the Pacific region surpassed the Atlantic market in the early 1990s, and by 2000 was 20% higher. Today more than 100 firms/producers are active on the world market, which together with domestic markets gives the aggregate coal market the appearance of a competitive network — and according to some observers considerably more than an appearance. At the same time though, reading the chapters on perfect competition in your favorite microeconomics or price theory textbook will not provide you with an ideal introduction to the kind of logic needed to understand the conditions under which this important resource is produced, bought, sold, and priced.

For instance, it is impossible to conceive of those 100+ firms operating at the bottom of their long-run cost curves as they would under ideal textbook conditions. Instead, equating supply to demand in the real-world coal market means the price rising at least to the bottom of the long-run cost curve of the highest cost firm in the market, which in turn means that the "intramarginal" (i.e., lower cost) enterprises will earn substantial economic rents (= profits greater than the amount needed to continue producing at their current level). The key explanatory factor for this phenomenon is, of course, a difference in the quality of coal deposits controlled by individual firms, which is a condition that cannot be eliminated in the short run, nor perhaps in the long run.

In the coal market, as everywhere else, there is a great deal of talk about replacing almost all long-term contracts by spot transactions. This kind of aberrant thinking comes from the present urge toward liberalization, and in some cases makes absolutely no sense at all. The ostensible justification is that spot prices respond rapidly to the existing market situation, rising when the market is tight, and falling when there are excess supplies, which is true. A problem here, though, is that enormously expensive investments are essential if markets like oil, gas and coal are to function in a manner that benefits households, small businesses, and energy intensive large businesses, and these investments will not be forthcoming if the managers of oil, gas, or coal suppliers are constantly faced with highly volatile spot prices that sometimes give the impression of a price collapse. With long-term contracts this volatility can be partially ignored.

Let us put this in a slightly different way. In finance theory, volatility is a common proxy for uncertainty. It can be easily demonstrated with some elementary algebra that, e.g., in the neo-classical models featured in conventional economics textbooks, a high price volatility (and thus a high uncertainty) reduces physical investment. This is also common sense, and has to do with risk aversion. As it happens, although there is not a single world market for coal, nor a unique coal price, it is clear that coal has displayed a more stable price over recent decades than oil and gas, and as a result we have not had to entertain the kind of complaints about inadequate investment that we constantly encounter about the other two.

There has already been a reference to energy units, but that can be expanded on somewhat here, and also in the sequel. Several units are used to measure energy. Physicists seem to prefer joules, while engineers are often partial to British thermal units (Btu), or kilowatt hours (which will be considered later). Another unit is calories (or kilocalories). The transformation between joules and Btu has been carefully measured: $1\,\text{Btu} = 1.055 \times 10^3$ joules. Since different coals have different calorific contents, a standard measure of energy content for coal can be extremely useful. This is the ton of coal equivalent (= tce), which is defined as a *metric* ton (= 1 tonne = 2205 pounds) of coal with a specific heating value of 12,600 Btu/pound. Consequently, more than one metric tonne of coal might be necessary to produce the heating value of 1 tce. For example, 1 tce = 1.4 tonnes of sub-bituminous coal, using the heating value of 9000 Btu/pound given earlier. (*Note*: 1 kg = 2.204 pounds).

Consider also that in 1977 world coal production came to 3400 million metric tons of raw coal, which was 2500 million metric tons of coal equivalent (= 2500 mtce), which in turn had the energy content (in Btu or joules) of 33 million barrels of oil per day (= 33 mb/d). This last figure is obtained from the following equivalency between oil and coal: 1 tce converts to 4.8 barrels of oil, and 76 mtce/year is equivalent to 1 mb/d of oil. To a certain extent, tce is an artificial unit, since its heating value is almost certainly higher than the heating value of an average tonne of coal extracted during any given year, but even so it is extremely useful.

It was mentioned earlier that the average global efficiency of coal using power generation equipment is 33%. Thus a standard pound of coal equivalent functioning as an input in this equipment would have an energy output of only $12,600 \times 0.33 = 4150$ Btu *electric* = 4150 Btu(e). Readers should note the difference between "equivalent" and "electric".

One more thing can be looked at here. Coal is sometimes referred to as a *backstop resource*, where the expression "backstop" (or even input into a backstop technology) was introduced by William Nordhaus (1973) in a brilliant article, and involves the availability of a substitute to which no "scarcity royalty" can be attached. For instance, at the present time coal has been described as a backstop for motor fuel since it can be transformed to synthetic oil (as Marlon Brando assured us at some length in the film "The Formula"); however, hydrogen that is produced employing uranium or thorium in a breeder reactor probably comes closer to the strict definition, as perhaps does hydrogen obtained via electricity generated in wind installations. Of course, coal might not be as plentiful as some people believe, and in any event it is not certain that using enormous quantities of "uncleaned" coal is a good idea. What we can do now is to examine the effect of the growth rate "g" on the availability of coal, noting that our result is only an approximation. Taking X_t as the consumption of coal in period "t", we can write

$$X_t = X_0 e^{gt}. \tag{1}$$

The term X_0 is the consumption of the resource in the initial period. Cumulative resource use is then defined as the integral from the initial period to a terminal period T, whatever that happens to be:

$$X = \int_0^T X_t dt = \int_0^T X_0 e^{gt} dt \text{ or } X = \frac{X_0}{g}(e^{gT} - 1). \tag{2}$$

If X^* is the total amount of the resource available at an initial period, we obtain for the approximate time to exhaustion T_e the following relationship:

$$T_e = \frac{1}{g} \ln \left(\frac{g X^*}{X_0} + 1 \right). \tag{3}$$

It is also interesting to observe the effect of changes in X^* on T_e. Differentiating we get

$$\frac{d T_e}{d X^*} = \frac{1}{g X^* + X_0}. \tag{4}$$

What we see here is that the substantial changes in X^* are not reflected in time to exhaustion (T_e). We can also compare the difference between the static time to exhaustion (where $g = 0$) and the dynamic — where, e.g., the value of g is taken as 2.5%/year. The static value ($= X^*/X_0$) is approximately 260 years. Now, adjusting this for growth by employing Eq. (3) we get $T_e = (1/0.025) \ln[(0.025 \times 260) + 1] = 80.5$ years for the "dynamic" value, which is a sizable difference. This is enough to make us wonder just how much coal the great grandchildren will actually have at their disposal.

The word "approximate" was used several times above. This is because although the *annual* rate of growth is, e.g., 2.5%, the compounding in the derivation is continuous, and so the *effective* growth rate turns out to be greater than 2.5%. Thus, "g" in the calculation is overstated. This means that the actual T_e would be greater than 80.5 years, and if increases in X^* took place, which is likely, there would be a further increase. Of course T_e will not come anywhere near the static value. Readers who want to avoid the effect of continuous compounding can work with $(1+r)^t$ instead of e^{rt}.

2. The World Coal Scene

This section begins with a short review of the coal situation in various parts of the world — "short" because the rapid change that often takes place does not justify a more thorough perusal. More important for me, however, is the suggested "commoditization" of the world coal market, which refers to the irrational desire by various buyers and/or sellers to increase the use of "spot" transactions while decreasing the employment of long-term arrangements. We have seen this sort of thing in other energy markets, and the results have not been encouraging.

Coal in North America is dominated by the large production and consumption of the United States. Coal not only heats more than 50% of US homes, but the energy in US coal reserves (measured in Btu or joules) is well in excess of the energy in the Saudi Arabian oil. The former situation is probably an important (though apparently unspoken) reason why the United States could not sign the Kyoto Protocol — aside from the fact that the world would probably be better off without the Protocol and the conference in which it was produced. Coal can fairly easily be transformed into motor fuel, although — unlike natural gas — with present technology this does not appear to be a very profitable activity.

In South and Central America, only Colombia and Venezuela are major coal countries, and at the present time only Colombia is making a large contribution to the world market. Most of the mining in these two countries is of the opencast variety, which suggests a high productivity, but this is not the case as yet. Much, however, is expected of these two countries.

In Europe (outside the Former Soviet Union), Germany is the largest coal producer if lignite is counted, and it should be taken into consideration because it supplies the largest input for German power plants. Germany is similar to the United Kingdom in that it is a country where quality of coal produced is increasing, while until recently quantity was decreasing, although a possible difference is that the remaining coal mines in the United Kingdom are the most productive in Europe. Quantitatively, Poland comes after Germany, but it has often been said that coal industry executives in Poland do not fully understand that the world hard coal market is a very competitive place. Of course, if economic growth in Asia continues at its present pace, then the financial prospects for all the large coal producers in every part of the world will be greatly improved, regardless of their technical or business acumen.

As with oil and gas, Russia ranks close to the top of the coal production league. At the same time its productivity (in output/man-year) is well below international averages. The World Bank has taken a strong interest in that country, providing it with financial and technical assistance for the so-called restructuring/privatizing purposes. Since I happen to find it inconceivable that Russia would need technical assistance from an extravagant refuge for high-flown mediocrity, I find it easy to conclude that the basic intention of the World Bank in this matter is to justify its budget in the eyes of its most persistent critic, which happens to be the US government.

Two highly productive and large coal producers and exporters are Australia (which specializes in coking coal) and South Africa. Of late, though, the progress of exporters like China and Indonesia should hinder an expansion in their market shares. Surprisingly, the United States is no longer the expansive force in the world coal export sector that it was during various periods of the last century. It is occasionally claimed that the reason for this situation is that high wages and salaries have decreased the international competitiveness of US coal, and it might also have something to do with the power plant sector of that country consuming a very large (and perhaps increasing) fraction of the domestic coal output. Along with China, the United States occupies the top positions in global consumption (as well as production).

Much more could probably be added to the above discussion; however, I think that everyone reading this chapter appreciates that for good or evil, coal is extremely important in both the present and future energy pictures. Globally, trade in steam coal is expected to increase at a fairly high rate between now and 2030, and because the price of coal is seen as stabilizing in comparison to oil and gas, increasing amounts of coal-fired generating capacity will likely be the rule in much of the world. Japan has not been mentioned here yet; however, Japan is an extremely important coal importer. At the same time, coal has a poor image in Japan, and I happen to believe that the implicit desire of the Japanese energy establishment is to minimize its use, while drastically increasing nuclear based capacity — if (or when) that is politically possible.

Unfortunately, it seems to me that it is highly unlikely that the huge amount of coal that is being used, and will be used, can be "processed/treated" in such a way as to substantially and efficiently reduce the amount of carbon dioxide (CO_2) that it produces. As you undoubtedly know, CO_2 is a key element in global warming, which in one sense happens to be good rather than bad, because without it the earth would be uninhabitable; but on the other hand there is the possibility that too much of it is currently being produced, and perhaps this excess supply is due to anthropogenic (i.e., man-made) sources rather than the various quirks of nature. The opinion of this teacher of economics and finance is that regardless of the actual situation, an assumption should be made that the overwhelming majority of the elite of climate scientists who say that there are dangerously excessive CO_2 emissions know what they are talking about.

Furthermore, the excess production of CO_2 should be negotiated down by heads of states, and not jet-setters from the environmental bureaucracies. To my way of thinking, the failure of the Kyoto exercise is precisely the inability of its participants to detect this option, and to recommend its immediate adoption. Of course, one reason they failed to do so is because half-baked talk-shops of the Kyoto variety are the life-blood of many footloose busybodies whose speciality is pseudo-intellectual environmentalism, and the waffle at these congresses counts for much more to many of them than attempting to evaluate a topic whose details are almost a total mystery to them. As for emissions trading, which is a highly advertised offshoot of Kyoto, this is hardly more than a scam, and as an advisor to President Putin remarked, it is about making money rather than curbing emissions.

Something else that is about making money is the attempt to "commoditize" the trading of coal. In the words of Robert Murray, president and CEO of Murray Energy — the largest independent, publicly owned coal producer in the United States — trying to make a true commodity out of coal is like "trying to fit a square peg in a round hole" (*Petroleum Economist*, October 2002). He continued by calling coal trading "an unnecessary fad" and "a doomed concept". The economic issue here involves putting an intermediary between buyers and sellers in the mold of a formal exchange of one sort or another; however, for the time being the idea is that "over-the-counter (OTC)" establishments are to fulfill, this function. Here I should make it clear that there is a very great difference between an OTC market and a genuine exchange — roughly the difference between the Fulton Fish Market and the New York Stock Exchange.

To me the kind of language employed by Mr Murray is perfect for describing electricity deregulation and the attempt to commoditize electricity, although that bogus escapade is rapidly losing popularity. The new–old argument being used in the case of coal is that both buyers and sellers would be better off if they accepted the beauty of OTC trading and short-term contracts because — as we teach our beginners — genuine competition always provides better outcomes to all involved. This is undoubtedly true for many items, but I doubt whether it applies to a market like coal, where tremendous amounts are involved under very special circumstances.

In an ideal situation the OTC market would have many of the features of an auction market (like the stock exchanges), with full price transparency, and where the possibility exists for participants to buy or sell almost any amount of the commodity at any time. It could then be argued that prices would correspond closely to the theoretically correct prices that would prevail in a textbook market. Moving beyond elementary theory, this would mean that the large inventories of coal held by, e.g., sellers could be reduced because these ladies and gentlemen would *always* be in position to provide coal from their own mines or from the trading marketplace, and, presumably, any saving they achieved would be shared to some extent by consumers. Some consumers (i.e., distributors) also maintain large stockpiles, but these could also be reduced because these consumers could also use the open market.

Here the reader should be aware that this kind of argument was employed in California when the electric deregulation fiasco was being sold to the television audience and their representatives in the California legislature. By putting an exchange or pseudo auction market for large scale trading between buyers and sellers, the theory was that it would be unnecessary for sellers to maintain a large reserve capacity, which in turn should eventually work to the benefit of everybody. The outcome of this less than brilliant gambit was, among other things, the ruining of the state budget and an electricity price explosion in San Diego; however, it did give some whole-salers (i.e., generators) an opportunity to charge outrageous prices for filling the gap between the local supply and demand.

Moreover, in a "super-ideal" situation some serious hedging (i.e., insuring against price risk) could take place, because the OTC contracts being used — or a spin-off of these contracts — could function in a manner similar to genuine futures (or perhaps even futures options) contracts, which would allow buyers and sellers to "lock in" present prices and thus avoid being faced with ruin in the event of having to fulfill any unfavorable commitments that they might have entered into. Naturally, all of this was a "hype", but as with the electricity markets in California and Scandinavia, it was treated with complete seriousness by some very intelligent and highly educated academics and businesspersons.

That brings us to a comment on the difference between real markets and ideal markets. In ideal markets there are large numbers of participants on both the buy and sell side, completely transparent prices, and a great deal of liquidity — which means that it is always possible to buy or sell any quantity without drastically altering these transparent prices. Furthermore, the prices that are formed are theoretically correct prices, which are sometimes called "scarcity" prices, in that they accurately reflect the intentions and capabilities of buyers and sellers. In addition, in the light of the bad news from, e.g., California, neither these prices nor the conditions under which they are formed encourage or facilitate "gaming the market" by ambitious market agents.

Reality is very different from this. Although the physical coal market has many competitive aspects, various changes have taken place during the past few years, and in particular some large consolidations (i.e., mergers) have undoubtedly reduced the degree of competition. Most important for this discussion, liquidity (and probably transparency) in the OTC market is too low to make it attractive for hedging large volumes. As with electricity, the best hedging item for buyers and sellers are long-term contracts. In addition, and this is crucial, Mr Murray berates the (OTC) intermediaries for their lack of knowledge of the industry. The same is even more true of the electricity market, where the gap between "quants" and traders in the exchanges, and the men and women involved within the physical market is enormous.

3. Coal Prices and Price Theory

One of the great mistakes of mainstream academic economics was/is the emphasis placed on the Hotelling model of exhaustible resources (1931) as a valid representation of the way that an industry such as coal (or oil or bauxite or whatever) functions. Then why bother with it here? The answer is that my presentation will be brief, and my explanations of what is wrong with that construction should be useful to serious students of resource economics.

We can begin with the case of a manager who has a fixed stock of coal, R, that can be extracted a unit at a time at a constant marginal cost, c. Let the *net* selling price in the present period be $p_0 = p' - c$, where p' is the market price. Similarly, for the next period, take p'' as the market price, and $p_1 = p'' - c$ is the expected net selling price in that period.

The manager's choice problem for each unit of coal is as follows: produce an extra unit in this period, and invest the proceeds (p_0) at the market interest rate (r) in order to receive $p_0(1 + r)$ in the next period; or defer production of that unit until the next period, when it will be extracted and yield an *expected* profit of p_1. The manager will be indifferent as to the date of extraction if $p_0(1 + r) = p_1$, and if this expression is rearranged we get Hotelling's famous result $(p_1 - p_0)/p_0 = r$ — which is usually written as $\Delta p/p = r$. If this expression holds, it makes no difference in which period we extract the resource; but if this equality does not hold, then because marginal cost is constant, we end up extracting all the coal in either this period or the next. For instance, if $\Delta p/p < r$, extraction will take place today because $p_0(1 + r)$ is greater than p_1 (or, what amounts to the same thing, the rate of growth of the net price is less than the interest rate).

During the period from the first oil price shock until a few years ago, when people like myself were able to convince many of the great and good in resource economics that Hotelling's logic was highly suspicious (and its study a blatant waste of time for innocent students), the equilibrium result derived above was treated with the same veneration in the learned journals of economics as was shown with Einstein's $E = mc^2$ elsewhere. However, if we take a careful look at a disequilibrium situation — e.g., $\Delta p/p > r$ — we will be able to comprehend just how hopeless it is.

With this kind of disequilibrium the expected rise in net prices is greater than the rate of interest, and so no production takes place in the present period. In terms of large real world coal mines this is nonsense, because with the exception of mom-and-pop type operations, in the real world, coal mining is a very capital intensive activity, and some production might have to take place in any and all circumstances in order, e.g., to obtain money to pay interest and amortization costs on the equipment being used. In my previous energy economics textbook (2000) I have provided a graphical analysis of the course of production in a multi-period situation, but should fixed capital be present that analysis would have to be greatly amended to consider the behavior of producers in periods where the Hotelling result might indicate no production.

As it happens, there is a *real option* associated with things like producing or not producing, leaving equipment idle, dismissing employees, etc. (*Note*: a *real* option as compared to the kind of *financial* options is discussed in Chapter 8 of this book.) Remembering that, e.g., p_1 is the *expected* price, it may happen — and often does happen — that the actual price in the next period is very different from the expected price. Given this possibility, and employing the assumed disequilibrium condition ($\Delta p / p > r$) posited above, it could be argued that at least some production should take place in the present period until a clearer picture is obtained of what market conditions will or are liable to be in the next period. The cost of this limited production corresponds to what in finance theory (and Chapter 8) is known as an *option premium*, where by paying this premium the manager hopes to dispel some of the uncertainty associated with the (at present) unknown future price. Incidentally, the theory here is not as important as the terminology.

It should also be recognized that there are explicit costs associated with stopping and starting production. Allowing production to continue for a while at an unchanged or slightly different level could be regarded as another (real) option for dealing with uncertainty concerning the future price. In the face of all this, I think we can conclude that since Hotelling's work did not take into consideration fixed capital, or real options, it is not comparable to anything Albert Einstein did in his real or fantasy life. Let me put it this way: it is virtually without any scientific value, although as explained above it might give readers some idea of what real option theory is all about.

The upshot of all this is that anyone trying to explain the movement of current coal prices with the Hotelling apparatus will not get very far. One theoretical reason of course is that the Hotelling approach is intended to explain the behavior of individual firms in a make-believe, perfect-competition textbook world, where there is a smooth extension from the behavior of firms to that of the relevant industry. This assumes that curious readers ignore the fact that in the coal market some firms are in possession of very rich deposits, and as a result they enjoy an (*ceteris paribus*) unbeatable advantage over their rivals. Of course, large firms with exceptional management and state-of-the-art technology can occasionally merge with firms that have superior resources, and apparently a great deal of this has been taking place in the last few years.

Most coal is probably still sold on long-term contracts for reasons given in the previous section, but the spot market is not insignificant. Naturally, spot prices influence (long-term) contract prices, as many buyers have discovered. Here we have one of those pretentious puzzles of the type often considered in graduate level seminars and the more abstract learned journals; however, as compared to physics what we are dealing with in this case is abstraction for its own sake, where in truth an apparently attractive solution is no better or worse than any other.

For example, spot prices were generally lower than contract prices in 2003, and many utilities thought it in their interest to purchase coal off-contract. As bad luck would have it for some of these establishments, spot prices began to increase at a rapid rate, and when buyers turned to the contract market, prices there had been dutifully adjusted up. A bystander unacquainted with the more elevated levels of economic theory might suggest that the spot market was mainly for risk takers, which is not only true but to my way of thinking indisputable; but as to be expected, the theory that eventually these prices must converge has been offered in some up-market publications and seminars. This happens to be a piece of academic wisdom that is basically without consequence outside the alpine heights of pure theory — regardless of whether or not it occasionally comes to pass. What it comes down to for sellers with a speculative bent is being in the spot market when prices are escalating, and being heavy in contracts in a buyer's market; while for buyers the opposite is true. This is no more than commonplace street-wisdom, although its embellishing might require long sessions in lecture and seminar rooms. Whether these sessions will produce players who can make the right moves most of the time in the real world is highly uncertain.

China has become a major operator in the world coal market, but on the selling as opposed to the buying side, where they do most of their oil business. Despite the talk about China's growing role as a coal exporter, about 65% of China's energy requirements are satisfied by coal (and 25% with oil), and it has been said that there is an insufficient supply of coal to satisfy the rapidly growing domestic demand, given the shortcomings of China's rail transportation network, and the location of major coal deposits. Essentially this means that when these defects are remedied, exports might be decreased. Since in the short run the possible loss of Chinese coal from the export market cannot be compensated for by other exporters or other energy media, it appears that a steady global price escalation cannot be avoided.

The last project in this section involves a short examination of the input–output situation for a large coal-based power plant, but to get the maximum benefit from this, a closer look at units is required. It has already been mentioned that the units in which heat is measured are Btu and joule, and calorie (or kilocalorie) was also mentioned. One of the great discoveries of science was that heat and work are equivalent, and so if we have some coal we know that if used in the right way the energy in this coal might suffice to, e.g., move a cable-car up Coogee Bay Road (in Sydney, Australia), or keep the large red light burning outside Molly Mae's delightful Dine and Dance establishment (near Fort Jackson, South Carolina). In discussing *power* with Molly Mae's scholarly clients, the units mentioned might be horsepower (= hp), which applies to the engine rating of their late model cadillacs; and kilowatts (or kW), as in the reading lamps in their plush libraries. Unfortunately, we need to go deeper into this subject, and exploit the fact that energy in all forms but heat is the ability to do work: once we have heat we are dissipating the latent energy in the coal.

The next thing to understand is that power is the *rate* at which work can be done (with the emphasis on "rate"). Thus watts or kilowatts (= 1000 watts) and horsepower can be expressed in terms of joules or Btu per second. A watt is a rate of one joule per second, and thus a kilowatt is 1000 joules per second. Since 1 hp = 0.746 kW, we get 1 hp = 746 joules per second. As pointed out earlier 1 Btu = 1055 joules (= 0.252 kilocalories). From here, moving from seconds to hours, it is a simple matter to get $1\,Wh = 3.6 \times 10^3$ joules $= 3.412\,Btu$, or $1\,kWh = 3412\,Btu$. Accordingly, $1\,kWh = 1.34\,hp$. All of this might seem tedious, but it is stimulating to realize that the man often considered the best brain of the 20th century — John von Neumann — specialized in remembering all sorts of physical and chemical constants. Summing up we can write 1 megajoule ($= 10^6$ joules) $= 948.6\,Btu = 239$ kilocalories $= 0.375\,hph = 0.2778\,kWh$.

Take special notice of the last two equivalents: joules go to hph and kWh, and *not* hp and kW. This is where we introduce "time" into the analysis. Thus if we know the Btu in a pile of coal, we can calculate the hours that the bulb burning outside Molly Mae's place of business will provide a welcoming beacon for weary travelers, assuming that we also know the power rating of the bulb (in watts or kilowatts).

Suppose that the pile of coal weighs one tonne. This particular tonne may contain approximately 27,800,000 Btu of (latent) heat energy — approximately because different coals have different heat contents. Suppose also that the bulb in question is 1000 watts ($= 1$ kW). A simple calculation using the above figures tells us that $27,800,000\,Btu = 8148$ kilowatt-hours. Looking at the units (or dimensions) we see that this bulb will burn for $8148/1.000 = 8148\,h$ if all the energy in the coal can be turned into electricity. In reality the efficiency with which the energy in the coal can be converted to electricity is well under 100%. Thirty-three percent might be reasonable for this example, and so Ms Molly Mae will only have about $8148\,h \times 0.33 = 2689\,h$ of precious illumination. Even so, given the music and gaiety offered inside, her guests will probably be glad to provide a certain compensation for any thermodynamic or engineering frailties that the lady might encounter in the valuable work she and her associates are carrying out.

Now we can ask about the fuel requirements for a coal-based power plant. Suppose that the plant generates 1000 megawatts (1000 MW) of electricity, where $1\,MW = 1,000,000$ watts $= 10^3$ kilowatts. Thus 1000 megawatts $= 10^6$ kilowatts, and this is the power rating of the plant. The energy that the plant's managers would expect it to generate in 24 h of operation is 24×10^6 kWh. It has also been pointed out that $1\,kWh = 3412\,Btu$ in a perfect system, but because of heat loss and other thermodynamic phenomena it takes 10,342 Btu to obtain $1\,kWh$. Thus 24×10^6 kWh is equal to $24 \times 10^6 \times 10{,}342 = 24.820 \times 10^{10}$ Btu. The 10,342 here is often called the "heat rate".

The next step, whose purpose is to get the daily (24 h) input of coal to the plant, is equally simple. If the coal has a heating value of 12,600 Btu per pound, a tonne of this coal ($= 2205$ pounds) has a heating value of 2.78×10^7 Btu. If 24.820×10^{10} is the number of Btu required per day, we immediately find that the daily coal requirement is $24.820 \times 10^{10}/2.78 \times 10^7 = 8928$ tonnes.

Finding the cost of the coal does not require much effort. One tonne has a heating value of 2.78×10^7 Btu. With an efficiency of 33%, the heat rate is $3412/0.33 = 10{,}340$ Btu/kWh. The number of kWh in a tonne of coal then turns out to be 27,800,000 divided by $10{,}340 = 2689$ kWh. If the average cost of a tonne of coal is \$45/pound, one dollar will buy $2689/45 = 60$ kWh. Or we could say the coal cost of a kWh is 1.66 cents.

The above is gone over in a more leisurely fashion in Chapter 7, and so before leaving this section some remarks can be added to about the optimal deployment of coal-based power plants. The theory associated with this topic is presented at considerable length in both my previous textbook and book on coal, but even so teachers of economics often fail to get the message. The essential point here is that peaky, short duration loads should be carried by equipment with low fixed costs, since this equipment might be idle a large part of the time. Prior to the development of combined cycle gas-based equipment, the so-called "merit order" called for natural gas to perform this function, but later it became conceivable that natural gas could compete with coal, nuclear, and hydro for carrying the base load — which is the load that is always on the line. Accordingly, as long as the price of gas was low, it was perhaps the most versatile member of the merit order.

When I deal with the subject of an ideal electricity generating system, I of course cite Sweden, where the base load is traditionally produced by nuclear and hydro. Hydro also carries most of the peak load, because it can be easily switched on and off, or output raised or lowered. Naturally, it also produces a large part of the base load, and nuclear and hydro together almost divide evenly the total electricity output of the country. For what it is worth, Sweden has often had the lowest electricity generating costs in the world, and is one of the lowest producers of CO_2 from its electricity sector.

Norway is the other winner in the low-cost league, and in that country almost all electricity production is hydro based. Accordingly, for many of us who remember our secondary school mathematics, this means that since electricity costs in the two countries are almost equal, nuclear based electricity is very inexpensive. I have unfortunately had to entertain arguments that nuclear is in reality very expensive for Sweden, and this will continue to be the case; however, the situation here is that if someone does not understand why this belief is incorrect, they would hardly be able to comprehend a simple argument to the contrary.

A good example here would be the so-called "energy professor", Gordon McKerron. In a recent article in the *Observer* (4 November 2005) he wants to know "who puts up the cash" for a new generation of nuclear power stations. The answer to that question is that according to the economics that I teach it should be the persons who benefit from these facilities — whether they know it or not — and that means just about everybody. In the case of Sweden one of the highest living standards in the world was created on the basis of the inexpensive power supplied by nuclear. Like McKerron, however, this fact is unknown to the present Swedish government, who have foolishly tied their economic future to the fortunes of the European Union.

Something that should be emphasized is that some of the logic being employed above is different from that provided in your microeconomics textbooks. Nuclear has a lower marginal cost than, e.g., gas, but if you construct a conventional supply curve and attempt to justify the use of nuclear to produce the peak load, you would be wrong: obviously, it does not make sense to construct a nuclear plant that might be idle for a considerable period.

4. From Coal to Liquids

In his recent testimony to the Australian Parliament, the director of the Australian Bureau of Resources and Energy (ABARE) painted a bright picture for his country where oil and oil products are concerned, saying that Australian coal could provide Australia with "thousands of years of oil" (and presumably oil products such as motor fuel), and moreover what was true for Australia was valid to only a slightly lesser extent for the rest of the world: the price of oil was sure to fall in his account of the energy future. Forty dollars per barrrel was his estimate of where the oil price would end up.

Coal may turn out to be a valuable source of liquids (oil and oil products), but hardly the panacea that Mr Fisher imagined. We should realize this immediately if we take a careful look at the situation in three coal rich countries: Germany during the Second World War, South Africa during the embargo of the l980s, and the United States today as it increasingly faces bad news on the motor fuel front.

Germany produced synthetic crude of a somewhat inferior quality from coal, and from this "ersatz" crude refined products which included aviation and vehicle fuel, diesel and heating oil, and lubricants. We hear a great deal about the German success in this endeavor, but at most the German syncrude industry produced 100,000 b/d of oil and oil products, which was not much for a country engaged in a war on two fronts, without any conventional oil, and with thousands of tanks, trucks and planes that were involved in combat virtually every hour of every day.

South Africa had better luck, and may have satisfied as much of 40% of their requirements by transforming coal to various liquids. In any event, during the embargo, the firm Sasol Ltd methodically improved the Fisher–Tropsch process that came to prominence in Germany during the war, and as result obtained the technology and expertise that made them an extremely profitable firm after the embargo period. Something that is very seldom discussed is the oil that was brought into South Africa by "smugglers" of various descriptions; however, I am of the opinion that without that oil the output of Sasol would have not have been sufficient to keep the standard of living in that country from greatly deteriorating.

The thing to appreciate here is that making liquids from coal is much more expensive than moving it in a pseudo-surreptitious manner across an extremely long border. Sasol still apparently make some liquids from coal, but they seem to be primarily interested in turning gas into liquids. For example, they have large GTL (gas-to-liquids) operations planned in gas rich Qatar and Nigeria, where a spin-off of the coal-to-liquids technology will produce liquid fuels from gas.

All this sounds very attractive, and it is attractive for Sasol executives and owners, but when output figures are examined, it becomes clear that

Mr Fisher's enthusiasm was not really justified. The widely viewed television program "60 minutes" presented a reportage in which coal-to-liquids enthusiasts in the coal rich western United States explained how the oil price could be pressed down or restrained by a more intensive application of the technologies already in use by Sasol; however, in terms of output if all present plans were translated into reality, the output of coal based liquids would at most be increased by 2.5 mb/d in 25 years.

The output (2.5 mb/d) is a great deal if it were available today, or during the present decade, but it will not be much in 25 years if present consumption and production trends continue. There are also some important cost considerations that deserve to be mentioned. It has been said that on average a GTL plant will provide products at a cost of $40,000 per daily barrel of capacity, as compared to $15,000/b from a conventional oil refinery (*Business Week*, 27 February 2006). A coal based barrel would hardly cost less.

What it all comes down to again is that solving the energy problem may eventually require a heavy dose of conservation, and here there are some questions as to how well this can work in a day and age in which technology rather than self-restraint is often proclaimed what we need.

5. Environmental Issues

> *"Danger invites rescue"*
> — Benjamin Cardoso

Until further notice, my position on the environment is similar — though not identical — to that of Professor David Goodstein (2004) of the California Institute of Technology. Oil and gas are much scarcer than commonly thought, and rather than reduce their consumption of energy, and particularly motor fuel, Mr and Ms Consumer will insist on — and by one means or another obtain — the continued use of coal at the present intensity, or even higher. It is not certain, but some observers have suggested that this could place a dangerous burden on the environment.

It would be nice to believe that along with the increasing consumption of coal, environmental considerations will be given their proper weight; however, this is far from certain. It is for this reason that I take the liberty of agitating for a direct and immediate attack on environmental dangers, which includes a Manhattan-Project type crusade in favor of safe nuclear energy and certain renewables, as well as an expansion of the kind of legislation that Governor Arnold Schwarzenegger is attempting to introduce in California. "The debate is over", he has said. "We know the science. We see the threat. And we know the time for action is now".

The lovely thing about the governor's agenda is that it is not explicitly based on fools-gold or pie-in-the-sky type initiatives such as emissions trading. One reason, of course, is that California is in the worst possible geographical position if global warning actually triggers some of the environmental catastrophes that have been mooted. I am referring to floods and a rise in the sea level that could obliterate some very choice real estate. According to an article by Petit in *Nature* (2005), California is one of the places where legislators "have begun their own versions of Kyoto-like regulations". What this apparently involves is capping carbon dioxide (CO_2) from more than 600 power plants in California and the northeast, which is a grand idea, assuming that "capping" does not mean tempting fate by playing trading games that involve institutions such as the Scandinavian exchange NordPool.

Some time ago I was informed that emissions trading had been shown both theoretically and experimentally to be the most efficient means for ensuring a healthier environment. Like the Russian submarine commander in Tom Clancy's *Hunt for Red October*, as soon as I heard this silly comment I knew what it meant: that gentleman was in line for a piece of the research and/or travel grants that for some bizarre reason are being passed out to supporters of this crackpot scheme.

To get some idea of what we are dealing with here, readers should find out the kind and quantities of pollution that are associated with a typical coal-fired power plant, and in particular mull over the millions of tons of CO_2 that are emitted into the atmosphere annually. Reducing or sequestering in the ground or oceans more than a small percentage of these emissions via half-baked market mechanisms is completely out of the question. No proof of that will be offered here; however, for those readers who want proof let me suggest that they examine the quantities of CO_2 that are involved, and then contact their local exchange to find out how much it has cost on the market for emission permits to get rid of substantial quantities of CO_2 when that market is in a "bull" mode. Some energy intensive firms in Sweden have performed this exercise and concluded that if they have to accept expenditures of this magnitude, then everything under their control that is movable should be transferred to another part of the world as soon as possible. Needless to say, this would be economically ruinous for Sweden, and in particular for every part of the Swedish welfare system. Similarly, "carbon capture" is probably a pipe-dream if very large quantities are involved. Another description might be "play for the gallery".

Professor Eric Smith (of Tulane University) has informed me that combined cycle generation mated to coal gasification units, located typically at a "mine mouth" in the United States, has acceptable pollution features, though capital costs can be slightly above the average. (What we have here is coal gasification, and the resulting hydrogen and carbon monoxide used to spin the wheels of a turbine.) He also notes that at present no "hydrogen economy" is possible without using nuclear to produce hydrogen. As the brilliant US jurist Benjamin Cardoso once noted, "danger invites rescue"; however, rescue in the form of a large input of nuclear would not be easy to sell.

Now let us consider some more complicated issues. When I wrote my coal book, I identified two worrisome environmental threats: an immediate threat from sulfur dioxide (SO_2) and a distant threat from carbon dioxide (CO_2). We do not hear much about SO_2 these days because it was possible to reduce these emissions to a considerable extent by the intensive use of new technologies such as fluidized-bed combustion.

Also important was the fact that at the time I wrote that book, about 160 times as much CO_2 (measured in tonnes) as SO_2 was emitted from a coal-fired electricity generation plant, and while acid rain — largely due to SO_2 emissions — was bad news, it might be small potatoes as compared to the problems that could eventually be posed by overloading the atmosphere with CO_2, which is the greenhouse gas that justly attracts the majority of attention at the present time.

The basic issue causing the acrimony and bad feelings where greenhouse emissions are concerned is uncertainty. Environmentalists emphasize that since expectations are not always fulfilled, optimal economic policies should turn on discerning the kind of uncertainty being confronted with a view toward keeping future options open. Needless to say, this advice should not be dismissed, because uncertainty exists in almost all human endeavors, together with the presence of risk aversion on the part of a majority of market actors. The irreversibility or near-irreversibility of many economic processes is also an acknowledged fact of life. The result of this situation is that flexibility is an attractive proposition for all except the most dogmatic legislator and his or her economic advisor.

Flexibility where a fossil fuel such as coal is concerned means either a lower than anticipated rate of growth of coal consumption, or a resort to expensive investments in equipment and techniques for "cleaning" coal. This issue has been clouded by a magnificent outpouring of hot air from various faculties of economics in the form of so-called scientific analyses, but the bare bones of the matter come down to the following.

The environmental and ecological effects of excessive CO_2 emissions will most likely only be felt in the distant future. As a result, it often happens that uncertainty about the damage resulting from these emissions cannot be resolved for years, perhaps decades, by which time irreparable harm might have been done. Accordingly, current resource use (in this case coal consumption) should be more conservative than in situations where decisions made today do not entail a foreclosing of tomorrow's alternatives.

This is what the sometimes complex subject of option value is all about, and obviously the subject has a lot to recommend it — even within the domain of common sense. It will be considered in Chapter 10, and also briefly below, but what I do not want to do here is to confuse the issue by suggesting to readers that they will be able to find in some advanced textbook or journal article a magic formula that can be used when or if they encounter one of the pseudo-experts dealing with this subject who, like former President Ronald Reagan's science advisor, viewed almost all talk about atmospheric pollution as "unnecessarily alarmist".

Option value is the amount that a risk averse person would be willing to pay to prevent an irreversible investment from being made when he or she cannot fully ensure against certain risks associated with that investment. For instance, if global warming has the deleterious effects that they say it has, and you have invested in a luxurious house in a Bangladesh beach colony, you might like to know that you could pay insurance firm "X" an amount every year of "y" that would make it possible for you to continue to enjoy the satisfaction you experienced in that house if the weather turns ugly. Of course, a certain amount of insurance of this nature may exist, but given the very negative experience of some of the largest insurance firms over the past few years, it would not be inexpensive. I can also note that you might have to enjoy that satisfaction in Switzerland, but perhaps this is not the place for an elaboration of that theme, given the complexity of defining "satisfaction".

By the same token, *quasi-option value* has to do with the willingness to pay for information about choices when a given investment decision is irreversible. It is an objective value determined by persons who place a monetary amount on delaying an irreversible investment decision until the information they seek can be revealed. As is probably obvious to everyone reading this book, information is — or should be — more valuable for someone who is very risk averse than someone who is only slightly risk averse, or risk neutral. By extension, the larger the penalties resulting from making the wrong decision, the more valuable the information. In the present discussion the main actor is the government, who makes the decision in the name of its constituents.

(In simple terms, a risk neutral person would accept a fair bet: if she bet a dollar on the flip of an unbiased coin, she would accept a dollar if she won and the loss of a dollar if she lost. The expected value here is zero, which means that it is a *fair* bet. In addition, in principle, she would not be concerned about the size of the bet. On the other hand, a risk averse person would not be interested in a fair bet. For instance in order to take this bet he might require $1.25 if he won, or give $0.75 if he lost, although the mathematical expectation here is $(1/2) \times 1.25 + (1/2) \times 0.75 = \$1.00$.)

In the context of our present discussion, the cost of information might be measured in terms of the goods and services that have to be foregone during the period when the environmental damage that could be caused by the burning of a fossil fuel was being assessed, and the use of such things as coal was being kept below the level which would have prevailed if the suspected or alleged environmental damage did not exist. A few years ago this cost — whatever it was — was regarded as excessive by many businessmen and women, politicians, commentators, and other important personalities who were charged with keeping the wheels of progress spinning. The attitude of many of these persons has changed a great deal over the last few years.

I would like to mention again the work of von Neumann and Morgenstern (1944). If you take the logic in their book and apply it to the kind of environmental matters that we are discussing in this section, you come to the mantra SAFETY FIRST! — in other words, ruling out high risk activities as long as other reasonable choices are available. "You know that the best you can expect is to avoid the worst", Italo Calvino once remarked, and according to William Poundstone (1992), this neatly summarizes the central paradigm of *The Theory of Games and Economic Behavior*, which is the widely known but not always well understood minimax principle. This can be put in another and, I believe, a better way, since real life is not like a poker party where many hands are dealt. The optimal strategy turns on avoiding a catastrophic loss! (And note, in the poker party where a few dollars are in the pot every hand, a catastrophic loss is not likely; but forgetting to insure your castle or private plane is another matter.) As noted elsewhere, Erich Röpke once called game theory "Viennese coffee house gossip", but it is difficult to accept that a man who was often called the best brain of the 20th century did not know what he was talking about.

6. Concluding Remarks

In the film mentioned earlier, "The Formula", Marlon Brando says to a Swiss colleague, "Today it's coal. In ten years it will be gold". As owner of a large part of the hard coal deposits in the United States, as well as a superior process for producing synthetic oil (from coal), the Brando character may well have known what he was talking about. Of course his time frame was very wrong: it would not be 10 years, but 30 or 40 years, or longer, before the billions of dollars started to roll in, but in terms of historical time it hardly makes a difference. Besides, in showing what they know about the future importance and use of coal, the writers, directors, producers, and maybe even the actors involved with this film gave the impression that they were better informed about coal than many academic energy economists.

Coal provides the majority of the world's electric power, which means that clean or dirty it is indispensable: oil is too expensive and is also "dirty", nuclear is unpopular, and while the capital cost of gas-based facilities is lower than coal, over the last few years the volatility of gas prices has been alarming. Everyone today is talking about coal gasification, since "syngas" is more acceptable environmentally than raw coal. The problem here could be price, with the average cost of a kilowatt of power from a syngas plant reputedly somewhere in the neighborhood of 1750 dollars (= \$1750/kW).

Everything considered, this might barely make it competitive to nuclear, where base load considerations are concerned, assuming that the environmental "bit" is not discussed. It has been suggested that "emerging technologies" will brighten the horizon for coal, which may be true, but even so it may turn out to be a matter of "too little and too late".

At several instances in this book I have pointed out that one of the things making nuclear highly competitive is the increasing length of life of nuclear installations. Sixty years is the present figure for new or refurbished facilities. Coal-based power plants are also being spruced up. In South Africa the Kriel Power complex consisting of six units and with a power rating of 3000 MW will have its longevity extended from 30 to (ostensibly) 50 years by the Siemens Corporation. South Africa's nuclear capabilities are definitely world class; however, it would be difficult to argue that that country can afford to ignore the energy that is available in low-cost domestic coal.

The largest Swedish utility, Vattenfall, is building a pilot coal-burning generating plant in Germany in which CO_2 emissions into the atmosphere are supposedly close to zero. (This sometimes comes under the heading of "FutureGen".) Nothing has been said about efficiency, but undoubtedly the intention is to get this well over the comparatively low level of 35–40% that characterizes many coal-based installations at the present time. (What this means is that only 35–40% of the energy input is converted into output. In Chapter 7 of this book the expression *heat rate* is used to describe this situation, and its logic carefully explained.) This facility of a few (or perhaps a few hundred) megawatts — as compared to a thousand megawatts for optimally sized installations — will be ready for evaluation in 10 years. If the news is good, a 250 MW demonstration plant will be constructed. Hopefully the Germans will be pleased by these (symbolic) arrangements, because according to the Hamburg branch of the German Industrial Association, the pricing practices of Vattenfall have threatened the industrial viability of a large part of the Hamburg region, and also parts of East Germany. Vattenfall, of course, has met these charges with a song-and-dance about free competition; however, in a letter to the Swedish ambassador in Berlin, the Germans insisted that they were confronted by a monopoly — a monopoly brought into existence by deregulation.

The 10-year horizon mentioned above also appeared in a speech of President George Bush on 27 February 2003. He announced a $1 billion,

10-year demonstration project whose purpose was to construct a coal based, zero-emission electricity and hydrogen facility of 275 MW. Coal will be transformed to gas, in the course of which it becomes mostly hydrogen and CO_2. The hydrogen will be used to generate electricity (in turbines or fuel cells), while the carbon dioxide will be stored. It goes without saying that eventually this technology or something like it will be essential, but a question needs to be asked as to why a decade is necessary to provide a 275 MW power plant whose basic technology has been discussed for many years. Of course, the important thing is not to expect too much quantitatively from this technology. Even if it shows itself to be a winner, it will still take years to replace the electric capacity and output coming on stream in the period before 2013.

In economics, as compared to physics, there are many trivialities, and I am afraid that our students are too occupied with them to get the message. The crucial thing here is that (1) there is going to be a huge increase in the use of coal, and (2) most of this coal will be an extremely large contributor to greenhouse gases. What happens as a result of this situation is left for interested readers to think about and/or investigate.

Key Concepts

anthropogenic	megawatts
black coal	opencast mining
brown coal	option value
Btu	primary energy sources
CO_2	scarcity royalty
hard coal	secondary energy sources
heating value	soft cola
intermediary	syngas
liquidity and transparency	western coal

Questions for Discussion

1. Construct a numerical example illustrating the "dynamic length of life of coal reserves if demand/production grows by 2%/y".
2. What is a "swing producer"? Who are considered the swing producers for coal, oil, and gas?

3. What is the suggested commoditization of the world oil and coal markets all about?
4. What are the characteristics of an ideal market?
5. Derive the Hotelling result and discuss! Does it remind you of Albert Einstein's famous equation?
6. Why would the scarcity royalty of coal be higher in, e.g., Indonesia than in Australia?
7. What did Marlon Brando have to say about coal in the film "The Formula"?
8. What is an auction market? Do you think the world coal market can be considered a market in "perfect competition"?
9. What is the "heat rate"? The "merit order"?
10. Suppose that coal with a rating of 11,000 Btu/pound costs $45 a tonne. What is the oil equivalent price?

Bibliography

Allen, Zach (2005). Comments on present manuscript.
Banks, Ferdinand E. (2006). "Logic and the oil future". *Energy Sources*, II(1): 1–22.
—— (2004). "Economic theory and a faith-based approach to global warming". *Energy and Environment*, 15(5): 837–852.
—— (2001). *Global Finance and Financial Markets*. Singapore and London: World Scientific.
—— (2000). *Energy Economics: A Modern Introduction*. Dordrecht: Kluwer Academic.
—— (1985). *The Political Economy of Coal*. Lexington, MA: Lexington Books.
—— (1974). "A note on some theoretical issues of resource depletion". *Journal of Economic Theory*, 9(2): 238–243.
Brendow, Klaus (2004). "Global and regional coal demand perspectives to 2030 and beyond". In *Sustainable Global Energy Development: The Case of Coal*. London: World Energy Council.
Duffin, Murray (2004). "The energy challenge — 2004". *EnergyPulse* (www.energypulse.net).
Goodstein, David (2004). *Out of Gas: The End of the Age of Oil*. New York and London: Norton.
Hansson, Bengt (1981). "Svalet kan elimineras". *Svenska Dagbladet*, 24 Juli.
Harlinger, Hildegard (1975). "Neue modelle für die zukunft der menscheit". IFO-Institut Für Wirtschaftforschung, Munich.

Hotelling, Harold (1931). "The economics of exhaustible resources". *Journal of Political Economy*, 39(2): 137–175.

Janssens, Leopold and Christopher Cosack (2004). "Forging internationally consistent energy and coal policies". In *Sustainable Energy Development: The Case of Coal*. London: World Energy Council.

Malinvaud, E. (1969). *Lecons de Theorie Microeconomique*. Paris: Dunod.

Neumann, John von and Oscar Morgenstern (1944). *Theory of Games and Economic Behavior*. Princeton: Princeton University Press.

Nordhaus, William D. (1973). "The allocation of energy resources". *Brookings Papers on Economic Activity*, 3: 529–576.

Petit, Charles (2005). "Power struggle". *Nature*, 438(7067): 410–412.

Poundstone, William (1992). *Prisoner's Dilemma*. Oxford: Oxford University Press.

Schultz, Walter (1984). "Die langfristige kosten entwicklung fûr steinkohle am weltmarkt". *Zeitschrift für Energiewirtschaft*, (1).

CHAPTER 6

AN INTRODUCTORY SURVEY OF ECONOMICS AND NUCLEAR ENERGY

President George W. Bush has finally presented the long awaited energy policy of his government. Nuclear energy was specifically mentioned as a main weapon to combat the build-up of excessive greenhouse gases — whose existence was thus explicitly acknowledged — as well as to provide the energy that will be needed in the possible transition to what might eventually turn out to be a less energy intensive economy. As pointed out in my previous energy economics textbook (2000a), in such a transition more energy might initially be required than ever for such things as the production of, e.g., hydrogen: although thermodynamically hydrogen has occasionally been called a loser, hydrogen might eventually merit the status of an economic winner in a world where oil is scarce and motor fuel is valuable. Something else that seems to be needed is a better understanding of the simple economics pertaining to nuclear energy and its optimal use in electricity generation, since recent economics textbooks and other publications seem reluctant to take up this topic.

I also present in the appendix a moderately long discussion of nuclear energy in Sweden. The situation in that country seems quite clear to me, although it has confused some readers of my papers on this subject. The Swedish nuclear sector is probably the most efficient in the world in terms of cost and reliability, and it is becoming more efficient all the time because of technical change and improved procedures. In a recent issue of *Business Week* (10 July) it was stated that "smart money is placing multi-billion dollar bets on ethanol, wind power, and solar, it's not throwing buckets of cash at nukes". The money may be smart, but not the young ladies and gentlemen making the calculations in the investment banks that deal with energy matters: nuclear plants with a "life" approaching 70 years and where capacity costs might fall to $1500–2000 per kilowatt are unbeatable. In fact they are unbeatable at a higher capacity cost. Moreover, when it becomes politically possible to exploit a larger amount of the energy in uranium, it should be clear where smart money belongs to.

My main intention here is to simplify and/or extend some of the discussion of nuclear energy presented in my previous textbook on energy economics (2000a). I also attempt to update and correct an earlier survey paper (2000b) on the same subject. The incentive for this project was provided by the announcement of President Bush that nuclear energy will be a cornerstone of his government's long awaited energy policy. Interestingly enough, on the day when this announcement was made, a gentleman from a country that is overwhelmingly unfriendly to nuclear energy informed me that an opinion is gaining ground among his colleagues that the only way to achieve the Kyoto stipulations on greenhouse gases is via the decreased consumption of energy intensive activities by all categories of consumers, and/or a greater reliance on nuclear energy. Since the first of these can be completely excluded in the real as opposed to a soap-opera world, an increased resort to nuclear energy seems unavoidable.

Regardless of any decisions taken in Washington — or anywhere else — nuclear based electricity with its almost negligible output of greenhouse gases is about to enjoy a renewed popularity, sooner or later. It is impossible to verify the absolute *certainty* of excess "anthropocentric" (or man-made) global warming — even if this assumption is supported by an overwhelming majority of top-level scientific opinion — however a mention of additional evidence to that effect appears constantly in both the popular and the scientific press. Just as important, the widely advertised "fuel of the future", natural gas, is far less plentiful than widely believed. Well before the middle of the present century, the global output of gas will very likely peak, which means that even before then it should be clear that its price has departed permanently from the bargain-basement levels it achieved at various times during the last decade of the 20th century.

An important reason given by the Bush government for rejecting the Kyoto Protocol had to do with it placing the United States at an economic disadvantage. But nothing would be more disadvantageous to *any* country than to reject nuclear energy in favor of alternatives that in reality are

economically unsure, regardless of what your favorite politicians and journalists say or think. As I have mentioned at various places in this book,
the optimal energy portfolio at the present time will contain a number of
assets. Arguments have been presented in virtually every part of the world
that nuclear energy (from *best practice* installations) is more expensive than
that obtained from, e.g., fossil fuels or renewables, but this is mostly a gross
misunderstanding with some prominent neurotic overtones: for instance, in
what could only be called a neurotic outburst, the previous Swedish prime
minister called nuclear energy "obsolete".

Economics is not an experimental science, but it so happens that important experiments take place all the time, and there is one involving nuclear
energy and its comparative cost that deserves particular attention. I am
speaking here of the introduction of nuclear energy into the Swedish energy
picture. On average, over the past decade, Sweden has produced electricity whose cost is the lowest or second lowest in the industrial world. The
other contender for the championship is Norway, where more than 95% of
electric power originates with water — which is universally regarded as the
least expensive means to produce electricity. For those persons who have
decided to think otherwise, let me refer them to the cost and market price of
Norwegian electricity over the past few decades where, until deregulation
raised its illogical head, electricity consumers were especially favored.

About 43% of Swedish power is produced in nuclear establishments,
while water is the source of most of the rest. Just by knowing this, and
the near equality of electricity cost in the two countries, it can be shown
by a few minutes of secondary school algebra that best practice nuclear
installations of the Swedish variety rank with hydro as the least-cost producers of electricity. And there is more: if the recycling of nuclear fuel
were permitted, then the average cost of electricity (in dollars per kilowatt-
hours) would unambiguously fall beneath that of water based electricity.
Of course, this might already be the case, since extending the "life" of
many nuclear reactors from 40 to 60 years, and beyond will in some cases
mean a drastic decrease in the capital cost. (A non-technical review of
this issue can be found in Hellman and Hellman (1983) as well as in the
next chapter of this textbook, but it is obvious that we can perceive the
logic of this result by simply examining the basic "annuity" formula, or
$P_c = rP(1+r)^T/[(1+r)^T - 1]$, where P_c is the total "periodic" capital

cost (= interest + amortization), r, the discount factor, P, the price of the asset, and T is the "length of life of the asset". *Ceteris paribus*, as T increases, P_c falls. The decline in P_c as T increases can be obtained immediately by differentiation, but intuitively, as T increases, the amortization cost falls. Readers should verify this by taking several different values of T.)

What about the disposal of nuclear waste? My approach to this matter is not very politically correct since it has to do with my belief that the nuclear reactor might deserve the title of the pre-eminent scientific invention of the 20th century. Disposing of nuclear waste should turn out to be a far less complicated scientific problem, although it definitely is not the kind of thing that deserves to be treated lightly. *Ceteris paribus*, the assumption that I feel most comfortable with is that the same kind of persons who designed the first reactors will have no great problem solving the disposal problem — if they are allowed to. It has also been suggested that nuclear waste is not really waste but, because of its energy content, may eventually turn out to be a valuable source of additional reactor fuel. If this is true, it would be disposed of by feeding it into the next generation of reactors.

According to the International Atomic Energy Agency, on 1 May 2005, there were 441 nuclear plants in operation, with at least 32 being constructed. Commercial reactors are in operation in 31 countries, and they provide about 17% of global energy. Furthermore, expectations are that at least 20 additional plants will come on line in the next 15 years. (South Korea, for example, is thinking in terms of eventually constructing 20 new plants, and the present US Energy Secretary has made it clear that if he had his way, as many as 15 or 20 new nuclear facilities would be constructed in his country as soon as possible.) Just as important, many installations are now being upgraded. For instance, for political reasons two nuclear plants had to be taken out of service in Sweden; however, upgrading the remaining 10 has enabled more than the lost *energy* (in kilowatt-hours) to be regained. What we can expect is that energy output in almost all countries with nuclear assets will probably be increasing all the time, even without the addition of new capacity. (*Note*: energy is measured in kilowatt-hours, while capacity is measured in, e.g., kilowatts or megawatts. In Sweden, capacity has decreased, while energy has marginally increased.)

Moreover, although no nuclear facilities have been constructed in the United States for more than 30 years, the Nuclear Regulatory Commission has approved and certified new designs by the Westinghouse and General Electric (GE) corporations. The new generation of GE reactors will be constructed in less than four years in Japan, which means that the cost of power from these reactors might be even lower than what is generally advertised. (The cost of power from a reactor that takes a short time to construct will be lower than the one that takes a long time, *ceteris paribus*, because the former will be producing earlier, and therefore earning the money to repay the interest and amortization costs of the facility sooner.)

Perhaps the most attractive plant under construction at the present time is located in Finland. This plant has the largest "nameplate" capacity in the world, 1600 MW, and according to the Finnish government, it will "enhance Finland's ability to meet its Kyoto greenhouse gas targets". Finland's environmentalists have declared the new installation "dangerous", but possibly they have confused it with those in neighboring Russia and/or the Baltic countries, where there is a large amount of equipment (of the Chernoble type) still operating that could not possibly obtain a licence to produce electric power in Western Europe or North America. In any event, little or no mention was made by the government of the need to have access to inexpensive, reliable electricity, since in Finland as elsewhere arguments on that level are not likely to be welcome or comprehended by many persons who will be crucially dependent on that commodity. On this point I can add that if the nuclear reactors that were closed in Sweden had been kept open, and the profits it earned were turned over to the schools in Malmö (where the facility is located), the educational decline now being experienced in that city could easily have been reversed. The same applies to Malmö's health sector.

This might also be a good place to note that a key statistic where nuclear energy is concerned is the capacity factor (which can be defined as *The actual energy produced in a given period divided by the (rated) capacity of the installation multiplied by the number of hours in the period*. This can be turned into percent by multiplying by 100). In considering the United States, the average capacity factor is now above 80%, as compared to 58% in 1980, where these figures do not consider annual "down time" (which usually is about three or four weeks) for maintenance and inspection, while in Finland this down time is taken into account. Unfortunately, in many countries no clarification is provided concerning the method used to calculate the capacity factor, although it should be obvious that the second method is being used when we observe a reference to capacity factors that are greater than 100.

Finally, let me stress that I am not trying to formulate a comprehensive argument for an immediate mass expansion of nuclear energy, because according to, e.g., the real options theory it probably makes sense to go slow and wait for the next generation of nuclear equipment — which should soon be available — instead of rushing madly into what in the long run might be viewed as a technically sub-optimal nuclear inventory.

1.   Some Basic Physics and Economics of Nuclear Energy

The input–output description of a nuclear reactor is simple. (Natural) uranium — which as clarified below is not the same thing as uranium ore — is transformed by a nuclear reaction to a substance that heats water and produces steam. The energy in the steam is transmitted by turbine blades to a generator shaft whose rotation produces electricity.

The reaction referred to above is nuclear (or atomic) fission. For example, a large uranium atom breaks into two smaller parts, releasing energy and neutrons. The neutrons trigger (via collisions) further break-ups, which is where we get the expression "chain reaction". Controlling this chain reaction in order to obtain the desired (stable) reaction rate is a crucial operation, and one way this is done is by passing the neutrons through water in order to increase the frequency of collisions. By keeping the water under a fairly high pressure (e.g., 150 atmospheres), it remains liquid even at high temperatures. (Obviously, a mathematical relationship can be formulated here in which the reaction rate is the dependent variable, with the water pressure a key (independent) variable on the other side of the equation.)

Right away a dilemma is suggested by the possibility of insufficient water unexpectedly flowing next to the fuel, causing the kind of heating that leads to a literal "meltdown" that particularly impacts on the base of the reactor. This is the kind of thing that voters in most countries do not want to have any part of, and so designers have provided equipment that shuts down automatically if control systems stop working, and in addition dissipates the heat produced by the reactions in the core, while stopping both fuel and radioactive waste from escaping. In other words we have a "fails safe" scenario, whose components are classified as "passive". Equipment is now available — such as the *pebble bed reactor* — that is optimally passive, and instead of water features graphite to regulate the flow of neutrons. More unique, instead of producing steam the heat generated is applied to a semi-inert gas such as helium, nitrogen, or carbon dioxide. It is this gas that drives the turbine.

Before going to more complicated matters, it needs to be appreciated that while energy produced from fossil fuel is the result of an uncomplicated chemical process, energy derived from nuclear fuel originates in the force binding the constituent parts of the fuel's atoms together, and its release necessitates the alteration of the structure of the atom itself. This can be an extremely complex process, though highly rewarding in terms of the energy that can be obtained.

The most common reactor is the light water reactor (LWR), of which the pressurized water reactor (PWR) is one variant, and the boiling water reactor (BWR) is another. The actual reactor operation is only a single element in what is known as the nuclear fuel cycle, because the storage and management of wastes is such an important activity. The total cycle begins with the mining, milling and treatment of (uranium) ore, and concludes with the management of uranium waste. (At present the cycle employed in the United States is a "once through" cycle in that it is not completed (or closed) by the reprocessing of spent fuel. Instead there is both interim- and long-term storage. In a complete cycle spent fuel is partially or totally reprocessed in order to extract more energy from uranium than is obtainable from a "once through" arrangement. The problem here is that plutonium comes into the picture.

Next it should be understood that uranium — or better *natural uranium*, which is the reactor input — has three naturally occurring isotopes: U-235, U-238, and minute amounts of U-234. In this context an isotope can be regarded as a component of natural uranium (which will be explained in the next paragraph). The word "isotope" literally means "same place", and these isotopes occupy the same place in the periodic table of the elements, although there is a difference in their mass because they have a different number of neutrons in their nucleus. Of these three only U-235 is naturally fissionable, and thus capable of providing the kind of reaction that leads to the generation of electricity.

Unlike the others, U-235 can be made to split if its nucleus is struck by a slowly moving neutron. The mass of these fragments and neutrons is now somewhat less than that of the original nucleus and, most important, the reduction in mass has been transformed into kinetic energy (i.e., motion), which in turn is converted into heat as the fission products collide with surrounding atoms and are brought to rest. Other U-235 atoms may absorb the neutrons released by a previous fission, and themselves undergo fission. The release of neutrons leading to further fissions constitutes the *chain reaction* mentioned earlier.

Now we take a look at how natural uranium comes about. Prior to the activity just described, we have the mining of uranium ore, after which it is mechanically crushed, and uranium in the form of (impure) uranium oxide (U_3O_8) is extracted. This is commonly known as *yellowcake*, and much of the trade literature involves the availability of this commodity and its price. The production of yellowcake is the key step on the way to *natural uranium*. Further purification and processing will yield uranium hexaflouride (UF_6), which is a feedstock for the *enrichment process* that will be considered directly below. *It is at this point in the fuel cycle that we have natural uranium*! (For some reason natural uranium is sometimes referred to as "uranium metal" (U), and according to basic chemistry, it comprises 84.8% of U_3O_8.) Readers should focus on the difference between uranium ore and natural uranium.

The problem is that natural uranium contains only 0.7% U-235 (or about 1 part in 140), and most reactors require fuel containing, on average, 3% U-235. (That is to say, between 2.7% and 3.3% U-235.) Thus *if* enriched uranium is desired, an upgrading of natural uranium must take place. (If we wanted weapons grade uranium, enrichment would have to produce about 93% U-235.) In the United States the gaseous diffusion method of enrichment developed during the second world war is still used. UF_6 is pumped through a series of porous membranes, where the molecules of the lighter isotope (U-235) pass through the membrane walls more rapidly than the heavier isotope (U-238). When extracted the gas has an increased content of U-235, and obviously this process can be repeated until the desired enrichment is achieved.

The *front end* of the nuclear cycle is basically concerned with upgrading (or enriching) natural uranium to the required quality (i.e., richness). The "non-upgraded" portion of the U-235 involved in the process is called *depleted uranium*, or *tails*. Professor Owen (1985) provides a valuable example in which 5.5 kg of natural uranium (with 0.711% U-235) becomes 1 kg of enriched uranium plus 4.4 kg of depleted uranium (i.e., tails) containing 0.2% of U-235. The front end consists of the first four stages of the nuclear fuel cycle, and stretches from the mine to the reactor core. The last two stages, whose purpose is to resolve the spent fuel problem, are called the *back end*. Here it can be noted that uranium typically accounts for 20–30% of nuclear fuel costs, which in turn account for 10–15% of total generating costs. The remaining fuel costs are due to various nuclear fuel services, such as conversion, enrichment, and fuel fabrication. (It should be noted that in a *full* cycle, it would be unnecessary to distinguish between a front and back end.)

The enriched product is converted into uranium dioxide (UO_2) pellets, which are further processed into a form (e.g., fuel rods) which can be inserted into a reactor core. Now, with fission induced heat available, steam can be produced, which is eventually transformed to the motive power for a conventional electric generator. The power output is controlled by varying the population of neutrons in the reactor core. According to Hecht (2006), the fuel for the next generation of reactors will be enriched uranium formed into tiny "pebbles". This is the so-called "pebble bed" approach mentioned earlier, and basically it seems to provide an absolutely safe reactor.

Now let us pick up the story from the point where the upgrading is complete. What takes place in the reactor is a mass-to-energy conversion in which the amount of energy that can eventually become available is huge. (The expression "mass-to-energy" deserves attention because it is here that we have an overtone of Albert Einstein's work.) In theory, the energy output of 1 kg of U-235 is equal to that contained in 2000 metric-tons (or *tonnes*) of oil, which is 2 million times as much in terms of weight. As mentioned, only about 0.71% of natural uranium is U-235. All except a minute amount of the remainder is U-238, which is unsuitable for the direct production of energy, because it captures neutrons without undergoing fission. This would greatly reduce the total energy produced by a given amount of natural uranium (U) were it not for another phenomenon. After capturing a neutron, the nuclei of U-238 transmute into an unstable element that is not found in nature: plutonium 239 (= Pu-239). Plutonium can also undergo fission, and thus both U-235 and Pu-239 are fissile elements, while U-238 is called a fertile element. The process by which a fertile element is converted to a fissile element is called breeding, and the breeder reactor is specifically designed to capture the enormous amount of energy that is inherent in U-238 should intentional breeding take place. (Another fertile element is thorium 232, which is at least as abundant in nature as uranium.)

Reprocessing is one of two approaches to spent fuel management, and it involves chemically separating the plutonium, uranium, and radioactive residues found in irradiated fuel. The alternative is storing spent fuel in an untreated or partially untreated form. There is a genuine economic dilemma here due to the difference in the *expected* present value of the cost of the two options, particularly since these costs are dependent on the forecasts of the future fuel supply, and the efficiency of waste management. Accordingly, there is scope for some ugly mistakes due to the inability to forecast future costs and prices with a high degree of accuracy.

In natural uranium the ratio of fissile to fertile atoms is 1/140, which indicates that without upgrading there would be a difficulty in maintaining the fission process, although slowing down neutrons with the help of a non-absorbent medium called a *moderator* will increase the probability of a neutron being absorbed by a U-235 nucleus. It might also be useful to know that heavy water reactors (HWR) of the Canadian deuterium uranium (*CANDU*) type differ from the equipment mentioned earlier, since its basic fuel is non-enriched (natural) uranium instead of the enriched commodity. (There is a widespread tendency to ignore CANDU reactors, but this may be a serious mistake.) Magnox reactors in the United Kingdom also use non-enriched inputs, and there are other designs. LWRs are shut down several weeks annually for inspection and maintenance, and during this period about one-third of the fuel rods are replaced. CANDU reactors are refueled continuously without interrupting their operation.

At least nine-tenths of all uranium used at present is enriched, and the enrichment stage accounts for about 50% of the cost of the nuclear fuel cycle. (The implication here is that it might be more economical to use equipment where enrichment is unnecessary; however, this is not necessarily true.) The costs of enrichment are measured in *separative work units*

(SWUs), which are a function of the effort required to separate U-235 from U-238. The proportion of U-235 remaining in the depleted uranium (the tails) that results from enrichment is called the *tails assay*.

Professor Owen and others have stressed the importance of the enrichment stage. New enrichment technologies (e.g., centrifuge and laser) have greatly reduced the energy needed to perform this activity. As a result these technologies display a tails assay of around 0.10% instead of the usual 0.30% (on average). Since about 10% of the OECD's uranium requirements are met from the supply of enriched tails, the large-scale adoption of these more efficient technologies could reduce the need for uranium by a significant amount. Adopting new technologies is a cost question, however, and these investments are unlikely to be made before the price of uranium begins to escalate.

The back end of the cycle begins with the used (or "spent") fuel elements being removed from the reactor: a reactor needs refueling when not enough U-235 remains to sustain a chain reaction. After being cooled, they are shipped to a reprocessing facility, where the fuel elements are reduced in size, dissolved in nitric acid, and various fission products are separated out. These are processed in various ways until shipment to a permanent repository become feasible. The thing to be aware of here is that the fuel has used up only a small amount of the total energy it contains. There is still some "unburned" U-235 in the residue, and from an energy point of view, the plutonium in spent fuel contains a large multiple of the amount released by the "burning" of the original load.

A 1000 MW installation can annually produce 15,000 cubic meters ($= 15,000\,\mathrm{m}^3$) of low-level waste, 1500 of intermediate-level waste, and $20\,\mathrm{m}^3$ of high-level waste. The high-level waste is difficult to neutralize. The first step is often vitrification (i.e., enclosing the waste in glass, which is then enclosed in steel containers). Final disposal might consist of burying these containers in deep holes in geologically inactive areas, etc. Eventually it may be possible to solve the nuclear waste problem by developing a reactor that completely burns up most or all of its fuel.

Uranium ore is mined in either underground or open pit installations from ores having a concentration that averages about 0.25% if the concentration is measured in terms of uranium. It is sometimes measured in terms of uranium oxide, but this could cause some confusion because uranium oxide can be considered a processed form of "raw" uranium. Australia has 40% of the world's uranium reserves, but voters in that country do not seem to be in a mood to exploit this bounty.

The above numbers imply that about 400 tonnes of ore must be removed in order to obtain 1 tonne of natural uranium. The general abundance of uranium averages about 4 parts per million ($= 4\,$ppm) in the earth's crust, and 3 parts per billion in seawater. There are many estimates in circulation as to the amount of uranium that can ultimately be extracted from both onshore deposits and seawater, but all the figures that I have seen concerning possible extraction amounts strike me as being mostly guesswork, and so they will not be discussed here. Yellowcake prices have been low since the first (commercial) nuclear power station has begun operating (in the United Kingdom in 1956), but given the enormous electricity demand that could emerge during this century should, for example, a fraction of the 2 billion or more persons without access to electricity express their dissatisfaction politically or otherwise, this situation cannot be taken for granted. Persons contributing to the important forum EnergyPulse, however, generally conclude that with present and future technology, the supply of exploitable uranium is huge.

2.   The Uranium Price, the Fast Breeder and MOX

A very important part of Professor Owen's book for the present topic has to do with his discussion of the pricing of uranium and its various components. Among other things he has clarified the key role of inventories in this pricing. That immediately suggests the validity of the stock-flow model shown in Fig. 6.1. Before examining this it might be useful to have a brief look at the stock-flow model presented in Chapter 2, because they amount to the same thing.

The current (or flow) supply goes into stocks (i.e., inventories) and current (i.e., flow demand. Price is formed by the relationship of actual stocks (AI) to desired stocks (DI), with the flow equilibrium $[s(p) = h(p)]$ playing a secondary (but important) role. The equilibrium expression is therefore AI $=$ DI, and when this situation prevails, $s = h$ (because there is no addition or subtraction from inventories due to current supply and demand, and price is constant). To put it another way, a stock equilibrium

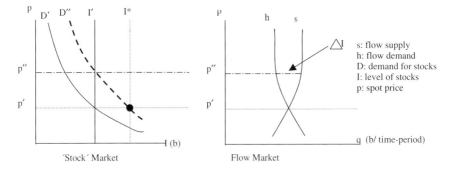

Figure 6.1. A Stock-Flow Pricing Model

implies a flow equilibrium, while a flow equilibrium does *not* imply a stock equilibrium. In this type of model, expectations are very important because of their influence on desired stocks, and in the real world, expected prices are undoubtedly more difficult to describe than via the simple expression of the type $p^e = f(p)$. Once again readers should note the similarity between this discussion and the much more important one in Chapter 2 dealing with oil.

There is probably no point in exploring the mechanics of the fast breeder reactor (FBR) in this book, except to say that it is principally concerned with converting as much as possible the U-238 in natural uranium into fissile material, as rapidly and efficiently as possible, and then using it to generate electricity. It does the same thing for thorium. These reactors can also use depleted uranium produced in the enrichment process. This is why, in Japan and perhaps several other countries, the FBR is considered the ultimate solution to the electricity supply problem, although it is not the kind of thing to be sung at the top of one's voice in the local karaoke club. Some of the directors of the Japanese energy bureaucracy have made it abundantly clear that, as far as they are concerned, the conventional nuclear power station, which exploits just about 1% of the energy in its fuel, will ultimately be as extinct as the dinosaur, and must be replaced by the fast breeder, which extracts about 80%. They will also tell you, in private, that a Japan that can reduce its energy costs could have a substantial commercial advantage over those countries utilizing high-cost energy.

An intermediate step in this process may be a resort to mixed oxide (MOX) fuels. What we have here is the extraction of plutonium and uranium from spent fuel, and mixed with new fuel. The problem here is the possible contribution of MOX fuel to an "explicit" plutonium economy, although since a recycling of plutonium can multiply the amount of electricity generated by the original load by a very large amount, the widespread concern for avoiding the highly disturbing presence of plutonium is unlikely to characterize the thinking of politicians for many more decades.

The price of yellowcake has moved in cycles for most of the past four decades; however, I have never heard any serious complaints from firms on the buy side of the market. It may also be the case that the comparatively low price of that commodity has kept greater investment away from more out-of-the-way regions where uranium ore is found.

A factor that has complicated the uranium supply–demand situation is the use of blended-down highly enriched uranium (HEU) from nuclear weapons as fuel for nuclear reactors. Present expectations are that at least 15% of OECD uranium requirements will be satisfied by Russian HEU, and perhaps some HEU originating in the United States. As in the case of yellowcake, I cannot detect any scarcity of nuclear fuel nor the services for its provision. If there is a sign of a shortage, however, then it may happen that attitudes toward utilization of the breeder could change, and change rapidly, because in the not too distant future it will become clear to many observers that the energy situation in the world does not provide grounds for optimism.

Although it is not widely discussed, reprocessed Pu-239 can substitute for U-235 in that it can be mixed with U-238 (in the form of uranium oxide) to provide MOX (for mixed oxides). This activity consumes more plutonium than it creates, and thus is not equivalent to "breeding", but even so, the presence of plutonium on the input side of the process greatly offends environmentalists and the anti-nuclear movement, as well as many persons who are pro-nuclear. They claim that it is safer and more economical to store spent nuclear fuel than to reprocess it for reuse. The mixing referred to above takes place in a reprocessing plant of the type that the UK government has approved of for British Nuclear Fuels (BNF) Sellafield complex in northwest England. A great deal of attention has been paid to this installation, and the opinion here is that in the name of safety, the more attention the better.

3. Nuclear in the Light of "Kyoto"

Several years ago I published a paper in *Geopolitics of Energy* with the title "Some Aspects of Nuclear Energy and the Kyoto Protocol" (2002). On the first page of that issue, the editor of the journal, Vincent Lauerman, asked the following important question: "Is 'Kyoto' a lost cause without the mass deployment of nuclear power plants? He added that "the current debate on this topic is long on ideology and short on reason".

That almost sums it up. "Almost" because basically what we are dealing with here is a shortage of the kind of information that would encourage not the "mass" but the *optimal* employment of nuclear facilities. (Optimal is a very important term in mainstream economics. It means choosing the *best* patterns of affordable consumption or production, given the presence of adequate information about available choices, and enough rationality to distinguish between different (e.g., good and bad) outcomes. In the *real* world, where intertemporal considerations dominate, this is asking for a great deal.) In any event, in theory, the general public's uncertainty where nuclear safety and waste disposal are concerned must be respected, while at the same time recognizing that a majority of this same public desires inexpensive and reliable electricity, as well as an end to the rapid build-up of greenhouse gases. In particular, an excessive accumulation of carbon dioxide (CO_2) is to be avoided. When all this is taken into consideration, we have an optimization problem that is analogous to those in, e.g., your favorite intermediate-level microeconomics textbook.

Ordinarily my approach to this quandary would begin with a reference to one of the greatest of all scientists, William Shakespeare: *"Time's glory is to calm contending kings, to unmask falsehoods, and to bring truth to light"*. The problem here is that we may not possess sufficient time to profit from this superb advice. My research has often been focused on the bad things that could happen due to, e.g., electricity deregulation and an unexpected shortage of oil, but these are trivial as compared to a bad global warming scene. Pacala and Socolow (2004) are absolutely correct in saying that in confronting the problem of global (or greenhouse) warming, "the choice is between action and delay", and as far as I am concerned, "action" means giving more weight to the nuclear option, beginning at once.

On the other hand, the possible consequences of delay can be inferred from the following brilliant observation by Gelbspan (1997):

> "Scientists do not know what hidden thresholds lie ahead. They do not know what feedbacks will take effect, or when. They do not know at what point an unstable climate will become a cascade down a steep slope. They cannot yet predict whether or when the rate of warming will accelerate. So those who are trying to avert the crisis are left groping in the dark, forced to choose arbitrary emissions-reduction targets that are determined more by their political viability than by their correspondence to the actual climate situation."

Returning to the first paragraph of this section, we are entitled to ask if an increased deployment of nuclear assets can "save Kyoto" — or more correctly, the United Nations Framework Convention on Climate Change that was broached at Kyoto, Japan, in December 1997. The implicit conclusion presented below is that nothing can save "Kyoto" except its (formal or informal) abandonment, and replacement by a more realistic alternative. As I pointed out elsewhere, "finding compromises that can satisfy all participants in the environmental wars must be as frustrating as the search for the Holy Grail (or the Fountain of Youth), but had the delegates at Kyoto genuinely believed that global warming (due to increasing atmospheric concentrations of greenhouse gases) constitutes a clear and imminent danger, they would also have realized that the final document served up to them by the behind-the-scenes grandees was grossly inadequate, and unless a radical extension of its provisions can be adopted (and implemented) in the very near future, greenhouse gases will continue their build-up in the same way that they have during the past few decades" (2000a).

(Something else those delegates would have done, if they had been serious persons capable of comprehending the subtler aspects of global warming, was to insist on the rapid adoption — if only in a token sense — of measures capable of reducing atmospheric pollution. As it happened though, most of them were too busy trying to ensure that they qualified for a ticket to the 1998 climate warming get-together in Buenos Aires to become heavily involved with theoretical considerations.)

Will this accretion of greenhouse gas be instrumental in bringing about a collapse of our civilization and the destitution of coming generations? A large majority of our scientific elite say that it is definitely possible unless there are some drastic alterations in our outlook and behavior. Once again I would like to emphasize that to me this means doing something about the uncertainty mentioned earlier, which in turn calls for a greater reliance on nuclear energy. *With nuclear energy we know what we are getting. We are not investing in a CO_2 lottery!* Most of the rest — and particularly playing games with emissions permits — maintain or increase uncertainty via the fabrication and retailing of unproved and/or impossible-to-prove hypotheses and/or conclusions.

In the very long run, of course, we are moving toward what could be an exciting panorama that featured a large stock of renewables and quasi-renewables. Whether this will turn out to be a comprehensive paradise on earth remains to be seen, although I for one have some problem believing that on a global scale, the corpus of economic and social losers will greatly diminish in size. The thing to remember here is that according to the OECD, two-thirds of the increase in the energy demand between 2000 and 2020 will come from developing countries, where, as already mentioned, several billion persons lack an adequate or reliable supply of electricity. Some question should then be asked whether the persons experiencing this shortage prefer their future prosperity to depend on renewables or traditional sources of energy — where traditional in the present context means uranium or fossil fuels. If they choose the latter, then we might be talking about irreparable damage to the environment — and this could happen even if fossil fuels are quickly exhausted. (See Goodstein (2004) for an elementary examination of some aspects of this quandary.) But if that happens, then we are worse off than ever because of the steady increase in global population.

That brings us to the inescapable topics of natural gas and emissions trading. The best way to begin though is to compare the prospects for nuclear energy with those for oil. As I stated above, in my opinion the nuclear reactor was the most impressive scientific achievement of the 20th century, and if governments become more cooperative, enormous improvements in this equipment are not only possible, but certain. It is also clear that science and technology have performed miracles where the search for and production of oil are concerned, and many observers expect that the oil wolf will never appear at the door because even more magnificent achievements are possible with the full utilization of things like supercomputers. However, *unlike* the situation with nuclear energy, some of us believe that these achievements are aimed toward finding and producing oil that — according to a large and growing consensus of geologists — will never be found because it does not exist. Eventually the same situation will prevail for gas.

There are many topics that are appropriate and accessible for a discussion of this nature; however, there are certain issues that need to be brought in the most direct manner to the attention of everyone with the slightest interest in the subject.

The first has to do with the increased use of natural gas to reduce greenhouse emissions: gas has often been portrayed as the perfect replacement for nuclear energy. Gas contains much less CO_2 than oil, and a great deal less than coal. Moreover, there is a very large amount of gas in the crust of the earth, and prospects are that a considerable amount will still be uncovered. Thus, in the light of what we have seen in the first six or seven years of the last decade — particularly in places like California and the United Kingdom — gas appeared to be just the thing needed to fuel the electric sector (instead of, e.g., coal and nuclear). And it needs to be unconditionally recognized that that sector is going to need a great deal of fueling, because the demand for electric power is increasing at a much faster rate than often predicted. In addition, technology has provided some good news for consumers of gas: as a result of the development of combined cycle equipment that has greatly increased the efficiency of gas turbines, the cost of a unit of gas-based electricity has been palpably reduced (*ceteris paribus*).

Now we move on to the bad news. Even persons who have studied economics at the advanced level often fail to note that when comparing the cost of electricity generated in nuclear installations to that of gas-based facilities, there is a widespread tendency to concentrate on *capital costs*, where (on a per-unit of electricity generated basis) the cost of gas (on average) appears to be one-half that of nuclear. However, in a short article in *The Spectator* (2004), Rod Liddle says that according to the UK Royal Academy of Engineering, nuclear is the least expensive way to generate a unit of electricity: on average, it is one-half the cost of coal, and about 40% less than the cost of gas. *Some observers might be offended by this claim; however, it is quite clear to me that when the present and likely future variable costs of generation are taken into consideration, and not just capital costs, nuclear is not at a disadvantage to any other technology!*

I can also refer here to a recent piece in the Financial Times by Andrew Taylor in which he discusses the cost of nuclear electricity with respect to gas-based power, but considers only the capital cost of nuclear. Once this mistake is corrected, we get an entirely different picture. The future price of natural gas relative to uranium — particularly as the global peak output of gas approaches — could reach a level where nuclear has an enormous cost advantage. A nuclear plant constructed today will have a "life" of at least 60 years, and halfway through this period the price of gas could go into orbit.

The same kind of reasoning has turned up in France, where a former prime minister, Lional Jospin, organized a study to clarify the competitiveness of gas with respect to nuclear energy. Jospin's instructions were to take *all* costs into consideration, to include those of an external nature (e.g., environmental costs). The conclusion, which was put into a 288 page report, was that there would not be great cost differences between gas and nuclear as long as there was no escalation in gas prices. As things turned out though, not long after the contents of the report had been fully digested by anxious readers, the price of gas almost doubled. Thus, another potential controversy involving "greens" and their adversaries could be removed from the government's table, although those persons with a "no thanks" approach to nuclear power continued to be unimpressed or for that matter uninterested in arguments with a pronounced reliance on facts and figures.

One more point is discussed on this subject. Michael Meacher in *Guardian Weekly* (21–27 July) wants to know why we (the United Kingdom) should "plan for a nuclear futures when uranium supplies are running out". "Running out" is precisely the wrong way of putting this matter, but even if it were true, uranium is certainly more plentiful than gas, and no effort is made to conceal the energy plans of the present and probable governments of the United Kingdom, since they are in favor of contracting for gas from sources that are thousands of kilometres away from where it would be consumed.

As in the United States and elsewhere, the "life" of *existing* Swedish nuclear installations are now being extended to 60 years, and it can go higher. By itself, this would mean that it pays to upgrade these facilities, but in addition there has also been a steady increase in *capacity factors* that makes upgrading even more attractive. On this point it should be mentioned that in the new deregulated Swedish electricity market, any decrease in nuclear capacity will increase the price of electricity in such a way that with the increased profits accruing to electricity wholesalers (i.e., generators), it will be possible for Swedish energy firms to increase their purchase of assets in, e.g., Eastern Europe, many of which are heavy contributors to atmospheric pollution. As for Swedish consumers, they no longer count for much in this game, since it was their sheep-like passivity that allowed misfortunes like electricity deregulation and the dismantling of the nuclear sector to begin.

Life extensions are also almost certain for the bulk of the United Kingdom's nuclear capacity, especially since the prime minister, Tony Blair, has said that "if you are serious about climate change, then it's wrong to close the door on new nuclear development". A group in Sweden called "Environmentalists in favor of nuclear energy" would almost certainly agree with this evaluation. Another item that is relevant here is that natural gas not only contains CO_2 (though not nearly as much as oil), but methane, and some researchers say that if very large quantities are involved, methane can pose environmental dangers on the order of excessive CO_2.

At the Kyoto meeting, nuclear energy was by and large overlooked, and probably was not even on the agenda; however, it was decided that a market would be established for the trading of emission permits. For some reason this concept has captured the enthusiasm of the high-and-mighty, and once this emission bazaar is fleshed out with confused buyers and sellers of permits, and bright-eyed young people functioning as market makers and/or brokers, it will fit perfectly the role of a *pseudo-market*, to use the terminology of the New Zealand economist Owen McShane. In concept, though perhaps not in layout, it will likely be similar to the uniformly inefficient establishments introduced to enable the risk associated with electricity deregulation to be hedged.

I hope that I am not revealing my basic frame of mind in this matter when I say that emission permits are one of the worst ideas ever formulated, and the cost — both in dollars and millions of tons of CO_2 launched into the atmosphere — would make it a distinguished non-starter if there had not been a small group of academic economists, and a large group of finance professionals, who expected to gain personally from their introduction. These ladies and gentlemen were able to take advantage of the lack of genuine economics expertise that characterizes the environmental ministries of most governments, to include exterior experts at their disposal.

"Most governments" however do not include the US government, where the shortcomings of emissions trading — though not extensively discussed — are perfectly understood. A deputy US energy secretary once informed a Senate committee that an excessive dependence on gas was a threat to US energy security, and made it clear that more nuclear power belonged in the US electricity generating portfolio. What he undoubtedly meant was that a threat to energy security was a threat to the US macroeconomy. This kind of logic is very definitely understood — though not perfectly — in Sweden, and therefore Swedish industrialists do not hesitate to make it clear that among the costs of emissions trading and the higher energy prices that will almost certainly be entailed, an accelerated movement of Swedish industry toward what are sometimes called "low wage" countries should be included. At the same time though, many of these "captains of industry" have not made a substantial effort to convince their counterparts in the government to become more enthusiastic about nuclear energy, because their primary loyalty is to salaries and bonuses, and these can be maintained even if their manufacturing facilities are in Poland or the Baltic countries or Pago-Pago.

I doubt whether all readers of this book will appreciate merely being told that emissions trading is a costly misadventure, and the best thing to do is to ignore it. Let me therefore suggest that they should ask their favorite economics teacher for a deeper insight into the interior logic of this undertaking, or for that matter consult the superb microeconomics textbooks that are now available. At the same time I feel obligated to assure them that all the pages in all the textbooks that have been written since Adam and Eve will not help those noble economists, civil servants, and students who hope to secure the expertise required to give an explanation of emissions trading that is capable of getting intelligent persons to see its merits. As President Vladimir Putin was summarily informed, "it's a scheme to make money, and has nothing to do with suppressing pollution". Let us put this another way: by adopting emissions trading instead of a direct and systematic program for reducing greenhouse emissions (via, e.g., nuclear energy, and emission taxes and subsidies), a lottery has been chosen instead of what might be a sure thing. There are, of course, good reasons for choosing lotteries instead of sure or near-sure things, but not when it might involve the future of the planet.

At the 1998 European Nuclear Conference, Dr Hans Blix — who later became heavily occupied in the search for "weapons of mass destruction" — provided delegates with a series of highly relevant queries. These were reviewed in some detail by Smosarski (1998), and one of the most interesting was that in France, which generates close to 80% of its electricity in nuclear installations, the emissions of CO_2 per kilowatt hour were about 64 g, while in the United Kingdom, which had a much smaller amount of nuclear, and as a result uses a considerable gas and coal, emissions were 10 times larger. Similarly, in Sweden, where nuclear and hydro generated most of the electricity, the figure was 58 g/kWh, as compared to Denmark — which even at that time had a large inventory of wind turbines, but relied for the most part on coal — the figure was 917 g/kWh.

What is not generally understood is that the Danish resort to windpower can be justified by the high cost and pollution that characterizes their dependence on coal. This situation does not apply to neighboring countries, and in particular Sweden and Norway. It is also interesting to note that the use of windpower in Denmark appears to be peaking at the present time, which may be due to the inability to fit it into the deregulated Danish electricity market — which like most deregulated electricity markets on the face of the earth has encountered considerable difficulty in honoring its promises to the households and firms of that country. This might also be the place to inform coal intensive Denmark that a 1000 MW(e) coal-fired power plant releases almost 100 times as much radioactivity into the environment as does a comparable nuclear plant. In addition, as the World Nuclear Association pointed out, "if all the world's nuclear power were replaced by coal-fired power, electricity's carbon dioxide emissions would rise by a third".

While on this subject it can be noted that according to Liddell, 18 million tonnes per year of CO_2 is avoided because of the presence of the United Kingdom's nuclear energy, which he states is equivalent to five car-free days per month. For Europe as a whole, Dr Blix says that nuclear power helps to avoid the emission of approximately 700 million tonnes of carbon dioxide a year. This is a very large number, and one would like to think that had it been circulated to the several thousand delegates at Kyoto, or the 60,000 at Capetown for the so-called "World Summit", enough of them would have been sufficiently motivated to put their eating and drinking aside long enough to realize that there was a short cut to environmental sanity that did not involve the uncertainties implicit in the "green message".

The problem here is one of rationality on the part of the taxpayers who sponsor and support elephantine holiday outings like those at Kyoto, Capetown, and elsewhere. My favorite example has to do with the willingness of a large number of the Swedish people to accept a program for nuclear retreat that is completely inconsistent with their overall "revealed preferences". A great majority of Swedes want full employment, adequate pensions, lower taxes, high-quality health care and education, a great deal of leisure, public order, and an efficient defence. They have also shown themselves to be willing to accept a high level of expensive immigration, at the same time aspiring to spend 1% of the Swedish gross national product on what they think of as aid to developing countries (but which to a considerable extent has been spent on weapons and plane tickets).

All of these goals — laudable and otherwise — are in the danger zone if the wrong kind of decision is taken about Sweden's energy supply. As bad luck would have it, sub-optimal decisions on this front are not just possible but likely, because the uncertainties associated with the present Swedish economy have greatly inhibited clear thinking on the part of the electorate. For instance, it is widely recognized in Sweden that raising the energy efficiency of homes and other structures, and vehicles, can yield sizable economic gains, but enormous expenditures associated with the Swedish entrance into the European Union have greatly reduced the scope for almost all socially profitable energy investments (to include health and education). There is also a remarkable lack of clarity in thinking about the proposed use of natural gas, where the issue is not just pollution, but the inevitable escalation of its price.

4. A Conclusion

Philip Abelson (2000) was the energy editor of *Science*, one of the top scientific publications in the world. Several years ago he published a short article called "Decreasing reliability of energy". The word "nuclear" did not appear in Abelson's exposition until the last paragraph, and then in conjunction with a warning that because of the changes that often take place in global energy realities, energy policies will need continuous monitoring and periodic revision. However, on the basis of the considerable shortcomings displayed by gas and coal that he mentioned previously, it might be suspected that a larger nuclear commitment might avoid some of this bother. Unfortunately, there is still this business of nuclear waste in the picture, but for anyone with a genuine faith in mainstream science, it is quite obvious that in the long run dealing with this matter is less of a problem than designing the equipment that caused it.

A caveat might be in order here. Discomforts due to decreased reliability and higher prices are of less interest to me than the global warming puzzle. I can live with higher electricity prices, but news of rising water on the Reeperbahn (in Hamburg) or Canal Street (in Amsterdam) might be more difficult to shrug off. Observers like Sonja Boehmer-Christensen (the editor of *Energy and Economics*) and Leonard Brookes (now a consultant and analyst, and formerly responsible for economic forecasting and energy policy at the London headquarters of the UKAEA) have assured me that the global warming issue contains some facets that cast a shadow on my "faith based" approach to the subject; however, I must confess that I am powerless to resist the kind of argument that might have been presented by a man often called "the best brain of the 20th century", the late John von Neumann. In his seminal articles and the famous book that he wrote with Oscar Morgenstern (1944), he concluded that *SAFETY FIRST* was almost always the best strategy for high-risk activities — i.e., activities where there is a significant probability of "ruin". I hope that I do not have to say that this is essentially what the former Prime Minister of the United Kingdom, Margaret Thatcher, meant when she once suggested that where global warming is concerned, it might be a good idea for political decision makers to avoid making wagers that their foot-soldiers cannot afford to lose.

One more observation seems useful here. Almost 25 years ago I attended a conference in Canberra, Australia, in which one speaker said that the sooner the breeder reactor was put into use the better. I did not talk to anybody who agreed with him — in fact, many listeners obviously thought that he had to be suffering from a serious mental disability in order to entertain those thoughts — and I believe that such would be the case at the present time in that country, but even so I now suspect that the plutonium community is inevitable. The huge amount of energy in plutonium will eventually overcome arguments that it is an undesirable component of the future energy economy.

Of course, it is impossible to say exactly when this will happen, but I suspect that a sustained movement will begin in that direction fairly soon after the global output of oil and/or gas peaks, or even if a strong belief emerges that there is not enough uranium to supply conventional reactor fuel: either one of these events will be the Pearl Harbor or 9/11 of the energy decision makers in the United States, and after that the rest of the world will have no choice but to join the parade. Everything considered, this is not something to look forward to, however one hopes that wise voters and decision makers will do everything possible to ensure that *if* it is destined, the plutonium economy arrives very late, and leaves very early, and during its visit it does as little damage as possible.

Appendix: Swedish Nuclear Energy

Winston Churchill occasionally used the expression "an enigma within an enigma" when attempting to evaluate the former Soviet Union. I have employed similar terminology when discussing the attitude of Swedish politicians toward nuclear-based electricity (since, on the whole, their position differs markedly from that of their constituents). Both statistics and a simple algebraic calculation make it clear that in terms of the *cost* of electricity, and safety, the Swedish nuclear sector is perhaps the most efficient in the world at the present time, although reliability has suffered because of the deregulation of electricity.

Moreover, the nuclear situation will soon be better, because all or some of the 10 remaining reactors are being upgraded to such an extent that they can more than replace the energy lost due to the illogical closing of two of the three reactors at Bärsebäck (in Malmö). But despite the steady deterioration of the Swedish welfare state, and even more depressing the fall in the quality of life in Sweden due to entry into the European Union (EU), it might happen that at any time another giant step will be taken in the Swedish nuclear retreat.

Lenin once remarked that socialism should be defined as communism plus electricity. The implicit assumption in Sweden after the Social

Democrats assumed power was that something called the "Swedish welfare state" was social democracy plus electricity. The way this was pictured as working is straightforward, and turns on mainstream economic
logic: a high electricity intensity, combined with a high level of industrial investment and the technological skill created by a modern educational system, would lead to a high industrial productivity, which in turn
would result in a steady increase in employment, personal real incomes,
and almost all the components of social security (such as health care and
pensions).

This is exactly what happened, and a relevant question of late is whether
a century of Social Democratic aspirations can be kept afloat if some of the
most modern electricity generating facilities in the world are scrapped for
what are clearly short-term political considerations. (Before continuing it
should be emphasized that the relation between "socialism" and Swedish
social democracy is about the same as that between the words and music
of a conventional rap standard and a Cole Porter "evergreen".)

For some obscure reason, in 1978, all the major political parties in Sweden agreed that the growing controversy over the future of nuclear energy
should be settled by holding a national referendum. The electorate was
asked to choose between something close to (but not quite) nuclear acceptance, the immediate closing of as many nuclear facilities as possible, or a
gradual phase-out that was to be complete by 2010. Confronted by a whirl-
wind of neurotic fictions launched by a technophobic nuclear opposition,
the latter option was chosen. Although not fully comprehended by most
Swedes even now, a key factor in that incomprehensible burlesque was the
assumption that the rising prosperity of Sweden could be maintained even
if the country's nuclear assets were massacred.

To a considerable extent, that ill-advised assumption no longer exists,
which is why a large majority of Swedish voters are no longer hostile to
nuclear. In the United Kingdom, on the other hand, some polls indicate that
most voters want to see nuclear and coal-based installations phased out in
favor of renewables, while the government of that country desires a nuclear
revival. This is because, as Prime Minister Blair points out, without such a
departure it will be impossible to achieve large reductions in carbon dioxide
(CO_2). And not only Mr Blair: James Lovelock, a founder of Greenpeace,
ostensibly proclaimed that "Only nuclear power can halt global warming",

(which did not boost his status with the leadership of that highly vocal organization).

The difference between the two nations is that no country has made as great an effort to introduce renewables as Sweden, but even so the result in terms of energy being generated is slight. Consequently, as compared to UK residents, Swedes have come to realize that while technically it is possible to greatly increase the use of renewables, the benefit–cost outcome is unacceptable.

One of the explanations for the often labile situation with Swedish nuclear politics is that a large percentage of the journalists and economists who maintain good relations with the government and its advisors are without even the slightest glimmer of how energy functions in a modern economy, and even worse, they are singularly uninterested in curing this deficiency. Energy economics is either not taught in the universities, or taught badly, and the exact manner in which the availability of electricity influences economic progress has never been properly understood, although a brilliant introduction to this subject can be found in a non-technical article by the late Samuel Schurr (1984).

Concentrating on the United States, Schurr demonstrated that the total energy use in what he termed the "business sector" more than doubled over the 1920–1973 period, and in relation to capital (= machinery + structures) increased by 50%. The observed slight fall in the energy intensity of *output* was then shown to be due to technical change (largely motivated by increasingly energy intensive *inputs*), raising output by so much that, *percentage-wise*, output increased by more than energy consumption. (And it was from the failure to understand the details of this phenomenon that Swedes were forced to confront the bogus argument that output could be maintained or increased even if the input of energy declined.) He also hypothesized that electrification meant a flexibility in industrial operations that would have been impossible with any other form of energy, and this was the cardinal reason for productivity growth. Equally as important, electricity would play an indispensible role in the employment of items such as computers, whose revolutionary promise was just being realized.

In Sweden, at that time, this kind of thinking was not encouraged, and I can recall students who attained the highest grades, and proceeded to rewarding careers, expressing a belief that the way to confront higher energy prices was to change the aggregate industrial structure of the country in such a way as to make it less energy intensive. They provided no examples, but it is conceivable that if given the opportunity a few of them might have put in a good word for the social and economic splendors of some stone-age province on the rim of the Kalihari. It is here that we can obtain an insight into why economics is "easy but subtle", to paraphrase the physicist Paul Ehrenfest, because while it was easy for those high achievers, it was very definitely too subtle.

On the basis of the evidence, an intelligent economist living in complete isolation from the "real world" — which, unfortunately, is a world in which security problems cannot be ignored — might suggest that the best strategy for stabilizing or reducing the inventory of atmospheric greenhouse gases is a *massive* program of nuclear construction in North America and, e.g., Western Europe, and it should be commenced as soon as possible. The present analysis is definitely in favor of more nuclear, but at the same time it seems optimal to wait until the security problem assumes another dimension before anything resembling a "massive" commitment is undertaken.

The Swedish nuclear past and its many enigmas

Before taking a closer look at the present day Swedish nuclear scene, it might be useful to understand that a large part of the antipathy toward nuclear energy in Sweden (and perhaps elsewhere) has its origin in something called "Den Kungliga Svenska Avundsjukan" (or The Royal Swedish Envy). The envy in this case was directed toward the scientists and technicians who — in the words of Professor (and Nobel Laureate) Gunnar Myrdal — were in the coveted (but unforgivable) position of "living to work instead of working to live". There was no question in the minds of the pseudo-intelligensia in the universities and liberal professions that these arrogant winners (or "school stars" as I heard one of the high-and-mighty at Stockholm University call them) had to be put in their place, which finally happened when a law was passed that forbade the scientific research aimed at developing more efficient reactors. (These new reactors included "safe" reactors of, e.g., the PIUS design, which would have made accidents of the type advertised by the nuclear opposition impossible.)

Observing the Swedish nuclear past provides a valuable but generally unappreciated insight into the almost certain arrival of what Professor Kenichi Matsui (1998) calls the "Seventh Energy Revolution", which he believes will be based on nuclear energy. When the first oil price shock took place, six reactors were rushed to completion, while work on four others commenced, and planning began for two others. I think it is possible to predict that when world oil output peaks in a decade or so, a similar phenomenon will be observed everywhere, because among other things an enormous quantity of electricity will be necessary to avoid a partial deterioration of the transportation system. In a country like Sweden (where for many politicians and academics, plane tickets are more precious than good health), neither nuclear haters nor nuclear lovers have the slightest intention of losing access to "the friendly skies" or the "open roads": the open roads leading, e.g., to the skiing and partying at Åre and Riksgränsen.

Something else that is not widely known is that as early as 1945, informal planning started in Sweden on the civilian application of nuclear energy. By 1954, the first pilot installation was ready, and 10 years later the highly efficient "Agesta" nuclear reactor was in operation, providing a small amount of electricity and heat. Although the next nuclear project — the "Marviken" reactor — turned out badly, there is no doubt that Sweden could have produced a large reactor about the same time that the first successful commercial installation opened in the United Kingdom. The decision to build the reactors mentioned in the previous paragraph was probably one of the most important in modern Swedish history, and when discussing Swedish technical skill it might also be appropriate to mention that during the 1960s, one million new housing units were constructed (in a country of slightly less than 8 million people). This demonstrates what is possible in a technologically advanced country if the political will exists.

According to Torsten Gustafson, chief scientific advisor to the Social Democratic government of Tage Erlander, there was a positive attitude toward nuclear energy in Sweden until about 1970. After that time, two of the five major political parties in Sweden — the "farmer party" and the communists — came to the crank conclusion that the "friendly atom" was bad for Sweden and just about everyone else, although there were a number of opponents to nuclear energy in all political and social factions. There is no rational explanation for the strong aversion developed by any political grouping to nuclear energy, since, e.g., farmers and industrial workers were clearly important benefactors of inexpensive electricity.

This situation could probably be compared to something like the "tulip *bubble*" in Holland in the 17th century, when intelligent people suddenly and inexplicably discerned enormously valuable qualities in the humble tulip, and paid fantastic prices for a commodity that eventually turned out to have no commercial and little intrinsic worth. The commodity in the present case is the belief in nuclear disengagement, which might provide a large slice of the voting public with a tangible psychological satisfaction in the short run, but in the long run would deprive Swedish industries and households of the comparatively low-priced access to an indispensable input.

Something can now be said about the difference between the cost and the price of electricity, since deregulation and open borders are progressively worsening the situation for energy-intensive buyers of electricity in Sweden, which includes a key portion of the industrial sector, as well as perhaps the most energy intensive households in the world. (The latter is due not only to the modernity of Swedish households, but also to the weather.)

The cost of a nuclear plant can in some respects be compared to the expenses associated with the purchase of an automobile. There are acquisition costs, possession costs, and operational costs. What about the costs highlighted in your economics textbook — fixed and variable costs. In reality, these are somewhat ambivalent, since they can and are used in several conceptual senses, but even so they can easily fit into the present non-technical discussion if desired.

If you could buy a nuclear plant exactly the way that you buy a car, then you can speak of a fixed cost (for the reactor and accessories, and the structure housing it), and possession and operating costs that as in the case of an auto involve fuel, maintenance, taxes, etc. The mechanics of this procedure are spelled out at an elementary level in my energy economics textbook (2000a), where it is explained how an estimate of these costs over a period of time is *discounted* back to the present. Given an output program over the same period, the *expected* unit cost of electricity is the total discounted cost divided by the total output.

There is no point in going over the details of this exercise here; however, I can state with considerable confidence that if this procedure were better understood, it would be difficult to claim that the natural gas network now being constructed on the Swedish west coast makes the slightest economic sense.

The main advantage with nuclear as compared to gas is in the cost of fuel: gas has been expensive relative to uranium, and this expense placed gas at a disadvantage (for carrying the base load), although the capital cost of a nuclear facility was much greater. When, however, combined cycle gas-burning equipment became widely available, and the price of gas fell, it was claimed by persons who should have known better that gas would *always* be much more economical than nuclear (for generating *both* the base and peak loads). With the price of gas in the vicinity of 3.5 dollars per million Btu ($= \$3.5/mBtu$), it was easy to argue that gas was a better economic bet than nuclear. (The gas price is much higher now.)

In Sweden, of course, if an accurate (and comprehensive) calculation had been made, and there was less technofobia in and around the political establishment, that claim would have been openly ridiculed, because it was obvious to many of us even then that the infinite supply of gas that many so-called energy experts were thinking of was indisputably finite — as everybody is either finding out or will find out; and since environmental considerations dealing with CO_2 were becoming more important, nuclear displays a clear (social) cost advantage over gas.

Another example might be useful here. The first time when I taught in Australia it was widely advertised that the Maui gas field in New Zealand was virtually inexhaustible. The reserve situation is quite different at the present time; however, that field is still spoken of as being extremely valuable. *Not*, it should be emphasized, for producing natural gas, but for storing — or "sequestering" as they say — as much as possible of the CO_2 that will be generated in the coal-based generating facilities that will eventually be required later in the century to provide New Zealand with an increasing fraction of its electricity. It can also be mentioned that the New Zealand electricity deregulation, which at one time was praised as the most satisfactory in the world, was very likely based on beliefs about the availability of gas that were completely illusory. I suspect that this was an important factor in establishing a natural gas price that was probably a great deal lower than what in economic theory is sometimes termed the "scarcity price" (or the theoretically correct market price).

Something else that deserves to be referred to is that a very large amount of low-grade uranium is located in Sweden: ignoring costs, and on the basis of its energy content, Swedish uranium has considerably more to offer than all the gas in the North Sea at the beginning of its exploitation. (This uranium is mostly found in shale form in Närke (Kvarntorp) and Västergötland (Billingen).) Assuming that the price of electricity continues to rise, this uranium could eventually be worth very many billions of dollars, enough, in fact, to provide the most modern health-care facilities for the nuclear opponents and their families, as well as high-quality educations for themselves and their descendents. Of course, it might also turn out that it provides a large number of Kalashnikoff assault rifles and/or plane tickets for certain lucky recipients of Swedish "bistånd" (i.e., development aid), but that delicate issue cannot be taken up here.

What about the price of electricity to businesses and households? In the case of Sweden, the low cost of nuclear and hydro power, and fairly smart regulation, made it possible to provide electricity to the industrial sector at the lowest price in the world. This being the case, nothing is more disheartening than hearing about the "subsidies" paid to the nuclear sector, because cheap electricity meant the establishment of new businesses, and more important the expansion of existing industries, and the tax income generated by these activities more than compensated for any "subsidies" that might have been dispensed by the government. (This tax income was received from both firms and their employees.) Households could also purchase electricity at reasonable prices, although occasionally this good might have cost more in Sweden than in Norway, parts of Canada, and Australia. Accordingly, had the Swedish government been in a rational mode, the two reactors that were closed would have been kept open, and another very large installation constructed.

In addition, regulation would have been continued (although it might be true that the comparatively low salaries of power plant executives and technicians should have been adjusted). The borders would quite simply have been closed to natural gas. In case anyone is interested in the "fruits" of deregulation in this country, the largest energy intensive industries have now threatened to form a syndicate in order to purchase electricity from Poland and Russia. Of course, were it possible, they would simply move their operations out of this country, and someday this may take place for many of these industries — in which case Sweden would lose still more thousands of highly paid jobs.

This is another of those topics that politicians prefer to overlook, because for the most part those ladies and gentlemen can look forward to a lifestyle which enables them to avoid indignities like unemployment and declining social services. Another reason for avoiding debate is that it would question the near sacred resolve to become even more deeply imbedded in the politics and philosophy of the EU. *For Sweden, membership in the EU is definitely the worst social, and arguably the worst economic venture in modern times*! By way of contrast, it was a godsend for politicians like Ms Margot Wallström, who became the EU's environmental minister, and was therefore able to declaim to a wider audience what to her mind was the lack of importance of nuclear energy for reducing the build-up of greenhouse gases.

Although only discussed en passant, the great winner in the Swedish deregulation circus is the government, whose good fortune can be attributed to the structure of energy taxes and pricing. *The Nordic Electricity Exchange* (NordPool) plays a key role in the pricing of Swedish electricity, and here it is instructive to notice that when the price of oil rises, an upward pressure exists on the price of electricity in Sweden, although oil has virtually an insignificant role in the domestic provision of electricity.

The story here is that oil-based power is important for some of the other countries involved with NordPool, and so an increased price of oil raises the price of the electricity to these other countries, which, via the trade taking place in NordPool, and marginal cost pricing, raises the price of electricity to Swedish buyers. Moreover, as Braconier (2005) indicates, the same phenomenon applies for emissions trading, since generators that must purchase "rights" will (*ceteris paribus*) increase electricity prices. (Aside from this situation, since the price of gas is to some extent directly indexed to the price of oil, and coal is to some extent a substitute, even countries that do not generate much electricity with oil, but instead use gas or coal, can contribute to increased Swedish electricity prices.)

Several items of general interest

It was mentioned above that Sweden possesses large quantities of low-grade uranium, and thus it can be suggested that science and technology could make it feasible to exploit these resources much earlier than presently expected. The same is true of the low-grade resources in many other countries.

One of the assumptions in my work is that even if gas were still available at bargain basement prices, when the likely development of its future price is considered, it would be sub-optimal to regard it as preferable to nuclear where new investments are concerned. The global output of gas might peak in 20 or 30 years, while a new nuclear installation should be on line for more than 60 years, and should also have access to comparatively inexpensive uranium during that period. In these circumstances I find it extremely difficult to comprehend why anyone in a highly literate country like Sweden would find it possible to disregard the advantages of having access to inexpensive energy within their lifetime, and probably even the lifetime of their immediate descendents.

By way of comparison, the *Economist* (9 July 2005) presents estimates from several sources for average electricity costs. For German utilities the Union Bank of Switzerland (UBS) gives 1.5 cents/kWh for nuclear, 3.1–3.8 cents for gas, and 3.8–4.4 cents for coal. Similarly, they give 1.7 cents/kWh for nuclear in the United States, 2 cents for coal, and 5.7 cents for gas. The International Energy Agency (IEA), employing a discount rate of 5%, argues that nuclear is $21–31/MWh, while gas is in the $37–60/MWh ranges. Other sources (e.g., Massachusetts Institute of Technology (MIT) and Britain's Royal Institute of International Affairs) disagree; however, since I believe that nuclear is optimal, and make a practice of ignoring *everything* originating with the energy economists of MIT and the RIIA, I think that when the gas peak is taken into consideration, nuclear has a clear economic advantage. It is true though that just now uranium prices are rising, even if many uranium mines are being reopened.

According to estimates of the World Nuclear Association in 2000, the country with the largest uranium reserves is Australia, whose reserves at that time were 622,000 metric tons (= 622,000 tonnes = 622,000 t), and whose production was 7720 t. In the sequel I denote this as (622,000; 7720). This discrepancy seems very large, but not when I remember the negative attitudes toward the production of uranium by my students in mathematical economics in that country. The largest producer was Canada, with a production of 12,520 t and reserves of 331,000 t = (331,000; 12,520). Other important countries were Kazakhstan (439,200; 2018), Namibia (156,120; 2239), Niger (69,960; 3095), Russia (145,000; 2000), United States (110,000; 1000), Uzbekistan (66,210; 2400), other (306,940; 2774). Total estimated reserves in 2000 were thus 2,246,430 t, while production was 35,767 t.

For technical details see Owen (1985), but the total input of uranium in, e.g., the production of electricity exceeds 35,767 t because a great deal of the resource can be obtained from the recycling of spent fuel and former military ordnance.

Sweden does not appear above because exploiting its low-grade reserves is uneconomical at the present time. Eventually this situation could change because of scientific and technological improvements in mining and processing. Something that might cause a quantum jump in the value of Swedish uranium, however, would be the breeder reactor becoming a commercial proposition, because in that case the output of energy (due to the exploitation of the plutonium that could be bred) would be enormous even for low-grade uranium.

As it happens, my opinion of the breeder remains the same as in my previous work, and it is reinforced by a casual and, I hope, impartial appraisal of the Swedish government where any kind of security matters is concerned. There was a time when various "controlled" or proscribed substances were sold openly in front of the Swedish Riksdag (i.e., parliament), virtually in front of law enforcement, and visible to any legislator or government official or anybody else with an interest in this trade.

This particular problem was solved by moving the Riksdag and its crew of EU groupies to more genteel surroundings; however, the drug trade flourishes more intensely than ever, because as a result of its EU membership, Sweden has only a nominal control of its borders. Incidentally, this is not true of many other countries, but Swedish politicians and bureaucrats were terrified that they would lose access to future (tax-free) employment opportunities in Brussels or other EU strongholds if they were to put Swedish interests before those of foreigners.

As far as I am concerned, the Swedish government (and most other governments) are at present completely incapable of solving the security problems that would be posed by a greater presence of and/or reliance on plutonium. This is probably the only point on which I happen to be in agreement with people like Ralph Nader and Amory Lovins. Unlike them,

296 The Political Economy of World Energy

however, I happen to believe that by partially rejecting the energy in uranium when used in "conventional" reactors, the (psychological) conditions are being created for a panic-stricken rush into the breeder when the fundamental scarcity of oil and gas is revealed to the television audience. In his important book on the depletion of oil and gas, Professor Goodstein (2004) seems to think that uranium is also scarce, but its scarcity is dubious if it is used as an input in the breeder.

The present Swedish prime minister, Göran Persson, has pronounced nuclear power "obsolete", and he has been joined in this loony judgment by the energy minister, Ms Sahlin, and the "economics" minister, Mr Östros. When the latter was a graduate student at Uppsala University, he assured me that if Sweden did not enter the EU, it would become another Albania.

An interesting factor here is that Sweden is literally surrounded by comparatively unsafe reactors: a total of six can be found at Sosnowy Bor outside St Petersburg (Russia), and Ignalina in Lithuania. In the film *The Deer Hunter*, Christopher Walken sang a drunken version of the marvelous tune "I've got my eyes on you", and many nuclear experts in Sweden have had their eyes on Ignalina as an installation (of the Chernobyl type) that could pose a danger to this country, but not the "Greens". Their eyes instead have been fixed on safe reactors in Sweden, as well as the new super-safe facility that will be under construction in Finland, and which will have a rated output of 1600 MW, or as much as the two Swedish reactors that were closed at Barsebäck (near Malmö).

Somebody else with a keen interest in reactors is Mr Romano Prodi of the EU, who is one of the overseers of the ridiculous attempt to deregulate Europe's electricity and gas. (Mr Prodi is now prime minister of Italy.) Among the reactors in which he has taken a particular interest are those of Bulgaria, which the International Atomic Energy Agency (IAEA) considers to be on a par with the average in Western Europe. According to John Ritch, the US ambassador to the IAEA, the European Commission has decided to "blackmail" Bulgaria in such a way as to make its entry into the EU contingent on its willingness to reduce its nuclear capacity.

Even a combination of John Maynard Keynes and Sigmund Freud would have a difficult time comprehending the reasoning here, although Mr Ritch feels that this scheme originates with the "antinuclear environmentalists" that play an important role in the Prodi team. This may be true, but as I pointed out in a talk in Milan several years ago, it may also have to do with a belief by the Prodi brainstrust that since half of Bulgaria's electricity came from nuclear reactors (as compared to 30% in Europe overall), electricity deregulation in that corner of Europe would be easier if Bulgaria's nuclear capability was reduced. Theoretically this makes sense, because in Sweden competition — which was supposed to be the object of deregulation — *decreased* rather than increased after deregulation was introduced, and one reason is that large generators have been able to merge with smaller firms. On the other hand, it is possible to conclude that deregulation has achieved one of its goals due to the opening of the NordPool pseudo-market for the trading of a fraction of Scandinavia's electricity.

Nuclear and the Kyoto hobby-horse

As I have found out, it would not be a good idea in Sweden (and probably elsewhere) to belittle the Kyoto Protocol if you are planning to impress the television audience with your message — or at least that portion of them with the typically "deep interest" in environmental matters that character-izes the young ladies and gentlemen employed at various research institutes in Sweden. The basic problem here is that this sub-set of the population does not really understand the issue. They do not understand that at bot-tom the Kyoto Conference itself had little or nothing to do with reducing Greenhouse gases, and might best be described as an outstanding example of what George Orwell called *a system of indoor welfare*. Michael Hanlon (2005), the science editor of the *Daily Mail* (UK), puts it as follows:

> "According to the environmentalist mullahs, there is only One Solution to global warming, and its name is Kyoto. The Japanese city in which a rather shambolic agreement to curb carbon dioxide emissions was signed some years ago has acquired talismanic status among people who one suspects have little idea what 'Kyoto' is, would do or how it works."

Among the "people" that Mr Hanlon is describing were most of the "del-egates" to Kyoto, whose principal interest was to obtain tickets for the next climate warming jamboree. According to Professor Sven Kullander and several colleagues in the Swedish Academy of Science (2002), Kyoto was an important first step for reducing greenhouse gases, but "helt otillräckligt för en reell förbättring" (= completely insufficient for a real improvement).

If readers can accept the latter portion of this judgment, then I accept the first part — although in reality I put the Kyoto meeting in the same category as the "World Summit" in Capetown, where perhaps 60,000 freeloaders assembled to solve in their own unique way the many and varied problems confronting contemporary societies.

Swedes accept Kyoto for the same reason that they accept electricity deregulation and the EU: they were told to accept it by celebrity politicians and journalists. Physicist Richard Feynman once said that in matters of the above nature the logic of science is superior to that of the authorities, but a hypothesis of that nature has no place in the pretentious deliberations and pronouncements of globalist and internationalist media favorites, which assures that it is taboo for a large part of their audiences.

Many people are unaware that George W. Bush (and many Republican members of Congress) accept the consensus opinion of elite climate scientists that excessive climate warming has an anthropocentric origin. In addition, as an English "boffin" recently said, half of the up-market climate skeptics are cranks, which is a perfect description of some persons who contradict my interpretation of Swedish "enigmas". Mr Bush infuriates many Swedish commentators because his approach to the problem is via technology. They want the billions that will be added to the many billions already spent by his government to address global warming to concentrate on "renewables". No attention is paid to the scam known as "emissions trading", although an advisor to President Putin once called it a scheme to make money that is irrelevant for suppressing greenhouse gases.

I will finish by summing up what I said in a recent article in the journal *Energy and Environment* (2004a). We do *not* know if global warming is the real deal, or just part of a cycle; but we do know that gas and oil are running out, although it may take a few decades. In these circumstances the optimal behavior is to get friendlier with the friendly atom, and do what Prime Minister Blair and the founder of Greenpeace suggest, which is to increase the use of nuclear energy.

According to one person who yearns for a public debate with me, letting nature take its course makes sense, because even if we find ourselves in deep trouble, after a few hundred years of heavy ice and other discomforts, beautiful Stockholm might be more attractive. I ignore that kind of advice, since the only place that it could possibly be taken seriously is here in the Kingdom of Sweden, where things like electricity deregulation make it clear to me that rationality has greatly declined in value.

Key Concepts

CANDU–reactor	natural uranium
chain reaction	once-through cycle
emissions trading	pebble-bed reactor
enrichment	plutonium
excessive greenhouse gases	"reactor life"
fast-breeder reactor	Russian HEU
fossil fuels	U-235
front end	U-238
meltdown	uranium ore
MOX	yellowcake

Questions for Discussion

1. The cost of electric power in Sweden is perhaps the lowest in the world, and nuclear energy is about 43 of the mix: the rest is mostly hydro. What do you think about the contention that nuclear energy in Sweden is expensive?
2. Discuss the disposal problem for nuclear waste.
3. Distinguish between energy and power!
4. Was it right or wrong for Sweden to begin a "nuclear retreat"?
5. Distinguish between natural uranium and uranium ore.
6. Discuss the productivity of electricity as presented by Dr Sam Schurr.
7. Discuss the Swedish nuclear past.
8. Discuss the stock-flow model in this chapter.
9. Do you think that there is any relation between emissions trading and the price of electricity in a country like, e.g., Sweden?
10. Do you think that natural gas can compete with nuclear in the electric sector? Some believe tht fast-breeder reactors are the future. What do you think?

Bibliography

Abelson, Philip H. (2000). "Decreasing reliability of energy". *Science*, 290(5493): 931.

Baltscheffsky, S. (1997). "Världen samlas för att kyla klotet". *Svenska-Dagbladet*.

Banks, Ferdinand E. (2006). "Economic theory and the logic of the oil future". *Energy Sources*.

—— (2005). "An uninvited rejoinder to climate warming skeptics". *Geopolitics of Energy*, 24(7).

—— (2004a). "A faith-based approach to global warming". *Energy and Environment*, 15(5): 837–852.

—— (2004b). "A new world oil market". *Geopolitics of Energy*, December.

—— (2004c). "Not the climate warming movie". *Energy Politics*, Summer.

—— (2003). "A perspective on natural gas". *OPEC Bulletin*, November-December.

—— (2002). "Some aspects of nuclear energy and the Kyoto Protocol". *Geopolitics of Energy*, July/August.

—— (2001). *Global Finance and Financial Markets*. Singapore, New York and London: World Scientific.

—— (2000a). *Energy Economics: A Modern Introduction*. Dordrecht, Boston and New York: Kluwer Academic.

—— (2000b). "Economic theory and nuclear energy". *OPEC Review*, 24(2): 115–142.

—— (2000c). "The Kyoto negotiations on climate change: an economic perspective". *Energy Sources*, 22(6): 481–496.

Bolin, Bert (1998). "The Kyoto negotiations on climate change: a science perspective". *Science*, 279: 330–331.

Braconier, Fredrik (2005). "Utsläppsrätter trissar upp redan högt elpris". *SvD*, 20 August.

Bronner, Nils (2005). "Sorgligt spel om kärndraften". *Svenska Dagbladet*, 1 February.

Crabbe, P.J. (1984). "Option values of natural resources". Department of Economics, University of Ottawa (Mimeo).

Dales, J.H. (1968). *Pollution, Property and Prices*. Toronto: University Press.

Dasgupta, Partha (1982). *The Control of Resources*. Oxford: Basil Blackwell.

Gelbspan, R. (1997). *The Heat Is On*. New York: Addison-Wesley.

Goodstein, David (2004). *Out of Gas: The End of the Age of Oil*. New York and London: Norton.

Hanlon, Michael (2005). "Why do greens hate machines". *The Spectator*, 6 August.

Harlinger, Hildegard (1975). *Neue Modelle für die Zukunft der Menshheit*. IFO Institut für Wirtschaftsforschung, Munich.

Hecht, Marjorie Mazel (2006). "The beauty of the nuclear fuel cycle". *21st Century*, 18(4): 66–69.

Hellman, Richard and Caroline J.C. Hellman (1983). *The Competitive Economics of Nuclear and Coal Power.* Lexington, MA and Toronto: Lexington Books.

Immordino, Giovanni (2003). "Looking for a guide to protect the environment: the development of the precautionary principle". *Journal of Economic Surveys,* 17(5): 629–644.

Kullander, Sven, Henning Rodhe, Mats Marms-Ringdahl and Dick Hedberg (2002). "Okunnig att avveckla kärnkraften". *Dagens Nyheter,* 7 April.

Liddle, Rod (2004). "Let's go nuclear". *The Spectator,* 21 August.

Matsui, Ken-Ichi (1998). "Global demand growth of power generation". *The Energy Journal,* 19(2): 93–107.

Montgomery, W. (1972). "Markets in licenses and efficient pollution control programs". *Journal of Economic Theory,* 5(3): 395–418.

Neumann, John von and Oscar Morgenstern (1944). *The Theory of Games and Economic Behavior.* Princeton: Princeton University Press.

Owen, Anthony David (1985). *The Economics of Uranium.* New York: Praeger.

Pacala, S. and R. Socolow (2004). "Stabilization wedges: solving the climate problem". *Science,* 305(5686): 968–972.

Schurr, S.H. (1984). "Energy use, technological change, and productive efficiency: an economic-historical interpretation". *Annual Review of Energy,* 9: 409–425.

Smosarski, Grog (1998). "Nuclear questions and a faustian bargain". *Financial Times Energy Economist,* November.

Stipp, David (2004). "Climate collapse". *Fortune,* 9 February.

CHAPTER 7

ECONOMICS AND ELECTRICITY

Books about energy economics — and particularly textbooks — generally make a practice of not bothering with electricity economics. This is one of the reasons why more textbooks are required, and as soon as possible, because electricity is one of the most important topics in economics. For instance, it is as important in development economics as in energy economics, because without adequate electricity, economic development is impossible — at least as we understand the expression. Some references have been made to this topic earlier in the present book, but much more is required. As a result, I intend to examine some of these materials again and add several important items.

1. A Preliminary Discussion

Nothing is more important for students of economics than to read and completely master a few of the superb intermediate microeconomics texts that are now available. A reason that I often cite for considering this option is that one of the great dreams of the electric deregulators is to convince the general public that *increasing returns to scale* (i.e., *decreasing costs*) do not exist, and so even in heavily populated regions, small-scale electric installations for producing the base load should be given more consideration. This pernicious delusion has been sold to many voters and at least a few decision-makers, but this does not make it a reality. It will be even less so in the future now that the inevitable rise in gas prices will tend to restore what historically appears to be, *on average*, the conventional "merit order" in electricity generation, which tells us *in what role* and *how much* of the currently and eventually available equipment should be used.

In nuclear-intensive countries — such as Sweden, France, Belgium, etc. — what we ideally have is very large nuclear plants generating (or "carrying") the *base load* — which is the load that is on the line all the time — while at the other end of the spectrum gas-based equipment will largely be earmarked for carrying the *peak* load, which is a load that is only on the line a comparatively small percentage of the time. (When I wrote my previous textbook, a weighted global average indicated that 60% of generating capacity was base load, while only 10% was designated peak load.) In very large countries such as Canada, the United States, and perhaps Brazil, a similar pattern would apply to certain regions (rather than to the entire country). Hydropower carries both the base and the peak load in Norway, since in that country more than 95% of the electric output is water-based, while in nearby Denmark coal is the main fuel for the base load. Hopefully, this section (and chapter) will help to clarify the terminology and logic of this deployment, which was discussed on a more technical level in my previous textbook, and is much more important than commonly realized. In addition, the algebraic content of the present exposition has been kept to a minimum.

In between the base and peak load, we have the intermediate load. Coal is often found here in the literature, although in theory this might be generated by any fossil fuel. It also appears to be the case that coal is often responsible for the base load in regions where there is no nuclear, and it probably is used for the peak load where there is no gas, although it can hardly be considered ideal for the latter assignment. The point is to be flexible in these matters, however it is not easy to envisage a situation in which nuclear would supply peak load energy. The reason for this is that given the large capital costs of nuclear, it would be uneconomical to have this equipment standing idle for long periods of time.

In Sweden the base load is generated by both nuclear and water, while the peak load is carried by water (because it is easy to switch hydro-installations on and off), but there is an impractical dream in Sweden to dispense with as much nuclear as possible and turn at least a part of the base load over to gas, since in the very recent past, the fall in the price of gas made it a good candidate for the base as well as the peak load. As the price of gas is now developing, the merit order in most countries appears to be reverting to the usual historical pattern. This will take time, because the unexpected increase in gas prices does not mean that gas burning equipment installed when gas prices were low, and now supplying the base or intermediate load, will be prematurely junked.

Some of the previous discussion probably caused a few readers difficulty, because there has been a widespread tendency in the non-technical literature to ignore the optimal plant (or firm) mix (i.e., merit order). This is unfortunate, because what we always see in the real world is a mix of electricity generating techniques, even though the application of conventional demand curves to the so-called electricity supply curves might suggest that — in the long run at least — only one generating technique is required. For example, in countries like Japan and France, it might be possible to argue on the basis of mainstream supply–demand analysis that all electricity should be generated by nuclear facilities, since the marginal cost of this electricity is appreciably lower than that obtained from, e.g., coal and gas. In general this argument is wrong.

What we need to understand is the crucial importance of the structure of demand: the demand for electricity typically varies during a day in the cyclic manner shown in Fig. 7.1(a). This is a different proposition from the scheme in Fig. 7.1(b), which occasionally appears in important documents as well as classrooms, where it is used to draw conclusions that are presented to politicians, students, etc. as scientifically credible, though actually they are false. (Note: the left-hand side diagram is for a day, and it may vary somewhat from day to day.)

Probably the most useful approach to these matters is to attempt to gain an insight into the different cost characteristics of various types of generating equipment. For instance, even though the marginal running cost of nuclear equipment is very low, while that of gas might be very high, the algebra required to show that it is much more economical to use gas rather than nuclear for generating peak load electricity is extremely simple. (It turns as expected on the capital cost of nuclear equipment being too high for it to stand idle during non-baseload periods.) This might also be the right place to emphasize that Fig. 7.1(b), which shows a conventional demand curve, and a more-or-less conventional supply curve, is without any genuine pedagogical value where the present subject is concerned, although the day before first writing these lines I suffered through an entire seminar where this reality was not understood.

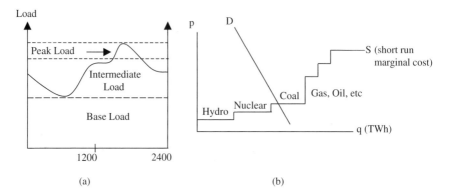

Figure 7.1. Daily Loading Curve and Apparent Supply-Demand Situation

There is a clear acceptance that low cost and high efficiency will continue to be desirable (and perhaps essential) characteristics of future power plants, and non-nuclear technologies are often pictured as rapidly developing in that direction. A great deal is relative in this world of ours, but even so I find an opinion of this nature not entirely correct. I am also discouraged by the failure of many observers to take into consideration such things as "best-practice (i.e., optimal) facilities" when discussing systems for delivering large amounts of electricity. For instance, if all nuclear facilities were of the same quality as those in Sweden, the global nuclear cost picture would be entirely different, and the attitude toward nuclear equipment might also be different. Interestingly enough, here in Sweden nuclear opponents claim that Swedish nuclear plants are too expensive and perhaps unsafe, when in truth they were probably the safest in the world until deregulation (i.e., restructuring) put in an appearance. As for being too expensive, they often produce the lowest cost electricity in the world.

It needs to be stressed that the discussion in this chapter has to do with the generating (or "wholesale") component of an electric system. The distribution (or retail) component is too special for a textbook of this nature.

2. Basic Investment Theory

Suppose that you have $100 at time t_0, which will be taken as the beginning of the period that ends at time t_1 (which is identical to the beginning of the period that in turn ends at t_2), while the rate of interest that is applicable for you is 10%. (By "applicable for you" I mean that there are many rates of interest, however if *you* want to borrow or lend money this is the applicable rate of interest.) Thus if you put this money in a bank or buy a bond, you can obtain \$110 in a year — i.e., at the end of period 1. The calculation here is $M_1 = M_0(1 + r) = 100(1 + 0.10) = 110$, where M_0 is money at the *beginning* of the first period (t_0), and M_1 is money in a year, or the end of the first period. r is the "applicable" rate of interest, and when written in decimal form 10% is 0.10.

Next, let us turn this around. With an interest rate of 10%, \$110 in a year is equivalent to \$100 now. The calculation this time is $M_0 = M_1/(1+r) = 110/(1 + 0.10) = 100$. Put in words, 100 is the *discounted* value of 110 at the given interest rate.

Using this logic we can proceed to a horizon of two years. \$100 today is equal to \$110 in a year, and if this money is left in the bank, and r is the same in the second period as in the first, it is equal to \$121 ($= M_2$) at the end of two years — i.e., at time t_2, which is the end of the second period (or year). The calculation in this case is $M_2 = [M_0(1+r)](1+r) = M_1(1+r) = M_0(1+r)^2 = 100(1 + 0.1)^2 = 100(1.1)^2 = 121$. This can also be turned around: \$121 in two years discounted at a rate of interest equal to 10% is equivalent to $121/(1 + 0.1)^2 = \$100$ today. At this point readers should derive in detail M_3, and calculate its value when $M_0 = 100$ and $r = 10\%$! After obtaining M_3, they should show how we work backwards to obtain M_0.

It is important to master the terminology, even if you think that the calculations are trivial! \$100 today is equivalent to \$110 in a year, at the (applicable) market rate of interest ($= r$). This "r" can also be regarded as a *market discount rate*. For example, \$121 in two years discounted at 10% is \$100 today, as shown above. It should be recognized though that I might have a different idea about discount rates than that associated with the "market", whose rate is sometimes thought of as an *objective* rate. I might only be willing to give up \$100 now if I obtain \$115 in a year. In that case my *subjective discount rate* is 15%, or 0.15. Looked at another way, \$110 in a year is only worth a sacrifice of $110/(1 + 0.15) = \$95.7$ at the present time. *There does not have to be any essential affiliation between my subjective discount rate and the market interest rate.*

There is occasionally some controversy in the scientific literature over what the (market) interest or (market) discount rate represents or does not represent, but there seems to be general agreement that it reflects the preference for (and perhaps convenience of) earlier as compared to later consumption, or more straightforward, the desirability of money now as compared to money in the future unless the lender receives a premium. One of the things that we are talking about here is the preference for assured consumption over contingent (i.e., possible) consumption due to the uncertainty attached to future income and consumption, and perhaps future social and political conditions, as well as future preferences: an apartment close to the Place St Michel in Paris may not be as attractive in 10 years as it is today. In addition, it could be argued that the interest rate could be thought of as a paramount determinant of the ability to increase income and/or satisfaction by means of productive investments (via the willingness to abstain from present consumption), but since no claim will be made here that markets for borrowing and lending are perfect, the Separation Theorem (involving the independence of production and preferences) does not apply.

Having said that, we can enter into a slightly more complex discussion, via a simple example. Suppose that the Queen of Norrland is coming to Stockholm in exactly a year from today, and she wrote me this morning saying that she wants to ride around the city in a custom-made late-model rickshaw pulled by my good self. In return she would pay me $250 dollars for being shown the city. After receiving her mail I immediately went to the rickshaw maker and ordered the desired vehicle, since it would take exactly a year to construct. Its cost was $100, and I paid this immediately. If there is no uncertainty involved, I might view this payment as a worthwhile investment.

Let us examine this situation at three dates, t_0 and t_1 to begin, and then t_2. At t_0, when I receive her letter, I make a quick calculation of *costs* and *benefits* which lead to my paying the rickshaw maker $100 in expectation of $250 in a year (at t_1, which is the end of the first period). Unfortunately, there is another cost: in order to chauffeur the lady during a day, it will be necessary to take official leave from my teaching position at the Stockholm College of Economic Knowledge, in which case I would lose $50 in income. Another possible cost might be notoriety associated with running through the streets of Stockholm pulling a rickshaw, however during a short period in the army I worked on a garbage truck as punishment for some imagined or real misdeed, and remembering my experiences during those splendid days, I decided that contemplating this aspect of my commitment was too abstract. (Also, in terms of the physical exercise that was involved, I might be dealing with a gain (or profit) rather than a cost, even though it would not be easy to translate this facet of the experience to monetary values, so that it could be used in a cost-benefit calculation.)

What the relevant calculation here will involve is summing *discounted* costs and expected costs, and discounted benefits and expected benefits at time t_0. Using my personal discount factor of 15%, what we get is: $-100 + 250/(1 + 0.15) - 50/(1 + 0.15) = \$74$. Even with the loss of 100 dollars for the construction of the rickshaw, and a day's pay of 50 dollars, my *income* — which is defined as the *net present value* of discounted present and expected future *net* income — has increased by \$74 dollars. This can be called the *net present value* of the expenditures $(-)$ and revenues $(+)$, which are represented by the vector $(-100; +250, -50)$, with -100 taking place at t_0 and the other two at t_1. The net *present* value applying to t_1 is $(250 - 50)/1.15$, where 250 is the revenue, 50 is the cost, and the discount factor $(1 + r)$ is 1.15. $250 - 50 = 200$ can thus be regarded as a *profit* that is experienced at t_1, however it is only a component in the *income* picture, since to determine the change in income, it must be discounted to the present, and the earlier expenditure (of \$100) taken into consideration. Please make sure that you understand this calculation and terminology before you proceed to the exercises, and it might be just as well if before continuing you give some thought to the discount rate that you personally might use if you had this remarkable opportunity.

Of course, there are things in this exposition that I perhaps should have considered but did not. For example, Madame Queen might (by accident or intention) leave Stockholm without paying me. To take account of this contingency I might raise my discount rate by 10% to 25%, which is very high. Now the calculation gives us for the net *expected* present value $-100 + 200/(1 + 0.25) = \$60$. Note the term "expected". This is employed because uncertainty has entered the picture. I have also implied in this book that given the importance of electricity, governments should try to remove uncertainty by giving certain guarantees to promising energy technologies. If this is done when, e.g., new generating facilities are under consideration, lower discount rates are probably relevant. Guarantees of this nature make investments much more attractive to financial institutions who are generally called upon for loans, and in the United States the government has started to play a more significant role on the energy scene. Readers should go through the calculations and terminology in this section carefully, and in addition do the next set of exercises as soon as possible.

Exercises

1. There is a numerical example above. Choose some symbols other than those used in the text and write this example out in symbolic form!
2. In the above example, suppose the rickshaw had to be ordered two years in advance. How would this have affected profits in the example given above? 10 years in advance? Suppose that the government guaranteed that anyone pulling a rickshaw containing foreign royalty would not lose money. Would this lead you to automatically agree to provide rickshaw transportation for all royal guests?
3. Suppose that exactly a year after the appearance of the Queen of Norrland, the King of Norrland has scheduled a visit and wants the same treatment. I am informed of His Majesty's visit at the same time that I receive the Queen's letter. Construct an example dealing with the visits of both dignitaries, considering maintenance that might be necessary on the rickshaw, and also assuming that you employ your "boss" at the College of Economic Knowledge to pull the rickshaw.

A few more comments might be useful before going to the next section. One of the most important concepts in economics is *opportunity cost*. In terms of the above discussion the opportunity cost can be identified as the cost associated with opportunities that are foregone by not putting the $100 invested in the rickshaw into its best alternative use. This might appear to be a complicated topic, but a possible answer focuses on the rate of interest "r", which is sometimes labeled the *opportunity cost of capital*. This is a kind of shorthand for the opportunity cost of investing money (e.g., $100) in a rickshaw instead of earning a guaranteed $100r (= 100 \times 0.10 = \$10$ if the interest rate is 10%) via, e.g., a bank account.

At this point we can put some of the above discussion in a symbolic form. Let us assume though that the rickshaw is paid for at t_0, which is the beginning of the first period, and used N years, where every year (i) there is a profit of V_i dollars (where profit in this case can be defined as (Revenue $-$ Cost) for the relevant period. Let us also assume that the discount rate for every period (e.g., year) will be called r, where r might be equal to the market rate of interest *or* alternatively a subjective discount rate, which is not expected to change over the relevant time horizon, and uncertainty does not explicitly enter the picture. We thus get what we can call the discounted present value at time t_0:

$$PV_0 = -C_0 + \frac{V_1}{(1+r)} + \frac{V_2}{(1+r)^2} + \cdots + \frac{V_N}{(1+r)^N}$$

$$= -C_0 + \sum_{i=1}^{N} \frac{V_i}{(1+r)^i}. \tag{1}$$

If we take the first numerical example dealing with the rickshaw we get $PV_1 = \$74$. This should be verified immediately with a formal presentation. When there is any degree of uncertainty, we can speak of an *expected* present value which, perhaps, could be called EPV, but to keep things simple it will still be referred to as present value (PV). The recognition of risk sometimes evokes a more abstract definition of the opportunity cost, which is that the correct value of the discount rate r is the return that could have been earned by making an investment with a similar risk to the investment being undertaken (e.g., the rickshaw). In thinking about the present example, where a (subjective) discount rate of 15% is used when the market rate of interest might be 10%, I might be tempted to argue that there is another investment with the same amount of risk paying 15% or thereabouts for which I could have used this $100, or for that matter a consumption "package" is available that is preferable to any investment that does not pay 15%. But neither might be preferable to a "riskless" 10%.

Since the PV can be positive or negative, depending on the size of the revenues and costs, the rule that is usually suggested is that the project (e.g., purchasing the rickshaw) is carried out if PV is greater than zero ($PV > 0$). Usually the suggestion is that PV must be considerably larger than zero, because when contemplating the future uncertainty is often unavoidable. Thus, "r" might be adjusted upward by a fairly large amount. A good elementary discussion of these matters can be found in Pindyck and Rubinfeld (2005), but make sure that you ignore their discussion of depletable resources.

Most business schools give courses in which the above exposition reduces to a simple procedure. First list the revenues (R_1 and R_2) = (0, 250) that an investment (in e.g., a rickshaw) will provide, and also the costs (C_0 and C_1) = (100, 50) that are entailed. Calling the differences between them $(V_0, V_1) = [(R_0 - C_0), (R_1 - C_1)] = [(0 - 100), (250 - 50)]$, their discounted values can be summed to obtain the (net) present value $PV_0 = V_0 + V_1/(1 + r_1)$. This can be generalized as $PV_0 = V_0 + \Sigma[V_i/(1 + r_i)]$, with the summation over the periods $i = 1, 2, \ldots, N$. In the above example $N = 1$ (i.e., $i = 1$) and $r_1 = 15\% = 0.15$, which is higher than a typical market rate of interest, but might be employed in order to account for uncertainty. V_0 is equal to -100 and V_1 is equal to 200. The fairly large value of PV_0 (or present value of the investment at time t_0) that was obtained suggests that the project should be undertaken.

Something that it might be worth pointing out here is that making and using calculations of this nature effectively is not something for enthusiastic amateurs. Making the right kind of investment decisions is generally an art more than a science.

3.   The Cost of Fuel

At several places in this book — e.g., the appendix to Chapter 1, and the chapter on coal (Chapter 5) — readers will find some materials that are useful for introducing the present chapter, however since many of the persons requiring some knowledge of electricity economics have a limited background in academic economics and/or the physical sciences, a certain amount of repetition seems appropriate. At the same time I would advise anyone who is serious about adding the information in this chapter to their intellectual armoury to read those earlier discussions.

Let us examine a few aspects of the physical background. The flow of energy is called work when it exerts a force, and it is called heat when it does not exert a force — like, for instance, the flow of energy in heat form when a pile of coal is burned below a water heater. The fuel (coal) is converted with little loss into "X" Btu of energy each second or minute that it burns, and this heats the water, but as things usually function, some energy is discharged into the air and/or lost through the sides of the heater. As a result, if the input of coal ceases, the water temperature descends to the ambient (i.e., air) temperature, and is no longer a force to be reckoned with. But if the coal input continues, steam at high temperature and pressure can be piped to the "blades" of a turbine whose rotation turns the shaft of a generator, and thus provides electricity. In the latter arrangement we have both heat and work, with the work associated with the rotating shaft of the generator.

Power is the rate at which energy is expended or work can be done, and the units of power that we are interested in this chapter are watts or kilowatts (kW) or some multiple thereof, which conveniently have an equivalent in horsepower. (The latter relationship is $1.00\,hp = 0.746\,kW$.) Watts are often mentioned when talking about the brightness of a bulb, and horsepower when talking about the capacity of an automobile engine. In this book the main unit in which energy is measured is the British Thermal Unit (Btu), which is the heat required to raise the temperature of one pound of water by one degree Fahrenheit. Btu can be easily transformed into another important energy unit which is kilowatt hours (kWh), with $1\,kWh = 3412\,Btu$. In your dwelling you may have a number of devices that are rated in watts or kW, but when you purchase them you should be aware that even if they are inexpensive, you must pay the electricity distribution company for the energy (in kWh) required to operate them. This energy originates in the fuel that is purchased by and consumed at, e.g., a generating station.

Pounds and Fahrenheit seem to be on their way out (but not Btu), and so eventually the kilocalorie (kcal) might become popular. The kcal is the heat (or its equivalent in work) required to raise the temperature of one kilogram of water ($= 2.2$ pounds) by one degree Celsius, and where equivalencies are concerned, $1\,kcal = 3.968\,Btu$. Finally, a unit that we sometimes encounter when talking about energy is the joule, and $1\,Btu = 1055\,joules = 0.252\,kcal$.

Now let us see what we can do with these observations. The bulb over the table in his kitchen where Professor B reads every day has a "power" of $100\,W$. If he reads 8 hrs a day, every day, the energy expended per day is $800\,Wh$, or $0.80\,kWh$. The brightness of the bulb is a function of its power rating, as is the price that he pays for the bulb, while the size of his electricity bill is a function of the energy (in kWh) that he utilizes. He has elected to buy a $100\,W$ bulb instead of a $60\,W$, but there is little difference in the price, and in truth he never thinks about the cost of bulbs. His problem is with the cost of energy that he consumes. Every month he gets a bill for this energy, and often when he sees it he becomes furious.

Suppose that he gets so disgusted with the size of his electric bill that he decides to buy a coal burning generator and put it in his basement. To be specific, he is going to buy a generator that will supply 100 W (= 0.1 kW) of electric power whenever he flips the switch. The output of the generator might be designated 100 W(e) or 0.1 kW(e) in some presentations. Assuming that he buys a small generator for $1000 at his local 7–11, and installs it himself in his house, his expenses are for the generator, which will be discussed in the next section, and for the coal it consumes. Also assume that at the beginning of every month he drives to a nearby coal yard to buy the coal that he believes he will require for that month, and puts it in his spare bedroom.

If that gentleman reads 8 h a day, every day of every year, then every day he requires $8 \times 100 = 800$ Wh $= 0.8$ kWh, or 0.8 kWh/d. Assuming that there are 30 days in every month, then the energy that he will require in a month is 0.8 kWh/d $\times$ 30 days $= 24$ kWh/month. As we pointed out above 1 kWh $= 3412$ Btu, and so each month the energy he requires from this coal is equal to 81,888 Btu ($= 24 \times 3412$).

In line with what was said earlier, a metric ton ($=$ tonne) of the available coal might contain on average 25,000,000 Btu, and so in a *perfect* system the professor needs $81,888/25,000,000 = 0.00327 = 3.27 \times 10^{-3}$ tonnes a month. We can convert this to pounds (#) by multiplying by 2205 ($\#/t$), and so we have $2205 \times 3.27 \times 10^{-3} = 7.21\#$ as the amount of coal that is required every month if the professor has a perfect system in his basement.

That brings us to the bad news. If the energy in the coal could be converted to electric energy with 100% efficiency, then 3412 Btu would be needed to generate a kWh of electric energy; but because efficiency is always less than 100%, more than 3412 Btu are required. In this example let us assume that instead of 3412 Btu to generate 1 kWh it requires 10,340 Btu of heat input to generate a kWh, where this number is called the *heat rate*. As a result it would be necessary to buy $(10,340/3412) \times 7.21 = 3.03 \times 7.21 = 21.84\#$. This still is not very much, and he could probably bring it home in a shopping bag. (We might also be able to think in terms of 1 kW(e) $= 3.03$ kW (coal).)

Obtaining the cost of coal in dollars/pounds (= \$/#) or \$/kg is a simple matter. At the present time the cost of coal at the 7–11 is \$50/tonne, or \$50 for 2205#, which is equal to 0.023 \$/#. 21.8# would then cost $21.8 \times 0.023 =$ \$0.502, or about 50 cents, remembering that 1 (US) dollar = 100 cents.

Knowing the number of pounds (= 21.8#), we can easily get the number of kilowatts in this coal from the heat rate, from which we could calculate the fuel cost of a kilowatt hour, but the fuel cost at a given time has nothing to do with the amount used by a small consumer like Professor B, and so this might be the time to use a small amount of "dimensional analysis". If we focus on dimensions it is obvious that [\$50/25,000,000 Btu] × [10,340 Btu/1 kWh] = 2.068 cents/kWh. (What is to be done here is to "cancel" the Btu in the numerator and denominator of the fractions, and then do the multiplication. It might thus be useful to write this expression without its numerical content: [\$/Btu]×[Btu/kWh] = \$/kWh; and for the fuel cost in cents/kWh multiply by 100.

These are simple but important computations, although not as important as being acquainted with various subtleties having to do with the cost of the generating equipment. But that will be taken up after a few exercises.

One more observation while we are on the subject of heat rates: in the United States in 2005, the Catawba Nuclear Station (owned by Duke Energy) had the lowest heat rate in the country with its Unit 2, while its Unit 1 was in second place. Low heat rates for these nuclear facilities meant that that electric rates for Duke Energy's customers in the Carolinas (United States) were about 20% below the natural average.

Exercises

1. In the example above, calculate the cost of coal in dollars per kilograms, in euros per pound and in euros per kilogram!
2. Suppose that Professor B decided to buy a generating system that burned oil. Assuming that the heat rate was 9000 Btu, and that the cost of a barrel of oil is \$70/b, how much oil would he have to buy, and what is the cost/kWh of his reading?
3. Suppose the Professor decided on a gas burning system. Using the information in the appendix to Chapter 1, formulate and solve as in the discussion in this section.

4. Investment and Capital Cost

Now we can look at the business of paying for the professor's generator. This is a topic that has not been adequately understood, and furthermore, we cannot rely on the conventional economics literature to provide us with everything we need. If we consider nuclear energy, the goal is to build plants where capacity costs will be between $1500 and $2000 per kW. $2000 or thereabouts is probably the most realistic figure at the present time, although I see no reason why it cannot be decreased.

In the United States, between 1975 and 1989, the average period required to complete a plant increased from 5 to 12 years. Naturally, this was devastating where costs were concerned, and since the electric bills of households and small businesses increased by a large amount, almost everybody was soured where the nuclear future was concerned. (Exercise: Explain why this was "devastating".)

Economics though is — or should be — about optimality: about optimal (or best practice) activities and procedures that can be transferred from region to region. The Japanese now expect to construct large nuclear plants in about four years, and if necessary less, and this is an important step toward reducing capacity cost under $2000/kW. Another important step is increasing the "life" of reactors. A reactor that is 33-years-old in Omaha Nebraska (United States) is having its life extended by 30 years, which tells me that new reactors will soon have "lives" of 70 years. Moreover, in an emergency, it may be possible to construct a nuclear plant in three years. Since these facilities have no direct emission of the main greenhouse gas CO_2, it is difficult to believe that electricity can be generated more cheaply if it is based on coal, gas, or wind — which are the main competitors to nuclear just now.

We can leave the real world and return to the travails of Professor B, who has purchased a small coal-based electric generator for $1000. The professor might choose to reach into his pocket and pay the seller immediately, or he might ask the 7–11 manager if he can have one or two years to pay. If the manager suggests one year, and the interest rate is 10%, the professor would be required to pay $1100 at the end of the year. The calculation here is $M_1 = M_0(1 + r) = 1000(1 + 0.1) = 1100$, where M_1 represents an amount at the end of this year or the beginning of next year, and r is the relevant interest rate. Now suppose that the manager agrees to two years. In that case the payment at the end of two years (M_2) is $[M_0(1+r)](1+r) = 1100(1+r) = 1210$. This can also be written $M_2 = M_1(1+r) = M_0(1+r)^2$.

More generally, with the interest rate fixed at r, and an agreement where the generator costing M_0 today will be paid for at the end of the Tth year, the amount that will have to be paid is $M_0(1+r)(1+r)\cdots(1+r) = M_0(1+r)^T = M_T$. Readers should verify these manipulations.

But there is another arrangement that both parties might find satisfactory. This is for a generator costing P_0 to be paid for over T years, with an equal payment A at the end of each year. The payment "A" for each of T years can be calculated using the "annuity" formula, which is:

$$A = \left[\frac{r(1+r)^T}{(1+r)^T - 1} \right] P_0. \tag{2}$$

If any of my students, anywhere, want a passing grade, then they are advised to always be able to reproduce and explain this equation at any hour of the day or night. Now, putting in the relevant numbers for $T = 2$, as in the example above, it is a simple matter to determine $A = (A_1 = A_2) = \{[r(1+r)^T]/[(1+r)^T - 1]\}P_0 = \{[0.10(1+0.10)^2]/[(1+0.10)^2 - 1]\}1000 = \$576$.

The annuity formula will be derived in the appendix, because the thing to stress now is what this annual annuity payment of $576 means.

The professor has in effect borrowed $1000, and at the end of the first year pays $576 of this amount. $100 is the interest cost for the year ($= 0.10 \times 1000$), and the remainder $576 - 100 = \$476$ is an *amortization* payment on the loan. At the beginning of the second year $524(= 1000 - 476$) is still owned on the borrowed sum, and this can be regarded as the remaining (or outstanding) balance (on the loan).

$576 is once again paid at the end of the second year. Of this, $524 \times 0.10 = \$52.4$ is the interest on the remaining balance ($= \$524$) of the loan, while the remainder ($576 - 52.4 = \$523.6 \approx \$524$) is the final amortization payment. Note that if the professor had desired, he could have paid the 7-11 a sum of $524 at the beginning of the second year ($=$ end of first year), in which case he would have repaid the $1000 he borrowed

($= 476 + 524 = 1000$), and he would not have another interest payment to make. (Why might he prefer an earlier payment?)

Exercises

1. Suppose that the 7–11 gave the professor three years to pay for the generator. What is the A for each year? Break A into interest and amortization charges!
2. Why might the professor decide to pay the remainder of his debt at the end of one year instead of waiting another year? At the end of two years the generator is fully amortized. Why is this an attractive situation for the professor?
3. Paying $1000 now, or $1210 at the end of two years, or $576 at the end of the each year for two years can be shown to be the same thing. Discuss!

Next we can look at some terminology that is often misused. The $1000 in the above example is the *investment cost* of the generator. The $576 is the *capital cost*. In a large generating station there are employees that must be paid for carrying out various duties, and in addition there is the cost of fuel, taxes of one sort or another, etc. Some or most of these can be taken as variable costs. When discussing the total cost for a year, these and the capital cost (and *not* the investment cost) go into the calculation.

It might be interesting to use the annuity equation to discuss what is the result of the interest rate increasing or decreasing, or for that matter changes in the amortization period. As can be easily verified by calculating a few values, or using the calculus, when r decreases, A falls, and when T increases A falls. An assured supply of energy is a good that is steadily becoming more important, and in the United States (and probably elsewhere) the government is prepared to extend certain guarantees so that suppliers of, e.g., nuclear energy and certain renewables, do not lose money in the event of something unexpected happening with the construction or operation of new facilities. If these guarantees are as comprehensive as I believe that they should be, it would mean that the builders of nuclear (and perhaps other) facilities would be able to borrow money at the absolute lowest interest rates, as would be the case if governments owned and operated these installations.

Something else that is happening in the United States and elsewhere is that licensing procedures are being speeded up, and the "life" of existing nuclear plants are being extended to 60 years, or in some cases higher. Readers should calculate the capital cost of 1 kW of nuclear capacity if its life is extended from 40 to 60 years, and the investment cost is $2000/kW. From 60 to 70 years! Would you suggest extending these lives to 100 years?

5. Capacity Factor, Efficiency and Some Thermodynamics

The materials in this chapter deserve your careful attention. They are elementary but important, and this is the kind of information that it pays to have at your fingertips in the highly competitive world in which we must make our way.

In the above discussion we noted that when the professor was buying coal, he had to take into consideration the imperfections in his generator–lamp system. For example, although in a perfect system 1 kWh(e) of energy could be generated with 3412 Btu, in the coal-based arrangement applicable to the professor it takes 10,340 Btu to obtain 1 kWh of energy. In this situation we spoke of something called the *heat rate* being equal to 10,340 Btu. The efficiency might therefore be defined as $3412/10,340 = 0.33 = 33\%$. Note that when efficiency increases the heat rate falls. A perfect system — with 100% efficiency — has a heat rate equal to 3412 Btu.

Now let us consider another example. Suppose that we buy some electric generating equipment for which we pay a price of $1500 kW. *Note*: this is a guaranteed price, and we do not have to worry about the kind of efficiency here that we discussed earlier. Now assume a discount rate of 9%, an amortization period (T) of 20 years, and as mentioned an investment cost (I) of $1500/kW. Using Eq. (2) we get approximately $164 as the capital cost per kilowatt. (The reader should check this, and also note that this example deals with capacity and not energy — i.e., kW and not kWh.)

Let us assume that the power rating of this equipment is only 1 kW — as compared with the power rating of 1000 MW(e) of the nuclear plant in your back yard. (We know of course that $1000\,\text{MW} = 1000 \times 10^6\,\text{W} = 10^9\,\text{W} = 10^6\,\text{kW} = 10^3\,\text{MW}$.) If this 1 kW piece of equipment functioned 24 h per day, every day of the year, then we would say that it is producing $1 \times 365 \times 24 = 8760\,\text{kWh/year}$, and so in this case the capital cost might be expressed as 164/8760 dollars kWh, which might best be expressed as 1.875 cents/kWh.

We can interrupt this discussion to look at some actual electric demands and prices for the United States. Total demand was 3830 billion kWh in 2005, and is expected to reach 3904 billion kWh in 2007. Residential customers paid an average of 9.43 cents/kWh in 2005 (and expected average rates are 10.16 in 2006 and 10.46 in 2007). In some parts of the United States rates were much lower than this. For example, The Southern Company (with headquarters in Atlanta Georgia) is a regulated utility serving about four million people. Its average price a few years ago was 8.5 cents/kWh, while deregulated firms in the same region charged on average about 11.33 cents/kWh.

But although mechanically the equipment mentioned above might be perfect and can deliver 1 kW when operating, there might be reasons why it cannot operate every hour of every day. One of the reasons might be that in order for it to retain this perfection, it must be taken out of operation for a certain length of time every period (e.g., year) for inspection and maintenance. Also, there may be unexpected "glitches" that keep rated output from being realized, or rated capacity from being employed.

Suppose that of 8760 h in a year, 876 h are normal "down time" in which inspection and maintenance take place. But in addition, during the same year, another 876 h were needed for unexpected repairs. It is here that we introduce the "capacity factor" (CF), the definition of which can be best written as $CF = $ (actual kWh)/(capacity $\times$ hours in period). In this example the capacity factor is $7008/1 \times 8760 = 0.80$. This is a simple matter, however it should be appreciated that CF is best thought of as an ex-post (i.e., after-the-fact) measure. This is because all down time cannot be predicted in advance. Think, for example, of wind installations. The rated capacity and therefore potential (energy) output of a wind park may be very impressive, ex-ante, but as often pointed out, ex-post capacity factors for these facilities have sometimes turned out to be very low. By way of contrast, the Wolf Creek nuclear plant in Kansas, 21 years "old", once operated continuously for 506 days before closing for a one-month refueling outage.

It is worth knowing that the definition of capacity factor sometimes takes as the relevant time period a year minus the period used for "normal" maintenance, to include refueling. In the above example the basis for calculating the capacity factor would be 7884 h, and calculated as $7008/(1 \times 7884) - 0.888$, as compared to the earlier 0.80. The US Energy Information Administration follows this practice, and as a result in their listing or evaluation of the nuclear units in the world in 1998, the top 10 had capacity factors that were very high. The capacity factor is sometimes confused with the load factor, but these are not the same. The load factor is the ratio of average daily deliveries to peak daily deliveries over a given time period.

In expressing the cost of a kWh of electricity as 1.875 cents it was assumed that the capital cost (of $164) was spread over 8760 h. But since only about 80% — or 7008 h — of this was available due to normal and otherwise down time, the cost of a kWh becomes $164/7008 = 2.34$ cents/kWh. Windpower for example can have very low capacity factors (CFs), and when this is taken into consideration, it can be very expensive power. It can also be very disappointing in providing certain amenities to which we have become accustomed. We can now examine some aspects of the concept known as efficiency with the help of Fig. 7.2.

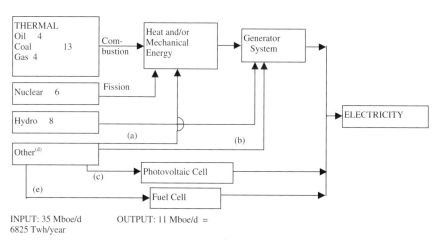

INPUT: 35 Mboe/d   OUTPUT: 11 Mboe/d =
6825 Twh/year

Solar-Thermal: Biomass, Geothermal, Solar
Wind, Tidal, Wave
Solar Source: Shell Briefing Service, 1986
Negligible
Hydrogen-Oxygen

Figure 7.2.   A Comprehensive Electric System: Inputs and Output

This figure shows the difference between the energy put into the global electric system by oil, coal, gas, etc, and the amount available in the form of electric energy. Energy to the extent of 35 million barrels of oil *equivalent* per day (= 35 mboe/d) on the average was put into the global electricity generating system in 1986, and the output was 11 mboe/d (= 6825 TWh(e)), where the "e" in the parenthesis signifies electric. This indicates a production and transmission efficiency of approximately 31.5%: only about one-third of the energy in the inputs was available to final consumers. As will be indicated below, thermodynamics provides an important clue as to why this is the case, but economics also must be brought into the picture. It was simply too expensive at that time to make the investments that would have raised the input–output efficiency by another few percent. The diagram applies to 1986, but in terms of the efficiency there is not much difference at the present time. The point quite simple is that technology will often come up against thermodynamic limits that it cannot surmount.

Mention was made above of the laws of thermodynamics, and to round out this section a short comment on the topic seems appropriate. Had he lived long enough to carry out the necessary public relations work, the French artillery officer Sadi Carnot might have found himself in the same class as Isaac Newton and Albert Einstein. In 1824 he not only founded the science of thermodynamics, but anticipated much of energy theory. Of course, maybe it was just as well that he left this vale of tears when he did, because one of his most brilliant successors — the German medical doctor Julius Robert Mayer — who in 1840 proposed the logical structure of the conservation of energy — aroused the envy of the scientific establishment to the extent that he was eventually hounded into an asylum for the insane.

The First Law of Thermodynamics — or the Law of Conservation of Energy — states that energy cannot be created or destroyed, but is always conserved. The second law — which is more subtle — states that heat cannot pass from a colder to a hotter body. Getting down to details we find out that in an isolated system in which there are two temperatures, energy tends to distribute equally across the system. Eventually an equilibrium (or state of rest) is attained from which no useful work can be obtained without energy being fed in from the outside.

In a conventional electric power station, heat is generated by a fuel (e.g., coal or gas). The steam produced from this heat and water can, in a properly designed system, perform work of one sort or another — such as turning a generator shaft. Eventually, however, this steam becomes water again at a lower temperature. Without more fuel this is the equilibrium. Carnot efficiency then comes into the picture, which in equation form is $(T_1' - T_2')/T_1'$. Here T_1 is the higher temperature, T_2 the lower, and if in Fahrenheit (F) they are transformed into absolute (i.e., Rankine) units using $T' = T + 460$. If we have $T_1 = 1000$ and $T_2 = 100$, then $T_1' = 1000 + 460 = 1460$, while $T_2' = 100 + 460 = 560$. The corresponding maximum theoretical efficiency is thus $(1460 - 560)/1460 = 62\%$. If the temperature was centigrade (C), Rankine units are $T' = T + 273$. (And remember $F = (9/5)C + 32$.)

6. The Economics of Load Division (1)

Screening curves show how the annual (energy) cost of a kW of electric generating capacity depends on the number of hours it is used. As a result it seems suitable to call them cost curves. For instance, a generator of 1 kW that is producing for a year of 8760 h, provides $1 \times 8760 = 8760$ kWh. If it uses a fuel that costs $0.2 kWh, then as calculated earlier in this chapter, the total fuel cost will be $1 \times 0.2 \times 8760 = \$1752$. Remembering your first course in economics, this can be considered a component of the total *variable cost*. In the discussion below the $0.2/kWh is the only relevant variable cost per unit. There are of course other costs, and in the sequel we identify what in microeconomics is called a fixed cost. Call this F, and for this example make it equal to $10,000. The total cost then for 8760 h of operation becomes $11,752.

As already indicated, this fixed cost (F) can be designated the *capital cost*. Its relation to the investment cost has been explained, but an even more simple example might be appropriate. Suppose that this 1 kW generator costs $100,000 ($= I$, the investment cost), and it will be financed with borrowed money, where the cost of borrowing — i.e., the interest rate — is 10%. Moreover, for this example, let us make the unrealistic assumption that the generator will last forever, with no depreciation, and can deliver 1 kW of power until the end of time. Thus for every year, possession of the generator will cost $r \times I = rI = 0.10 \times 100,000 = \$10,000$. This is how we obtained the $10,000 in the previous paragraph. (The assumption of no depreciation here includes "economic depreciation", and thus at any time in the future we could sell the generator for $100,000, put this money in the bank and draw $10,000 a year. This is the (annual) opportunity cost that is incurred as a result of buying the generator.)

In considering the above it is clear that we can write a cost equation (or screening curve) having the form $C = F + vt$. Where does the v come in? v is the 0.2 ($/kWh) above. It is the fuel or variable cost that is associated with operating the generator. The cost equation for the above example then becomes $C = F + vt = 10,000 + 0.2t$. Readers should do everything possible to understand this discussion before continuing! I can also mention that F is sometimes called the capacity cost, while "vt" is called the energy cost (for the period t).

Next, we can consider two types of generating equipment, gas (g) and coal (c). Historically, gas burning equipment has a relatively low fixed cost, but a high variable (i.e., fuel) cost, while coal has a high fixed cost but a low variable cost. For the important examples in the next section I take $C_g = 500 + (1 \times t) = 500 + t$, and $C_c = 1000 + 0.5t$. The values of v in these examples are thus unity ($= 1$) and 0.5. Now let us look at the cost of, e.g., producing for one week ($= 168$ h) and one year ($= 8760$ h). For the first period, $C_g = \$668$ and $C_c = \$1084$. The reader can check these! For the second production period ($= 1$ year) $C_g = \$9250$ and $C_c = \$5375$. It thus appears that gas was the least costly fuel when the production period was one week, while coal was the least costly when the production period was one year. This is an important observation for the present analysis.

One more operation is necessary before we go to some exercises. At what value of the time (t) is the cost of production equal for the two types of equipment. To get this we merely solve $C_c = C_g$, or $1000 + 0.5t = 500 + t$. The answer is 1000 h (i.e., $t = 1000$). Furthermore, when t is less than 1000 ($t < 1000$), $C_g < C_c$, and when $t > 1000$, $C_g > C_c$. Once again, this is an important observation and the reader should make sure that he or she understands it before proceeding.

Exercises

1. This section ended with a numerical example. Discuss this example and provide a numerical or formal proof that things are as I say they are, and write out the algebraic value of "t"!

2. $C_g = F_g + v_g t$. Write out C_c in the same form! Consider the following cost equations: $C_c = 1200 + 0.4t$ and $C_g = 600 + 0.6t$. Calculate the value of t when these costs are equal, and call it t^*. What is the situation when $t > t^*$ and $t < t^*$? Discuss!

3. In the above the fixed cost (or capital cost) is obtained by assuming that the equipment never depreciated, and so $F = rI$. Make the same assumption here, only take $I = \$100,000$ for coal and $\$70,000$ for gas. Calculate the values of F and write out the cost equations when $v_c = 0.4$, $v_g = 0.3$, and $r = 0.9\% (= 0.09)$. Calculate the values of t^*. Now assume that r falls to 6%, and make the same calculations. Can you draw any conclusions from this exercise?

4. Why does it make sense to call F in the previous discussion the "capacity cost", and v the "energy cost"? Expressions sometimes used are off-peak loads and off-peak periods. Can you identify these in the examples in this section?

This might be a good point to review some of what we have done. If we have $C_g = 500 + t$, and $C_c = 1000 + 0.5t$, then $C_g = C_c$ at time $t^* = 1000\,\text{h}$. If the intention is to have 1 kW available for greater than 1000 h then coal is cheaper, because its low variable costs more than compensates for its high fixed cost; but if the intention is to supply 1 kW for less than 1000 h, gas is less expensive. Basically this is due to its relatively low fixed cost.

Let us see how this plays out when we have two loads and two generators. Bill has a contract to supply a load of 1 kW for 8760 h (i.e., every hour of every day in a year), while Sally has agreed to service a load of 1 kW for 500 h. Bill must generate a total annual energy of 8760 kWh while Sally must generate 500 kWh. From our previous discussion we know that Bill will use coal and Sally gas. As for what this load might be, a possibility is lighting at one of the Uppsala University's student clubs. 1 kW is *always* on the line (for 8760 h) in the form of ten 100 W bulbs, however for 500 of these 8760 h, an extra ten bulbs of 100 W are on the line. Thus, for 500 h annually, twenty 100 W bulbs are on the line.

Suppose that Bill and Sally decide to form a company that will have 2 kW of capacity available every hour of the year, however 2 kW are required only 500 h of the year, and 1 kW the rest of the time. Therefore, there is considerable excess capacity available — though not, note, when the peak load (= 2 kW) is being generated. Assuming that they continue to sell to the student club mentioned earlier, this club now pays one firm instead of two. Here we have identified 1 kW as the base load, and 2 kW as the peak load. Where this 2 kW peak load is concerned, Bill supplies 1 kW and Sally adds 1 kW, although since they have formed a single firm, there is no point in identifying who-supplies-what. It should also be noted that it does not matter when the peak load is on the line. For instance, it might be on the line five hours a night for 100 nights of the year, with some of these nights being during the fall term, and some during the spring term. The total energy supplied during the year is 8760 + 500 = 9260 kWh, and as mentioned earlier the firm is paid on the basis of the energy supplied.

The presence of the large excess capacity in the above example brings to mind a question. Would not it have been less costly if Sally had only a one-half kilowatt (= 0.5 kW) generator that operated 1000 h of the year instead of a 1 kW generator that operated only 500 h? (In other words a 1000 h peak lower than the 500 h peak.) This equipment mostly supplies lighting to an Uppsala student club, and so it might have been possible through innovative pricing to redistribute the "load" — e.g., operate the disco over those 1000 h, with less lighting than before, but higher entrance costs for what have traditionally been peak hours. (For example, 8–10 during the week, and 10–12 on weekends.) If that was so then maybe the Sally–Bill firm could sell the 1 kW generator, buy a 0.5 kW generator with some of the money they received, and use the remainder of the money to hire a talented disc jockey who might increase total receipts, or simply take a long holiday on the west coast of Sweden during the summer.

Anyone who knows anything about student clubs in Uppsala knows that it is very difficult to make predictions about the attendance (on the dance floor or at the bar). As a result, another possibility might be to sell one of the 1 kW generators and buy several smaller units known as "peakers". This kind of equipment is designed to start up immediately in response to a sudden and perhaps unexpected need for energy.

Having to satisfy unexpected peak loads is a real problem, and a main purpose of innovative pricing that takes advantage of customer response is to smooth peaks or whenever possible to eliminate them. If you spend time examining contributions on the important forum *EnergyPulse* (www.energypulse.net) you will often encounter references to the peak load and the disproportional part it plays in the pricing of electric power.

7. The Economics of Load Division (2)

If the above discussion is understood, then you should not have any trouble with the slightly more complicated presentation below. We can begin this section by specifying three kinds of equipment that can produce electricity. These are gas-based, with a low capital cost (F_1), but a high variable cost (v_1); coal, with a capital cost (F_2) that is higher than gas, but a variable cost (v_2) that is lower; and finally nuclear with the highest capital cost (F_3), but the lowest variable cost (v_3). This arrangement can be seen in the top diagram of Fig. 7.3(a). Once again the cost relationships are linear and of the type $C = F + vt$ (or $C = F + tV$), with the applicable part of these curves being the solid lines that form the aggregate cost curve, In the previous section's example the discussion all the time involved a capacity of 1 kW, but these screening or cost curves are applicable for any capacity.

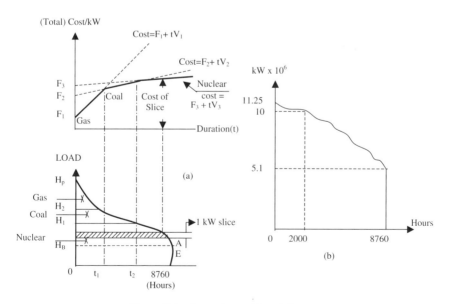

Figure 7.3.   Screening and Load Curves

In turning to Fig. 7.3, we can begin with 7.3(b), which shows the load on the line in Norway in 1975. The maximum load was 11.25×10^6 kW, while during 2000 h of the year the load varied between 11.25×10^6 and 10×10^6 kW. Between 2000 h and one year $(= 8760 \text{ h})$, the load was between 11.25×10^6 and 5.1×10^6 kW. As can be noticed, never during the year did it fall below 5.1×10^6 kW, and so it is clearly appropriate to designate 5.1×10^6 kW as the base load, although it could happen that the base load equipment supplies some of the intermediate load. What about the intermediate and peak load? This is more or less subjective, however I am sure that Norwegian engineers were capable of making the optimal choice, whatever it turned out to be.

The exposition will continue by extending the examples given in the previous section. The first step is to put the load diagram at the bottom of Fig. 7.3(a) into perspective with the screening (i.e., cost) curves at the top of Fig. 7.3(a). As in the previous section we can write the values of the costs as $C_1 = F_1 + v_1 t$, $C_2 = F_2 + v_2 t$ and $C_3 = F_3 + v_3 t$. Something that can be noted again is the expression *merit order*, where the intention is to determine which type of equipment carries which load, and over what portion of the year (of 8760 h).

What we are going to find out with some simple algebra is that in the arrangement in the figure, gas generates the peak load, coal generates a part of the intermediate load, and nuclear generates the remainder, which in this diagram means the base load plus a part of the intermediate load. Accordingly, during a part of the time nuclear is idle, and so it might be designated a reserve, since after all there is considerable uncertainty associated with the ex-ante (i.e., before the fact or predicted) load. It might be argued that this is a bad example, since it is a waste to have expensive nuclear equipment idle, however given the cost curves, the specification of cost-minimization leaves us with no choice. (It seems that a reserve of 15%–20% is usually deemed correct, although at the present time in the United States and perhaps other countries it has been suggested that there has been serious underinvestment in power sources and especially transmission lines.)

Using the algebra and elementary logic from the previous section, it is a simple matter to find t_1 and t_2 in Fig. 7.3(a). To get t_1 we start with $F_1 + v_1 t = F_2 + v_2 t$. This immediately gives us $F_2 - F_1 = t(v_1 - v_2)$, and so $t = t_1 = (F_2 - F_1)/(v_1 - v_2)$. Obtaining t_2 is just as easy, but it will be left for you to do as an exercise. Notice also that from the point of view of signs, the value of t_1 makes sense, because $F_2 > F_1$ and $v_1 > v_2$, and thus the quotient is positive.

Let us also notice that in this example if we say that we have a peak, intermediate, and base load, only the base load $0 - H_B$ is unambiguous. The peak load definitely appears to be $H_2 - H_P$ and the intermediate load $H_B - H_2$, but aside from the algebra there is a certain ambiguity about these two which is not important for the readers of this book — nor for its author. Even so, a generalization of this analysis is in the appendix!

We can imagine a number of hypothetical situations which would have a place in this discussion. For instance, one might be that after we make our calculations, gas carries none of the load. Why? The only possible answer is that it costs too much relative to coal and nuclear. On the other hand, it may carry the entire load. Why? The short answer is that it is less expensive than the other options. Consider the situation in California over the past decade. As a result of technology improving combined cycle gas-based equipment until it became very efficient, and the gas price remaining very low until the last few years, gas-based equipment became sufficiently economical to generate a much larger share of the electric load in that state than previously contemplated. The same thing happened in the United Kingdom with the so called "dash for gas". As bad luck would have it though, the gas price suddenly escalated, and while existing gas-based equipment could not be instantaneously discarded, when new generating equipment was considered, gas looked much less attractive. Accordingly there is a difference between the optimal merit order and the existing merit order.

Exercises

1. In the discussion dealing with Fig. 7.3(a), I say that nuclear not only generates the base load and part of the intermediate load, but might also function as a reserve. What does this mean?
2. In Fig. 7.3(a), I calculated t_1. You calculate t_2, and tell if the sign makes sense, and why. Can you say what it means in this figure if $F_3 - F_2 > 8760(v_2 - v_3)$?

3. Explain and expand on the sentence in which it is pointed out that there is a difference between the optimal merit order and the existing merit order, using a diagram if possible!

Readers who have come this far, and can solve most of the exercises can feel very satisfied. It is interesting to note that in Australia, plants that are designated intermediate load plants comprise about 40%–45% of total installed capacity, as compared to 50% for base load plants, and 5%–10% for peaking plants. This says something about the place of uncertainty in these matters and how it causes a deviation from the "ideal" or optimal merit order of the type being presented above where we get unambiguous answers as to the value of t_1 and t_2. Generally the peak load represents only a small fraction of the demand for electricity, and it can happen that only a portion of this capacity is in use, but since the available generating equipment must be able to satisfy the maximum demand that may appear in the system, capacity "*load factors*" for peak load facilities are often quite small. As a result, if possible, as much peak load power as possible should be purchased rather than generated in the system, and as a result many utilities do everything possible to satisfy these requirements by purchases from other cities, states, regions or countries. The expression "load factor" was used above. This can be defined as the Average Load divided by the Peak Load. Ideally this is fairly large (i.e., close to unity), but there can be some ugly surprises where electric generation is concerned, and so in some regions considerable excess or reserve capacity must be available because there can be a simultaneous peak in the neighboring regions.

8. Final Remarks and Conclusions

Among the things left out in this chapter is the demand side of the electric market. Too much has been written on that topic in the academic economics literature already, because much of this information is not applicable to the real world where electric demands are periodic, and the commodity itself (i.e., electricity) is essentially non-storable. In addition there can be considerable uncertainty in things like the physical characteristics (e.g., amplitudes and frequencies) of what can be a very volatile demand. At times demand will move very close to available supply, and given the explicit and implicit costs of unplanned outages, substantial reserve capacity should be available. It is not easy to calculate what "substantial" means here however. What can be done is to attempt to make sure that readers of this book have at least a rough idea of how a typical electric system looks. A simple example is found in Fig. 7.4.

This is a diagram that I expect students to be able to reproduce without paying excessive attention to the details. The point is that they should develop a reasonable familiarity with some of the terminology in the diagram. Besides, everything in the diagram is self-explanatory. The transformers for instance move voltages up or down — e.g., from the several thousand volts in the large power lines that almost everyone has noticed at one time or another, down to the several hundred volts that you might require to watch your prime-time favorites.

Another topic that deserves a few comments is transmission lines. Underground electric lines are more satisfactory aesthetically than the overhead variety, and suffer only a third of the outages, but according to the

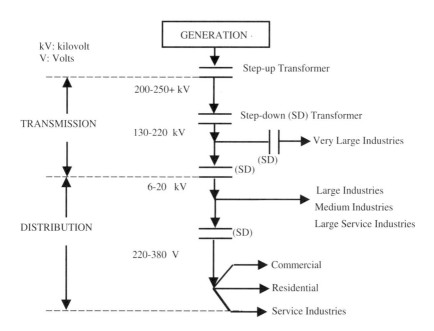

Figure 7.4.   An Electric Generating System

Edison Electric Institute they cost 10 times as much as overhead structures. They suffer a third of the outages as overhead lines, but they take
twice as long to repair. What this means is that the future of large scale
"undergrounding" is uncertain, although on the basis of the extended blackouts suffered in Sweden a year ago due to the damage inflicted on overhead
lines by wind and snow, the economic arguments of Swedish power companies are no longer well received.

One of the more unfavorable aspects of deregulation is that investment
has decreased in order to boost present profits, and so when electric demand
threatens to exceed supply, it is necessary to resort to reserve capacity that
is expensive to operate. In Sweden (and probably many other countries) this
means oil-based equipment, and if marginal cost pricing is being practiced,
then the price of every unit of output increases.

My intention in this chapter was to stress that when confronting a periodic demand, a mix of equipment will generally be resorted to, and these
facilities will have different operating and capital costs, where the capital
cost is derived from the investment cost. I was also careful to handle these
matters with a minimum of mathematics. As I pointed out at the beginning
of this book, there are a great many things in the economics literature that
you really do not want to spend your time trying to absorb, but the materials
in this chapter are not among them.

We very often read about the large amount of "nuclear" in the French
electric system, but what is not pointed out that this "large amount" refers to
energy (as measured in kWh) as compared to capacity (in kW). As I noted in
my previous energy economics textbook, there is also considerable difference between the marginal cost of electric generation in periods when most
of the load was being generated by base load equipment (mostly nuclear),
and periods when the peak load was being generated. Unfortunately, this
is somewhat trivial, because if we reflect on the discussion in this chapter
we should detect immediately that the value of "v" is the marginal cost for
a particular piece of equipment, and in the real world it can be much larger
for gas (or oil) than for nuclear. Spikes in electric demand often require
oil-based equipment to be put into service, and with the high price of oil
that is now being experienced and expected, and marginal cost pricing —
which causes all electricity to be priced at the value of the most expensive
unit being supplied — the price of electricity can occasionally be very high.

Appendix: Deriving an Important Equation, and Some Aspects of the Discount Rate

The annuity equation was presented and discussed above without a derivation. Hopefully readers understood it to an extent that the derivation below can go smoothly in the context of a debt incurred in order to finance an investment.

The first part of this analysis reviews the example in the text of a two period situation where $1000 was "invested" in an asset, a rickshaw, which was amortized in two payments. (Amortization means repaying the principal.) It was here that we introduced the term annuity, which is the amount paid every period (which was calculated as $A = \$576$), and which if it was invested by the receiver (i.e., the person making the loan) at the *notional* rate of interest ($=10\% = 0.10$) in the example, would be sufficient to repay the debt at the end of the second period (which in this example is the *amortization period*). Observe also that the debt "today" is $1000, and if unpaid for two periods would be $1000(1 + 0.1)^2 = \$1210$ if 10% is the applicable rate of interest.

Let us look closer at this. The first payment of $576 is at the end of the first year, and this is equivalent to $576(1 + 0.1) = \$633$ at the end of the second year. If we add this to the annuity payment of $576 at the end of the second year, it sums to approximately $1210, or the same as above. It can thus be specified that, *ceteris paribus*, paying $1000 now for the asset, or paying $1210 at the end of two years, or paying $576 at the end of the first and second years are equivalent where the person granting the loan is concerned, and 10% is the applicable rate of interest. Note the *ceteris paribus* criterion, because obviously in real life there are situations when this condition would not hold.

Something else that can be mentioned is that if the payment for the asset had not been borrowed, but paid for in cash at the time of the purchase, the concept of an annuity would still be valid. In this case the annuity payments represent the opportunity cost of purchasing this asset instead of, e.g., lending the cash and earning interest (amounting to, e.g., $210 after two years).

Observe also the term *notional*! This is important in finance, and here it means the value used in the calculation, regardless of the value of other discount or interest rates or whatever that may be in circulation. For instance, the *notional* value of the discount rate above was 10%, but the rate of interest that is relevant for this investor if he had wanted to be a lender instead of a borrower could have been something quite different. It could, for instance, have been the deposit rate at his local bank. (In the next chapter the term is used in connection with swaps.) What we are saying here is that someone who is going to make an investment in a rickshaw for the purpose mentioned in this chapter should achieve a profit (rate) of at least 10%, because this is available without having to take a risk. Since discounted profits were substantially greater than the size of the investment (= $1000), a profit rate greater than 10% was realized.

Now let us generalize this two-period example to T periods. Two equivalent arrangements for paying a debt of PV entered into at the beginning of the first period is to pay $PV(1+r)^T$ at the end of T periods, or via annuities A at the end of each period, beginning with the *end* of the first period, and ending at the end of the last period! Thus we get:

$$PV(1+r)^T = A + A(1+r) + A(1+r)^2 + \cdots + A(1+r)^{T-1}.$$

Multiplying both sides of this expression by $(1+r)$ we obtain:

$$(1+r)[PV(1+r)^T] = A(1+r) + \cdots + A(1+r)^T.$$

Subtracting the second of these expressions from the first yields:

$$[(1+r)^T]PV[1-(1+r)] = A - A(1+r)^T.$$

From this we get Eq. (2) in the text, which was

$$A = \left[\frac{r(1+r)^T}{(1+r)^T - 1}\right]PV. \tag{A.1}$$

This expression can also be derived using some elementary calculus, beginning with a fundamental (neo-classical) economic concept: the capital cost of an investment is the uniform return per period that an asset must earn, in order to achieve a net present value of zero. In other words, the asset price is the present value of future net yields (i.e., revenues minus costs). Notation in this derivation is changed somewhat in order to correspond to standard usage. Taking I as the asset price (i.e., the investment cost), P the capital cost per period, and r the market discount rate, we can write for T periods:

$$I = \int_0^T Pe^{-rt}dt = \frac{P}{r}\left(1 - \frac{1}{e^{rT}}\right). \tag{A.1}$$

It takes very little manipulation to obtain $P = re^{rT}I/(e^{rT}-1)$. Remembering that we can approximate e^{rT} by $(1+r)^T$ for small values of r, we get Eq. (2), though with a different notation. The discount rate here was the market interest rate, because in the neo-classical world, there is no risk/uncertainty on the part of lenders and borrowers, which means that the risk-free interest rate is always appropriate. This is not the kind of recommendation that needs to be taken seriously outside a seminar room.

A few more comments on the interest or discount rate are probably in order before concluding this chapter. First, real versus nominal (i.e., money) interest rates. The real interest rate is the nominal interest rate — i.e., the one you see on a "handout" in your bank or in the newspaper — *minus* the rate of inflation. In the examples in the chapter nominal values were used for investment, revenues and costs and so interest rates should be nominal. If real values — i.e., nominal values adjusted for inflation — had been used, then real interest rates should also have been used.

I also spoke of adjusting the discount rate for risk. As explained in my finance book this means distinguishing between *diversifiable* (or *non-systematic*) and *non-diversifiable* (or *systematic*) risks. For the gentleman lecturer in this chapter who moonlighted as a rickshaw chauffeur, his risk is non-diversifiable because any gain or loss that he might suffer is beyond his control. Moreover, even if it were otherwise, for one reason or another he is not in a mood or position to diversify what risk he is exposed to by, e.g., buying a fund that has many different types of investments. Of course, if he operated a fleet of rickshaws he might be receptive to a more scientific or businesslike train of thought. Mainstream theory informs us that if optimal diversification is possible, then a sensible player will take advantage of it, in which case any discounting exercise that we do should employ the risk-free interest rate (e.g., a bank rate offered by your favorite bank). As for myself, I do not mull over this kind of conjecture outside the classroom.

Instead, for our rickshaw person at the beginning of this chapter, he should think in terms of being confronted with an investment characterized by a non-diversifiable risk — if "think" is the right word. Conventional theory then informs him that the opportunity cost of investment is higher than the risk-free rate, and so a premium should be included in his discount rate. The discount rate used in the example was 15%, and given a risk-free rate in the real world of 6% or 7% at the present time, it is likely that a substantial risk premium is included in the 15%.

The *Capital Asset Pricing Model* provides a means for calculating a premium, but once again this is an academic device. In the real world so-called "hurdle rates" are used that are mostly subjective, and according to some researchers who have studied this topic, most of these hurdle rates are excessive. Of course, many of the persons employing these excessive hurdle rates are multi-millionaires or more whose fortunes show no signs of decreasing, and so perhaps there is little or no benefit to be gained from speculating on any deficiencies in their knowledge or behavior.

In some classroom discussions students want a formalization of the results presented above on "load division". Here I can point to an important article by Michael Einhorn (1983) whose mathematics I have altered somewhat to correspond to my classroom presentations of this topic. The following expression should be self-evident if the reader comprehends Fig. 7.3, and is familiar with integral calculus.

$$TC = F_1(H_p - H_2) + F_2(H_2 - H_1) + F_3(H_3 - 0)$$
$$+ v_1 \int_{H_p}^{H_2} t(H)dH + v_2 \int_{H_2}^{H_1} t(H)dH + v_3 \int_{H_1}^{0} t(H)dH.$$

Integrations take place horizontally, and involve slices of the capacity H bounded by the vertical axis and the systems load curve. This is synonymous to Eq. (A.2):

$$TC = \sum_{j=1}^{N} F_j(H_j - H_{j-1}) + \sum_{j=1}^{N} \{v_j \int_{H_j}^{H_{j-1}} t(H)dH\}. \qquad (A.2)$$

Next we differentiate TC with respect to, for example H_j, and set the resulting expression equal to zero. This gives us (A.3):

$$\frac{\partial TC}{\partial H_j} = F_j - F_{j-1} + v_j t(H_j) - v_{j+1} t(H_j) = 0. \qquad (A.3)$$

From this we obtain for a cross-over time:

$$t(H_j) = \frac{F_{j+1} \quad F_j}{v_j - v_{j+1}}. \tag{A.4}$$

For instance:

$$t(H_2) = t_2 = \frac{F_3 - F_2}{v_2 - v_3}. \tag{A.5}$$

We have an overtone of (Albert) Einstein's equivalence theorem here in that two approaches (informal and formal) lead us to the same result, which suggests that the same fundamental law is operating. The informal presentation was also about cost minimization.

Exercises

1. In Eq. (2), what is A if T = (or rather approaches) "infinity", $T = 0$, $T = 1$? Comment!
2. Derive A in Eq. (2) if $T = 3$. Show all steps!
3. I have only mentioned the expression "hurdle rates" *en-passant*! What do you think about it.
4. In Fig. 7.4, some transformers are shown. What are their purposes?
5. Is there any difference between the discount rate and the interest rate?
6. Do the small amount of algebra necessary to turn the equation for I above into the same form as Eq. (2)!
7. In the saga of Sally and Bill in this chapter, if you were Bill would you have gone into an "equal" partnership with Sally?

Key Concepts

amortization	merit order
base load	opportunity cost
capacity factor	peak load
capital cost	photoelectric cell
discounted cost	power (versus) energy
distribution	present value
fuel cell	retail price
fuel cost	transmission
heat rate	variable cost
increasing returns to scale	wholesale price

Bibliography

Banks, Ferdinand E. (2000). *Energy Economics: A Modern Introduction*. Dordrecht and New York: Kluwer Academic.

Einhorn, Michael (1983). "Optimal systems planning with fuel shortages and emissions constraints". *The Energy Journal*, 4(2): 73–90.

Fisher, John C. (1974). *Energy Crisis in Perspective*. New York: John Wiley.

Percebois, Jacques (1989). *Economie de L'energie*. Paris: Economica.

Pindyck, Robert S. and Daniel L. Rubinfeld (2005). *Microeconomics*. New Jersey: Prentice Hall.

Rees, Ray (1984). *Public Enterprise Economics*. London: Weidenfeld and Nicolson.

Siebert, Heintz (1979). "Erschopfbare ressourcen". *Wirtschaftsdienst*, (10).

Smith, Vernon (1961). *Investment and Production*. Cambridge (Mass): Harvard University Press.

CHAPTER 8

ENERGY AND MONEY

The escalation of the world oil price that so many experts said would never take place seems to have happened. The spot price of oil has exceeded 76 dollars a barrel (= $76/b) on several occasions, and even if adjusting this price for changes in exchange and inflation rates means that the "real" price is much lower, this is an unpleasant situation for many motorists to contemplate. "Why, why oh why?", General Robert E. Lee reportedly asked when confronted with the failure of Pickett's charge at Gettysburg, and a similar question can be posed here about the origins of this price rise. The answer happens to be supply and demand, which is the answer for a very large number of questions in this world. Another question that might be asked is why something so simple is not comprehended by important and well-positioned movers and shakers who, in theory, have access to the best information and expertise available.

In his testimony before the US Senate on 20 July 2006, the new chairman of the board of governors of the US Federal Reserve System constantly referred to the oil futures market as the logical predictor of global oil prices over the next few years. As alluded to above, the chairman could not obtain the right kind of expertise to handle this issue, because in truth the futures market has no more capacity to predict what will happen to the oil price during the next few years than it does to provide the names of the ladies and gentlemen who will win the major tennis tournaments during the same period. Of course, if all the players in and observers of that market read this book, which is unlikely, they might be able to offer better predictions than they provided in the past two or three years for the oil price that we must deal with at present.

This chapter will present enough basic theory of the main derivatives markets (i.e., futures and options) so that readers learn to see these institutions for what they are: places where transactors (= agents or actors or players) in things like (physical) oil and gas can obtain some price insurance if they are careful, and where big-ticket speculators gain access to what someone once called "the greatest game in town". (Some reference will also be made to swaps.) The "town" in that particular case was New York City, which was already overflowing with what Tom Wolfe called "Masters of the Universe": gentlemen and some ladies dealing in stocks (i.e., shares) and bonds for assorted clients, and big bucks for themselves via salaries and bonuses. There are however a number of other important venues for derivatives: Chicago, London, and Singapore are probably the best known, with the latter receiving a little extra attention because of the activities of a certain Mr Nick Leeson.

A film has been made about Mr Leeson with the name "Rogue Trader", which follows to some extent a book with the same title. Needless to say, the most important truth in those epics was grasped by only a small minority of viewers and readers, which is that Leeson was *not* a super-educated take-no-prisoners "quant" or "rocket scientist", but a young man who was capable of doing a great deal of work, and who completely grasped the essentials of his vocation. He had no knowledge of econometrics or the more fancy aspects of financial economics, nor did he need any. If he disappointed the investment bank that employed him — the celebrated "Barings" — it was because he failed to correct the trivial mistake that started him on his downfall.

One more thing is that pay close attention to the terminology! You will never be able to impress the "right people" in this game if you are not fluent in the language of finance.

1. A Futures Market Fable

John Q. is walking down 39th Street on the great south side of Chicago, on his way to purchase a ticket to the annual "Hustlers' Ball", when he passes a newsstand. Despite his haste he stops to buy a paper, and to scan its front page: ". . . tension in the western Mediterranean . . . Monaco calling up reserves . . . A shortage of Veuve Cliquot (champagne) in the grog shops of the famous Italian Riviera resorts Rapallo and Portofino results in . . .''. John suddenly remembers something that a brilliant friend on the troopship taking him to Europe published in the ship's newspaper: "You will never forget the Riviera". That was when he reached for his mobile phone. If the oil price does what I think it will do, I'll never forget it, he says to himself. John's basic frame of mind makes him a *bear* — or someone who anticipates a price decline — where oil is concerned, but at that moment he was a *bull*.

He calls his broker, since he has lately come to believe that tension anywhere in the Mediterranean can only mean that the oil price is going to rise, and fast. "Gordon G., buy me a million barrels of oil".

"*Actuals* (i.e. physical oil) or paper oil (futures contracts)?"

"Why would you ask one of your faithful clients that silly question?"

John means paper oil (as opposed to "wet" barrels or actuals), and Gordon knows it. A real or imagined conflict in the Mediterranean has a way of leading to an increase in the price of physical oil, but the logic of the oil derivatives market — which this chapter will explain on an elementary level — is such that it also means an increase in the price of paper oil, in this case futures contracts. The problem here was that whenever anyone submits a very large order, Gordon's brain starts working at a high speed, and he needs a few seconds to examine his computer screen. "One thousand futures contracts", he says, since each futures contract is for 1000 barrels. "The contract maturity I suggest is for 30 days", he says to John, at the same time punching in an order for 10 million barrels (or 10,000 contracts) for himself.

John is now the proud owner of 1,000,000 barrels of (paper) oil, but unless he reverses (or "offsets") his 1000 contracts before 30 days (the maturity or expiry period of the contracts) — which he has every intention of doing — a million barrels of physical oil will have to be delivered to a designated delivery point somewhere in . . . somewhere in . . . John shakes his head. He does not know or care where the designated delivery point is, because the only oil that he has seen or wants to see is the kind poured into his late-model Cadillac. (And note the expression "which he has every intention of doing"! What this means is that when he gives an order to buy it will be done with a minimum of trouble, and the same will be true when later he gives the order to sell that will close out his "exposure" — his exposure to possible bad news such as the oil price falling instead of rising. This is what (market) liquidity is all about, which is why it is one of the most important words in financial economics.)

John is also obligated to pay his broker a "security" deposit (called "margin") on these contracts, because although he believes that the oil price will go up, something could happen that would cause it to go in the other direction, and if this happens somebody has to lose. The purpose of margin is to ensure that "somebody" is John and not his broker.

Like all clients, John is required to have a margin account with his broker which contains a minimum amount of cash for each of John's contracts in the broker's possession, and Gordon usually demands 10% from his clients for all new contracts. The price of paper oil at that moment is exactly $70/b, and so for just this new transaction John will have to add $7 million to his margin account. There might already be some extra cash in John's margin account as a result of gains on previous transactions, but hardly $7 million. Luckily though, on this occasion Mr G. is so busy buying oil for himself that he forgets to remind John of his margin obligation. Besides, knowing what kind of person John is, Gordon suspects — although wrongly this time — that John is buying on the basis of insider information that has somehow come into his possession, and he is prone to believe that an investment opportunity based on the right kind of insider information could be the opportunity of a lifetime. This assumes that you are not accused of insider trading by the authorities, and if found guilty marched off to what they call the "slams" in that part of Chicago.

Before continuing, let us clear up several details. John has bought futures and not forward contracts. (To be precise, he is *long* in futures!) True, a futures contract is a forward contract, in that delivery is usually specified on the contract, but as you will soon learn, delivery does not have to take place: this is what "reversing" or "offsetting" a contract is all about. *Futures and forwards are entirely different assets* (where an asset is defined as anything that has value), although some people who should know better have a tendency to confuse them. It also needs to be emphasized that futures contracts are *standard* contracts, for a specific amount of a commodity, and should delivery take place because the holder of the contract does not reverse it before the maturity (or expiry) date, then delivery takes place to a specific location. (By reversing I mean that if he started out by buying (via the futures market) a good, reversal takes place when he sells the same amount. As for the delivery point for oil, in the United States, this specific location might be West Texas or New York harbor.) By way of contrast, forward contracts can be for *any* amount, for any maturity, while delivery is to any place agreed to by the "counterparties". These contracts are not traded on organized exchanges.

There are arrangements in some futures markets, however, in which a transfer of monies takes the place of the delivery of the physical commodity. "Cash-settlement" is the operative expression, and it will be mentioned later in this chapter. As for Gordon, he could be classified a broker–dealer, since he not only acts as an intermediary between buyers and sellers (brokerage), but (in this fable) can buy or sell for his own account and that of his firm (which makes him a dealer). Proprietary trading is what this is usually called when the dealer works for an investment bank. He is not, however, a *market maker* — i.e., someone whose function (at, e.g., an exchange) is to execute buy and sell orders on behalf of customers at posted prices, or on his own account. When the great stock market meltdown took place in 1987, there was a talk of "stand-up" or "macho" *specialists* (i.e., market makers) in New York who continued to buy everything coming their way until they did not have bus-fare to go home.

Now I interrupt the narrative in order to briefly elaborate on two extremely important definitions. The first, which was alluded to above, is margin! Margin is an "up-front" security deposit in the form of cash or some form of collateral (e.g., highly negotiable bonds) that is posted by transactors in the futures market with their brokers in case the value of a position deteriorates because the futures price moves in the wrong direction: down for a long position, and up for a short. Too great a deterioration leads to a margin call from brokers for "maintenance margin", and if this margin is not immediately forthcoming, the broker closes the position of the buyer or seller. Similarly, if the price of a long futures contract increases on a given day, then the owner of this contract receives an amount of money equal to the price change times the quantity on the contract. This profit may initially be placed in the transactor's margin account, however he/she can extract it if or when he/she wishes.

The second definition is Marking-to-Market! In order to determine whether maintenance margin is required, futures portfolios are valued during every 24-hour period — usually after the exchange closes by "back-room" employees of the brokerage or clearinghouse. The point here is that if there are any losses, the client is *immediately* accountable. Similarly, gains can be immediately extracted. To take John Q. as an example, assume that he opened his position at an oil price of F_0, and when he closed it the oil price was F_1. If $F_1 > F_0$, then his account with the broker increases by $[(F_1 - F_0)q_0 - C_b]$, where q_0 is the number of barrels of (paper) oil that John is buying, and C_b is the broker's fee or commission.

While John was purchasing his ticket to the ball, a radio announcer who calls himself Daddy Romance interrupts his philosophizing to announce that the oil price had spiked to $76/b. This is *physical* oil, as Mr Romance points out in a condescending tone of voice. Again John reaches for his phone. "What's the futures price?", he asks Gordon.

"Seventy-five dollars a barrel. In fifteen minutes you've made five million dollars — minus my commission, of course. I call that a nice payday".

"Sell my oil", John tells Gordon. "Dump it all". He is tempted to prolong his exposure, and maybe rack up another few million dollars this fine morning, but he has a bad feeling. Anything that went up so fast could fall at the same speed.

Just as Gordon opened John's position by contacting the "exchange" and buying a million barrels (= 1000 contracts), he now calls the exchange and sells a million barrels. *This closes John's position — he no longer has any exposure*; if the exchange is a viable establishment, with a high level of liquidity, buying and selling are very simple operations. It is just as easy as buying and selling shares on the New York Stock Exchange. As for liquidity, this refers to the amount of activity taking place in the market. A high level of liquidity means that transactions can take place at or close to the presently quoted price. An illiquid or "thin" market can cause a lot of trouble for a buyer or seller in the form of undesired price movements, and when these markets fail it is almost always because of a shortage of liquidity. Note also that as in the share (stock) market, transactors are for the most part anonymous. For instance, John did not know who took the "sell" side of the "buy" transaction that he had initiated earlier (although when we have an "exchange of futures for physicals" (EFP) this may not be true).

If readers do not consider the above discussion simple, then they should go through it once more before they continue! Now, let us turn the exercise around.

John Q. is walking down 39th Street in the other direction, and as he arrives at King Drive he sees a headline on a newspaper saying that a super-giant oil field (sometimes called an "elephant") has been located close to the Italian Riviera, near Genoa. That is an interesting place for a new oil field to be located if you can profit from a fall in the price, he tells himself, because Genoa has all the facilities needed to rapidly produce this oil and transport it to market. He pauses for a moment. Once he read a book on oil by a great economics teacher which claimed that if the price of physical oil (actuals) fell, then it was almost certain that the price of paper oil (futures) would follow. He reaches for Mr Mobile.

"Sell a million barrels of oil", he tells his broker, "and don't ask me whether it's physical or paper oil".

"Short a million barrels", Gordon says, confirming the order. He punches in John's order, and also a healthy order for his firm. Once again margin is forgotten.

And once again some explanation is in order. John does not own any physical oil, and since he has no intention on owning any, it appears that he is selling something that he does not have, but this is incorrect. Just as earlier he bought (i.e., went long) without intending to take delivery, now he sells (i.e., goes short) without any intention of making delivery. The reader will get a more thorough insight into these manipulations later, but they are perfectly straightforward: as in the previous example, an off-setting or reversing transaction (in this case long) will relieve him of the necessity of finding and delivering physical oil. The key elements in this particular fable remain John and Gordon — the other sellers or buyers or potential sellers and buyers have about as much significance as a Greek Chorus. We can also add some numbers to the story. The price of oil futures eventually climbed to $77/b, and it was at this level John gave his sell order to Gordon. Later that day it dropped to $73/b, at which point John decided that it was time to call Gordon again. "Close my position", he says, which meant that Gordon should buy a million barrels (= 1000 contracts). This time John had made $4 million (minus Gordon's fee). Quite enough to finance his skiing that winter in Åre (Sweden) or Courchevel

(France), he assures himself. Who said that there was no justice in this world?

A *caveat* might be in order here. What is the likelihood that in the real world John Q. could realize the kind of windfall described in the examples above? The answer to that is not very much. The Efficient Market Hypothesis (EMH) suggests that he would have a better chance of finding that sort of money in one of those garbage cans that he handled every day during a few weeks of his military service.

If we take the first part of the fable, where John comes to the conclusion that there is going to be some rifle play in the Mediterranean, the EMH says that some other "players" came to that conclusion long before John, and so when he goes into the market, the price of oil has already been boosted to a point where it is too late for him to make any genuinely large gains. Of course some players, somewhere, may have a good chance of making some really big bucks from hostilities in that part of the world, and someday it might be John, but most likely it would be a person like Gordon, who is in the business looking for these opportunities every waking moment of every day in the year. And statistically speaking, even Gordon would be too late more often than not.

Exercises

1. In the above discussion, John's luck was good. Suppose that it had been bad. What is the situation for this charming man? Explain in detail!
2. What is opening a position? Closing a position? What is the significance of the terms "long" and "short"? Can there sometimes be an advantage in using forwards rather than futures? If so, what is the difference between them? How was it possible for John to sell something that he does not own? The definition of position is "status in the market" as long or short. Clarify! What are "changes" in position?
3. Buying $70 million of oil for 7 million is called "leverage"! Are you impressed?

2. The Basic Mechanics of Futures Markets

Now that you know how you might make $9 million (minus brokerage fees) in the course of a pleasant stroll down 39th Street on the wonderful south side of Chicago, we can intensify our examination of some of the basic mechanics of the futures markets. Some of the following is familiar, but that is intentional. The point is to master these materials, to always have them at your finger tips.

Futures trading is centuries old. John Cary described the "disposal" of brandy on the Amsterdam market in 1695 via a scheme that did not require the commodity to be delivered, while it is said that during the Middle Ages techniques were developed in Japan designed to guarantee the forward delivery of silk at previously agreed on prices. Although such conveniences as clearinghouses for the settlement of contracts do not seem to have been a part of the Japanese experience, it is very possible that the mechanics of these transactions were akin to those employed on modern futures exchanges. ["OBSERVE: A clearinghouse is a "non-profit" entity affiliated with a futures or options exchange. It monitors/supervises clerical activities associated with buying and selling, paying particular attention to transactions that have to do with the offsetting (i.e., reversing) of "open" futures positions, since these "close out" those positions. If necessary, the clearinghouse makes sure that the commodity in question is delivered to or shipped from the official delivery point, and if contracts are settled by cash instead of delivery, it might do some of the necessary accounting.]

Futures markets operate as follows. Against a background of speculators "betting" on the direction and size of commodity price movements by buying and selling futures contracts, an impersonal agency can be created that permits producers, consumers, inventory holders, and various traders in physical products to reduce (i.e., hedge) undesired price risk. This process will be described below.

The success of a futures market is dependent on the satisfaction of several well-defined criteria. It is essential that the commodity in question can be traded in bulk, is susceptible to grading, is relatively imperishable, attracts a lot of attention from market actors, and almost as important as the last item, the physical commodity is bought and sold in circumstances that cause its price to fluctuate in a random or non-systematic manner. Without this latter provision, speculators are unlikely to be attracted to the commodity, and without considerable speculation (i.e., liquidity), futures markets will not function properly. To put it another way, transactors in a physical commodity (e.g., buyers and sellers of physical crude oil and oil products) can employ futures markets to reduce price risk only if other traders and/or speculators are willing to accept this risk.

The social gain from futures trading derives from the voluntary redistribution of risk between speculators and risk-averse dealers in physical products. The belief here is that in the oil market this gain is considerable, and everyone is made better off by the presence of oil derivative markets. This does not, however, apply to all derivatives markets, by which I specifically mean electricity derivatives markets. (OBSERVE: A derivatives market can be based on organized exchanges, or over-the-counter arrangements. The price of derivatives — e.g., futures and options — is ultimately derived from the price of the *underlying* — e.g., barrels of oil. (The underlying is also called "actuals".) Exchange traded derivatives are standardized assets whose trading are characterized by margin requirements, while over-the-counter derivatives — which are often encountered for options and swaps — are privately negotiated bilateral agreements that are independent of organized exchanges.)

Now we can look at some aspects of hedging. As already noted, if a speculator believes that the price of a commodity is going to rise, she buys futures contracts — goes long. These contracts are referred to a certain delivery month, and often its first day, in which case we can speak of the expiry month or expiry date. In a very liquid market, before the contract matures, this "long" position can be easily offset — i.e., reversed — by the sale of futures for the same delivery date or month. When this is done, the position of Ms Speculator is registered as closed. If the sale price of the contracts is higher than that at which they were bought, then she has made a profit.

One measure of liquidity is *Open Interest*! This is the total number of *open* contracts, long or short — but not both — in a given market. A transaction involving a buyer and seller that is not a reversing trade will increase the open interest by one contract — *note, one and not two contracts*! The greater the open interest, the easier it should be to close a position. This is because there are a large number of (open) contracts that are candidates for a reversing transaction. Open interest can therefore be regarded as a measure of liquidity.

Similarly, if she had begun by selling contracts — going short — and (taking into consideration brokerage costs) the price at which she made an offsetting transaction (a buy) was lower than the original sale price, she has also made a profit.

Something that is often forgotten or ignored is that the maturity of these contracts is for the most part less than six months. The talk about futures contracts for oil or oil products with a maturity of three or four years does not deserve any credibility, because there is inadequate liquidity for contracts of that maturity. (OBSERVE: A semi-formal definition of liquidity might be the ability of individuals to obtain cash with minimal delay by selling an asset. *Market liquidity* means that large sales and purchases can take place without unduly moving market prices. In a "thin" market some dramatic price movements can take place.)

If this is clear, the mechanics of hedging can be considered. Hedgers also buy and sell futures contracts, depending upon whether they want to guard against price rises or price falls. Consider, for example, someone who has contracted for a given quantity of crude oil, but does not know the price at which this oil will be delivered because the seller insists that buyers will be charged the price prevailing on the spot market at the time of delivery. The buyer thus faces considerable price risk in that the price of oil might rise sharply; however, a risk-averting buyer can "lock in" a price in this situation by *buying* futures contracts at or around the same time they contract for their oil that have a maturity (expiry) date at or close to the date on which the oil will be delivered. Then, around the time that the oil is delivered, they make an offsetting (reversing) sale of futures. If the spot (i.e., market) price of the oil rises, this gentleman takes a loss on the physical transaction, however compensation will be gained on the sale of the futures.

Note also that even if no contract is signed between a specific buyer and seller, for someone who is going to buy oil in the future, a resort to futures might be judged wise. If both physical and paper prices rise, which should happen, the loss on the physical purchase will be (partially or totally) compensated for by the gain on the futures transaction. What about sellers of oil? If they are afraid of a price fall they sell futures (i.e., go short). If the price of physical oil falls, the price of paper oil should also fall, with the loss on the physical transaction being compensated for by the gain on the futures contracts. (Make sure you understand this before proceeding!)

One thing remains to be done in this section, which is to provide a brief discussion of the convergence of physical and futures prices. This topic will be discussed at greater length later, however readers should make an effort to comprehend the following.

Formally, the proposition that is being put forward is that in the delivery month or date specified on a futures contract, the futures price and the physical market price of the commodity (e.g., oil) must be very close. If this is not the case, arbitrage comes into the picture! If there was a discrepancy between the two prices, either buyers or sellers of the contract would become involved with delivering or taking delivery of the commodity, as well as buying or selling on the physical market. (OBSERVE: Arbitrage can be explicitly tied to the law of one price: there cannot be different prices in the same market for identical goods! Stockholm and Uppsala are essentially in the same market for certain goods. If the price of a designer shirt is higher in Uppsala than in Stockholm, then I might travel to Stockholm and buy the shirt, which I sell in Uppsala.)

Suppose, for example, that the price of oil on a futures contract was posted as $75/b, while the price of oil in the physical (spot) market was $80/b. Someone who has bought a futures contract perceives this difference, and does not make an offsetting (i.e., reversing) sale. Instead they accept delivery on the contract, and immediately sell it on the spot market. This yields a profit of $5/b. Arbitrage of this nature — i.e., taking delivery and selling the commodity will tend to drive down its spot price. There will also be an increased demand for futures (in order to take advantage of this arbitrage situation) which should raise their price. In a very short time the futures and spot prices should be very close. (They might not be identical however because of "transaction costs".)

Deliveries are not common in the oil futures market, and cash settlement of course reduces deliveries even more. The detailed mechanics of cash settlement will not be taken up in this book because this is really a simple matter. If we take the fable at the beginning of the chapter, if the excellent John Q. forgot to close out his position and cash settlement prevailed, then at what was defined as the expiry date, he or his broker would receive whatever he had gained on that transaction — assuming that it was a gain. The price employed to calculate gains or losses was either the market price or a price close to the market price and specified (or authorized) by the clearinghouse. It should also be apparent that cash settlement reduces transaction costs because it is unnecessary to be concerned with moving and storing physical oil.

Exercises

1. Consider a geographically single market for some good — e.g., Los Angeles and San Diego — but with "different" supply and demand curves that result in different equilibrium prices for these cities. Discuss how arbitrage would work using these curves!
2. Explain in detail hedging for someone selling oil!
3. Do you think that John Q. in the above fable would engage in arbitrage if he saw that there was a difference in the futures and spot prices? What about Gordon?

That brings us to an artificial but pedagogically useful example of a futures market with only three traders — speculators X, Y, and Z — who became involved in transactions on only three trading days of the month in question, which were the 14th, 22nd and 30th. They could have traded at any time, but given the prices on other days as well as their inclinations and expectations, they abstained. The situation is as follows. These gentlemen were in the first class lounge of an airport, and prices — originating on an exchange with many traders — were announced once an hour on the PA system. During the month in question they were alone in this exclusive venue. Contracts are available at the information desk in the lounge, all trades are for one contract, and their maturity is such that the expiry date is the last day of the month, regardless of when transactions take place. Thus a contract that is bought or sold on, e.g., the 26th of the month expires four or five days later, depending on the length of the month. Finally, their contracts are only marked to the market on the 22nd and 30th.

What we see in Table 8.1 is the price (per barrel) on the relevant trading days (P), the "names" of the traders (X, Y, Z), their (net) behavior on the day that they trade — i.e., whether they end up as buyers (B), or sellers (S); the result of marking-to-the-market (MM) for each of them on the 22nd and 30th if they have an open contract, and the number of transactions (V) and open interest (OI) on those days, and the 14th. Figures in the table are for only one barrel, but they apply to the 1000 barrels on a contract.

Table 8.1.   Players in Action (Ex Post for July), One Barrel

Day	P	X	MM$_X$	Y	MM$_y$	Z	MM$_z$	V	OI
14	38	B (long)	—	S (short)	—	—	—	2	1
22	25	—	−13	B (long)	+13	S (short)	—	2	1
30	35	S (short)	+10	—	—	B (long)	−10	2	0
Σ			−3		+13		−10		

The details that are important for understanding this table have already been reviewed, and in addition we do not need to discuss the financial status of the traders, such as whether they can manage margin payments, or the size of their margin accounts, and in the event of a gain for their positions whether they want the money involved paid to them in cash or cigar store coupons. The transactions in the table take place in July, and like John Q. in the previous fable they are not interested in delivery, and therefore have no problem closing out their positions before their contracts mature. Trading ceases at 1800 on the 30th of the month, and all trading is for one contract (= 1000 barrels). Something that should be remembered is that open interest — which is very important — is defined as the number of contracts, in the bought or sold category (but not both), that are open at the end of each trading day, but only for these three persons.

Now let us see what we have in this very special market! On the 14th X buys and Y sells a contract. The number of transactions is taken as two, since both of them deal with their brokers, and through their brokers the clearinghouse. (Arguments have been presented that this should be booked as only one transaction, but this will not be taken up here.) Open interest is unambiguously unity. It should also be appreciated that on the 14th X and Z could have traded in the morning, but Z could have closed out his (short) position in the afternoon with a buy from Y. This would have meant that Z was no longer of interest for that day, but the number of transactions would have been 4. Open interest however (at the end of the day) would only be 1.

The next trading day for these three speculators was the 22nd. Y offsets his (short) position with a long, and Z buys this contract. X's contract was marked-to-market, and as noted it declined by 13. On the other hand, Y had started with a short, and so he gains 13 when he offsets. Finally, on the last trading day of the month the two players with open contracts — X and Z — must close their positions, which they do. X turns out to be lucky, while Z loses 10. Notice that there is no longer any open interest.

Where money is concerned, P is the per-barrel price. It therefore appears that Y has gained $13,000 if the trading was for one contract (= 1000 barrels). X has lost $3000 and Z $10,000. However as they say in the gambling world, there is always tomorrow.

3. Simple Options Theory

In a lecture presented to the Fifth Annual Meeting of the German Finance Association, the Nobel laureate Professor Merton Miller said that if he were starting over and entering the field of finance, he would specialize in options. He pictured options theory as being at the center of gravity of financial economics.

Maybe it is, and maybe it is not; but certain aspects of options theory are extremely important — and not just for finance. In any event, I cannot think of any subjects in economics whose rudimentary logic is as easily acquired as that dealing with futures and options. Of course, trying to keep track of the details requires a certain amount of concentration. The basic building blocks that will be covered in this book are futures and options, and swaps are mentioned; but things like caps, swaptions, floors, collars, etc. have become very important in the great world of derivatives. These are constructed from the basic elements, and if you understand this chapter you will have no problem with them unless you read the wrong books, which is always possible.

As already made clear, derivatives can be used for speculation or hedging, where hedging refers to "price insurance", and sometimes "risk management". But regardless of what derivatives we are talking about, or where they are used, a widespread opinion outside the financial community is that these are complicated assets. "The wild cards in international finance", US Congressman James A. Leach labeled them. The contention here is that history does not fully support this judgment, although it must be admitted that the presence of derivatives widens the scope for some very suspicious behavior by various actors in the financial markets.

How do derivatives derive their value? The term derivative indicates that the value is derived from some other asset. For instance, if you buy an option on Standard Oil share (i.e., stock), paying the seller of the option (i.e., the writer) the premium (= the option price), then the purchase of that option gives you the right to buy or sell a certain amount of Standard before a specified date (the maturity or expiry date), for a specified price (called the strike or exercise price). As you will be able to understand soon, the writer (seller) does not want to see this option exercised: more than anything in the world she wants to see an option price at a level that while the option would be attractive to a purchaser, the likelihood of its being exercised would be miniscule. The buyer, though, wants the price to move in such a way that the option can be exercised, and occasionally a great deal of money can be made.

If you have bought the right to buy an asset (e.g., the Standard Oil share), then you have purchased a *call* option; while if you have bought the right to sell an asset (i.e., the Standard Oil share), then you have bought a *put* option. From the time you made your purchase until the maturity (i.e., expiry or settlement) date of the option, the value of your option depends on what happens to Standard Oil in the share market, and so the share is called the *underlying*. [OBSERVE: As in the futures market, we can distinguish between the paper market and the "actuals" market — where in this example the "actual" is also paper (the share).]

Now let us consider how we measure the option's value. If you purchase a call option on, e.g., the Standard Oil share, and the share price climbs in such a way that it exceeds the exercise price, then you could be in a position to make a lot of money: buy (i.e., call) Standard (from the writer) at the exercise price, and then, e.g., sell it in the spot market at the prevailing (market) price. (The *spot* market is the market for immediate delivery.) On the other hand, if the share price does not climb, then you lose the premium, but that is all that you lose. Apart from that there is no downside risk!

What about a put option? Here you start out with a belief that Standard's price will fall, and so you pay a premium to sell Standard at some exercise price. What you desire now is for the price of the share to collapse — i.e., move well below the exercise price. If that happens you exercise your option: you buy the share at its bargain-basement (market) price, and sell it (to the writer) at the (higher) exercise price. Once again, as above, if the share price does not descend below the exercise price, then you simply throw the option into the waste paper basket. You have lost your premium. There is something else about options: you might buy an option and change your mind about its prospects, in which case there is a sort of "secondhand market" in which you might be able to sell it.

Now let us forget about things like stocks and paper markets and construct a simple (but not entirely realistic) example in which the *underlying* is one barrel of physical oil. You suspect that the price of oil (= $100) will collapse, and so you go to an over-the-counter option emporium (i.e., market) and examine the premiums and exercise prices for (physical) oil. You see something you like and so you *buy* a put (i.e., sell) option specifying one barrel of oil, paying the option writer (who might be another speculator, or even the emporium in a speculative mode) a premium of 3 dollars for an option whose exercise (or strike) price is 95 dollars, and whose expiry date is in a week. (Which means that if you do not exercise the option in a week, it is worthless.) The next day the oil price collapses to 50 dollars, and so you decide to exercise the option. (You might also have decided to wait a few days, hoping that the price would go lower.) How is this exercising done? You go to a seller of physical oil, pay 50 dollars for a barrel of oil, put it in the back seat of your Ferrari Convertible and take it to the OTC emporium, who must pay you 95 dollars (the exercise price). Your net profit is obvious: the price of the put option minus the market price of the oil you bought minus the premium (or option price), or $95 – $50 – $3 = $42. There might also be a small fee that has to be paid to the emporium for their help.

You might ask how does the emporium management feel about all this. If they are simply acting as an intermediate, it should not bother them at all, because the money they pay you comes from the option writer. But if it was a proprietary operation on their part, they might feel slightly annoyed at having made such a bad bet. And what about margin? The buyers of options do not need to be concerned with this, but since the writers of options can face a great deal of risk, they begin their commitment by paying *initial margin*, and if the price moves against them in such a way that they are in the danger zone, they must pay enough *variation margin* to cover their losses. Should they go into liquidation, then the emporium (or its clearinghouse) honors the debt, and their lawyers have a talk with the option writer.

Let us sum this discussion up, and add something. (1) A call option gives the right to buy an asset at a specified price, the exercise price, before a certain date (the expiry date). A put option gives the right to sell an asset at a specified price (the exercise price) and before a certain date. (2) If the strike (or exercise) price P_E of a call option is equal to the actual market (i.e., spot) price S, then the option is said to be at-the-money. If $S > P_E$, then a call option is in-the-money. If $S < P_E$, then a call option is out-of-the-money. For a put option, the opposite is the case, which you should immediately explain! (3) Often, instead of going through the trouble of exercising an in-the-money option, and becoming involved with the underlying, you might be able to simply sell the option. Finally, and trivially, in-the-money and out-of-the-money are important expressions!.

Unfortunately, as easy as all of the above seem — and is — the expression "derivatives disaster" has crept into the language, and apparently it can happen at any time. Metallgesellschaft lost about $1.5 billion on a bad hedging strategy, while in 1992 traders employed by the government of Malaysia were said to have lost several billion dollars on unsound bets. Some observers have called these enormous losses part of the learning process, but what it comes down to is simple (but expensive) carelessness.

Now the price of the option is considered. Basically this depends on three things: the relation of the exercise price to the market price of the underlying; the amount of time that the option has to run before expiry; and the volatility of the market price of the underlying. The logic here is simple. The closer the exercise price is to the market price of the underlying, the more expensive is the option — i.e., the higher the premium. This is because the closer it is, the more probable it is that the market price will reach and move beyond the fixed exercise price. Similarly, the longer the amount of time to expiry, the longer the time the option has to move into a position where its owner will exercise it. As for volatility, a highly volatile option might "jump" past the exercise price, which means that it can be immediately exercised. That makes it expensive.

Take the oil price for 14 July (i.e., Bastille Day) 2006, of $74/b, and consider an imaginary option of oil with an exercise price of $80/b, with an expiry date of, e.g., the first of September 2006. Oil has never reached a price of $80/b, but the oil price is very volatile, and so it is fully conceivable that it would reach (and perhaps go beyond) $80/b, even though it would only stay there for a very short time. This would not make the writer of the option happy, and so she would likely set a high premium before entering into this transaction. It might even be so high that the person buying this option today would not exercise it immediately even if the market price reached $80/b. If, e.g., the premium were 5 dollars, then the buyer of the option would not realize a net gain from exercising the option unless the market price reached at least $85/b. Explain why, and also explain why it might be exercised anyway before it reaches $85/b!

What we are saying here once again is that the writer sets the premium according to the likelihood of the option being exercised. Basically a writer wants the so-called "premium income", since there is no possibility of the kind of windfall that the buyer of the option has a chance of experiencing. If the option is exercised, then the writer might be exposed to serious losses. Given the kind of losses that option writers are occasionally exposed to, it might be thought that option writers would be scarce, but this is not so.

Is there any deeper reason for the availability of option writers? Speculation is a large part of the option market, but so is hedging. Where the latter is concerned, option writers are providing a sort of insurance. Firms that provide insurance expect to be paid for this service, and so statistically one expects the corpus of option writers not to lose. Some do, but very many win, and it is knowing this that sends them to the market.

Exercises

1. For a call option, if the market price is higher than the exercise price, then the option is in the money. Suppose that in the discussion above premium P is $5, market price S is $62, and the exercise price is $58. Is this option in the money? Suppose that the option has a maturity of one month, and three weeks have passed. Would you exercise the option?

2. In the above example, suppose that $P = 5$, $S = 58$, and $P_E = 55$. Would you exercise the option?

3. Construct an example for a put option where the option is out-of-the-money (i.e., it does not pay to exercise the option)!

4. What do you think is the relationship between the present price of an asset (e.g., Standard Oil stock), the exercise price, and the premium? What do you think about an option writer who sells an option for $5

when the exercise price is $53 and the market price is $60? What do you think would be a reasonable premium for this option?

Something that needs to be noted is that since an option can always go unexercised, delivery does not appear to be an important factor for the buyer of an option. However, if a "buy" (i.e., call) option for, e.g., crude oil is exercised, then some physical oil is supposed to change hands (unless, for example, a special agreement can be entered into between the buyer and seller in which there is a movement of cash instead of product). Delivery is one of the things that might make options on commodities more complicated than options on financial assets (stocks, currencies, bonds, etc.). However, one way to forget about having to handle physical oil is to deal in "options on futures". In this case if the options are exercised, then the delivery is of oil futures contracts and not barrels of physical oil. If we take the fable at the beginning of this chapter, it would be impossible to think of John Q. being interested in physical commodities, but he might be prepared to deal in options on futures.

Two important expressions have not been used as yet, although we know something about them. These are "time value" and "intrinsic value". Intrinsic value is defined as the difference between the exercise (= strike) price and the market price of the underlying. (EXERCISE: Would a profit always be made if an option is exercised when its intrinsic value is greater than zero? The answer is no! Explain?) As for time value, an option has time value if it has not reached expiry. As noted above, the longer the time the option has to run before expiry, the greater the chance that it will not only go "in-the-money", but deep in the money, with more than enough intrinsic value to cover the premium. It might be useful to speak of a "breakeven" point here, which is the exercise price *plus* the premium. The reason is that when an option has intrinsic value it is commonly spoken of as being in the money, but whether it is sufficiently deep in the money to make immediate exercise attractive is quite another thing. There is still the matter of recovering the premium.

One of the reasons that many students of the subject find options interesting is that there can be hidden or implied options in many situations; for instance, buying the right to explore for offshore oil. The option comes about in that while the "right" to explore is purchased, the exploration may

not actually take place unless the oil price rises, and then there may only
be a minimum of exploration. Here we are talking about a subject known
as "real options". Unfortunately, I am not as enthusiastic about this topic
as many teachers. There is also an innovation called "one touch options",
in which the investor gets a payout if the price of the underlying reaches or
surpasses a predetermined level.

4.   Another Look at Futures

Let us begin by examining an interesting hedging exercise. Several years
ago Mr T. Boone Pickens — then of Mesa Petroleum, but now a billionaire
fund manager — came to the conclusion that the oil price might fall. He
reacted by selling a number of futures contracts equal to the entire production of Mesa Petroleum over some particular period: in other words,
he opened his position by going short. In viable futures markets, as we
indicated in the previous section, this is no more complicated than going
long, although it should never be believed that the market is sufficiently
liquid that all the big oil producers (the *majors*) can hedge most of their
production against price declines, even if this is exactly what the head of
a large brokerage announced to delegates at a conference in France that I
once attended.

Later, when the price of physical oil fell, Mr Pickens offset his opening
(short) position by buying futures contracts for the same amount. The loss
on his physical position when the price actually fell was balanced by the
gain on the "paper" transaction.

Mr Pickens deserves our congratulations; however, as Carol Loomis
noted, "hedges may be difficult to put on". She quoted a Washington lawyer,
Eugene Rotberg: "The only perfect hedge is in a Japanese garden". This
is not completely true, but as former economics professor Heinz Schimmelbusch — once named manager of the year by *TopBusiness*, a German
magazine — found out, the downside risk with futures can be enormous,
especially when you adopt a flawed hedging strategy that is put on automatic
pilot.

A transactor whose position in *the cash market* — i.e., spot or forward
market for actuals (or underlyings) — is offset by his position in the futures
market is conventionally labeled a hedger, and if the market functions the

way a textbook market is supposed to function, then price risk will be greatly decreased, and in some cases even eliminated. But, unfortunately, since any gain in the futures market will be canceled out by a loss in the actuals market, it follows that any profits due to spectacularly favorable price movements for the underlying will be eliminated due to a loss in the paper market. Large profits or losses in a futures market that accrue to hedgers who are fully hedged are due to shortcomings in the conventional (i.e., textbook) structure of these markets, and it is here that *basis risk* deserves special attention. (Basis risk will be taken up below.) It is not unheard of, however, that a transactor who is unequivocally a hedger will assume a position in which some of the physical product is left "uncovered". This kind of arrangement is briefly touched on in the appendix.

What we are talking about here is the ability of a transactor to lock in a price. For instance, an oil refiner might be worried about the price of oil that he intends to buy at some point in the future. Suppose that the present (spot) price of (physical) oil is 20 dollars/barrel (= \$20/b), and the futures price is \$20.5/b. It may be possible for the refiner to lock in a price of \$20.5/b by going long in futures. (Oil futures contracts are for 1000 barrels. Thus the hedger in this example would initially have to pay \$20,500 for a contract, or rather the margin on this contract of perhaps 5% or 10%. This is what *leverage* is all about!)

Assume that one contract was purchased, and that during this month the price of paper oil increased at the rate of \$1/d for each barrel (or \$1000/d for the contract). During the month the contract will be marked to the market every day, and so in 30 days the value of each barrel will increase by \$30/b. But as already mentioned, and will be elaborated on below, at the expiry date of the contract, the futures price and the price of the underlying must be equal (or almost equal). Thus, at the end of the month, the refiner might have to pay \$50.5/b for oil, but has received \$30/b for the increase in the contract's value. The net price paid for the oil is thus \$50.5 − \$30 = \$20.5/b.

Suppose that instead of increasing, the price of paper oil decreased, but this time by \$0.5/d for each barrel. If the hedger starts out by going long, then each decrease reduces the value of the contract by \$0.5/b, and so a succession of margin calls is involved. (Even if margin calls are not involved, the transactor's margin account at his broker is decreased.) However, if the futures and actuals price should converge at the end of the month, the refiner pays only $5.50 for the physical oil. The net cost is thus $5.50 + $15 = $20.5. (Observe, $15/b is the loss on the futures contract that was initially purchased for $20.5/d. When the buyer closes her position by selling her contract, she receives only $5.5/b).

Exercises

1. Why would a transactor who is worried about price risk employ a futures contract instead of a forward contract? (In the forward market arrangements are made for the delivery or receipt of an item at an agreed upon price.)
2. Suppose that a hedger told his broker to go long in futures, but the broker misunderstood and went short. What might happen?
3. I say that the futures market is not sufficiently liquid so that the major oil companies can hedge all of their production. Can you explain why? In the last example in the text, discuss the situation if the (actuals) price did not move over the maturity period, but the futures price did. Would this example "work" if I turned it around: a stable futures price but a volatile actuals price?

Next, we can take a look at convergence again as an introduction to the important topic of "convenience yield". Convergence has been mentioned on several occasions, while convenience yield and especially what it implies is one of the (unfortunately many) concepts that you need to know if you plan to feel at home in the financial world's corridors and restaurants of power.

The simplest way to talk about price convergence is to bring in the delivery mechanism. Conventionally, when a contract reaches maturity (i.e., the expiry date), the shorts who have not offset their position must deliver the item in the manner designated by the contract, while the longs with open positions must accept and pay for what they have bought. Thus, at the time of delivery, if the spot price (S) of the underlying is greater than the futures price (F), the longs (in position to do so) will accept delivery and sell on the spot market. The arbitrage taking place here should work to bring about an equality between S and F — or, in reality, a near equality — at the expiry date. Similarly, if $F > S$, the shorts will buy on the spot market and make delivery in order to obtain the higher futures price. Once again, arbitrage will work to equalize prices, since the increased demand for oil will raise its price. People like John Q. of course do no delivering or taking delivery. These activities are a mystery to them!

But we can go farther. The shorts would not deliver anything that could be sold at a higher price in the spot market, and so, as the delivery date approaches, if $S > F$ many of them would offset their contracts. This amounts to an increase in the demand for futures contracts that raises their price, and thus drives F closer to S. Similarly, the longs would not want to take delivery of anything that they could buy more cheaply elsewhere. Thus, if $F > S$ as the delivery date approaches, "longs" will offset their contracts. This amounts to an increase in the supply of futures, which tends to depress F, while if there is an increased demand for the underlying, its price will be raised.

As mentioned earlier, there is a growing tendency for cash settlement to replace delivery. This amounts to a great simplification as long as there is a single price that can be used as an index to calculate the gains and losses of transactors — which in theory should be easy to arrange. Pedagogically, however, the presence of cash settlement does not require modifying the previous exposition to any great degree.

Now to the matter of intertemporal arbitrage. *This is an important theoretical approach to the price setting mechanism when inventories are in the picture, and if we are talking about items like oil, it is useful to utilize it.* As the reader might remember, inventories were explicitly introduced into the analysis twice in this book — in Chapter 2 on oil, and Chapter 6 on uranium. The thing to focus on here is that oil is expensive, inventories are huge, and since their owners are usually in the profit-maximization business they have to be managed. For John Q. and various persons in the brokerages and investment banks it is the outcome of this management that they must know something about to one degree or another, even if these ladies and gentlemen are not physically in contact with oil. For example, when there is war or rumors of war, inventories are increased, and as a result the oil price will move in such a way as to yield an outcome that we do not often see in mainstream economics textbooks.

Discussing this topic on a theoretical level brings into the picture the topic known as the *convenience yield*, but we can begin by saying something about "equilibrium". This term has already been used, and in economics and finance, as well as physics, it is often defined as a state of rest. In the context of the forthcoming discussion this will mean that all arbitrage possibilities are exhausted, and so for the — probably extremely short — period being examined, all buying and selling having to do with inventories ceases due to the perceived absence of profit opportunities. Let us put this in a slightly different way: equilibrium is equivalent to the *no-arbitrage* condition that pops up occasionally in financial economics.

I prefer to deal with this matter semi-formally. *If* the futures price of a commodity is high compared to the spot price, and expectations are that the spot price at some point in the future will be high, then a reasonable strategy for inventory holders might be to go short in futures, buy the item (e.g., oil), store the item, and eventually offset the (short) futures (with a long) in conjunction with selling the oil that was stored. If the numbers are right, this simple piece of intertemporal arbitrage might yield a nice profit.

Let us use some symbols, with signs, to describe this procedure, and to identify the profit. Begin by selling futures $(+F_0)$ at t_0, buy oil $(-S_0)$ at the same time, and store oil at a cost of $R S_0$ $(= -R S_0$ since this is a cost), and where R can be taken as an "adjusted" interest rate that takes into consideration storage costs. Finally, offset the earlier futures sale with a buy $(-F_1)$ at time t_1, and sell the stored inventories for $(+S_1)$ at the same time. Something to notice carefully here is that *if* convergence takes place, $S_1 = F_1$; however, it might seem judicious to offset the futures and sell inventories before the expiry date, and so we do not have this equality. Needless to say, in this phase of the discussion, we are only considering one unit of the commodity, since the prices are for one unit!

Now we can ask what a (per unit) profit (V) implies. Using the above we get $V = F_0 - S_0 - R S_0 - F_1 + S_1$, and this will be equal to $F_0 - S_0 - R S_0$ if convergence $(F_1 = S_1)$ is relevant. This last expression can be easily simplified to give $F_0 > S_0(1 + R)$ if $V > 0$ (or $V > 0 \to F_0 > S_0(1 + R)$, where $\to$ signifies "implies"). Naturally, extensive buying and selling at the *market* level will cause changes in the prices of both futures and actuals, and so *conceptually* we might think of a single firm carrying out this arbitrage barrel by barrel, or perhaps in lots of 1000 barrels (since this is the size of a futures contract) even if the actions of all except the largest firms have no effect on the market price. The main point though is that, beginning with $F > S$, as long as we have $F > S(1 + R)$ for the "unit" in question, "arbitrage" based on changes in inventories seems like an attractive proposition.

Suppose that for one reason or another convergence does not prevail. In looking at the expression $V = F_0 - S_0 - RS_0 - F_1 + S_1$ we might still have expectations about S_1 and F_1, which would lead us to carry out the purchase of additional inventories. [EXERCISE: What might these expectations be?] In addition, for pedagogical reasons, I temporarily assume that $F = S(1 + R)$ is our equilibrium or no-arbitrage condition if we are buying the physical commodity (e.g., oil), and postulate that convergence will take place.

At this point it looks like smooth sailing, because the above was perfectly straightforward, but if we begin our discussion with the disequilibrium arrangement $S(1 + R) > F$, and we are talking about an item such as oil, we run into complications that lead to our having to introduce convenience yield.

Just as $F > S(1 + R)$ resulted in our defining an arbitrage-type situation (with emphasis on "type", since by definition *arbitrage* is supposed to involve riskless profits), the opposite arrangement $S(1 + R) > F$ also suggests the possibility of arbitrage. Here it appears that holders of inventories should replace at least some of these inventories by futures contracts. Later they could replenish these inventories by buying the commodity in the market or even taking delivery on the futures.

Let us go through the same procedure as above. Begin by selling some inventories ($+S_0$), and buying futures ($-F_0$), where these are per-barrel prices, but might pertain to "units" of 1000 barrels. By selling these inventories interest and/or storage costs are reduced, so now we have $+RS_0$. Then, at some point in or at the end of the period being discussed the long futures is offset with a sell ($+F_1$), and all or some of the inventories that were sold are replaced ($-S_1$). Once again convergence means $F_1 = S_1$, and writing out these expressions as above means that $S(1 + R) > F$ implies a profit, which in turn makes us to think once more that the no-arbitrage condition is $S(1 + R) = F$.

But in the present case we have overlooked something. The problem is that inventories provide their owners with a *convenience yield* that is derived from their being available when inventory holders need them, and these occasions — or emergencies in some cases — are usually not known in advance. Obviously, the size of the convenience yield depends on the size of inventories: if they are large, then the marginal convenience yield (i.e., the convenience yield of the marginal "unit" of inventories) is small, or even zero; while if inventories are small, the marginal convenience yield could be relatively large. Thus, in this situation, $F = S(1+R)$ is inadequate as an equilibrium condition. (And notice again: a unit could be 1000 barrels, which is the amount of a futures contract.)

The no-arbitrage condition that we should be working with instead (which is formally derived in my previous energy economics textbook) is obviously $F = S(1 + R - \beta)$, with β (i.e., *Beta*) defined as the *marginal convenience yield* of a unit: the marginal convenience yield of a single barrel, or for that matter of a thousand barrels, since futures contracts are in the picture. Rather than go off on a mathematical bender, let us put it as follows: if inventories are large, then β is small, and if inventories are small, then β is large. Accordingly, if transactors have $S(1 + R - \beta) > F$, they reduce (sell) inventories and buy futures contracts, and in theory would continue until they get $F = S(1 + R - \beta)$. The thing to carefully notice here is that β is *not* constant — instead β is a function of the size of inventories, or $\beta = f(I)$, where I is the inventory, or even $\beta = f(I/q)$, where q is the consumption of the item, and I/q might be labeled inventory coverage (in days). If you read the financial press, e.g., the *Financial Times*, you will find this kind of reasoning, but without the mathematics.

Before continuing, we should take note of the following: there are two equilibrium conditions introduced above, $F = S(1 + R)$ and $F = S(1 + R - \beta)$. This is not particularly elegant; however, it seems obvious that we can incorporate the first of these expressions into the second. For instance, if $S(1 + R - \beta) > F$, then inventories (I) are reduced, which brings about an increase in the marginal convenience yield β, and the relationship indicates (*ceteris paribus*) that it is progressively less attractive to reduce inventories. What we expect is that the equality (i.e., equilibrium) would be restored. Similarly, if $F > S(1 + R - \beta)$, then (*ceteris paribus*) the appropriate behavior appears to be increasing the size of inventories, although if $\beta = f(I)$ as proposed, this becomes progressively less attractive as "I" increases, because β decreases. The relationship tells us that once again we move toward the equilibrium (or no-arbitrage) condition.

Notice something else here: selling inventories and buying futures contracts do not necessarily mean "using up" these inventories, since they may have been purchased by other inventory holders, and not routed into a current production process. What usually happens is that, due to the act of selling, the price of these inventories will be driven down to a level that will make some transactors willing to buy and hold them. Thus, when inventories are placed on the market, S falls. This contributes to decreasing the left-hand-side (LHS) of the first inequality in the previous paragraph. Moreover, as additional futures contracts are demanded, F rises. Considered in the aggregate, the redistribution of inventories might raise β, although the outcome here is essentially indeterminate.

A slight problem arises because logically the discussion of inventory behavior should turn on the behavior of individual transactors, since convenience yield is almost certainly a subjective variable: what one market actor thinks is an excess of inventories, another might think is a deficit. However as long as we stick to theory it is useful to think of inventory holders in the aggregate. Consider again oil. When a great deal of oil is available it invariably happens that many — though perhaps not all — inventory holders immediately elect to reduce their inventories by selling or trying to sell them to others before the over-supply reduces the price, reasoning that if they decide to rebuild inventories, it might be possible to do so later at a lower price. Those who make this decision early enough might be happy with the outcome, but many end up holding inventories whose value will have to be written down by a considerable amount.

Now we come to a topic that anyone who thinks that he/she might work with or take an interest in commodity futures markets should pay particular attention to. Common sense tells us that in the relationship between S and F, F should be larger than S. In other words, in the usual textbook situation it is easy to find an expression such as $F = S(1 + R)$, and since R is greater than zero, we get $F > S$. To put it another way, it hardly seems logical to deliberately buy large amounts of various goods for the purpose of selling them later at a lower price.

But due to the presence and importance of, e.g., oil and gas inventories, we can — and do — have something quite different a large part of the time. An equilibrium relationship that we have examined is $F = S(1 + R - \beta)$, and immediately we see that if β is large enough, we can have

$F < S$. (EXERCISE: demonstrate this immediately with some numbers!) This is the condition called *backwardation*, and it turns out that there are commodity markets — like oil — which are in backwardation much more often, percentage-wise, than they are in *contango* (with $F > S$).

A more down-to-earth explanation here is that when consumption jumps, or is expected to jump, the spot price (S) must rise in order for producers to raise production by the amount necessary to boost inventories. Take the Gulf Crisis as an interesting example. Transactors expected that the availability of oil would decline relative to consumption, and in the light of the trouble ahead (in terms of increasing prices), existing inventories were regarded as inadequate. The increasing of inventories, particularly by the consumers of oil, resulted in an increase in S that was sufficiently large to cause a sharp backwardation.

Expressed in a slightly different way, the rise in the spot price, along with the rise in the demand for near-term futures contracts (relative to distant-term contracts), resulted in a declining term structure of oil prices: a term structure with a prominent negative slope which meant that the spot price was higher than futures prices, and/or near-term futures higher than distant-term futures.

I cannot remember first year students experiencing any great difficulties with the previous discussion. The following presentation, however, should be examined carefully because basis risk is a very important topic.

5. Basis Risk

I will now begin an elementary discussion of basis risk. Suppose that you have a portfolio of 15 US shares, and you are worried that the price of these securities is about to fall. Having read the previous sections in this chapter, you come to the conclusion that you can protect yourself by *selling* a stock index futures contract based on, e.g., the S&P 500 index. The idea here, of course, is that if the price of your shares fell, the index futures "should" also fall, and what you lose on your portfolio, you "should" gain on your futures position. This is so since in the offsetting transaction, you expect that you can close your position with a "buy" that is lower than the sell price at which you opened your position. This was what the mechanics of portfolio insurance was all about.

Unfortunately, things might not work out the way you planned. Your particular portfolio and the index futures contract are two entirely different animals. You could lose on your portfolio, and also lose on your futures position, because the price of the index futures appreciated instead of fell. In that case the offsetting transaction takes place at a higher price than that of the short transaction with which you opened your position. This is clearly possible, since S&P 500 contains many shares that are not in your portfolio. This is a simple and unambiguous example of *basis risk*. If, however, there was an S&P 15 futures contract comprising the same shares as in your portfolio, then you might be able to satisfactorily hedge the risk in your portfolio.

Consider the following statement in an article by Liz Gall (1990): "... the basis risk across the Atlantic is now so large that a substantial movement in absolute prices must be anticipated before the differential risk becomes worth taking". What this is about is hedging one commodity (North Sea Crude) by using futures contracts originating on the New York Mercantile Exchange (NYMEX), but with these latter contracts based on West Texas oil — i.e., West Texas Intermediate (WTI). Yes, we have crude oil in both cases, and for the most part when the price of one of these is rising or falling on international markets, the price of the other tends to follow, but over short (and sometimes long) periods there can be substantial differences in the direction and/or size of these prices, as suggested by Ms Gall. (This has been partially corrected because of the enlarged presence of the International Petroleum Exchange in London.)

Some very elementary algebra should illuminate this issue, and also help serve as a "soft" transition to more technical presentations. To begin, let me point out that I will be using something below called an expectations operator, which will be designated E. For instance, in thinking about the price of oil on 1 January of 2030, I might write $E(P)$ or $E(P_{2030})$; while in thinking about the price of the same commodity in January of last year, I would simply write P, or P_{2005}. It is also useful to think of $E(P)$ as the ex-ante (i.e., expected) price, and P as the ex-post (i.e., realized) price.

The basis (B) is usually defined as $(S - F)$, where again S is the spot price, while F is the futures price. I will also designate S_0 as the spot price at time "t_0", which can be taken as the time at which a transaction might be initiated, and F_0 as the futures price at that time. The starting basis is thus $B_0 = (S_0 - F_0)$! S_1 and F_1 are the spot and futures prices at the time at which the transaction is terminated, and so the terminal or final basis is $B_1 = (S_1 - F_1)$. It is especially important to remember that when $S > F$ we have *backwardation*, while $F > S$ is designated *contango*. As noted on several occasions earlier, normally we expect the latter because of the expense of purchasing a commodity (like oil) today, and holding it in inventory until it is sold at a later date, but, on the average, backwardation has been the usual situation for oil. This is a key observation!

Now we consider an algebraic approach to a possible *long* hedging exercise. Hedging might take place because a buyer of oil has $E(S_1) > S_0$: expectations are that the spot price at time "t_1" could be larger than the spot price at time "t_0", and as a result a loss could be experienced. Another assumption however is that this possible loss could be compensated for (i.e., *hedged*) by a rising futures price: $E(F_1) > F_0$, since as pointed out earlier, if the spot price increases, so should the futures price. These inequalities indicate that $[E(F_1) - F_0]$ and $[E(S_1) - S_0]$ are both positive, and so we can write as our expectation of the *outcome* $[E(V)]$ from a long hedged position the (ex-ante) relationship, shown immediately below:

$$E(V) = [E(F_1) - F_0] - [E(S_1) - S_0]. \qquad (1)$$

Equation (1) can now be rewritten in such a way as to make the bases explicit:

$$E(V) = [S_0 - F_0] - [E(S_1) - E(F_1)] = B_0 - E(B_1). \qquad (2)$$

The important thing to understand now is that the long hedger hopes or expects that the basis will decrease. We can get this result from Eq. (2), but the underlying logic does not require an equation. The basis is $S - F$, and if this declines it means that S falls or F increases, or both. This in turn signifies that the buyer pays less for the oil, or obtains more money on the offsetting transaction for the futures, or both. Thus, if initially there was backwardation ($S > F$), the long hedger wants it to decrease, or if there was contango ($F > S$), he wants it to increase. This is perfectly straightforward, and thus is one of those concepts that the reader should make certain that he or she understands it perfectly.

Bad news for the long hedger is naturally the opposite: backwardation increases, or contango decreases. [EXERCISE: Explain why using the same approach as above.]

A slightly more complicated way to deal with this topic is to look at an ex-post version of (2), with $E(B_1)$ replaced by B_1, and $E(V)$ replaced by V. That gives us $V = B_0 - B_1$, which immediately raises three possibilities: B_1 is equal to, greater than, or less than B_0. (In words, the terminal basis is equal to, greater than, or less than the starting basis.) Taking the first of these, $V = B_0 - B_1 = 0 : S$ and/or F may change, but the bases remain constant. This implies that S and F moved in the same direction by the same amount. How do we know this? Write $V = (S_0 - F_0) - (S_1 - F_1) = 0$, and so $S_1 - F_1 = S_0 - F_0$, or $B_1 = B_0$ (and, trivially and algebraically, B_0 does not change after t_0).

But if the basis moves in the wrong direction, it could result in an unfavorable outcome for, e.g., the long hedger, or $V < 0$. This is what basis risk is all about! How did we get this? Well, obviously, the basis increased: i.e., $B_1 > B_0$, or $(S_1 - F_1) > (S_0 - F_0)$, which in turn means that S increased relative to F, or F decreased relative to S: we have an increase in backwardation or a decline in contango, which meant that the buyer had to pay more for oil, while obtaining less on the offsetting futures transaction! This immediately allows us to state that if this is bad news for a long hedger, good news must consists of a decline in backwardation, or an increase in contango, as pointed out in the earlier heuristic analysis!

Concomitantly, if we had started out with a short instead of a long hedge, then the bad news would have consisted of a fall in backwardation, or an increase in contango. The long hedger in the previous example (e.g., a buyer) was afraid of a price rise, whereas with a short hedge the hedger (e.g., a seller) is afraid of a price fall, or $E(S_1) < S_0$. He/she therefore starts out by selling a futures, and without any algebra we know that what she wants is the futures price to fall so that she will not have to pay as much in the offsetting transaction, or the spot price to rise so that she gets more for her oil, or both. Expectations-wise he/she has $F_0 > E(F_1)$. Thus it will turn out that the best arrangement for him/her is for backwardation to increase, or if there was contango to begin for it to decrease, or even to move into backwardation.

We can get this result in a semi-formal manner by forming an expression similar to Eqs. (1) and (2):

$$E(V) = [F_0 - E(F_1)] - [S_0 - E(S_1)]$$
$$= [E(S_1) - E(F_1)] - [S_0 - F_0]. \tag{3}$$

In terms of expected outcomes the first two parentheses in (3) are positive, so as a rationale for hedging it is specified again that losses are minimized or eliminated, and not — as someone suggested — $E(V)$ should be non-negative. In the exercise mentioned above the reader should perform those manipulations which show that good news for a short hedger consists of an increase in backwardation, or a decrease in contango. Some very heavy losses have been taken when hedgers ran into situations where instead of the good news suggested by the history of the oil market, backwardation/contango functioned in a contrary manner. In order to avoid basis risk, swaps often turn out to be the derivative of choice, and these will be touched on later in this chapter.

One more thing is to be noticed. Now that we have Eq. (3) we can go to the ex-post version, which is $V = B_1 - B_0$ for short hedging. We can easily obtain the result above by a straightforward application of the delta operator. We can start with $\Delta V = \Delta(B_1 - B_0) = \Delta B_1 - 0 = \Delta B_1$, where ΔB_0 was obviously zero. $\Delta V = \Delta B_1$. For V to go up, B_1 must go up, and for bad news B_1 must go down. (EXERCISE: Go through the procedure in this paragraph for a long hedger!)

Exercises

1. What is arbitrage? If arbitrage is possible, why do futures and spot prices converge at the terminal date of a contract? Can you see any use for *total* convenience yield? "Good news for a long hedger is a decline in backwardation or an increase in contango". Discuss!

2. Algebraically, what is the basis? What is basis risk? Suppose that there was no futures contract for crude oil, and you decided to hedge your purchases of crude oil with futures for heating oil. Why might this work, and why might this not work?

3. What does the clearinghouse do? What is marking-to-market? What is a margin call? Assume that the demand for oil is stagnant, and you own

huge inventories of oil. Say something about the marginal convenience yield of your inventories!

4. Just above the exercises there is a simple algebraic discussion of what could happen if you hedge long, and basis risk is possible. Complete that discussion by explaining what happened to make $V_1 > 0$!

5. Now take the case of short hedging, and repeat the discussion referred to in the previous exercise, taking up all three possible outcomes for V_1!

6. Some Further Aspects of Options

It is a fairly common belief that options are much more difficult to understand than futures. This is not true up to a certain point, and it behooves everyone with even a slight interest in the subject to attempt to master the basic operations associated with this particular derivative, as well as the terminology. To me the word "master" implies repetition, and so I do not hesitate to repeat some earlier materials. The reader knows that he or she is getting somewhere when it is possible to say "But I already know that".

An option provides the buyer of the option the right to buy (call) or sell (put) a given amount of an underlying asset at a fixed price, called the exercise or strike price, within a given period that is called the expiry or maturity period. As noted earlier, the physical or financial asset in question is often called the "underlying", or the "actual". The end of the period is called the expiry or maturity or settlement date. The two types of options are American options, which can be exercised at any time prior to the expiry date, and European options, which can only be exercised at the expiry date. Most options are American.

But remember, an option does not have to be exercised. It can be discarded if the purchaser so desires, and so as compared to futures, no reversing transaction is necessary. In fact the seller of the option, the writer, wants nothing more than to see the option go unexercised.

When the initial transaction takes place, the buyer of a put or call option pays a premium to the option writer. This premium is the option price, and ideally it would be formed in an auction type market (similar to a stock or futures exchange) by the interaction of supply and demand. Supply and demand undoubtedly plays a part in option pricing, but for the most part these assets are sold on an over-the counter (OTC) basis by financial institutions such as brokerages. OTC products do not have to be standardized, and often to some extent can be tailored to the needs of the buyer. On the other hand, exchange traded assets are often easily sold back to the exchange. Even when this is possible for OTC products, a liquidity shortage could make the price uncertain.

Once a position is opened in a futures market, it stays open until the expiry date of the contract or, in the usual case, the contract is closed by a reversing transaction. During the time a futures position is open, its owner must face the possibility of margin calls if the price of the contract moves in the "wrong" direction — as well, of course, as margin windfalls if the price moves in the right direction. ("Right" means up in the case of a long position, and down if the buyer is short.)

As for the option buyer, once the premium is paid, the downside is fully accounted for. On the other hand, with a call option, if the market price of the underlying rises and moves past the exercise price, the option buyer still has the right to purchase the underlying at the exercise price. Similarly, if the market price falls beneath the exercise price of a put option, the underlying can still be sold at the exercise price. Expressed another way, the option writer has the obligation to deliver the commodity if a call option is exercised, and the obligation to take delivery (at the exercise price) if a put option is exercised. Obviously, a cash settlement can replace delivery, and often does. As for "margin", this is something that the option writer might have to deal with.

Clearly, some categories of option sellers could be in an uncomfortable situation if the options that they have written are exercised — so much so that the question must be raised as to why anyone would write options. The answer is that the options writer intends to sell an option at a price which, he/she thinks, will provide a comparatively small profit with a very large probability, although it means accepting a small probability of a large loss. This loss, large or small, is the (absolute) difference between the market price of the underlying and the exercise price of the option.

On the other side of the transaction, the buyer of a put or call option is accepting a high probability of a comparatively small loss in return for a small probability of a large gain. When expressed this way, we are clearly thinking about speculators. Hedgers, of course, are in the position of insurance buyers: we do not think of ourselves as losers if our house does not burn down, and as a result we do not gain access to the amount for which it has been insured. In fact, when looked at from this point of view, it suggests that speculators as a group make money in the options market for performing an insurance or risk-bearing function.

Next, let us introduce two important concepts. Calling the exercise price P_E, and the market (spot) price of the underlying S, the intrinsic value I_p of a put option is $I_p = P_E - S$. If $P_E > S$, then $I_p > 0$, and the option is said to be in-the-money. By way of contrast, if $S > P_E$, a put option is out-of-the-money. (In addition, trivially, if $S = P_E$, then the option is at-the-money). Conventionally, the intrinsic value of an out-of-the-money option is set equal to zero, and so $I_p = \text{Max}(P_E - S, 0)$. Similarly, for a call option we can write, $I_c = \text{Max}(S - P_E, 0)$.

Once we have added these simple concepts to our vocabulary, we can proceed to a short discussion of price formation for an option. The factors that are most important in explaining this price are the exercise price of the underlying in relation to the market price of that asset; the time to expiration of the option; the interest rate; and most important of all, the volatility of the underlying.

If there is a very large difference between the exercise price and the market price, then (*ceteris paribus*) the price of the option will be low. The reason is obvious: it is unlikely that the option will move into the money and be exercised. Thus writers will be generous in specifying their premiums.

Taking the same approach, if there is a very short time before expiry, then (*ceteris paribus*) the option price will be relatively low. An option can have time value as well as intrinsic value, and the shorter the time to expiry, the lower the probability that the option will move into the money and be exercised. An out-of-the-money option has no intrinsic value, but it does have time value; however, this time value is very small for an option that only has a few days to "run".

The lower the volatility, the lower the price. A low volatility means less likelihood of the option jumping into the money. Obviously, with everything else being the same, an American-type option has a higher price than a European-type option, since the American-type option can be exercised at any time during the maturity period. Volatility is the most important factor in determining the option price.

The interest rate might also have to be taken into account, and not just by big-ticket players. This is because instead of buying an option, a potential option buyer can, e.g., purchase a bond. As a result, theoretically, the option price is inversely related to the interest rate: the higher the interest rate, the lower the option price must be (*ceteris paribus*) to attract buyers. The same is true for writers of options. Why write options if you can get 25% on a high-quality bond from Pago-Pago?

These conditions furnish a starting point for obtaining the price of an option employing the famous Black–Scholes formula — or as it is sometimes called, the Black–Scholes–Merton formula, since Professor Robert Merton solved an important mathematical puzzle that had stalled Fisher Black and Myron Scholes. The original formula was for a European option referred to a non-dividend paying share, and it has presumably been modified by various well-paid "quants" to take into consideration other underlyings, which mean bonds and possibly commodities such as oil and gas. Personally, I find references to it largely a play for the gallery, and definitely not something that serious players want to emphasize in serious operations involving serious money, but if important persons are impressed then I say "go with the flow".

An article in *The Economist* once cited a well-known finance scholar as saying that the Black–Scholes–Merton (B–S–M) option pricing formula is "the most successful theory not only in finance but in all economics". *This is precisely what it is not*, and anyone using it in that spirit in the real world could find their credibility seriously undermined. I will not bother to reproduce it at this point because in engineering and gunnery I was taught not to use formulae indiscriminately, but I say a few words about it in the appendix.

I close this section by noting that according to a journalist in the *Financial Times*, a quick brain and unbridled self-confidence will no longer be enough to succeed in the new computer-driven exchanges. I certainly hope that nobody reading nonsense like that takes it to heart and concludes that this chapter should be abandoned before it is completely absorbed. Regardless of your luck in the genetic draw, rest assured that both a quick brain and unlimited self-confidence can be acquired by patience, concentration, and meticulous attention to important details as well as an uncompromising avoidance of nonsense. And ladies and gentlemen, it is never too late to start!

Exercises

1. "Buying an option gives you the right to buy or sell..." Buy or sell what? And if you buy, haven't you paid twice for the option?
2. Why did Mr T. Boone Pickens use futures instead of options?
3. What happens to the marginal convenience yield when (I/q) increases?
4. Volatility is important when considering both futures and options. Explain!
5. What is "contango"? Backwardation? At the beginning of the first Gulf War, there was an enormous backwardation in the oil market. Why?
6. I have memorized the original Black–Scholes formula because I never know when I might need it. Why would I say something like this?

7. Three More Topics: Exchange of Futures for Physicals, Options on Futures and Swaps

If you want a great deal of information about futures, then the book you should read is Duffie (1989). Among other things he defines the Exchange of Futures for Physicals (EFP) as "a spot market trade between two agents who have previously established futures positions as hedges against their spot commitments". This can be put another way: EFP is the transfer of a position between the physical market and the futures market by closing out an existing position in one market (the futures) while simultaneously entering into an equal and opposite position in the other market (the actuals).

In terms of our earlier discussion this means that if one party is long, and if her contract (position) is not closed out prior to the expiry date, she would have to receive a commodity (e.g., oil), while the other agent must be a short, who would have to deliver a commodity if his contract were not closed out. Obviously, there are situations in which it might be advantageous for these two parties or their brokers to contact each other before their contracts expire and exchange offers and/or suggestions about delivery conditions together with prices and quantities. Making this happen when it is convenient for agents (i.e., buyers and sellers) rather than just convenient for brokers and exchanges could be interpreted as expanding the flexibility of the market. Moreover, in theory this should not provide any headaches for the clearinghouse, since the accounting is straightforward.

If there are any mysteries here, the main one concerns how the counterparties found each other. Duffie's solution is via an independent broker
who spends his working hours looking for likely counterparties. In terms
of the definitions above a problem might arise concerning the quantities
involved, because Mr Short may not want or be able to deliver as much as
Ms Long desires, or vice versa. As far as the accounting is concerned, if a
deal was struck, one or both could be left with a residual futures position.

We can take a simple example here. Sally and Bill have open contracts
of 100 units, and they enter into an EFP. Sally is long and Bill is short, so
a complete closing out would mean that Bill delivers 100 units to Sally. In
terms of the definitions above they have closed out their futures positions
and entered into an arrangement involving physicals. (Perhaps Bill is a
producer of oil, and Sally is a refiner.) But suppose Bill wants to keep
10 units. In that case, if they deal with each other, each is left with open
positions, but 10 units instead of 100. Presumably these could be eventually
closed as easily as their original positions. Of course, the independent broker
might have found George, who started out with an open (short) position of
300 units, and was glad to provide Sally with 100. Sally's position is thus
closed in that she no longer has any exposure, while George still has an
open position of 200 units. In a highly liquid market, however, he should
have no problem closing his position later by an offsetting trade, an outright
sale of his contract, or even a delivery on the contract.

Where options on futures are concerned, NYMEX has an arrangement
where it is possible to trade in options on crude oil futures, where one options
contract corresponds to one futures (= 1000 barrels). These function so that
the option expires at or just before the delivery (= expiry) date on the futures
contract, which is a very important stipulation.

There is little in this discussion that is new for readers who comprehend
the earlier presentation of futures and options, although some of the details
might deserve a closer examination than provided here in case you find
yourself dealing in these assets. Where options on futures are concerned, a
call option gives the buyer right to take a long position in the futures market
if the option is exercised, and a put option gives the right to take a short
position in this market if exercising takes place.

The special feature of all this perhaps is that the option writer takes the
opposite position if the option is exercised: short for a call and long for a

put. Moreover, the price on the futures is set equal to the option's exercise price. Bailey (2005) goes into these matters, but not very clearly as far as I am concerned, and so let us look at a very simple example.

Consider a call option on a futures contract for a single "unit" of something with a strike price of $100. If this option is exercised, the writer must deliver a long futures contract with a price of $100, but marked-to-market. Suppose that the actual futures price at the time of exercise is $110. Then the writer hands the buyer a long futures contract with a value of $100, together with $10, while he takes a corresponding short position in the futures market. This payment (of $10) is obviously necessary because as marked-to-market, the value of the position is $110. The only loose end here is how the option buyer manages the futures that she now possesses: instead of selling it immediately (to the option writer) she might hold it hoping that its price will rise and a larger gain might be possible. (Of course, the opposite could happen) How long can she hold it? We have already said that the expiration date on any futures that enters the picture must be the same as that on the option she originally bought.

Some of the quantitative intricacies of this topic are discussed by David Luenberger (1998). One possible "adjustment" of the above arrangement might be the option writer simply buying a futures for $110 and selling it to the option buyer for the exercise price of $100 if the option was exercised. The buyer's gain in this case is $10 (minus the premium originally paid), and she has the choice of immediately offsetting the futures or holding it. There might be some problem here, however, because the necessary maturities might not be available: the writer might not have been able to buy a futures with a maturity that was equal to the remainder of the original maturity period. Had the writer been holding the short side of the position, however, then the maturity issue would not be relevant.

Now we can look at swaps. As one insider said, above a maturity of six months, swaps *are* the derivatives market! One well-established scholar who got this wrong was Professor Henrik Houthakker of Harvard University. That gentleman actually promulgated the fiction that it was unnecessary to worry about an escalating oil price because of the hedging possibilities afforded by the futures market. In the short run these possibilities may be considerable, but are definitely limited where the long term is concerned, if not nonexistent.

The most straightforward swap might be one where Bill (an oil producer) is worried about an oil price fall, and Sally (a refiner) is worried about a possible oil price increase. Given a "*notional*" price and quantity, a swap become much easier to understand than a futures or options transaction. (A definition of "notional" that applies here is the quantity (which is typically not exchanged) on which the cash flows of a derivatives contract are based. We can also speak of a notional price which applies for the transaction, regardless of, e.g., the market price.)

Suppose that Bill and Sally settle on a notional quantity of 3000 barrels a month, and a notional price of $68/b. When the market price is over $68/b, Bill pays Sally the difference between the market and notional price, and when under, Sally pays Bill. The accounting for the payments may take place on a daily basis, or, e.g., a monthly basis using an average price for the relevant month. Suppose that for July the average price turned out to be $71/b. Then Bill pays Sally $(71 - 68)3000 = \$9000/b$ for that month. The actual prices and quantitites for the output of Bill and purchases by Sally are irrelevant, since they are exterior to swap considerations. Also, as posed in this particular example, this is strictly a financial transaction: they are not dealing with each other where physical oil is concerned.

Things are not usually so uncomplicated, however. Suppose that Sally, who uses 4000 barrels of crude a month in her refinery, wants to fix her costs for most of this oil, or 3000 barrels. Why most and not all? Because she is not absolutely certain that the oil price will escalate, and also feels that in the negotiations with a swap arranger (i.e., an intermediary) she can get a better deal with, e.g., 3000 barrels than 4000. What might happen is that instead of trying to find Bill she goes to a swap arranger — usually a very large financial institution — and agrees to pay the arranger a fixed price of $65/b for each of $3000/30 = 100$ barrels that on average she buys every day on the spot market, with the payment taking place at the end of the month. Thus every month she is obligated to pay the arranger $3000 \times 65 = 195,000$ dollars.

Why 65 instead of 66. Perhaps it is because the swap arranger is captivated by Sally's smile, or perhaps it is because he feels that the price of oil will settle in the low 60s for the duration of the contract. This is important, because the other side of the swap is that the arranger agrees to pay Sally the market rate for oil for the duration of the contract, taken on a daily basis, and with payment at the end of the month. Thus, on a day when the market rate is $63/b, the swap arranger comes out 2 dollars ahead on each barrel, which on 100 barrels means 200 dollars. On that day Sally would have been better off buying these 100 barrels on the open market, although it should be recognized that she has a certain peace of mind from knowing that she will not have to pay more than $65/b in case the price spiked to the upper 70s or beyond. And observe, she has not hedged all of her requirements with a swap, and so she obtains some oil that day for $63/b.

Suppose that every day in this month the price of oil is $63/b. Sally buys the oil on the market for $3000 \times 63 = \$189,000$, but is obligated to pay the arranger (3000×65), or 195,000, *minus* $189,000 for that month. It is the difference that changes hands, and so $6000 goes from Sally to the arranger. Had the market price been $67, then Sally would have received $6000.

Since swap arrangers not only dislike losing money, they often go to a great deal of trouble to run "matched books", which means finding somebody else to carry the risk that is involved, while they simply pocket a fee for bringing these two players together. The person they might be thinking of is Bill, who has gradually become convinced that the oil price will fall. He produces 3000 barrels a month, and he wants to hedge all of it. Unlike Sally, who entered into careful negotiations with the swap arranger, Bill runs to the office of Mr Arranger, and as soon as he is in the door agrees to accept a nominal price of $64/b for his monthly production of 3000 barrels: he will pay the swap arranger every month 3000 times the difference between the market price and $64/b if the market price is over $64/b, while receiving for each barrel $64 minus the market price if this price is under $64/b.

Instead of dealing with a swap arranger, why he did not try to find Sally — because she was willing to accept a notional price of $65/b. One reason might be that he did not know that she existed: her business might be in Seattle, and his in offshore Miami. In addition, he feels more certain that where the receipt of money is concerned, the swap arranger is more reliable than Sally. Similarly, Sally feels that it is easier for her to obtain oil from nearby producers than to enter into an arrangement with Bill, and she wants some certainty where the price is concerned. A swap arranger can probably provide this better than Bill, since financial institutions have access to expertise and financial resources that are superior to all except the largest energy firms.

In addition to making considerable amount of money on price spreads of the type mentioned above, financial institutions are usually very skillful in the use of options and futures to "lay off" risk if they sense that things are developing in such a way where they can suffer a substantial loss. The policy of swap arrangers (or intermediaries) is usually to find counterparties as soon as possible; however, the most successful arrangers are not fanatics when it comes to running matched books, since this is too restrictive where the number and range of transactions into which they can enter are concerned. Instead they often accept large exposures, which they count on closing later if necessary by a matching or nearly matching transaction.

8. A Final Comment

As noted in the preface to this book, this is an elementary presentation of energy economics. My expectations are that everyone interested in this topic should be able to read and understand most of the book, and that includes the present chapter. For some reason, however, many potential readers find this topic a burden, which is an outcome that I am unable to accept. On the basis of my contact with persons in the financial market in Sydney (Australia) and Singapore, I think I can say that a perfect comprehension of this chapter is a very attractive investment, even if it is far from a complete education in financial economics.

Appendix: Some Further Aspects of Hedging and Options, and the Optimal Hedge Ratio

Although it seems to be disappearing from the journals, the Metallgesellschaft (MG) fiasco of 1973 has started to appear in books on finance and financial engineering. The study of that incident is a simple application of what you have learned in the present chapter.

Even though in theory you break even (or close to even) in the long run when hedging with futures — assuming no basis risk, and ignoring the time value of money — if the margin calls start coming in, and really large amounts of money are involved, then decision makers must decide whether to pay these margin calls (with money that could be used for other purposes), or to shut the position down. As it happened, after finding themselves more than a billion dollars in the hole, MG's management and advisors decided to head for the emergency exit.

MG was in the following situation. As traders they were obtaining and selling oil and oil products, while at the same time being engaged in long hedging with futures and OTC swaps. The last item has been widely overlooked, largely because it did not lead to any misery (and to my way of thinking, when bad news appeared on the futures front, MG's presence in the swaps market should have increased if possible). As emphasized in this chapter, the futures were of short duration because contrary to what certain so-called experts think, there is insufficient liquidity to make large-scale, long-term hedging an attractive proposition in the oil markets.

How did MG's hedging team go about their work? What they did was to simply look at the futures market and note that it was in backwardation most of the time, with near-term contracts selling for more than distant contracts. Convenience yield probably had a great deal to do with this. In any event we can depict this situation by merely writing $F_0 > F_1 > F_2 \cdots$, although we should be careful to specify that this applies *most* of the time as compared to *all* of the time. F_0 is the contract selling at time t_0, F_1 is the contract selling at the end of t_1 (or the beginning of t_2), and so on.

Now we can consider a situation where we have a two-period perspective, where buying and selling is concerned. To be specific a contract bought at time t_0 with a two-period maturity will be sold at the end of the first period (t_1), which can also be taken as the beginning of the second period (t_2). That closes the position of the buyer where that contract is concerned, but the contract still has a maturity of one period left. This last point is irrelevant, however, because the lady or gentleman that we are talking about buys a new two-period contract at the end of the first period (or beginning of the second). This is sold at the end of the second period, and another two-period contract is bought which is sold at the end of the third period, etc.

Buying and selling will be distinguished here by the number of subscripts. The initial purchase was F_{02}, which means bought at time t_0 (the beginning of the first period) with a maturity date at the end of the second period (or beginning of the third). F_{13} then is the contract bought at the end of the first period (or beginning of the second) with a maturity date at the end of the third period, etc. As for selling, I use the notation F_{ijk}, where

"i" is the contract bought at time t_i with a maturity date of t_k, but which is sold at t_j. For instance, if we have F_{345}, this is a contract bought at the beginning of period 3 with a maturity date at the beginning of period 5, but which is sold at the beginning of period 4 (or end of period 3). Once again, the hedger that we are talking about closes out her position after one period, and buys a new two-period contract, but the contract still has a year to its maturity date. Diagramatically

$$[t_0; F_{02}]\_\_\_\_\_[t_8; F_{13}, F_{123}]\_\_\_\_\_$$
$$[t_2; F_{24}, F_{234}]\_\_\_\_\_[t_3; F_{35}, F_{345}]\ldots$$

The sign pattern is important in this discussion, and if we call G the gain (or loss) from the hedging program we have

$$G = -F_{02} + (F_{012} - F_{13}) + (F_{123} - F_{24}) + (F_{234} - F_{35}) + \cdots \quad \text{(A.1)}$$

If backwardation works its magic, then the values in parentheses are mostly positive, and in the long run G is positive. In examining this expression we see that while we start out long (with a buy), F_{02} is negative, as are the other two-subscript values, while the three subscript values are all positive, but there is no guarantee that all the values in parentheses will be positive. The assumption seems to have been, though, that they are positive about 70% of the time, and so MG's hedging team felt comfortable with the no-brainer of continuously rolling their positions forward in the manner described above, concluding that despite an occasional setback, it was a statistical certainty that in the long run a profit would be registered. According to the boss of the hedging team, he believed in backwardation, and he believed in it because it had served him well in the past.

Where did things go wrong? According to Professor Stephen Ross the market is too efficient to allow profits to be made so easily. The issue of course was not so much profits as avoiding losses, and in a viable futures market this seems quite reasonable. Thus, when there was a long stretch of bad news, it might be argued that the hedging team should have paid the margin calls that came in, or so reasoned Professor Merton Miller. Maybe so, but the margin calls here were not "chump change" but millions of dollars. The interest on the money borrowed to pay this margin — or for that matter the opportunity cost if payment did not involve borrowed money — would have been very large, and perhaps much too large.

A consortium of banks rescued MG from bankruptcy, but insisted that they go slow with their hedging activities. A few months later the prices of the commodities that MG was dealing in rose, and as a result their unhedged exposure resulted in another spell of bad news.

The original B–S–M analysis deals with a non-dividend bearing European call option instead of the almost universally traded American options, and the many costly attempts that have been made — and are being made — to generalize it to more prevalent instruments have not been particularly successful. As a concept, however, it cannot be dismissed.

A great deal of work apparently went into deriving the B–S–M equation, but it is simple enough for you to remember. If we take P_E as the exercise price, S the spot price, and P the premium (i.e., the option price), we can write $P = SN(d_1) - P_E e^{-rT} N(d_2)$. In addition to the variables already mentioned, σ is the instantaneous standard deviation — a surrogate for volatility; T is the time to expiry in fractions of a year $(0 < T < 1)$; r is the riskless rate of interest; $d_1 = [Ln(S/P_E) + (r + 0.5\sigma^2)T]/\sigma T^{1/2}$, and $N(d_1) =$ cumulative probability distribution for the standard normal variate, from $-\infty$ to d_1. $N(d_2)$ is the same for d_2, where $d_2 = d_1 - \sigma T^{1/2}$. There are tables supplying the values of N_1 and N_2 when d_1 and d_2 are calculated. Bodie and Merton (2000) give an interesting linear approximation for the above equation. This is for $T < 1$ year, and is $P = \sigma S(T/2\pi)^{1/2}$.

A couple of questions always appear when students initially confront the above analysis. The first concerns the absence in this equation of the *probability* of the asset price rising or falling: this absence is highly counter-intuitive. The answer here turns on the asymmetric nature of an option: the downside is limited to the premium, while the potential profit depends on how far the price might move on the "upside", and the volatility — where the volatility is in the B–S–M equation. As for the presence of the risk-free interest rate, this says something about the attractiveness — or lack thereof — of investing in an option instead of an asset such as a short-term government bond that is essentially risk free.

And how, *in theory*, is the B–S–M relationship used? One answer is that P is calculated, and then compared to the existing (market) P. If they are not the same, then arbitrage is *theoretically* possible. Note the emphasis on *in theory* and *theoretically*! In his Nobel Prize lecture at Uppsala University, Professor Scholes made it clear that carrying out this kind of "arbitrage" is far from riskless, and whoever is involved with it should have a good relationship with his or her banking "support".

It may not be a good idea to overload beginners with algebra, but it seems likely that some readers will be interested to know a little more about some of the rudimentary algebraic concepts that are associated with options.

The profit of buyers of put options can be written as follows: $V_{Bp} = $ Max$\{(P_E - S - P_p), -P_p\}$. Sellers' profit is $V_{Sp} = $ Min$\{(P_p + S - P_E), P_p\}$. If, for example, the option is exercised, then the profit is $(P_E - S - P_p)$. Otherwise it goes into the waste paper basket and the buyer loses P_p, which happens to be the gain to the writer. Suppose that we take a situation where $S = 15$, $P_E = 30$, and $P_p = 5$. The buyers profit is then Max$\{(30 - 15 - 5), -5\} = 10$. The seller's profit is -10. If S were 50, then $V_{Bp} = -5$ and $V_{Sp} = 5$. You should verify this result.

One more topic can be considered here, since many students of finance are not given a formal introduction to the so-called "hedge ratio". Instead they tend to think that when hedging takes place it is of the all-or-nothing variety.

Suppose that we are planning to hedge a total amount T of a homogeneous commodity, and are considering hedging an amount H, with $0 \leq H \leq T$. Hedging in this example will mean that there is a futures market where, due to the absence of basis risk, it is possible to lock in a price F_0 for the amount H. As for the remainder, or $N = T - H$, the actual price at which it can be sold is unknown, and so we must resort to expectations: the expected spot price at the end of an arbitrary maturity (or expiry) period can be written as $E(S_1)$. This enables us to write the expected yield $E(R)$ of a portfolio consisting of the hedged amount, H, and the unhedged amount N:

$$E(R) = (T - H)E(S_1) + HF_0. \tag{A.2}$$

The uncertainty associated with the outcome is, as usual, measured by the variance or standard deviation of the stochastic component. This will be called Var $S = \sigma_s^2$, and in theory could be estimated from a time series of spot prices. With no basis risk, there is no uncertainty about the price of the hedged component, and so the uncertainty of the entire portfolio is the same as that of the unhedged portion, or

$$\sigma_R^2 = (T - H)^2 \sigma_s^2. \tag{A.3}$$

I will now introduce what seems like a logical expected utility function, where $E(U)$ signifies expected utility. Taking α to be a constant larger than zero ($\alpha > 0$), the function is

$$E(U) = E(R) - \lambda \sigma_R^2. \tag{A.4}$$

Substituting from (A.2) and (A.3) we get

$$E(U) = (T - H)E(S_1) + H F_0 - \lambda(T - H)^2 \sigma_s^2. \tag{A.5}$$

In order to determine the optimal hedge we have only to set the derivative of this expression with respect to H equal to zero: $dE(U)/dH = -E(S_1) + F_0 + 2\lambda\sigma_s^2 T - 2\lambda\sigma_s^2 H = 0$. We immediately obtain

$$H = [F_0 - E(S_1) + 2\lambda\sigma_s^2 T]/2\lambda\sigma_s^2. \tag{A.6}$$

Rather than trying to interpret Eq. (A.4), we can formulate an expression for the "hedge ratio". Defining this as $H^* = H/T$ we get

$$H^* = 1 - \{[E(S_1) - F_0]/2\lambda\sigma_s^2 T\}. \tag{A.7}$$

Perhaps the most important observation here is that when $E(S_1) = F_0$, H^* is equal to unity, or $H = T$. This is hardly a revolutionary result, but my intention is merely to suggest that hedging is not an all-or-nothing proposition, and this can be demonstrated for a textbook world.

Key Concepts

actuals	long
assets	margin
basis risk	marking-to-market
call vs. out option	maturity
cash settlement	option writer; option buyer
clearinghouse	paper oil
convenience yield	proprietary trading
exposure	short
forwards vs. futures	speculating vs. hedging
liquidity	underlying

Bibliography

Bailey, Roy E. (2005). *The Economics of Financial Markets*. Cambridge: Cambridge University Press.

Banks, Ferdinand E. (2001). *Global Finance and Financial Markets: A Modern Introduction*. Singapore and London: World Scientific.

—— (2000). *Energy Economics: A Modern Introduction*. Dordrecht and New York: Kluwer Academic.

Bodie, Zvi and Robert C. Merton (2000). *Finance*. Upper Saddle River: Prentice Hall.

Cuthbertson, Keith and Dirk Nitzsche (2001). *Financial Engineering*. New York: John Wiley and Sons.

Duffie, Darrell (1989). *Futures Markets*. New Jersey: Prentice Hall.

Gall, Liz (1990). "How a nonintegrated North Sea producer views oil price risk". *Oil and Gas Journal*, 88(4).

Hull, John (2003). *Options, Futures and Other Derivatives*. New Jersey: Prentice Hall.

Luenberger, David G (1998). *Investment Science*. New York and Oxford: Oxford University Press.

CHAPTER 9

A FAITH-BASED APPROACH TO GLOBAL WARMING

This chapter is a non-technical examination of some aspects of global warming that are generally neglected in the academic economics literature. The discussion features several basic issues considered by Professor David Goodstein (2004) in his short and easily read book, and particularly the serious consequences that might result from a peaking of the global oil output. The same topic is considered to a lesser extent in my previous energy economics textbook (2000). In addition I have emphasized that, as Victor (2001) makes it clear, the provisions of the Kyoto Protocol are meaningless unless emissions trading is effective. A key argument here is that since exchange-based financial instruments have been unsatisfactory in the electricity markets, to include those associated with the Nordic Electricity Exchange (NordPool), it could happen that the trading of exchange-based emission permits will also be ineffectual: for example, the emissions trading program broached by the European Union is likely to result in serious problems for the electricity-intensive firms of industrial countries, since one result of that program is that a large increase in electricity prices may be unavoidable. *Furthermore, it may also be true that even if there is no man-made component of global warming, the curtailing of greenhouse gas emissions (by, e.g., reducing the use of fossil fuels and increasing energy efficiencies) could result in sizable economic and social gains.*

1. Introduction

To get started, let us consider two groups of people who might have a far-ranging interest in climate warming. I call these (physical) scientists and economists, although classifications which specifically took account of other groups and/or persons might be more suitable. (Ideally it would be possible to include partnerships such as the Climate Group, which comprises a number of influential firms that want governments to take immediate practical action on climate warming; or for that matter observers who do not question the reality of the "greenhouse effect", but at the same time believe that many of the conclusions reached by conventional science as to its intensity and management are mostly irrelevant. This might be a good place to note that several of the largest insurance groups in the world have become members of the Climate Group: they have already experienced an increase in the frequency and severity of weather related events that has cost them many millions of dollars.)

By way of continuing, I designate two subsets: those who believe that there is danger ahead because of a too rapid expansion of the stock of greenhouse gases — primarily carbon dioxide (CO_2) — in the atmosphere; and those who are of another opinion. In the real world the believers are, as far as I can tell, *at least* 90% of the total considered here, and they want this matter addressed as soon as possible. This might also be a good place to stress that although the President of the United States was not customarily regarded as a climate warming enthusiast, and in 2001 the United States abandoned any intention to comply with the Kyoto Protocol on climate change because of the economic restrictions that it ostensibly placed on the US economy, the US government is an impressive supporter of climate research, and President Bush is *not* a climate-warming denier.

Immordino (2003) has said that the reason for the divergence of views on climate matters between the United States and Europe can be explained by "scientific uncertainty". In point of truth, there is a universal scientific agreement on these items. A divergence of views characterizes the television audience, and is mostly due to cultural and geographical considerations. In the United States, climate risk has been managed relatively successful for two centuries, although there have been short-term discomforts. For example, the bad news in Oklahoma during the 1930s (in the form of the "dust bowl") meant good news for California (in the form of many new residents). Moreover, the present explosive growth of Las Vegas may have to do with many Californians wanting to put as much distance as possible between themselves and the Pacific Ocean. The hurricane Katrina that leveled a large part of New Orleans was undoubtedly a shock, but the final judgment about the United States by Wehrmacht Sergeant Christian Diestl in Irwin Shaw's brilliant war novel *The Young Lions* — "Untouched and Untouchable" — might still apply. Many North-Americans almost certainly think in those terms when the discussion about climate turns serious.

Before continuing, I would like to remind readers of the basic issue being treated in this chapter. In a world free of the multifarious activities of human beings, the natural emissions (i.e., *flows*) of CO_2 and other greenhouse gases would probably be matched by any excess being eventually removed from the atmosphere by absorption in large bodies of water or by plant photosynthesis. ("Excess", because without the presence of these gases, the earth would be uninhabitable.) Most climate scientists now agree that human (i.e., *anthropocentric*) activities disturb this "equilibrium", but a system imbalance *per se* (in the form of a rapidly expanding *stock* of greenhouse gases) hardly constitutes a clear and present danger, since the capacity of the atmosphere is obviously huge. The problem arrives when this imbalance reaches inordinate proportions, as may be happening at the present time due to large-scale electricity generation, transportation, and industrial activities generating an amount of, e.g., CO_2 that cannot be assimilated. The possible consequences of this situation are spelled out in a short paper in the prominent business periodical *Fortune* by Stipp (2004).

Next we can turn to academic economists. The majority of these ladies and gentlemen almost certainly do not feel inclined to oppose the colossal amount of anecdotal and scientific evidence dealing with climate warming, at least not in public. I count myself among this group, and moreover, given the near unanimity among climatologists (as well as Nobel laureates in science who are interested in this topic), I am unable to muster any genuine doubt at the present time about the purported dangers of global warming — *although I do accept that the overwhelming consensus referred to above could be completely wrong. In other words, my approach is based on faith!* — faith in the competence and dedication of most of the scientists who have the opportunity to do systematic research on this topic, and to only a slightly less extent faith in their honesty.

Similarly, I must unfortunately express a lack of faith in those individuals working — the other side of the street, and not just because it is possible to detect among them a few high-profile charlatans: it certainly is not unthinkable that some of the most vocal skeptics are highly competent, and perhaps heartbreakingly honest. In other words, I am rendering a value judgment, but I am comfortable with this even though it has been made clear to me that there are also a few hypocrites marching with heads held high in the ranks of influential climate-warming believers.

When it comes to doing something about reducing atmospheric CO_2, I am particularly dubious of emissions trading. Here I would like to note that most of the academic economics literature on emissions trading is completely without any scientific value; however, even in the case of important contributions (such as Farrell and Lave, 2004), there seems to be an implicit assumption that this trading takes place between firms and/or governments — which, strangely enough, might turn out to be the optimal arrangement. *The often expressed intention, however, is to have an exchange-based product, and as I shall claim in Section 3 called "Emissions Trading", my work on electricity deregulation leads me to believe that this kind of platform could result in some unpleasant surprises for buyers and sellers of "emission permits".*

There is a large amount of non-technical literature on the subject of global warming, but I am going to recommend two short and easily read papers, and one very short and easily read book. In other words, a few hours of reading. The papers are by Hansen (2004), whose testimony to US Congressional committees in the 1980s was instrumental in raising awareness of global warming issues, and the already mentioned journalist Stipp (2004) — who considers the reaction of the US Department of Defence (i.e., the Pentagon) to the consequences of climate warming.

As for the book (which also provides a crucial ingredient for the present contribution), this is by Professor (of physics) David Goodstein (2004), of the California Institute of Technology. I choose Goodstein's book because its (sub)title is "*The End of the Age of Oil*", and his main thesis is as follows: Oil is in short supply, and when this situation is revealed by the "peaking" of oil production, or perhaps just before, the production and use of coal will accelerate. As a result, the stock of CO_2 in the atmosphere could attain some sort of "critical" magnitude, and by a fairly complicated process, cause some very ugly things to take place here on earth, where the main feature of this ugliness is its irreversibility.

Goodstein wants careful attention paid to this matter, and so do many economists who profess an academic interest in environmental topics.

Unfortunately, however, what many of this latter congregation are mainly focused on is access to the generous research and travel grants that too often become available to persons who (mistakenly) feel that they can make a significant contribution to the understanding of environmental issues by publishing a few pages in some unread journal or conference volume. The vast majority of literature originating with this research is naïve and/or counterproductive, and in the case of, e.g., Sweden is perhaps best described as a methodical affront to human intelligence. For instance, how did Swedish economists draw the bizarre conclusion that authoritative discussions about marketable emission permits could take place without examining the mechanics of trading these items?

No claim will be made that the presentation in this chapter is all-inclusive in any respect. As a teacher of economics and finance, my principal interest is marketable emission permits. Apparently the World Resource Institute, an American "think tank", believes that "the market is a good place to tackle environmental problems", but considering the many electricity deregulation fiascoes, it might turn out that a resort to marketable permits is the worst possible option.

An important and intelligent Swedish civil servant has claimed that marketable permits are capable of playing a decisive role in the reduction of CO_2 emissions, but this might be a good place to inform him and all other interested parties that this hypothesis has not been proved, and in fact it may be impossible to prove. Something that deserves to be observed and remembered is that in Sweden the main beneficiary of electricity deregulation has turned out to be the Swedish government, and very definitely *not* households or small businesses, and it may be the case that in the corridors and restaurants of power it has been decided that the structure of the Swedish tax system is such that the use of emission permits could provide still another avenue for helping to finance the kind of foolishness so dear to the heart of recent Swedish governments.

Goodstein makes a few remarks about nuclear energy, and like myself believes it essential for helping to reduce the use of fossil fuel. My position on this topic has been given on several occasions in this book, but I do not hesitate to give it again. The basic technical and psychological problem with nuclear energy has to do with the disposal of nuclear waste; however, while scientists may not be able to find oil and gas that does not exist —

which many observers seem to find surprising — it is highly conceivable that eventually they will find some way to recycle this waste in an attractive way, and/or develop reactors that almost completely eliminate it from the production cycle. Similarly, "safe" reactors are not really a mystery to scientists, because they have already been developed in Sweden in pilot form (e.g., PIUS and SECURE), although the Swedish government has thoughtlessly banned further research. This is a departure which will almost certainly have the effect of adding huge amounts of greenhouse gases to the existing stock.

Something that is often forgotten is that the *activity* called "reducing CO_2 in the atmosphere" probably qualifies as a *public good*, and in these circumstances it makes both political and economic sense for it to be paid for by the community as a whole, instead of allowing, e.g., marketable permits to place the *largest part* of this burden on energy intensive industries — which is very definitely possible, and which industry spokespersons in Sweden, Germany, and the United Kingdom say is a certainty. (But make no mistake: consumers are also going to come into the line of fire.) It is because of issues of this sort that Goodstein hopes that electorates will become sufficiently interested in the welfare of themselves and their descendents to take the steps that are necessary to obtain political leaderships capable of designing optimal carbon constraints. It needs to be added that it is important for this awareness to make an appearance in the near as opposed to the distant future.

It would be nice to see a closing of the gap between forward-looking multinationals (such as BP and DuPont) that are already taking extensive measures to reduce emissions and increase energy efficiency, and the many large enterprises that recognize the possible deleterious effects of climate change on their operations, but are essentially passive. In considering my research on the topics mentioned above, I am afraid that I cannot be especially optimistic on this point; however, miracles do happen, and more often than people think.

2. Climate Change and Politics

"Climate Change and Politics" is the sub-title of a brief discussion in *The Economist* (5 February 2005). Its purpose was to make readers believe that a large collection of high-profile physical scientists (and others) regard the climate warming controversy as biased in such a way that it favors "believers". The discussion began with a quotation from the sci-fi novelist Michael Crichton, who tells us that "science and politics is a bad combination with a bad history". He concludes his evaluation of climate warming and its believers by insisting that "critics (i.e., skeptics) are few and harshly dealt with", which suggests that his complete lack of perception and perspective should logically serve to make him a worthless commentator on what some observers call the most crucial scientific question of the 21st century.

Critics are indeed few, and in the foremost scientific circles they are generally considered lightweights whose research and/or teaching does not merit consideration. However, when they gain entrance to learned forums they tend to be treated with a leniency that hardly any of them deserves. Fortunately though, the pre-eminent journals *Science* and *Nature* contain hardly a paper by the skeptics, because these publications prefer that "experts" who obtain this designation in popularity contests rather than through the quality of their work should find other outlets for their precious wisdom.

Among the observations by *The Economist* is a blurb about the utilization of the wrong exchange rates by scientists working with the Intergovernmental Panel on Climate Change (IPCC). Apparently this insignificant deficiency was pointed out by two London economists who are also providing the IPCC with detail critiques; however, I would like to inform these two gentlemen and their publicists that things like exchange rates are completely irrelevant to the scientific aspects of this issue. It was also noted in this "piece" that the statistical issues associated with this subject are complicated, which is true, but fortunately they are not complicated to the Nobel Laureates and PhDs in mathematical statistics who have informed the governments of the leading industrial countries that in all likelihood climate warming is real and not science fiction.

Something that is badly in need of comprehension where this matter is concerned is that the basic issue where global warming is concerned is not science or economics, but rationality. It is about whether voters and serious politicians — or for that matters non-voters and/or political hacks and crackpots — adopt or accept strategies that are consistent with their ambitions in life, love, and the pursuit of power. An overwhelming majority of the world's scientific elite have lined up behind the even larger majority of climatologists who say that global warming is a clear and imminent danger, while the general public in some countries has been systematically led to believe that global warming skeptics and believers in excessive global warming are evenly divided in numbers and quality. This is the precise opposite of the truth.

Bjorn Lomborg — one of the poster boys of the skeptics — went so far as to assemble a pseudo-congress that he called "The Copenhagen Consensus". The *Economist* article mentioned above said that three Nobel laureate economists making appearances at Lomborg's spectacle labeled investments to counter global warming "bad" (as compared to money spent to, e.g., reduce the incidence of AIDS and HIV). As it happens though, two of these laureates were economic historians without any advanced qualifications in economic theory or empirical work, while the third was a brilliant economist — Professor Vernon Smith — who unfortunately was instrumental in the establishing of a failed scheme for trading electricity in Sydney (Australia).

Other skeptics are mentioned en passant in a recent issue of the important journal *Energy and Environment* (Vol. 15, No. 5, 2004), with a long reference to the Leipzig Manifesto, which is a pronunciamento claiming that global warming is an unproved and unprovable hypothesis. I think that I can say that many of the people signing that bogus document would have signed their own death warrants if they thought that a television camera was pointed in their direction. Like Mr Lomborg's absurd Copenhagen Consensus, the Leipzig arrangement was nothing more than a publicity stunt disguised as a scientific platform. It needs to be asked then why should an informed audience respect a denial lobby that features the ravings of novelist Michael Crichton or — for that matter — highly qualified scientists who are not climatologists. It also needs to be made clear that many very large corporations that once loudly declared their sympathy for the skeptics are now believers. For instance, in 1997, BP withdrew from the Global Climate Commission — an industry group opposing action to reduce greenhouse gas emissions — and by 2006 had reduced emissions to 1990 levels, while developing CO_2 capture and storage facilities at its production sites. All of this was done without materially reducing profits. That firm is also heavily committed in activities involving wind, hydrogen, and solar panels, which will serve them well regardless of how the climate warming imbroglio is resolved.

Interestingly enough, almost all of the climate skeptics with which I am familiar are also strong believers in the long-run availability of oil and gas. Dr Lomborg, for example, has stated publicly that oil will last at least 100 years. He is certainly correct with this judgment; however, even if it were close to a million it makes little or no difference. The correct way to define scarcity is in terms of the peaking of the world oil supply, and this will take place long before 100 years have passed. It can also be mentioned that in Stipp's article the Pentagon plays the role of concerned observer in the climate warming drama, and unless I am mistaken, any indication that oil production was peaking or about to peak would cause the lights to burn longer than usual in that impressive structure. This is why, unlike many students of the oil market, I find it difficult to believe that oil production will be allowed to peak in the near future.

3. Emissions Trading

About 50 years ago, I and some colleagues were treated to an impromptu lecture by the commanding officer of the second (US) Infantry Division in which he remarked (at the top of his voice) that "If you aint got communication you aint got nothing". Apparently the general had slept through his English classes at West Point; however, this particular mode of expression might apply to financial markets of the exchange (i.e., *auction*) variety, if we substitute *liquidity* for communication.

The electricity financial markets failed or are failing because of a shortage of liquidity, and the same could easily happen to an exchange-based market for emission permits. When I speak of an "exchange" I think primarily of The New York Mercantile Exchange (NYMEX), the world's largest energy exchange, with the most competent management, traders, and analysts in the world, and not a storefront operation in Beverly Hills or Carmel. Some time ago NYMEX delisted its electricity futures contracts because of a lack of liquidity, although the intention apparently was/is to eventually introduce other contracts of the over-the-counter (OTC) type. A renewed effort of one sort or another is (or was) almost certain, because with a little luck, as well as some help from paid and unpaid publicists, assets of this nature might be capable of turning a financial winter into summer. On the other hand, like marketable emission contracts, there is no guarantee that they are capable of providing appreciable benefits to producers or consumers or to anybody else not engaged in the rewarding profession of selling them to persons who do not understand that in reality they should not exist.

In a recent issue of the Newsletter of the *International Association for Energy Economics* (IAEE) (2004), Mr Erling Mork accused me of failing to understand the magnificent service that he feels is being rendered to electricity consumers and producers by the presence on this earth of the Nordic Electricity Exchange (NordPool). The truth is that I am one of the few persons in the academic world who is fully cognizant of the makeup and functioning of that establishment: among other things I am aware that without NordPool and the deregulation "scam" of which it is a part, my electricity bill and that of my colleagues would be considerably lower. Luckily, in his comment, Mr Mork begins by admitting that NordPool has suffered liquidity problems, which was a signal for me to immediately tune out, because it is a well-known fact in theoretical economics — dating back at least to the work of Leon Walras — that if an auction market has inadequate liquidity, then it is best for both its present and potential customers if it closes its doors without delay. Looked at in a down-to-earth manner, if it is dealing in contracts that are generally ignored, then these contracts should be taken out of circulation.

As to be expected, the head of NYMEX has said that he believes that emissions trading will "evolve to be big business", *but at the same time he has made it clear that NYMEX will not swing into action until, in his words, he sees which of the existing contracts "developed gravity".* By gravity he "probably" means liquidity, and if I ever found myself enjoying the hospitality of an old soldiers' home in which the General mentioned at the beginning of this section was residing, I would inquire if he would be so kind as to assist me in turning that bizarre expression into plain English.

Many of the same persons that are or will be working with emissions trading have been involved with electricity derivatives, but even those who are new to this game use the same "lingo" of the financial world that I explained at great length in my elementary textbook on international financial markets (2001). But for those persons uninterested in reading my finance book, or any book for that matter, everything that they need to know about emissions trading will sooner or later be found on the financial pages of their local newspapers, or in various periodicals, and the information in these sources is inevitably more reliable than that found in many of the unnoticed and/or unread learned journals gathering dust on the shelves of almost every university library in the world.

According to Andrei Marcu of the International Emissions Trading Association, "Europe is now clearly committed to action on climate change, whatever happens to the Kyoto treaty". I am sure that he is sincere in this belief, because his salary (and bonuses) will depend on the trading successes of carbon permits, and not the fate of the Kyoto Protocol nor the reduction in the output of physical carbon in the atmosphere. For him and his collaborators, cash comes first, and carbon in its various forms somewhere to the rear. Another heavyweight player in this burlesque, Michael Grubb of London's Imperial College, as well as the inanely named "Carbon Trust", informed *The Economist* (UK) that "Kyoto was designed for the rich countries to miss their domestic targets. That's why we included international emissions trading" (3 April 2004). The identity of the "we" to whom he was referring was not clarified; however, for the purpose of the present contribution it could apply to everyone with expectations of a first-class ticket on what they hope will become an emission-trading gravy train.

In the latest edition of *Energivärlden*, a periodical distributed by the Swedish Energy Agency (*Energimyndigheten*), there was an enthusiastic description of a purchase of emission credits by the Netherlands from New Zealand. I see no point in discussing this transaction at length, because I happen to consider it absurd. The money that was used to buy these credits should have gone to various firms in the Netherlands so that they could invest in CO_2 suppression and energy efficiency, and if that was not sufficient, then steps should have been taken to obtain more funding, since carbon suppression is a public good. Even better, the government of the Netherlands could have refrained from some of its least productive spending in order to help finance this and other projects. However, at some point in the future, a transaction in emission credits might turn out to be even more preposterous, because it could be carried out via an intermediary such as a broker. In other words, an organization such as NordPool — or even NordPool Itself — might be able to pocket a few million dollars every month because some politician or civil servant elects to carry out his country's carbon suppression business with the aid of a market that should never have been established, instead of just picking up a telephone or logging onto the Internet.

The Swedish minister of industry has just announced that Swedish firms that are heavy users of energy will have their energy taxes reduced if they take steps to become more energy efficient. Although the minister or his advisors may not understand the significance of this arrangement, I think that it can be interpreted as an (elementary) technology based approach to CO_2 suppression, and a sensible alternative to emissions trading. (*But note: although it makes sense to me, it does not make sense to the bureaucrats of the EU, since they do not intend to allow any tax adjustments of a non-general nature!*) In addition, the Swedish government could assist in this endeavor by restarting the nuclear reactors in the south of Sweden that were closed, while at the same time making realistic plans for another large facility that makes full use of the latest technology. If these things were done, then whatever commitments that Sweden has made for reducing CO_2 will be completely fulfilled without having to utilize the services of socially retrograde organizations of the NordPool variety, because nuclear installations permit enormous gains to be made in the reduction of CO_2.

Some readers of this chapter may not be satisfied with the manner in which I have approached emissions trading — i.e., comparing it to the financial side of electricity deregulation. I have heard from several readers, and would be genuinely overjoyed if they appeared in Uppsala for the purpose of ventilating their objections in an open forum. Among other things, I would make it clear to those ladies and gentlemen that the directors of large energy intensive companies in Sweden — despite their sincere preferences for market-based solutions, and the large salaries and bonuses that these often mean — are unyielding in their insistence that emissions trading is one of the worst ideas ever hatched, and may cause irreparable harm to both producers and consumers. This is sufficient cause for me to denigrate what the prominent New Zealand economist Owen McShane calls a "pseudo market" whenever it is possible.

At this point some algebra might be useful, but since I prefer more readers to less, that departure can wait until a later contribution. It might be argued, though, that what we are dealing with here is so obvious and so elementary that no algebra is necessary, although apparently I failed to convince one of my former mathematical economics students that he should accept the above assertions at face value. The Swedish government plans to issue one group of energy companies emission permits for 250,000 tonnes of CO_2 per year. The emissions from these companies were 450,000 tonnes last year. The implication thus is that if they want to produce the same amount this year as that in last year, they will have to purchase from somewhere permits giving them the right to emit about 200,000 tonnes of CO_2. I hope that I do not have to explain that this is equivalent to a tax on those companies, and as we know from elementary and intermediate microeconomics textbooks, the tax will be divided between these producers and the persons who purchase energy from them — depending upon the elasticities of supply and demand curves. Of course, consumers who use the services of these firms could avoid increased electricity prices by spending next winter on the rim of the Kalihari or in exotic Guadacanal, or if that option is too expensive they could try wearing thick fur underware and fur-lined baseball caps indoors, but despite the proven ability of the Swedish electorate to accept all sorts of nonsense from their political masters, I suspect that they will soon learn that emissions trading has a number of disadvantages.

4. Kyoto and Nuclear

At this point it might be useful to say that the present section will be brief, because the word "nuclear" tends to diminish the enthusiasm of many readers and potential readers. I would like for everyone to know, however, that as far as I am concerned, mastadon talk-shops of the Kyoto and Rio variety should not take place if the intention is to ensure that useful answers will be obtained for dealing with what might turn out to be the major environmental challenge of modern times. Instead, I believe that it is much more efficient to handle this issue at the highest political level, with heads of state and the executives of organizations such as the United Nations and OECD making the key decisions.

I have no doubt at all that sufficient financial resources can be mobilized to put into place optimal emission suppression and energy efficiency programs. The energy and environmental "commissions" of the European Union should also be involved in this endeavor, even if up to now they have proved to be oblivious to conventional economic logic, and even though it might also happen that in some future perfect world, Europeans might come to their senses and vote this illogical undertaking out of existence. (Among other things, the EU is in the process of sponsoring an economically senseless program for the deregulation of natural gas. It also appears that European fund managers have launched what the *Financial Times* has labeled an "unprecedented attack" on Brussels, which evidently was provoked by the unbelievable incompetence of officials who are charged with reshaping the European financial scene.)

Whenever I become involved with discussions of this kind, I always begin with the statement by Donald Johnson, a former Secretary General of the OECD, that greenhouse gas emissions are "putting the world on a fast track to unhealthy global consequences for future generations". He goes on to say that, "if we are to hand on to future generations a planet that will meet their needs, as we have met ours, it can only be done by incorporating the nuclear option". This is not what many persons want to hear, which is probably why it was largely ignored at Kyoto. Besides, it should be clear that a world containing 8–10 billion human beings who are recklessly consuming whatever fossil fuels that are still available will not be an especially pleasant place for the readers of this humble paper, regardless of any gratuitous brainwashings to which they have or will be subjected about the utility of an immediate mass deployment of windmills and solar energy. Eventually these and other "soft" energy options will have an important role to play in a new energy economy, but not yet. It might also be appropriate to suggest that when the time comes to exploit these items, an effort on the scale of the "Manhattan Project" may be in order.

Similarly, the National Research Council of the United States once stated that environmental hazards were carrying our planet into "largely unknown territory". To this Jean-Claude Charrault of the Directorate General for Energy of the Commission of the European Communities added "...the decisions we take now (and those already taken) will affect our children, grandchildren, and great grandchildren for many generations. We've got to get it right".

Getting it right includes recognizing that a good environment is too important to be reduced to the status of a prize in a lottery, and by extension it is a waste of valuable time to pay attention to *chic* algebraic demonstrations designed to obtain research grants for their authors, but with no application to the real world. *It means standards, and not compromises!* In May 1990, when an international panel of scientists warned that if the discharge into the atmosphere of large amounts of carbon dioxide, methane, etc. were not reduced by a substantial amount, unpleasant consequences were possible for the entire human race, the British Prime Minister at the time, Baroness Thatcher, immediately dissociated her government from the skepticism of the US government, and stated that if other governments did their part, Britain would attempt to stabilize its CO_2 emissions at the 1990 level by 2005. The German government also took a strong pro-environment stand on that occasion. Obviously, if everyone had done their part, the Kyoto circus would have been unnecessary, and we would already be well on our way into an economically optimal emissions suppression and energy efficiency future.

Nuclear energy can be thought of as necessary but not sufficient, and so it is wise to consider some "no-regret" measures that can be initiated in the near future, and which might generate substantial environmental benefits even if global warming turns out to be over-exaggerated. These include maintaining the rain forests (which may be capable of absorbing large amounts of atmospheric CO_2), developing strategies for diverting more greenhouse gases into acquifers and/or the oceans, centralizing and/or expanding research on such things as fuel cells, clean coal, energy storage, the utilization of CO_2 in the chemical and metal industries, and improving nuclear technology, while ensuring that this research and its application is adequately but not extravagantly financed. An *optimum* employment of wind energy should be promoted, which will probably mean much less than the amount being planned at the present time. I can also comment on why I have come to consider nuclear energy a "no-regret" option. This is provably the case for Sweden, because the high standard of living enjoyed by this country is largely based on cheap (nuclear based) power, as well as a high quality educational system that, to a considerable (but indirect) extent, was financed by an electricity-intensive industry.

Something that needs to be stressed is that many of the activities mentioned above are both socially and privately profitable, and not just because — as the government of Alberta (Canada) once pointed out — it is necessary to place a value on the environment. (This is a concept that possibly originated at the Stockholm Conference on the Environment in 1972.) In addition, as Cairncross (1992) has noted, making environmental improvements does not necessarily mean sacrificing economic growth. Sweden was once a perfect example of this before becoming a victim of a particularly deleterious species of globalism that can be attributed to joining the EU.

I would also like to suggest that many of the persons attending conferences like those at Rio (with its 25,000 delegates) and Kyoto (with its 2500) were not the least bit serious about doing something positive to reduce global warming: *serious people would have insisted upon immediate action, and would not have accepted a 10-year lapse before a measure as unavailing as emissions trading was installed*! What many of them wanted more than anything else was a ticket to attend the next global warming jamboree. With certain exceptions they were the kind of individuals who are incapable of comprehending the subtler aspects of global warming, and the same is true of many energy "experts" lounging about the offices of the EU headquarters in Brussels, or so-called "researchers" at several environmental establishments in Sweden: places that are best described by George Orwell's phrase *"systems of indoor welfare"*.

Shortly after the Kyoto meeting, Professor Michael Hoel — winner of the 1996 IAEE award for outstanding contributions to energy economics — summed up his many theoretical papers on the topic of emissions trading by making it clear that only under "ideal" conditions are marketable permits capable of obtaining the desirable results. Unfortunately, it can also be shown that even under ideal conditions, marketable permits might be a sub-optimal policy measure; however, regardless of what has or could be shown, Hoel's results were completely ignored. In these circumstances, it is easy to understand why it is impossible to eliminate the gross misunderstandings about emissions trading that circulate at the highest levels of many governments.

Unless I am mistaken, it is the hypocrisy and posturing by many self-serving "experts" that is one of the reasons why the government of President Bush is so cavalier in its approach to the Kyoto Protocol, although attention is not usually paid to the fact that the emphasis on emissions trading was mainly the work of the US government, which later ignored its handiwork and denounced the protocol. Of course, if the protocol had made genuine economic and political sense, then there is no evidence that the President would be unwilling to give it his support. After all, it was his father who — when occupying the same office — signed into existence the Framework Convention on Climate Change, which is the instrument that initiated the process leading to Kyoto.

5. Final Comments and Conclusions

Because of many uncertainties, climate warming is not an easy problem to approach, but in some respects a partial solution is already available. This turns on a steady and systematic attack on all fronts that takes particular care to reduce emissions and improve energy efficiencies. More attention should also be paid to what I have called "no-regret" measures or policies. Here it can be suggested that more hydrogen and ethanol could make economic sense even if heavy subsidies are necessary to initiate the process, regardless of the expected or actual outcome of climate warming.

As it happens though, recent Swedish governments have demonstrated an unprecedented willingness to accept a great deal of pseudo-scientific wish-thinking, the result of which could drive more Swedish firms out of the country, raise unemployment, and by reducing the tax base, make it more difficult to finance the public-good components of carbon suppression and energy efficiency. Why did this happen? The answer is an unhealthy and, to some extent, desperate love of airline tickets to romantic places (to paraphrase a passage of the marvelous song "These Foolish Things"). To this can be added an intensive adoration of expensive meals in these romantic places in order to freshen up after the boredom of insipid meetings which treat various topics that are enigmatic to most Swedish civil servants and politicians — and the same is true with their drowsy counterparts from other countries. There is also the thrill of having this travel and dining paid for by unalert taxpayers who have allowed themselves to be convinced that by indulging glib bunkum, their economic and social futures will be improved.

In Peter Bernstein's brilliant book, *Against the Gods* (1996), he goes into great detail about how risk and uncertainty have influenced human history. He comes to the conclusion that in modern times the development of insurance and derivatives markets have helped rational persons to deal with this central problem of modern life. But on the other hand they have also tended to make many decision makers in the political world overly comfortable with uncertainty, and thus unable to analyze the kind of dangers that might be associated with, e.g., erratic climate movements. There is also the question of whether these decision makers possess enough mental firepower to understand the catastropic results that wrong decisions can bring about. Here in Sweden this is the situation with the EU, although consequences are probably milder than would be experienced with a climate disaster. With the EU we are dealing with near certainties, and one is that the financial and social consequences of the mistake that was made in becoming involved with this enterprise will be quite evident to a great majority of the residents of this country in the not too distant future.

Some years ago in Australia I participated in a discussion about climate warming in which I suggested that climate turmoil could easily result in political turmoil, and as a result even social and economic elites might find themselves in the danger zone. I also suggested that while there might be a great deal of (science) fiction associated with environmental matters, it may not be a good idea to spend too much time entertaining the arguments disseminated by various skeptics — and this is true even if it turns out that they are correct. As I mentioned in Chapter 1, these persons seem to have confused global warming with a global tour by some rap artist that you can avoid simply by not buying a ticket; however, with global warming, you get a ticket whether you want one or not, and even worse, you might have to use it.

Everything considered, it makes sense to give some attention to a "no-regret" type scenario sketched by John Jennings, chairman of a Shell subsidiary, at the World Energy Congress in 1995, which among other things said that "We have to start to prepare for the *orderly* transition to new, renewable forms of energy...while sustaining secure supplies of conventional energy as the world economy hopefully continues to expand".

Key Concepts

anthropocentric	emissions trading
Climate Group	faith-based
CO_2	fuel cell vehicles
Copenhagen Consensus	global warming
derivatives markets	greenhouse effect

hybrid
Leipzig Declaration
liquidity
Manhattan Project
no-regret measure

NordPool
oil optimists
PIUS
risk aversion
SECURE

Questions for Discussion

1. Not being a scientist, I call my position in the climate debate "faith-based". Exactly what do I mean, and how do you feel about this issue?
2. Is the "Copenhagen Consensus" a real consensus? What is this all about?
3. The anti-climate warming booster club seems to contain a number of celebrities. Who are these people, and what are they after?
4. On the basis of reading this and other books, and this chapter, what do you think about wind, ethanol, nuclear, and especially hydrogen?
5. Suppose that you had been given the job of organizing the Kyoto Conference. How would you have gone about it?

Bibliography

Baltscheffsky, S. (1997). "Världen samlas för att kyla klotet". *Svenska Dagbladet* (Stockholm).

Banks, Ferdinand E. (2004). "Beautiful and not so beautiful minds: an introductory essay on economic theory and the supply of oil". *OPEC Review*, 28(1): 27–62.

——— (2001). *Global Finance and Financial Markets: A Modern Introduction.* London, New York, Singapore: World Scientific.

——— (2000). *Energy Economics: A Modern Introduction.* Boston and Dordrecht: Kluwer Academic.

——— (1987a). *The Political Economy of Natural Gas.* London, New York, Sydney: Croom Helm.

——— (1987b). "The reserve-production ratio". *The Energy Journal*, 8(2): 147–151.

——— (1974). "A note on some theoretical issues of resource depletion". *Journal of Economic Theory*, 9(2): 238–243.

Bernstein, Peter (1996). *Against the Gods.* Chicago: Wiley.

Cairncross, Frances (1992). "Corporate environmentalism". *Colombia Journal of World Business*, 28(3/4).

Easterbrook, Gregg (1997). "Cleaning up". *Newsweek*, July.

Farrell, Alexander E. and Lester B. Lave (2004). "Emissions trading and public health". *Annual Review of Public Health*, 25: 119–138.

Gelbspan, Ross (1997). *The Heat Is On*. New York: Addison-Wesley.

Goodstein, David (2004). *Out of Gas: The End of the Age of Oil*. New York and London: Norton.

Hansen, James (2004). "A paradox in the notion of human-made global warming". *Scientific American*, March.

Harlinger, Hildegard (1975). *Neue Modelle fur die Zukunft der Menshheit*. Munich: IFO Institut Fur Wirtschaftsforschung.

Hoel, Michael (1991). "Global environmental problems". University of Oslo (Seminar paper).

Immordino, Giovanni (2003). "Looking for a guide to protect the environment: the development of the precautionary principle". *Journal of Economic Surveys*, 17(5): 629–644.

Mork, Erling (2004). "Nordpool: a successful power market in difficult times". *IAEE Newsletter* (Second Quarter).

Stipp, David (2004). "Climate collapse". *Fortune*, 9 February.

Victor, David G. (2001). "Climate of doubt". *The Sciences*, 41(2): 18–23.

Yohe, Gary W. (1997). "First principles and the economic comparison of regulatory alternatives in global change". *OPEC Review*, 21(2): 75–83.

CHAPTER 10

AN ENERGY MESSAGE FOR THE 21ST CENTURY

"On every ship there is somebody who doesn't get the message"
— US Navy adage

Many years ago I had the opportunity to ask the late Sir John Hicks — who had recently received the "Nobel Prize" in economics — why he had such a great faith in neoclassical economics, when it was clear to me that certain assumptions which were ubiquitous in mainstream academic economics were questionable. The principal items that I was thinking about were rationality and information — that is, the unspoken assumption that there was always enough information available to make the kind of rational choices that would maximize the profits of producers and utility (i.e., satisfaction) of consumers, given the resources at their disposal. Despite his obvious offence at being accosted with my question, Sir John informed me that without this premise, a systematic economic theory could not be constructed. I waited until I was outside to shake my head and laugh, because it was clear that his concept of economic theory had little or nothing to do with the world in which both he and I had to make our way.

Someone has called the present century the energy century, and on the surface this designation may well be correct. I do not believe that I have used that expression in this textbook, however, because saying "The Energy Century" makes it sound as if we are facing an energy future that we will have a difficult time comprehending, and which will give rise to problems that are excruciatingly difficult to solve employing traditional means. In reality, if the decision-makers and their foot soldiers make a greater effort to be more rational, were less inclined to welcome with open arms the questionable information and expertise coming their way, and did not hesitate to reject the neo-classical fairytales fabricated by Professor Hicks and his devotees, the energy challenge could be met in style.

For example, serious students of energy economics no longer want off-the-cuff assurances that there is "plenty" of oil in the crust of the earth. Of course there is plenty, but unfortunately we have reached a point in human history in which plenty may not be enough. Instead it is necessary to become aware of and eventually be provided with the kind of technology and procedures that will enable us to make a smooth adjustment to any traumatic energy shocks that may unexpectedly appear, which in turn assumes that this technology will be used correctly and to the optimal extent. Here I can mention the guarantees that the US government now seems prepared to give energy companies in case their nuclear investments encounter excessive bureaucratic or legal hinders.

Among the persons insisting on an expanded governmental presence in energy matters are Frederick W. Smith, chairman, president, and CEO of Fed Express, and General P. X. Kelley, formerly commandant of the US Marine Corps. They are co-chairmen of the Energy Leadership Council in the United States, and they have made it clear that they are not impressed by the opinion of many of their colleagues that energy is something for the private sector, the market, to exclusively manage. Quite simply, they do not believe that the market is capable of dealing with potential disaster scenarios. As they have noted, each year the United States employs enormous military resources to protect the chronically vulnerable oil production and distribution network. This constitutes an unacceptable burden on the economy, and so they recommend a fundamental shift in the US energy policy in order to prevent the kind of economic and social calamity that could follow in the wake of a very large (and sustained) increase in the price of, e.g., oil.

In July 2006, leaders of the eight largest industrial countries in the world, the G8, met in Saint Petersburg to consider the various ramifications of what they called "energy security". As pointed out by Martin Rees, president of the Royal Society and professor of Cosmology at Cambridge University, the results were not spectacular, even if those ladies and gentlemen were inclined to accept the prediction of the International Energy Agency (IEA) that global demand for energy will rise by more than 50% in the next 25 years (and in addition annual energy-related emissions of carbon dioxide (CO_2) will be 52% higher in 2030 than in 2003). On most occasions I ignore forecasts of the IEA; however, of late I have come to the conclusion that even if not especially accurate, these prognostications can be useful when on the pessimistic side, because a heavy dose of pessimism might result in elected officials and their experts ultimately making greater efforts to choose optimal policies — something that they would ordinarily fail to do in the light of the illogical optimism to which they are occasionally exposed.

The IEA claims that by 2030, 80% of world energy demand will be met by fossil fuels, while nuclear, hydro, biomass, and waste will provide 17%. Renewables such as geothermal, solar, and wind energy that are popular with aggressive environmentalists will supply less than 2%. One of the arguments in this book, and elsewhere, is that this is an unacceptable mix, and not just because it implies that environmental goals cannot possibly be met. Given a choice, the leading exporters of oil and gas are no longer prepared to court the favor of the larger importing countries if it means having to satisfy their rapidly growing demand for motor fuel at bargain basement prices. Needless to say, miracles are expected from things like technological improvements and increased investment (spurred by higher petroleum prices), but as yet these miracles are scarce. An important commentator recently said that there is still an enormous amount of oil that new technology will find, which is probably correct, however my knowledge of oil discovery rates and the likely behavior of the major oil producers makes it clear to me that when considered in the light of future demand, this "enormous amount" will be insufficient.

Mr Rex Tillerson, CEO of ExxonMobil, recently assured a large conference in Norway that there are sufficient supplies for decades to come, thanks to new technology, increasing production from existing oil wells and extending the frontier for new oil exploration into even deeper water. He thinks that we underestimate the potential of technology, whereby he probably means people like myself, but I am quite satisfied that I am on the right track where this topic is concerned. The media in the United Kingdom frequently reports that the North Sea oil and gas industry has 30–40 years of prosperity left, but this is a very misleading contention, because there is a tremendous difference between prosperity and a large quantity of oil! If an earthquake destroyed the large shopping mall would near the neighborhood in Uppsala where I live, but the next day a large trailer that offered a wide selection of Thai food and pizzas appeared in the place where this mall was located, they would undoubtedly experience a high prosperity, but the many persons living near the former mall would continue to be greatly inconvenienced. Moreover, although the mall could be rebuilt in a short time, the mostly exhausted North Sea oil fields will probably not be restocked for a few million years, despite the "prosperity" of the firms feasting on the remains of those once impressive assets.

The amount of oil reserves discovered every decade has been falling for at least the last half century, and at the present time only one barrel of conventional oil is being located for every three or four consumed. Even more important, the discovery of conventional oil peaked about 1965, and 1980 was the last time that discovery matched consumption. This is the kind of information that everyone reading this book needs to have at hand when confronted with crank arguments as to why the global oil production will never peak. It is also useful to cite Chris Skrebowski's observation that of the 18 largest oil deposits, 12 are in decline, and to remember that while the much heralded deposits of unconventional oil (i.e., heavy oil and oil from tar sands and shale) may change the reserves picture, their effect on production will not be decisive for many years. Another heavyweight where this subject is concerned is the director of the French oil major Total. He insists that with luck global production can be raised to 100 mb/d from the present 85 mb/d, but *not* the 120 mb/d promoted by the IEA and the USDE. See also the web publication *Energy Politics*, edited by Jenny Considine.

Let me put it this way: many claims about unconventional and new oil are "hype", or worse. Of course, even if this was not true, you can be certain that some of the major oil exporters — and definitely Saudi Arabia — are not going to export as much oil as the IEA and USDE say that they will. Why should they? Would you if you were in their place?

Even more discouraging, Professor Rees suggests that the governments of the main industrial countries are not facing up to the "huge" energy challenges that he feels are ahead, in that their Research and Development (R&D) budgets are inadequate. What he does not say is that many important politicians no longer have any real influence over the destinies of the countries for which they are theoretically responsible, and very often they do not want any. What they want are plane tickets to high-profile conferences where they can bask in the presence of bona-fide movers and shakers.

1. More Aspects of World Energy and the 21st Century

"Seek truth from facts"
— Deng Xiaoping

Most of us know something about what is going to happen on the world energy scene during the 21st century. Conventional oil and probably conventional natural gas will eventually become very scarce, although we do not know exactly when, while the transition to renewables and unconventional energy sources will intensify. In addition, nuclear energy will see a new dawn. In a world which may contain 10 million people before the New Year's Eve parties begin in 2099, the energy in uranium is going to be invaluable. On this point I suggest examining an article by Sutherland in *EnergyPulse* (2006), and equally as important, the many comments that followed his contribution, to include those with another point of view.

In this long section, I will attempt to summarize in a non-technical form several of the arguments presented earlier in this book, and elsewhere. To a considerable extent this section originated in my reaction to some of the papers and comments made at the 1997 meeting of the British Institute of Energy Economics (BIEE), where one of the main themes was the imminent appearance of scientific miracles that we are capable of radically transforming the energy landscape. Somewhat later, at the 1999 international conference of the IAEE in Rome, this kind of London wine-bar gossip was supplemented by enthusiastic references to the "freeing of electricity markets". As it happens though, in Norway and Sweden, the deregulation/re-regulation of the electric market can best be described as an enormous deception foisted on those unlucky citizens who happen to be on the customer end of the distribution system. Here I want to repeat a mantra that is never far from surfacing in my lectures and talks, which is that electric deregulation has failed, is failing, or will fail everywhere except possibly in centers of luxury such as Monaco or Dubai, where ratepayers are mostly without interest in their electric bills. More on this topic will be found in the last section of this chapter.

In this book, and elsewhere, considerable attention has been paid to the Kyoto conference on global warming — or COP 3, to give it its official title (which means the Third Conference of Parties to the UN Framework Convention on Climate Change). Although I realize that they could be mistaken, I have decided to accept both the research and gut feelings of the more than 90% of legitimate climatologists who say that trouble is ahead if something is not done about anthropogenic (i.e., man-made) sources of carbon dioxide. And it is probably well over 90%, because an overwhelming percentage of those who work the other side of the street, and put their name on this-or-that petition disclaiming global warming, have no authentic scientific background, by which I mean that they would hardly qualify to teach introductory courses in physics and chemistry at Boston Public.

However, I want to emphasize that it does not make the slightest difference if the more-than-90% is completely wrong, while the other group is completely right. Confronting an increase in global warming of any extent with a more environmentally friendly energy economy is the correct strategy, regardless of the actual outcome, although here two things should be kept in mind. The first is that energy is the driving force of the global economy — the medium that puts the world's industries in motion. Despite what some people believe, they would not want to inhabit an energy constrained society if they knew what that really entailed. In addition, as we learned in elementary game theory, whenever there are elements of common interest in potential conflict situations, and cooperation is feasible, attempts at cooperation should be resorted to as soon as possible, and not after the alarm bells start ringing. As a result, voters should give some thought to excluding from the decision-making process those players who are uninterested in cooperation having to do with matters of this nature. Here some advice of Aristotle might be relevant: it is impossible to be ethically good in the most comprehensive sense without being in possession of what he called "practical wisdom", which is the ability to see things as they really are.

More on the great world of oil

In 1980, the Stanford Energy Modeling Forum invited 10 leading oil forecasters to demonstrate the virtuosity of their computer models, and if they had no models the virtuosity of their thinking. According to *Business Week* (10 November 1997), the average forecast for 1997 among the six forecasters responding with predictions was $98/b. It also claimed in the same article that as recently as 1991, experts were predicting a 1997 oil price of

$45/b, as compared to the value in the vicinity of $20 which prevailed at the time.

In the late 1970s the Swedish newspaper *Dagens Industri* published a more extensive review of forecasts. The mean forecast for the turn of the century was $75/b. For example, Dr Armand Hammar — the CEO of Occidental Oil — gave his estimate as $100/b. Somewhat later Dr Michael Lynch of the Massachusetts Institute of Technology (MIT) assured interested parties that oil prices cannot rise because technology will always overwhelm depletion. In his words: "Oil-price forecasters make sheep seem like independent thinkers".

By "sheep", I suspect that Michael meant persons like myself, and if not it does not matter, because others have called me much worse. Although some readers of my oil book came to the conclusion that I also forecast an oil price of $100/b, this is probably untrue. The confusion is probably due to the fact that I have always emphasized that an unexpected shortage of energy, and oil in particular, would jeopardize the global macroeconomy: this is a certainty regardless of the pseudo-scientific bunkum that we encounter in seminars on macroeconomics. As geologist Craig Bond Hatfield (1997) notes: "It is better to recognize the impending reality of genuine shortage, and to prepare for it now. If we wait for oil shortages to arrive, as we did in the 1960s and 1970s, we shall once again experience greatly accelerated inflation, a serious reduction in economic growth, and strain on the global monetary system". Given that the exports of the major oil exporting countries rose by as much between 2002 and 2005 as they did between 1973 and 1981 (measured in 2005 dollars), we have every reason to suspect that the global monetary could be easily overstrained if the wrong kind of events takes place in certain parts of the world.

Normally, it would be unnecessary to prolong this discussion, since as compared to the scepticism prevailing when Hatfield published his paper, a large number of prominent geologists are now predicting in public an escalating oil price, just as any number of corporate high flyers are predicting the same thing in private. There is constant talk about how important the production of Saudi Arabia is to the oil importing world, but between now (2006) and 2015, just the global *increase* in demand for oil could be well in excess of the *total* present production of that country, even if they raise their output by the promised 2–2.5 mb/d (to 12–12.5 mb/d).

In light of the information available in the 1970s, an oil price forecast of $100/b made at least as much sense as predicting a 1998 oil price that turned out to be lower than the (ex post) price of a barrel of Coca Cola. In fact, if executives like Dr Hammar and the top management at the oil majors had listened to academic celebrities like Professor Milton Friedman when formulating their exploration and production scenarios, oil might indeed be at the $100/b mark today, and the main oil importing countries would be breaking apart at the seams, both economically and socially.

I have made it clear elsewhere that right or wrong, the judgment of highly trained climate scientists should be considered of greater value than that of itinerant dilettantes where global warming is concerned. Similarly, I have always considered it appropriate to ignore the commentary of sceptical economists on substantive matters relating to the production of oil, and this is particularly true now that a majority of the geological elite consider a production peak a certainty, and perhaps not much more than a decade away. (The relative arguments here can be found in Chapter 2 of this book.) As long as geologists appeared to be divided on this matter, I can understand how conference and workshop audiences would be moved to ecstasy by the stimulating phraseology of Professor Friedman, as well as the forecasting elite of certain "think tanks" with their talk about undulating production plateaux, but as things are now, I regard it as sensible to adhere to mainstream scientific traditions. Anything else is utopian fantasy blended with criminal stupidity, although it prompts me to paraphrase an interesting observation of Upton Sinclair: *It is difficult for a person to understand energy economics if their salary and career prospects depend on not understanding it!*

In the long run there is probably no reason to be dubious about the potential of technology, but at the present time, in the matter of oil, we are facing a kind of lottery (instead of a sure thing): technological progress on one side, and depletion and decreasing returns on the other, along with the unpleasant truth that lotteries have a way of not always presenting the desired result. Consider, for instance, the talk having to do with techniques for increasing the percentage of oil that can be extracted from a given deposit. In my opinion, these techniques are provably inadequate, and as a result the present 35% *average* rate of recovery (for global oil) is *not* going to reach the widely discussed (and longed for) 40% in the near future, nor perhaps in the distant future. Why not in the distant future? The answer here is that deposits are becoming leaner, and the conventional economic logic indicates that it is more difficult to increase the total extraction percentage when production is falling, or the *rate* of increase is declining. (See the articles of geologist Colin Campbell in every issue of *Energy Politics*.)

While ordinary citizens may not feel particularly risk averse when strolling into the Grand Casino in Monte Carlo with a few hundred francs to wager, most of these punters do not want their governments playing fast and loose with the energy futures of themselves and their children by joining irresponsible academic economists in theorizing that the price of a barrel of oil in 25 years may be in full decline. They also are becoming aware that technological marvels like three-dimensional seismology, and oil wells that would not disturb the filming of Baywatch because they could be put on the ocean floor near Santa Monica, are unlikely to reduce the huge and growing oil import bill of the United States — a situation that could have ugly consequences for exchange and interest rates in every country.

A topic that was mentioned earlier is substitutes for oil, such as ethanol and hydrogen. The director of the German auto maker Volkswagen has referred to ethanol as a lost cause, and hydrogen has also lost a great deal of its shine. It has been calculated that if the entire corn crop of the United States was turned into ethanol, it would only supply a few percent of the vehicle fuel being used. As for hydrogen, the technology appears to still be in its elementary stages. Hybrids appear to be the best bet just now.

Before finishing with this section, and as an introduction to the next, let me recommend the recent paper by Dennis Moran in *EnergyPulse* (2006), and also comments on this paper by Gould (2006), Kurtz (2006), Rawlingson (2006), Edward A. Reid and others.

Natural gas and coal

The chapters on natural gas and coal in this book are fairly straightforward, and in writing them I have received some excellent advice and information from Professor Eric Smith of the Energy Institute at Tulane University, and especially Mr Zach Allen. As a result, only a few comments will be offered below.

According to one of the editors of the widely read *Oil and Gas Journal*, Mr Bob Williams, "Because the hurdles in developing gas use infrastructure and in meeting future gas supply needs are much greater than they are for oil, any short-term supply shortfalls will have a relatively greater impact on markets than will oil supply shortages" (2003).

Everyone did not believe this, and a few of the doubters are named in that paper. Exactly what kind of hearing these ladies and gentlemen would get today is uncertain, because as things have turned out, their beliefs about the availability and price of conventional natural gas are palpably wrong. Perhaps the most interesting of these people is William L. Fisher, director of the School of Geosciences at the University of Texas, at Austin. The fact that gas production in the United States has peaked has gone unnoticed by that scholar, because his thoughts are focused on sources of "exotic" gas, and especially methane hydrates. As has been pointed out on several occasions by various observers, if only a few percent of the methane hydrate resources in the United States are producible, the entire US gas demand could be met for at least a century.

As Williams notes though, no knowledgeable source expects exotic gas sources to make a significant contribution to the gas supply of the United States or any other country for decades. By no one he excludes Professor Fisher and friends, who as with oil have completely abandoned reality. Once again I can suggest that if you want to know how the global gas economy will play out, it is only necessary to study the history of gas in the United States. As with oil, that country was a gas powerhouse, but at present is on the downward slope of its gas depletion curve, and this will not be reversed in the foreseeable future regardless of the amount of exotic reserves that have been located.

The attitude of people like Fisher and Michael Lynch toward unconventional gas resources is similar to that they have toward oil. They — and probably many others — do not consider some unconventional resources unconventional. The oil sands of Canada are an example, as is coal-bed methane where gas is concerned. I call this short-sighted, because the basic problem with both oil and gas is going to be price, and as a result of the comparatively modest quantities that will become available in, e.g., the next decade, the exploitation of unconventional assets will hardly have a significant effect on the price of oil and gas for many years, if ever.

When Williams wrote his article, the price of gas was still in the neighborhood of four dollars per million BTUs (= $4/MBtu), and this was considered high by millions of less well-off Americans. Since then gas has occasionally spiked to greater than $10/MBtu, although at the present time it seems to have stabilized at between $6/MBtu and $7/MBtu. These figures are considered a serious matter by a number of important civil servants in the United States, to include energy ministers and the former head of the Federal Reserve System, Alan Greenspan. They know that while it might be possible for many persons to greatly reduce their demand for motor fuel, they are often in no position to adjust the heating of their homes. Here I can quote Will Hutton (1998), who explains that electricity and gas are not commodities like designer dresses "where an interruption of supply poses no wider consequences: they are a precondition of successful modern life". The directors of gas-intensive firms have also taken notice, and some of them — e.g., petrochemicals in Louisiana — have served notice that they may have to pack their bags and depart for brighter energy horizons, taking with them many attractive jobs.

There is no shortage of references in this book to the environmental shortcomings of coal; however, it is not likely that these shortcomings will lead to a decrease in the steady growth of consumption of that commodity in the decades to come, given the increase in world population. In the United States and Europe, "clean air" legislation is becoming more prominent, and recognizable progress is also being made in China where this problem is concerned; however, taking demand (and production) into consideration, a great deal more will have to be done in order to convince certain observers that we are not on our way toward an environmental disaster.

According to the World Bank, the social cost of air pollution caused by the burning of coal in Beijing is almost equal to the cost of the coal itself. The same kind of observation is probably relevant for much of India and elsewhere. Worldwide, coal accounts for at least 40% of total carbon emissions from fossil fuel use, and this is likely to increase. There is a great deal of talk about "clean coal", but this is mostly a play for the gallery, because it happens that cleaning coal or storing CO_2 from its burning is too expensive an affair to be resorted to on other than a moderate level. This point is brilliantly elaborated on by Roger Arnold (2006) in a comment on an article by Valentine (2006). Another venture is FutureGen, or a very expensive coal power plant with *no* emissions of CO_2. Some work to obtain a semblance of this kind of installation is justified, although as a teacher of economics and finance my solution is a greater resort to nuclear energy, with some (or most) of the profits obtained being put into the cleaning of coal, because, like it or not, a great deal of coal is going to be used.

In some of the forums where environmental problems caused by coal use are mentioned, there are increasing references to game theory. I have attempted to play a part in this, because it is here that more attention needs to be paid to the work of John von Neumann who — in his prime — was referred to as "the best brain in the world", and whose work where the present topic is concerned can be summed up in the expression SAFETY FIRST! Amazingly, von Neumann's contributions are hardly known by many present day students of game theory, while at the same time both students and teachers have been led to believe that the most important figure in this discipline is the mathematician (and Nobel laureate in economics) John Nash. My position here is that if von Neumann had believed that Nash's version of the "Prisoner's Dilemma" was as important as many persons think that it is, he would have taken a few minutes to derive it, and perhaps included it in the famous book he wrote with Oscar Morgenstern, *The Theory of Games and Economic Behavior*. Whether Professor Erich Röpke examined this volume in detail is dubious, but his description of game theory as "Viennese coffeehouse gossip" is relevant to at least some of the work of Nash, and particularly as it was described in the Hollywood travesty "A Beautiful Mind".

Finally, before leaving this topic, let me note that a biofuel that is becoming popular in the United Kingdom is butanol, produced from sugar beet, and which according to present intentions is to be blended with gasoline and sold at more than 1200 service stations. It is considered more promising than other biofuels (e.g., ethanol) because it does not involve buying special automobiles or adapting engines. It also has a higher energy content than other biofuels, delivering 10% fewer miles per gallon than conventional fuels, as compared to the 30% for ethanol. It has been estimated by the UK Department of Transport that there is sufficient land available in the United Kingdom to satisfy a third of UK transport requirements from butanol by 2050, using sugar beet whose quality makes it unsuitable for export. I mention it because it may eventually be possible for these biological resources to play a greater part in power generation.

A point of interest here is that in the United Kingdom, the positive attitude toward butanol can be contrasted to a growing negative attitude toward wind in certain parts of the country. In the United States, wind farms were the second largest source of new power generation in 2005, although wind power is still less than 1% of the US electricity supply (as compared to 20% in Denmark). Apparently, in the United Kingdom the installation of 350–400 foot tall turbines is vehemently discouraged in some communities, while in the United States it is becoming clear almost everywhere that it is going to be impossible to avoid accepting wind energy, particularly if the endangering of migrating birds can be avoided. But even so, as noted early in this book, many observers consider wind energy badly overrated.

Not discussed above is this matter of "gas to liquids" (GTL). For this topic the reader is advised to read an article by Arnold (2006), and the accompanying comments.

Electricity, hydro and nuclear

The most visible topic in electricity at the present time is deregulation and/or privatization. For example, a large part of the financial press (e.g., *The Economist*) seems to still be claiming that the economic ills of the entire world are due to the failure to deregulate or privatize adequately, which is something like General Custer blaming the weather for his misfortunes.

Once I was of the opinion that it might be true that electric privatization and/or deregulation were perfectly in order in some (but definitely not all) highly developed countries, although it was not (and is not) true in those countries where the supply of electricity needed to be augmented by a very large amount in a fairly short time. In these latter (mostly developing) countries, taking advantage of the increasing returns to scale that characterize very large investments in integrated electric power generation and transmission systems could mean saving billions of dollars: dollars that should be spent on the low- and medium-level technical education that is probably the most crucial element in economic development, at least if the Scandinavian experience has any relevance.

At the Sixth Annual World Economic Development Congress in Hong Kong (1997), it was predicted that the world demand for energy could double by 2020 — or slightly after — since the growth in demand is increasing from an already high level. The main factors behind escalating demand were given as population growth, the population shift from rural to urban areas, and accelerating industrial and economic development, particularly in Asia. It was suggested that the amount of money required to meet the coming demand for electric power is somewhere in the vicinity of $3 trillion. This is not exactly walking-around-money, even though it could be on the low side, since I have heard it said that a serious electricity crisis could take place in the future. I have no real insight into how an electricity crisis would play out, although in a world with the population growth that is being experienced, virtually anything could happen.

At the same congress, the United Kingdom-based private power producer, PowerGen, presented a report claiming that there is likely to be a "convergence of electricity and futures markets" — whatever that means — allowing companies to "hedge against price volatility of a commodity which is impossible to store" (as reported by *The Asia Journal of Mining*, November/December, 1997). They are referring to electricity, I suppose, because it is not impossible that the person responsible for that opinion had little or no idea of what he was talking about.

In any event, many things can happen in the next 20 or 30 years, and so I will not say that the claim about hedging electric price volatility is impossible. What I will say is that almost everything written today about electricity futures and options is a naïve misrepresentation or, in most cases, a blatant falsehood. This is easy to prove, because if you examine the most sold and most praised textbooks in finance, and particularly those dealing exclusively with derivatives (futures, options, and swaps), you would hardly find a full page in any of them about the application of these derivatives to electricity markets. This is a non-subject, although there was a time when it was possible to find academics willing to ignore both what they learned and what they teach when asked by the gentlemen in the executive suites to sing the praises of electric deregulation.

Hydroelectricity is a subject that has interested me since my engineering studies. On the average, the least costly electricity in the world can be found in countries like Norway, Sweden, and Canada, where hydropower is especially important.

In China, some of the largest hydroelectric installations ever designed are now under construction, and will soon be on stream. When completed they will have a major role to play in keeping China on the road to becoming an industrial colossus. In 1992, the World Energy Council estimated that it was possible to increase the share of hydropower in world energy from 2% to 10%, but this seems unlikely for political reasons. Given the present concern about global warming, however, it seems wise to begin thinking about raising the output of hydropower from its present modest level, especially in those countries where large installations do not offend influential politicians and a large percentage of their supporters.

That brings us to nuclear energy. At the present time, 441 commercial reactors are in operation in 31 countries, and they produce about 17% of global electricity. Even governments that have been sceptical about nuclear seem to be changing their mind. Argentina is an interesting example, where new capacity and an upgrading of existing facilities may increase rated capacity by a factor of three.

An important dilemma with nuclear is that many voters are reluctant to trust their politicians, and undoubtedly with some justification. From an objective point of view, a great many new reactors should be constructed, and not just a few dozen: now that it is possible to build absolutely safe plants, a hundred or more should be in the building or planning stage at present. But this may be one of those very special situations where objective considerations should be subordinated to the popular feeling that we are not ready for a nuclear plant in every neighborhood. The optimal prescription therefore might be as many new nuclear facilities as are politically viable, and at the same time a large dose of renewables, even if the cost–benefit mathematics fails to justify the latter. Governor Arnold Schwarzenegger of California has signed a bill whose purpose is to encourage the installation of solar panels on one million California homes in the next decade, and while I am not sure that I would have signed this bill had I remained in California and been elected Governor, it may not be a bad idea. There is a great deal of friction that must be overcome in moving to a new energy economy, but it is worth initiating even if it costs more than what I might regard as the optimal solution.

One more point needs to be mentioned here. According to the director of the Russian nuclear administration, plans are being made to begin construction on two new nuclear plants every year, beginning in 2007, although if feasible, between 42 and 58 new reactors will be constructed up to 2030. Each of these is scheduled to have a capacity of 1150–1200 MW, and a life of 60 years. Among other things this means that while more gas might become available for export instead of being used to generate electricity domestically, Russia will become a serious contender for raw materials such as oil, copper, iron-ore, etc., because the electricity that will be supplied by these plants should greatly increase the rate of economic growth in Russia.

The Canadian energy scientist John Sutherland is in favor of expanded rail systems, with as much long distance transport as possible by rail. Electricity from many new reactors would be a major source of energy here. District heating would employ nuclear steam, while home heating would utilize electricity or steam, etc. The point is to obtain a smooth and expedient reduction in the use of oil (which in the long run is essential), and in addition there could be substantial environmental benefits. Where reducing the use of oil by increasing the use of electricity is concerned, this was the very effective policy resorted to by Switzerland during World War II.

It is also the case that this is the kind of program that we occasionally hear about in Sweden, and I feel sure that a large majority of voters and potential voters, as well as their legally elected and appointed representatives, would be willing to give it the necessary support if they had the opportunity; but for some reason their wishes are circumvented by a small environmentalist minority, led and supported by facile or naive politicians. This is perhaps why the famous mathematician Kurt Gödel, when he was in the final stages of taking his US citizenship, informed the judge who asked him if he was prepared to uphold the democratic ideals of his new country, assured the judge that democracy was unworkable. Fortunately, Gödel's sponsor was on hand to explain that Dr Gödel was joking, because otherwise he would have returned to Princeton as an Austrian rather than an American citizen. Nobody who knew Gödel, however, had ever heard him joking on that subject.

Professor Bert Bolin of the University of Stockholm is a meteorologist who enjoys talking about his integrity as a scientist. Some years ago (1988) he published an article in which he claimed that nuclear energy could not solve the problem of global warming. I agree, but it can *help* solve it, and I am sure that Bolin knows this as well as a huge majority of the world's physicists. But instead of saying it, he chose to put together a fiction about the availability of uranium.

The simple truth is that if the present rate of growth of energy demand continues for another two or three decades, then more nuclear-based power is indispensable. But even so, scientific research having to do with nuclear energy has been banned in Sweden. If this kind of thing happened in other countries, then in 30 or so years the fail-safe equipment using low-grade uranium or thorium that should be available will not be available, although by that time the voters might understand the economic benefit of comparatively inexpensive electricity, and many of them will insist on having it even if it means falling madly in love with the excessive use of plutonium. This is something that nobody in their right mind should look forward to.

The derivatives markets

Since this book already contains a long chapter on derivatives, very little needs to be said here. I would like to mention though that I played a small and, I hope, significant part in the popularizing of commodity derivatives markets, beginning with the book on the copper market that I wrote while at the United Nations Commission on Trade and Development (UNCTAD) Secretariat in Geneva, Switzerland. As a result there is no genuine evidence that I have ever been hostile to derivatives in commodity or financial markets. I enjoy teaching people about these markets, and studying them myself. In fact I enjoy it so much that I coined the phrase "finance is the physics of economics". Even so, my very negative attitude toward electric derivatives has raised a few hackles.

The futures markets in, e.g., oil and financial assets make a lot of sense, and not just because they increase what some people call "price visibility". If you remember your courses in microeconomics, you might also remember that uncertainty was assumed away: the agents making all those efficient and impressive consumption and production decisions never for a moment found themselves thinking that nothing is more certain in life than uncertainty, or that uncertainty is a good candidate for the central fact of life.

In the work of several great analytical economists, a theory has been offered that uncertainty could be handled if there was a complete system of futures and insurance markets. As bad luck would have it, a complete system is impossible, and even when we have futures markets that function magnificently, we cannot speak of anything close to a complete system. (One reason might be the absence of a continuum of maturities.) But even so, certain influential amateur economists in the media and the academy have told the television audience that sufficient "completeness" is available to provide the kind of price visibility and hedging possibilities that will make the world a better place.

The well-known result of this error is that a number of risk managers who peddled a misconception of this nature to various firms and consumers were eventually rewarded with pink slips or early retirement. They deserved this, perhaps, although more than a few of these persons were able to retire in luxury; but as to be expected, many of the households that bought this swindle found their access to the discos of Paris and the beach life of Portafino greatly reduced.

The Scandinavian spot and derivatives market for electricity (NordPool) has been pronounced a shining example for the entire world to emulate. In the case of Sweden, however, a country that may still produce electricity at the lowest cost in the world, it has been estimated to have one of the highest electric prices in Western Europe, and perhaps all of Europe and North America. What we have here is not just hypocrisy and falsification, but the more serious gratuitous failure of electricity consumers to protect their standard of living. The pipedreams about present and future electricity prices that Swedish households have been asked to accept by their politicians and the directors of electric generating firms cannot be supported by the most elementary and accessible economic logic, and I strongly doubt that even the most fanatical believer in free markets is willing to accept an arrangement in which he or she must pay outrageous electric bills in order to turn executives in the electric industry into millionaires. The most grotesque element in the Scandinavian picture is the Nordic Electric Exchange (NordPool), and its curse has been intensified by the Kyoto inspired introduction of emissions trading.

In looking for a statement to conclude this long section, I turn to the superb book of Earl Cook (1976) in which he says, "There is no reason to expect the transition from a low energy society to a high energy society to be irreversible. If the energy support of a high energy society fails, it must again become a low energy society. The great difficulty is that the low energy phase can be regained only at the expense of a degeneration in living standards and life-styles".

A degeneration in living standards and life-styles! Sounds pretty grim, doesn't it, although many of the young party-animals to whom I had the pleasure of teaching economics and finance in Stockholm and Uppsala would feel proud to inform anyone who inquired that they were willing and able to reduce their use of energy if it were for the general good. On the same occasion, though, most of them — and especially the finance students — would make it clear that they wanted and expected full employment, pensions, high quality healthcare and education for themselves and their families, "summer houses" near a beach, a very great deal of leisure that involved extensive foreign travel, public order, and interior temperatures high enough so that "pile caps" and padded dinner jackets did not displace Armani and Boetang creations in the more fashionable restaurants and discos. Defence was also occasionally mentioned; however, with the end of the cold war this is not so important, and in any event the Swedish military has been gutted in order to scrape together a few battalions for service somewhere on the rim of the Kalihari.

2. A Loose End: Option Value

I was tempted to place this section in an earlier chapter; however, I am very aware that option value is one of those topics that cause many persons to close their book before the *grand finale*. In any event, much of the option value literature is pedagogically confusing; however, the logic is quite elementary, and involves no more than realizing that if the environmental effects of today's investment and/or consumption activities are irreversible and uncertain, then we should think about ensuring that future options (i.e., alternatives/choices/preferences) are not foreclosed or unduly restricted by present actions — assuming of course that we are concerned about the future. This is a very simple concept — but even so much more important than any conclusions that can be drawn from the equations in the following discussion.

The way this problem is usually tackled is to calculate a sum of money that we would require in order to undertake a risky and irreversible project.

Put more formally, option value is sometimes described as the amount a risk-averse person would be willing to pay to prevent an irreversible investment taking place which involves a risk that cannot be avoided through conventional insurance. Of course, in the light of the above, this could be put another way: it is the amount that a risk-averse person would have to be paid (above a normal profit) to make this investment.

Option value is often — though not always — distinguished from *quasi-option value*, which is the amount that a person would pay for information (about future states of nature) when the outcome of a given investment or consumption activity is irreversible. The finer points of these two definitions will not be mulled over in this short discussion; however, I consider it appropriate to note my faith in the great majority of scientists who proclaim that the atmospheric environment should be kept as close to its present state as possible until adequate information is available about the costs *and* benefits of making large changes that for all practical purposes are irreversible.

The following algebra will derive a result that I first presented to a seminar at the Australian National University. I begin with the following diagram:

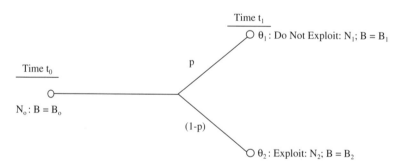

Figure 10.1.   States of the World and Decisions under Risk

(1) The possible states of the world are θ_1 and θ_2, with probabilities p and $(1 - p)$. θ_1 involves a situation in which the exploitation of an atmospheric asset results an unfavorable outcome, while the state θ_2 is favorable socially and/or economically. For example, an investment that (ex post) turns out to not cause any appreciable harm to the atmosphere.

(2) The social benefit (measured in money) from being in the two states are B_1 and B_2, as shown in the diagram. In addition $B_1 < 0$ (i.e., a loss), and $B_2 > 0$. The sign of B_0 can be considered later.

(3) N_0 is the *marginal* amount of the atmospheric asset exploited at time $t = t_0$. It is taken as unity, and so we have $0 \leq N_0 \leq 1$, but, e.g., the "1" could signify one million units of "something".

(4) We can now write an expression for the present value (= PV) of the *expected* social benefit realized because of the exploitation of an amount N_0 of the atmospheric asset. Here, it can be noted that the atmospheric asset might be "unpolluted" — or relatively unpolluted — air, or something similar, that can be "exploited" at t_0 by, e.g., investing in a new power plant that burns a fossil fuel. A *social* rate of discount "r" is applied to the *expected* benefit in period t_1 (which is the numerator in the second term on the right-hand side of the following equation). In some cases this can be taken to be the interest rate.

$$PV = B_0 N_0 + \frac{p B_1 N_1 + (1 - p) B_2 N_2}{(1 + r)}.$$

(5) *If* we find ourselves in the bad state then we choose N_1, while if we find ourselves in the good state, then we choose N_2. Something else that should be appreciated here is that whoever is making the decisions is risk neutral, otherwise the Bs would have to be expressed in "utility" rather than monetary units. We can also specify that $0 \leq N_1, N_2 \leq 1$, and soon we will discover what we should have for the sign of B_0.

(6) At this point the language becomes important. Given N_0, if $\theta = \theta_1$ (the bad state) results, then N_1 should be N_0: there should be no further exploitation of the asset, and irreversibility keeps us from making $N_1 = 0$. But if $\theta = \theta_2$, then we would choose $N_2 = 1 - N_0 = 0$, which is obtained by full exploitation of the (marginal) atmospheric asset in period t_0, or $N_0 = 1$. *Observe what is happening: we are thinking about how we should act now (i.e., at the present time) in dealing with the possible outcomes of a risky, irreversible situation.* This allows us to write the expression for PV as

$$PV = \left[B_0 + \frac{p B_1}{(1 + r)} \right] N_0.$$

(7) We see immediately from this expression that in order to have PV > 0 we must have $[B_0 + (pB_1/(1+r))] > 0$, or $B_0 > -[pB_1/(1+r)]$. B_0 *is the option value and it is positive, since B_1 is negative*! In looking at this expression we should be able to see why I once called it trivial, but something that is often missed (along with getting the sign of B_0 wrong) is that the larger the p and/or the smaller the r, the larger is the option value. For example, if we were thinking in terms of private enterprise, B_0 is the amount that the potential exploiter/investor would have to receive in order to undertake this particular risky project, in addition to the normal profit.

If we were thinking in a "social" sense, it is the amount that he would have to pay to the persons liable to be damaged by his investment, and who would be in a particularly bad situation because of the irreversibility of the arrangement. This makes sense because, for example, if r (the social discount rate) were put equal to zero, it means that whoever is making the decisions considers that *at the present time* the welfare of future generations should be valued as highly as the present (decision making) generation. This might have been viewed skeptically a decade or so ago because at that time almost everyone believed that, on the average, future generations would live in luxury as compared to the present.

There is some ambiguity associated with the above analysis; however, this is in the nature of academic economics, where for the most part practitioners deal with "models" rather than reality. The original presentation of option value many years ago had to do with transactors who were obliged to sell options, although had it been possible — which ostensibly it was not — they would have hedged against uncertainty by purchasing insurance. Needless to say, "efficient" markets for option transactions that are based on the possibility of *immense* climate changes are unlikely, nor is it conceivable that they will ever be available — despite the claims about "catastrophe derivatives" in various financial publications. On the other hand, institutions are supposedly coming into existence that will make possible the large-scale trading of emissions permits, but since *maintaining* the atmospheric environment is an important *public good*, it could be argued that a carbon tax is more appropriate than a lottery — given the ruinous outcome of the experiment with electricity deregulation. Put somewhat differently, we might be better off if, instead of working overtime to demonstrate their cleverness, economists and heavy-duty thinkers who are in a position to influence the high and mighty of this world would focus on prudence and clarity.

3. Final Statement: Sweden's Electric Deregulation Failure

> *"Who will carry the message?"*
> — *Ronald R. Cooke (2006)*

After reading the article of Ronald Cooke, I volunteered to carry the message, although as usual — regardless of the topic — any message that I carry is strictly mine, and usually has to do with oil or, as in the present case, electric deregulation. Someone else, though, who might be a good messenger is Mr Harry Lind who, in the (conservative) Swedish newspaper *Svenska Dagbladet* (11 September 2006), wrote the following: re-regulate for the sake of the citizens (i.e., ratepayers), industry and the country. And he is not alone. Deregulation in Texas (United States) was once called "the best in the world", but now Texans on the average pay more than most Americans — 13.33 cents/kWh in June 2006 as compared to the US average of 10.84 cents/kWh. See Weinberger (2007) for more bad news!

The former Swedish industry minister, who is a warm friend of deregulation, once said that Swedish electricity prices are going to climb to record levels. He was very right about that. In addition, according to that gentleman, the "hard competition" in the electric industry has favored consumers, but now — in his opinion — the postponing or canceling of physical investments due to the negative price developments resulting from this so-called competition must come to an end, and in order to finance new production capacity, electricity prices must escalate.

No matter what you believe or do not believe about deregulation in Sweden, it is impossible to accept that it has favored consumers. In fact, a main reason for deregulation was to enable Swedish firms to sell low-cost Swedish electricity to Germany, which had the highest electricity prices in Western Europe. And although many recent Swedish finance ministers can hardly claim that they possess an advanced knowledge of economic theory, they understood perfectly that the ensuing rise in domestic (i.e., Swedish) power prices meant extra billions of Swedish crowns in tax revenues due to taxes and assorted "fees".

I think that I have made some good decisions as to how I should buy electricity, but even so I am very annoyed by my electricity bills, and the same is true for colleagues who are a great deal more careful in this matter than myself. Some observers say that the high electricity prices of the past few years have not been due to deregulation, but a shortage of rain which has kept reservoir levels low, and thus reduced the output of hydroelectric installations. As it happens, however, on a recent occasion the water that provides a large part of the Swedish electricity reserve was turned into electricity and sold at a time when it was judged highly profitable for the now deregulated power companies, but which happened to be wrong for the country as a whole. (These companies were also not vehemently opposed to the closing of two nuclear reactors, because unlike their favorite politicians, they understood enough of the first course in economics to accept that when supply goes down price goes up, and when price goes up their salaries and bonuses also rise.)

Supply down, prices up, profits up, and instead of an end to "monopoly", the largest power company in the country is now in a financial position to undercut its competition in the distribution segment of the electric system, and eventually take over their customer base. When that happens, prices will accelerate in northerly direction.

Another interesting facet of the deregulation burlesque is that the electricity reserves have occasionally fallen to a record low level — perhaps as low as 7%, as compared to a 12–14% normal level. While this was taking place, the competition that Mr Industry-Minister was so proud of led to the five or six firms that produced almost 90% of the (wholesale) electricity in Sweden, gradually being reinvented as three firms.

Before continuing, let me say that speaking as a student and teacher of economics and finance, I have nothing at all against this change in the composition of the electric sector. However, I am unable to be so blasé about those aspects of the Swedish deregulation picture in which some of the lowest cost electricity in the world drastically increased in price as a result of consumers allowing themselves to be convinced that it was beneficial to disregard their self-interest in the name of "competition", without being informed of the disadvantages that could result from this transition.

Facing the music

For the past few years I have been attempting to spread some useful information about certain existing and proposed deregulation experiments. It seems, however, that my uncompromising approach to this topic has made me lose the sympathy of many persons who attend the seminars and meetings where I carry out this important work.

Frankly, this does not bother me at all. One reason is because at a recent international meeting of the International Association for Energy Economics (IAEE), members of the electric deregulation booster club kept a low profile. Even Professor David Newbery, chairman of the Department of Applied Economics at Cambridge University and once a leading deregulation theorist, failed to assure his audience that the day would soon arrive when they could luxuriate in one of the deregulated paradises that he was working so hard to create. As to be expected though, the many failures of electric deregulation have escaped the attention of Swedish representatives of the club, and so given the opportunity they continue to encourage the kind of foolishness that could result in huge economic losses for their country.

Professor Nils-Henrik von der Fehr (2002), of Oslo University, once wrote that the Nordic power sector reform has been a definite success so far. *Actually it has been a failure from the start, if you compare results with expectations, although an academic in Sweden who plays fast and loose with this description can say goodbye to research and travel money.* I am certain that Professor von der Fehr knows this as well as I do and the majority of people in Sweden, because he has the kind of analytical ability that many academic members of the Nordic deregulation booster clubs would work night and day to acquire if they were not overwhelmed by a gargantuan lack of self confidence. He knows a few other things too. In the same review he wrote:

"However, it is also true that in some respects the model has not been tested. Although over-capacity has been reduced, the market has never been really tight except, perhaps, this winter. Consequently, we do not actually know how the model will perform in such circumstances. Is the market mechanism flexible enough so that demand will be met and rationing avoided? As over-capacity is eroded, will new investments be forthcoming at the required rate? And will tighter market conditions — in combination with increased concentration — mean that market power, which has not really been an issue so far, becomes more of a problem in the future."

Market power is not a future problem. Because of deregulation, it is a problem *today* in Sweden and Norway, and almost certainly elsewhere. As for the over-capacity syndrome, this is something that I never really understood — largely because in the context of Sweden and Norway, it is not worth understanding.

Von der Fehr says that new problems emerge as the power industry develops, and regulators must maintain their "alertness" in order to adjust the model as required. On the basis of existing evidence, however, it could be argued that many regulators have no alertness to maintain.

As I like to emphasize, the only thing that is necessary to comprehend what is taking place in the great world of electric deregulation is an open mind. J.A. Casazza (2001), an engineer and president of the American Education Institute, claims that the annual cost of a comprehensive electric market restructuring in the United States would be about $28 billion. This may or may not be true, but regardless of the cost, what I find interesting is his contention that when restructuring was initiated in California, some engineers were required to sign confidentiality agreements that kept them from discussing the problems that were almost certain to emerge in a deregulated setting. Casazza also suggests that economists from some of the most prestigious universities in the United States have failed to fully comprehend the electric power industry. He believes that the economic theory used in restructuring the electric power industry is badly flawed.

The problem is not the theory, but the people using it. The theory would more than suffice if there were not, as US Congressman Peter De Fazio observed, "millions and billions" on the table; millions and billions for the Enrons of this world; thousands and tens of thousands for certain academics who pointedly ignore discussions on this subject in the wonderful microeconomics textbooks that are now available, because they feel that it is not in their interest to discover that electric deregulation is a crusade whose justification has a pronounced voodoo content. There is also a near-conspiracy to ignore or downgrade the historical evidence, which includes outright failures in California and Ontario (Canada), fiascoes in Alberta (Canada), Brazil, and Montana (United States), and an ongoing botch in Sweden, Norway, and South Australia. I can also mention outlandish price variability in some of the midwestern and eastern states in the United States, as well as in Australia; and lower reliability just about everywhere. Unexpected and painful outcomes have occasionally surfaced in the United Kingdom, Germany, and New Zealand, although in these regions we will have to wait until the inevitable decrease in physical investment (and increases in the cost of inputs such as gas) leads to the price rises that, hopefully, will bring consumers of electricity to their senses.

Goodbye to all that

When I began this section, I gave some thought to explaining in detail why NordPool (i.e., the Nordic Electric Exchange) is a superfluous departure, despite the ability of untruths and pseudo-science to give it an undeserved respectability. The reason I will not is because examining the background and interior mechanics of this elaborate deception requires more than the comparatively short time available in conferences or workshops, where I plan to recycle this discussion.

But even so, I am satisfied that making an informal case against Nord-Pool is no more difficult than doing the same thing with a considerable amount of the (physical) electricity trading in the United States, which the international business press has now revealed as a gigantic bluff. By the same token, the mainstream economics journals are surprisingly void of work on electricity derivatives. Electricity derivatives were first mentioned about 10 years ago, and since that time hundreds of papers on various types of derivatives have appeared in the mainstream scientific periodicals, but to my knowledge none about electricity. I have, however, seen a few pathetic contributions on deregulation in specialized reviews, and the situation is not much better in the energy literature. Of course, these materials have only a few readers, and so perhaps it makes no difference.

Not too long ago, liquidity problems caused the New York Mercantile Exchange (NYMEX) to delist its electricity futures and options contracts. If this renowned New York Exchange — which has enjoyed great success for decades — found it unprofitable to trade these particular assets, it seems presumptuous to assume that NordPool deserves to be regarded as a permanent component of anybody's electric market. For reasons alluded to in my previous energy economics and international finance textbooks (2000, 2001), the trading of electricity futures and options involves enormous practical difficulties (due to basis risk for futures, and excessive premiums for options), and this is exactly what NYMEX and, among others, the futures market in Sydney experienced. Contracts for differences are more useful, although for final consumers of electricity — households and businesses — it would be better if *all* electric derivatives were marginalized, and the old system for selling and buying power reintroduced.

According to the CEO of a major Swedish power company, the large industries in the country still purchase energy on a long-term basis, and so they do not have to face the curse of short-term pricing via NordPool that plagues households. Maybe so, but firms in Sweden are closing their doors because of power prices, and moving elsewhere. It must be admitted, though, that the closing of two nuclear reactors was a principal cause of this unfortunate situation.

Recently, in an editorial in the *Financial Times* (5 July 2004), a plea was made to "set energy free". The most interesting point here was the confession that "proponents of liberalization no longer have the carrot of price cuts to lure people on". Instead it was suggested that consumers should be grateful for a more "efficient" energy pricing.

Deregulation was sold to electricity consumers on the basis of assurances that electricity prices would decrease. As for "efficiency", in the popular mind this means price cuts, and if it means something else, then the less said about it the better. It also needs to be pointed out that in Sweden, also on 5 July 2006, it was finally recognized (in the largest morning newspaper in the country) that the success of electricity deregulation is a myth. Consumers and most distribution firms are losers. Generators have scored record profits, which they use to invest outside Sweden. The largest winner is the government (via both its taxes and equity position in, e.g., the power company Vattenfall). In the US deregulation in Virginia, Delaware and Maryland were described as a success story at a conference I once attended. The truth is that consumers are facing price rises of 100%, and the economies of these states might be weakened.

Given the bizarre mispricing that often occurs in NordPool, it is only the lack of sophistication of NordPool's customers that keeps the doors of this operation from closing and staying closed forever. It has been said that new types of financial assets might appear soon, both in Oslo and New York, and this may well be the case; however, these will hardly mean a great deal to ratepayers and their families. Let me assure everyone reading this that the most valuable risk management tools in the electric market are still long-term contracts in a regulated environment.

On this last point I conclude by mentioning that I once contributed a very unfriendly lecture to a workshop in Sweden in which electric deregulation had been praised to the high heavens by a California member of the deregulation booster club. Fortunately though, he had come to the wrong country to get his dance card filled out. An increasingly vocal majority of Swedes now understand that regardless of how much they may adore electricity deregulation, it has no affection for them. "At the mercy of forces that have no mercy", is how former Governor Gray Davis of California put it, referring to large, energy intensive firms as well as households and small businesses.

Key Concepts

basis risk	marginal cost pricing
biofuels	monopoly/ologopoly
butanol	NordPool
clean coal	NYMEX
derivatives	option value
distributors and wholesalers	"practical wisdom"
Energy Leadership Council	ratepayers
exotic gas	social cost vs. private cost
FutureGen	tar sands
G8	Viennese coffee house gossip

Questions for Discussion

1. If you were the director of a large power company and you heard that deregulation was on the way because "consumers" (or ratepayers) wanted more competition in order to reduce prices, would you laugh or cry? Explain in detail!
2. Brazil thinks that it will be possible to eliminate the import of oil by the end of 2006, mostly because of the large-scale production of ethanol. Do you think that the United States can do the same in the foreseeable future?

3. Few things are more profitable at the present time than owning large oil drilling rigs that can be used off in the Gulf of Mexico off the coast of Texas and Louisiana. Recently a large driller, Todco, was getting $104,000 a day for rigs in the Gulf of Mexico. As far as I can tell, however, they are not finding very much oil, but even so they do not expect that there will be a decrease in the demand for these rigs in the near future. Discuss!

4. Almost every day now we hear about how the tar sands of Canada, and in the not too distant future, the oil shale in the western United States will save the energy day for the United States Comment on this on the basis of what you have read in this chapter, book, and elsewhere.

5. Russia recently exported more oil than Saudi Arabia, which has usually been considered the unchallenged king of oil exports. Do you regard this as a sustainable arrangement? In addition, I say that Saudi Arabia will not export as much oil in the future as they sometimes claim that they will, and the same is true of Russia. What is your opinion here?

6. Sweden has closed two nuclear reactors, but even so it retains its position close at the top of the nuclear league, with more than 46% of electric energy having a nuclear origin. Explain this — even if it means that you must refer to Chapter 6. Distinguish between capacity and energy. Both Argentina and Finland, countries that are almost at the opposite poles of the world, are concerned about a possible energy shortage, and both have chosen nuclear instead of natural gas, although a great deal of gas may be in nearby regions. Discuss.

7. The algebra in the section on option value seems straightforward to me, but some persons do not like algebra. Explain what the issue is using words instead of algebra, and as an example discuss replacing Notre Dame cathedral in Paris with a fast food restaurant, taking care to note who would be involved by an arrangement of this nature.

8. The great David Hilbert said "We must know. We will know". After reading this chapter what do you think that we absolutely must know about the future energy supply if we are going to feel at ease?

9. The pricing of oil as explained in this book is different from the way that it was explained in your favorite microeconomics textbook. Explain!

10. People have tried to explain to me that nuclear electricity is exorbitantly expensive, while I say that the fact that almost a half of Sweden's electricity has a nuclear basis, while almost all of the remainder has a hydro basis, shows that nuclear is inexpensive — since the cost of electricity in Sweden, Norway, and Eastern Canada is the lowest in the world. How do you handle this topic? And if electricity in Sweden is so inexpensive to produce, what are households and energy-intensive firms complaining about?

11. For diligent students and former students of economics — The Nordic Electricity Exchange employs marginal cost pricing in determining the announced price of electricity. I call this a curse for the Swedish consumers of electricity. Explain. The emissions trading that Kyoto thinks will reduce the generation of CO_2 is another curse for local firms and households. Explain!

12. The outgoing chief of the Australian Central Bank says that the oil importing world will not have any problem dealing with oil at \$80/b. Is he right or wrong, and why? What about oil at \$100/b? Some observers say that a global peak of world oil production will not take place because of technological progress. What do you say about all this? How much oil would you export if you were the chief decision maker in Saudi Arabia? At BP?

Bibliography

Arnold, Roger (2006). "Comment on Valentine". *EnergyPulse* (www.energypulse.net).

———— (2005). "Will GTL nail the coffin lid on cheap NG?" *EnergyPulse* (www.energypulse.net).

Banks, Ferdinand (2001). *Global Finance and Financial Markets*. Singapore, New York, and London: World Scientific.

———— (2000). *Energy Economics: A Modern Introduction*. Boston, Dordrecht, and London: Kluwer Academic Publishers.

———— (1983). *Resources and Energy*. Lexington, MA: Lexington Books.

———— (1980). *The Political Economy of Oil*. Lexington, MA: Lexington Books.

———— (1974). "A note on some theoretical issues of resource depletion". *Journal of Economic Theory*, 9(2): 238–243.

———— (1972). "An econometric model of the world tin economy: a comment". *Econometrica*, 40(4): 749–752.

Bolin, Bert (1988). "Karnkraft löser inte klimat problem". *Svenska Dagbladet*, 8 September.

Casazza, J.A. (2001). "Electricity choice: pick your poison". *Public Utilities Fortnightly*, 139(5): 42–49.

Cook, Earl (1976). *Man, Energy, Society*. San Francisco: W.H. Freeman & Company.

Cooke, Ronald R. (2006). "Depletion has changed the PR script". *EnergyPulse* (www.energypulse.net).

Darley, Julian (2003). "The North American gas crisis". *Petroleum Review*, 57(681): 35–38.

Gould, Len (2006). "Comment on Dennis Moran". *EnergyPulse* (www.energypulse.net).

Harlinger, Hildegard (1975). *Neue Modelle für die Zukunft der Menschheit*. Munich: IFO Institut für Wirtschaftsforschung.

Hatfield, Craig Bond (1997). "Oil back on the global agenda". *Nature*, 387(6629): 121.

Hutton, Will (1998). "Darkness at the heart of privatization". *The Observer*, 8 March.

Kurtz, Ellen (2006). "Comment on Dennis Moran". *EnergyPulse* (www.energypulse.net).

Losekann, Luciano and Joanne Evans (2003). "Optimal power reform design". Paper for the 2003 international meeting of the IAEE, Prague, 3–5 June.

Moran, Dennis (2006). "Energy supply and price projections (parts 1 and 2)". *EnergyPulse* (www.energypulse.net).

Rawlingson, Malcolm (2006). "Comment on Dennis Moran". *EnergyPulse* (www.energypulse.net).

Saunders, Harry D. (1984). "On the inevitable return of higher oil prices". *Energy Policy*, 12(September): 310–320.

Soddy, Frederick (1933). *Wealth, Virtual Wealth and Debt*. New York: Dutton.

Sutherland, John K. (2006). "The inevitable nuclear resurgence, and the inevitable panic attacks". *EnergyPulse* (www.energypulse.net).

Valentine, Harry (2006). "Synthetic hydrocarbon production in a low-carbon economy". *EnergyPulse* (www.energypulse.net).

von der Fehr, Nils-Henrik (2002). "Comment on Lars Bergman". *Swedish Economic Policy Review*.

Wallace, Charles P. (2003). "Power of the market". *TIME*, 3 March.

Weinberger, Paul (2007). "Utility deregulation revisited — still a bad idea". *EnergyPulse* (www.energypulse.net).

Williams, Bob (2003). "Debate grows over US gas supply crisis as harbinger of global gas production peak". *Oil and Gas Journal*, 101(30): 18–25.

Wolak, Frank A. (2003)."Measuring unilateral market power in wholesale electricity markets". *American Economic Review*, 93(2): 425–430.

INDEX

Åre (Sweden), 289, 345

ABARE, 249
Abraham, Spencer, 29, 209
actuals, 341, 348
Adelman, Morris, 83, 124
Alaminos Canyon, 103
Alhajji, A.F., 114
Allen, Zach, 259, 417
American options, 372
American Petroleum Institute (API)
  number, 120
Anderson, Roger, 114
annuity formula, 317
anthracite coal, 232
arbitrage, 30, 223, 350
Arctic National Wildlife Refuge (ANWR),
  108
Argentina, 51
Armani and Boetang creations, 427
Asia-Pacific refining capacity, 123
Association for the Study of Peak Oil
  (ASPO or ODAC), 159
auction market, 241, 398
Australia, 31, 294
Australian Bureau of Resources and
  Energy, 249
Australian School of the Environment, 6

average rate of recovery (for global oil),
  416

Bärsebäck, 285
backwardation, 367, 369
Bailey, Ronald, 162
Baily, Jed, 48
Baker Institute, 96
Bakhtiari, Ali Samsam, 44
Bardi, Ugo, 45
Bartlet, Jed, 90
base load, 53, 248, 304
basis, 360, 368
basis risk, 72, 216, 222, 367, 368
bear, 341
Bell, Ruth Greenspan, 90
Berlin, Irving, 28
Bernstein, Peter, 405
bituminous coals, 231
Black–Scholes formula, 375
Black–Scholes option pricing formula, 73
Blair, Tony, 280
Blix, Hans, 62, 282
BNF, 274
Boehmer-Christensen, Sonja, 284
Bogart, Humphrey, 141
Bois de Boulogne, 13
Boiteux, Marcel, 8
Bolin, Bert, 424

Bolivia, 48, 51
Borowitz, Sidney, 82
Boussena, Sadek, 158
Brando, Marlon, 256
Brazil, 31, 48, 51
breeding, 270
British Gas, 54, 180
British Nuclear Fuels (BNF), 274
Brookes, Leonard, 284
Brown, Lester, 12
bull, 341
burner tip, 53
Bush, George W., 65, 76, 142, 298
Business Week, 20
butanol, 420

California, 26
Calvino, Italo, 256
Camisea Field, 48
Canada, 294
Canal Street, 63, 284
CANDU reactors, 270
Cantarell, 107
capacity factor, 60, 193, 320
Caperan, Loic, 70
Capital Asset Pricing Model, 336
capital cost, 318, 323
carbon capture, 253
carbon dioxide (CO_2), 229, 240, 253
Cardoso, Benjamin, 251, 253
Carnot efficiency, 323
Carnot, Sadi, 234, 322
Caruso, Guy, 94
Casazza, J.A., 434
cash settlement, 343, 350, 362
Caspian basin, 117
Caspian region, 38
Cassandra, 167
Catawba Nuclear Station, 315
Cavaney, Red, 150
cellulosic ethanol, 13
chain reaction, 266
Charrault, Jean-Claude, 402
Chenery, Hollis, 83
Chiarelli, Bob, 17

China, 49, 163
Churchill, Winston, 115, 163, 285
Clancy, Tom, 252
Clark, Paul, 83
clean coal, 419
clearinghouse, 347
Climate Group, 390
Clinton, Bill, 67
coal, 52
Cohn, Laura, 29
cokers, 121
combined cycle, 47, 232
combined cycle equipment, 278
common carriage, 190
compressors, 188
conservation of energy, 233
contango, 367, 369
continuous compounding, 237
contract prices, 245
contracts for differences, 436
controlled or proscribed substances, 295
convenience yield, 194, 361, 364, 365
conventional oil, 101
Coogee Bay Road, 246
Cook, Earl, 426
Cooke, Ronald, 431
Cooper, Richard, 25, 34
Copenhagen Consensus, 396
Courchevel (France), 202, 346
crack spread, 120
Crandall, Maureen, 96, 160, 168
Crazy Horse, 107
Crichton, Michael, 395
critical R/q ratio, 41, 101
Crown Prince Fahd, 149, 150
cryogenic tankers, 207

Daddy Romance, 344
Dali, Salvador, 34
Damon, Matt, 148
Danish electricity market, 282
Darfur, 165
dash for gas, 329
Davis, Gray, 90, 179, 437
De Fazio, Peter, 82, 434

Dean, James, 14
DeGaulle, Charles, 77
Deng, Xiaoping, 413
deregulation, 53, 263
deregulatory uncertainty, 55
derivative(s), 50, 126, 354
Desmarest, Thierry, 118
Diestl, Christian, 391
dimensional analysis, 315
discounted present value, 311
discounted value, 307
district heating, 424
Doctor Strangelove, 119
Doha, 51
Dow Chemical, 57
downstream, 121
Dr Pangloss, 221
dry hole, 103
Duffin, Murray, 141
DuPont, 66

Econ 101, 57
economic depreciation, 324
EDC, 199
Edison Electric Institute, 332
efficiency prices, 40, 72
Efficient Market Hypothesis (EMH), 346
Ehrenfest, Paul, 221, 288
Einhorn, Michael, 336
Einstein, Albert, 124, 244, 322
Einstein's equivalence theorem, 337
El Paso Pipeline Company, 179
electric deregulation, 52, 53, 241, 422
electric deregulation experiment, 171
electricity deregulation, 2
emission permits, 69, 74
emissions trading, 67, 75, 240, 281
energy, 313
Energy Development Corporation (EDC), 199
Energy Leadership Council, 410
energy units, 235
EnergyPulse, 13, 19
enrichment, 268
Enron, 2, 28, 70, 78, 79, 90, 117, 172, 173

environmentalists in favor of nuclear energy, 280
equilibrium, 362
equivalence principle, 124
Erlander, Tage, 289
EROEI, 45, 47
estimates of gas reserves, 186
ethanol, 13, 261
European options, 372
European Union (EU), 172, 249
ex-ante (i.e., expected) price, 368
ex-post (i.e., realized) price, 368
exchange of futures for physicals (EFP), 344
exercise price, 354
expectations, 273
exposure, 341, 344
ExxonMobil, 18

Farrell, Michael, 81
Farren-Price, Bill, 168
fast breeder reactor (FBR), 273
FBR, 273
Federal Energy Regulatory Commission (FERC), 55
Federal Reserve System, 30
Feigenbaum, Edward, 57
Feinstein, Dianne, 33
fertile element, 270
Feynman, Richard, 298
financial economics, 353
Finland, 81, 265
Financial Times, 164
First Law of Thermodynamics, 233, 322
Fisher, William L., 418
Fisher–Tropsch process, 250
fissile elements, 270
fixed cost, 323
Flower, 100
fluidized-bed combustion, 253
Forbes, Steve, 143
Ford, Bill, 29, 51
Fort Jackson, 246
forward contracts, 342
fossil fuels, 49

Fountain of Youth, 276
Framework Convention on Climate
    Change, 66, 405
Franklin, Benjamin, 129
Franssen, Herman, 35, 148, 168
free flow, 14
Freud, Sigmund, 296
Friedman, Milton, 104, 416
Frisch, Morten, 184
Fulton Fish Market, 241
FutureGen, 257, 419
futures, 126, 127, 195
futures contracts, 72, 183
futures markets, 213

Gödel, Kurt, 424
game theory, 37
gaming, 198
gas demand, 49
gas deregulation, 54
gas production, 186
gas reserves, 19
Gazprom, 202
Gekko, Gordon, 89
Gell-Mann, Murray, 39
General Custer, 421
Genoa, 345
Germany, 59
Ghawar, 176
Ghost of Christmas Past, 200
Global Climate Commission, 396
global natural gas demand, 184
global oil supply, 42
globalization, 64, 145
going short, 214
Goldstein, Lawrence, 99
Goodstein, David, 251, 389
Gore, Al, 65
Greene, Graham, 223
greenhouse gases, 68
Greenpeace, 286
Greenspan, Alan, 30, 52, 144, 145, 201,
    419
Groningen gas field, 196
Grubb, Michael, 399

Gustafson, Torsten, 289

Hall, Darwin, 224
Hammar, Armand, 104, 415
Hanlon, Michael, 297
Hannibal, 203
hard coal, 231
Harvard, 156
heat rate, 248, 257, 314, 319
heavy oil, 40, 147
hedge ratio, 385
hedgers, 215, 222
Heller, Douglas, 70
Hemingway, Ernest, 114
Hennemeyer, Paul, 78
Henry Hub, 214
Herbert, John, 54
HEU, 274
Hicks, John, 409
highly enriched uranium (HEV), 274
Hoel, Michael, 404
Hollings, Ernest, 28
Holmes, Bob, 131
Holy Grail, 276
Hopper, Ron, 55, 56
Hotelling, Harold, 124
Houthakker, Henrik, 127, 378
Hoyos, Carola, 83, 164, 165
Hubbert, M. King, 34, 36, 38, 39, 105, 137
Huber, Peter, 13
hubs, 196
Huettner, David, 114
hurdle rates, 336
Hurricane Katrina, 230
Hustlers' Ball, 340
Hutton, Will, 72
hybrid, 7
hydrocrackers, 121
hydroelectricity, 422
hydrogen, 7, 13, 51, 261

IAEE, 97
IBM, 66
Iceberg Alley, 124, 131
IEA, 21, 35, 49, 50, 58, 94, 294

IHS Energy, 105
in-the-money, 356
increasing returns to scale, 27, 303
India, 163
innovative pricing, 326
Intergovernmental Panel on Climate
  Change (IPCC), 395
intermediate load, 304
International Association for Energy
  Economics (IAEE), 97, 218
International Atomic Energy Agency, 62,
  264
International Energy Agency (IEA), 94,
  144, 146, 173, 233, 294
International Petroleum Exchange (IPE),
  127
International Petroleum Exchange in
  London, 368
intertemporal arbitrage, 362
intrinsic value, 358
inventories, 195
Iran, 142
Iraq, 142, 147, 159, 160
isotope, 267
Italian Riviera, 341

Jennings, John, 406
Johnson, Donald, 5, 402
Jones, Digby, 172
Jones, Nicola, 131
Jospin, Lional, 279

Kahn, Alfred, 76
Kalihari, 427
Kay, John, 72
Kelley, P. X., 410
Keynes, John Maynard, 221, 296
Kielmas, Maria, 163
King Canute, 63
King Drive, 345
Kissinger, Henry, 131
Korea, 49
Korean War, 230
Korn, David, 15
Krell, Erik, 54

Kvint, Vladimir, 155
Kyoto conference on global warming, 413
Kyoto Protocol, 11, 66, 81, 82, 90, 238,
  297, 389

Lamont-Doherty Earth Conservatory, 114
Lansky, Meyer, 73
Lauerman, Vincent, 275
Laughlin, Robert, 59
Law of Conservation of Energy, 322
law of one price, 29, 212
Lee, Julian, 158
Leeson, Nick, 340
Leipzig Manifesto, 396
leverage, 360
Libya, 147, 162
licensing procedures, 319
Liddle, Rod, 278
light oil, 130
lignite, 231
Lind, Harry, 431
Lindahl, Mary, 126
Lindzen, Richard, 11
liquefied natural gas (LNG), 19, 48, 58
liquidity, 222, 342, 344, 349
Littlechild, Stephen, 78
Liveris, Andrew, 57
load factor, 193, 321
Locatelli, Catherine, 158
Locke, Gary, 29
Lomborg, Bjorn, 396
Loomis, Carol, 359
looping, 189
Lord (John) Browne, 37, 97
Lovelock, James, 286
Lovins, Amory, 295
Lugar, Richard G., 93
Lynch, Michael, 415

MacAvoy, Paul W., 33, 219
Madonna, 59
maintenance margin, 343
Mandil, Claude, 4, 5, 201, 202
Manhattan Project, 131
Marcu, Andrei, 399

margin, 342
margin account, 342
margin calls, 222
market centers, 197
market discount rate, 307
market liquidity, 349
market power, 28, 434
marketable emission permits, 393
Marking-to-Market, 343
mass-to-energy, 269
matched books, 380
Matsui, Ken-Ichi, 9
Maui gas field, 291
Mayer, Julius Robert, 322
McKerron, Gordon, 249
McShane, Owen, 280, 400
McTeer, Robert, 178, 375
meltdown, 266
merit order, 52, 248, 303, 328
Metallgesellschaft (MG), 381
Middle Eastern countries, 122
Mill, John Stuart, 76
Miller, Merton, 125, 383
Milov, Vladimir, 158
minimax principle, 256
mixed oxide (MOX) fuels, 274
MMC, 180
Monbiot, Georges, 7
Monte Carlo, 417
Morgan Stanley, 144
Morgenstern, Oscar, 168, 284, 420
Mork, Erling, 398
Munich Re, 61
Murphy's Law, 74
Murray, Robert, 240
Myrdal, Gunnar, 288

Nader, Ralph, 295
Nash, John, 172, 420
National Research Council of the United
    States, 402
natural decline, 187
natural decline rate, 18
natural depletion rate, 18
natural depreciation, 98, 210

natural gas, 47
natural uranium, 266–268
Neumann, John von, 168, 247, 284, 420
New Orleans, 230
New York Mercantile Exchange
    (NYMEX), 51, 70, 73, 127, 174, 397,
    435
New York Stock Exchange, 241
Newbery, David, 433
Newton, Isaac, 322
no-arbitrage condition, 364
Nordic Electricity Exchange (NordPool),
    293, 389, 398
NordPool, 73, 79, 252, 293, 426, 435, 436
North Dome, 176
Norway, 30, 263
Norwegian North Sea, 44
notional, 333
nuclear cycle, 61, 269
nuclear plants, 61
nuclear waste, 62, 264

O'Leary, Hazel, 33
O'Reilly, David, 14
Odd, Robert, 19
OECD, 49
offsetting, 214, 342
OFGAS, 180
OFGEM, 72
OFT, 180
oil futures market, 339
oil optimist, 36
oil reserves, 34
oil-in-place, 15, 97
Oman, 57
OPEC, 147
open access, 190
open interest, 348
opportunity cost, 310, 311
option, 126, 128, 195, 353, 372
option premium, 244
option price, 372
option value, 254, 427, 428
options on futures, 358, 377
Ormerod, Paul, 79

Orwell, George, 297
Oswald, Andrew, 129
out-of-the-money, 356
over-the-counter (OTC), 373
over-the-counter derivatives, 348

Palais des Nations, 67
paper oil, 341
Parente, Pedro, 32
peak load, 53, 248, 304
peak production, 42
peak shaving, 196
pebble bed reactor, 267
Pentagon, 3, 130, 131, 229
Peru, 48, 51
petrochemical industries, 219
petrochemical production, 120
Pew Center on Global Climate Change, 66
Pfaff, William, 71
PFC Energy, 144, 147
Pickens, T. Boone, 47, 359
Pindyck, Robert, 33, 220
pipelines, 49
plutonium, 425
Portafino, 426
Porter, Cole, 286
power, 313
PowerGen, 422
premium, 372
premium income, 357
price convergence, 217
primary energy, 232
Prodi, Romano, 296
Progress Energy Florida, 64
proprietary trading, 343
proved reserves, 42
Prudhoe Bay, 105
pseudo-market, 280
PUREX, 63
Putin, Vladimir, 74, 281

Qatar, 57
quasi-option value, 255, 428
Quebec, 192

R/q ratio, 39, 103
Radetzki, Marian, 205
Raymond, Lee, 18, 125
Reagan, Ronald, 202, 254
real interest rate, 335
real options theory, 190
recoverable reserves, 97
"Red" Adair, 131
Reeperbahn, 63, 284
Rees, Martin, 410
refinery margin, 120
refining, 119
regulation, 26
reprocessed Pu-239, 274
reprocessing, 270
reserve capacity, 332
restructuring, 55
reversing, 342
Reynolds, Douglas, 131, 168
Riksgränsen, 289
risk, 212
Ritch, John, 296
Roach, Stephen, 144
Rodenbeck, Max, 142
Roeber, Joe, 224
Röpke, Erich, 256, 420
Ross, Stephen, 383
Rotberg, Eugene, 359
Russia, 94, 153, 157, 159, 160
Russian nuclear administration, 423
RWE npower, 75

S&P 500 index, 367
safe reactors, 394
SAFETY FIRST, 256
Salameh, Mamdouh G., 160
San Diego, 242
Sanford Bernstein, 118
Sasol Ltd, 250
Saudi Arabia, 35, 94, 113, 118, 146, 148, 149, 151, 153, 159, 160, 167, 168, 234, 412, 415
Saudi Basic Industries Corporation (Sabic), 219
Saudi Petroleum Ministry, 115

scarcity prices, 46
scarcity rent, 109
Schimmelbusch, Heinz, 359
Schurr, Samuel, 287
Schwarzenegger, Arnold, 252, 423
screening curves, 323
Scuola Enrico Mattei, 73
Second Law of Thermodynamics, 234
secondary energy, 232
Senegal, 162
Separation Theorem, 308
Shakespeare, William, 275
shale, 52
Simmons, Matthew R., 35, 43, 152
Simon, Julian, 152
Sir Elton, 59
Skilling, Jeffrey K., 71
Skinner, Robert, 205
Skrebowski, Chris, 412
Smil, Vaclav, 166
Smith, Eric, 253, 417
Smith, Frederick W., 410
Smith, Gordon, 33
Snillen Speculerar (Genius Speculates), 59
solar, 261
South China Sea, 171
South Korea, 151
South Side of Chicago, 111
Southern Company, 71
speculation, 347
speculator, 214
spot gas, 183
spot markets, 55, 354
spot prices, 30, 245
spot transactions, 235
Stanford, 156
state of the world, 213
Stern, Jonathan, 200
stock-flow models, 132
Stockholm College of Economic
    Knowledge, 308
Stockholm Conference on the
    Environment, 403
storage sites, 194
Store, Jonas Gahe, 159

subjective discount, 307
surge capacity, 94, 150
Sutherland, John, 424
swap arranger, 379
swaps, 126, 128, 195
Sweden, 30, 59, 81, 85, 152
Swedish consumers, 280
Swedish Energy Agency, 399
Swedish military, 427
Swedish uranium, 292, 295
Swedish welfare state, 286
swing gas, 183
swing producer, 196
Swiss Re, 61
Switzerland, 424
synthetic crude, 250

tar sands, 40, 44, 142, 147, 148
Teece, David, 223
term structure, 367
Thatcher, Margaret, 82, 90, 284
The Energy Century, 409
The West Wing, 85
thermodynamics, 322
third-party access, 190
thorium, 273
Tillerson, Rex, 163, 411
time value, 358, 374
tough love, 29
transmission lines, 331
Travesso, Lutz David, 32
tulip *bubble*, 290
Tyson, Laura D'Andrea, 31

UBS, 294
UK North Sea, 17
UK Royal Academy of Engineering, 278
UK Royal Society, 8
ultimate reserves, 42, 58
uncertainty, 212
UNCTAD, 69, 425
underlying, 50, 216, 348
Union Bank of Switzerland (UBS), 294
United Nations Conference on Trade and
    Development, 69

United States, 37, 63, 66, 85, 144
United States Department of Energy
  (USDE), 153
United States National Defence
  University, 96
United Technologies, 66
upstream, 121
uranium ore, 266
uranium reserves, 294
US Congress, 66
US Department of Energy, 35, 144
US Energy Information Administration,
  197, 321
US Energy Information Agency, 94
US Geological Service, 186

Vaiteeswaran, Vijay, 4
Valero Energy, 121, 122
variable cost, 323
variation margin, 355
Vattenfall, 257
Venezuela, 48, 51
Veuve Cliquot, 340
Victor, David, 90
Vind, Karl, 116
Voltaire, 221

Walken, Christopher, 296
wall friction, 188
Walls, David, 223

Walras, Leon, 398
Washington Park, 13
Wayne, John, 33
wellhead, 53
West–East Pipeline, 173
Western Canada, 192
Western Canada Sedimentary Basin
  (WCSB), 191
wet barrels, 341
Weyer, Martin Vander, 143
wheeling, 197
Williams, Bob, 418
Willis, Bruce, 229
Wilson, Brian, 8
wind power, 261
Wise, Stan, 71
Wolfe, Tom, 340
Woolsey, R. James, 93
workaholics, 126
working gas, 197
World Bank, 419
World Energy Council, 423
World Nuclear Association, 282
World Resource Institute, 393
World Trade Center, 3

yellow cake, 268
Yergin, Daniel, 154
yield curve, 145